Emerging Technologies Transforming Higher Education:

Instructional Design and Student Success

Jacquelynne Anne Boivin
Bridgewater State University, USA

Jabbar A. Al-Obaidi
Bridgewater State University, USA

Madhusudana N. Rao
Bridgewater State University, USA

Published in the United States of America by
    IGI Global
    701 E. Chocolate Avenue
    Hershey PA, USA 17033
    Tel: 717-533-8845
    Fax: 717-533-8661
    E-mail: cust@igi-global.com
    Web site: https://www.igi-global.com

Library of Congress Cataloging-in-Publication Data

CIP PENDING

ISBN13: 9798369339046
EISBN13: 9798369339053

Vice President of Editorial: Melissa Wagner
Managing Editor of Acquisitions: Mikaela Felty
Managing Editor of Book Development: Jocelynn Hessler
Production Manager: Mike Brehm
Cover Design: Phillip Shickler

British Cataloguing in Publication Data
A Cataloguing in Publication record for this book is available from the British Library.

All work contributed to this book is new, previously-unpublished material.
The views expressed in this book are those of the authors, but not necessarily of the publisher.

Table of Contents

Section 1
Defining and Exploring Instructional Technologies

Section 2
Improving Instruction and Learning With Technology

Section 3
Instructional Technologies' Global Impact

Detailed Table of Contents

Section 1
Defining and Exploring Instructional Technologies

Chapter 1
Madhusudana N. Rao, Bridgewater State University, USA
Jabbar A. Al-Obaidi, Bridgewater State University, USA

The rapid advancement of artificial intelligence (AI) is reforming various sectors, and higher education is no exception. AI tools are increasingly being integrated into classrooms and learning environments, offering a range of opportunities for students and faculty alike. This chapter explores the various AI-powered tools that are being used in education today. These tools can potentially revolutionize how faculty teach and how students learn and engage. Providing personalized learning experiences, automating tasks, and making learning more engaging and effective. The literature review illustrates that AI enhances education by offering efficiency, personalization, and accessibility, catering to diverse learning styles. It enables adaptive learning, addressing individual needs and creating a more engaging and effective learning environment. his chapter discusses the benefits of building into a learning management system like Blackboard and other systems. Students can benefit from AI if faculty build it into their syllabus and teaching pedagogy.

Within this chapter, the author will address the multifaceted nature of artificial intelligence (AI), a machine's ability to simulate the human mind. The author evaluates generative AI and its pros, cons, and reliability. First, the author examines AI's effect on essay writing in higher-level education. Then, the author explores how preservice teachers can be equipped to address and implement proper usage in the classroom. The author includes literature reviews of scholarly texts that help address the research question: How do English professors and teacher educators negotiate AI as a tool for essay writing and teaching? The author will evaluate data through a theoretical framework that analyzes and assesses emergent data and is supported by pedagogical anecdotes. This framework is designed to guide teachers in their own evaluation of AI in the writing process. The findings will help equip teacher educators with tools to implement AI within their classrooms and identify the proper usage of AI for essay writing in higher education. The findings are designed to assist university boards, teacher educators, and preservice teachers in making informed decisions regarding AI in postsecondary classrooms.

Chapter 3

This chapter evaluates the qualitative studies on how AI chatbots impact HE, specifically their benefits and challenges. A systematic search was conducted across academic databases resulting in the inclusion of 27 research papers published between 2018 and 2023. The research in this involved utilizing the Critical Appraisal Skills Programme (CASP) checklist for Systematic Review to evaluate the quality and relevance of each study followed by a thematic analysis of the data using Braun and Clarke's approach to identify key themes. The first theme, " Improved Learning Experience," explores the benefits of including personalized support, increased engagement, user-friendliness, skills development, and efficiency. The second theme, ": Practical and Ethical Issues," delves into the practical and ethical issues, such as ethical concerns, pedagogical limitations, information accuracy, and technical challenges. A balanced approach to integrate AI chatbots in HE, addressing ethical and technical concerns while maximizing its benefits were given emphasis on the studies reviewed and evaluated.

This chapter explored the philosophical orientation, transformational instruction practices, flexible learning, and students' university experience. It utilized a phenomenological transcendental design with ten participants. The various sections in this chapter reveal that to stay competitive and relevant in the ever-evolving field of education, it is imperative that our faculty continually acquire new skills, upgrade existing ones, and engage in professional development. An effective approach to achieve this is by fostering a technology-infused collaborative environment, as such environments have been proven to enhance student learning. For our teachers' philosophical orientation, a particular focus can be placed on existentialism as a philosophy for study. By utilizing a qualitative phenomenological method, we can delve into the personal and profound experiences of learners, thereby uncovering humanism and exploring the perspective of the respondents in-depth.

Section 2
Improving Instruction and Learning With Technology

Youssef Laaraj, Faculty of Sciences and Techniques, Sidi Mohamed Ben
Abdellah University, Morocco

Morocco has been actively attempting to modernize its education system by embracing and promoting the use of information and communication technology (ICT), as outlined in official documents such as The National Charter and Loi Cadre 51-17. Initiatives like integrating digital tools and e-learning platforms have aimed to improve access to quality education for over two decades. This chapter investigates the innovative technology integration in Moroccan university classrooms at Sidi Mohamed Ben Abdellah University, and particularly examines its effects on class and time management. Using a mixed-methods approach, the research investigates university teachers' experiences with the use of modern technologies in their classes. Within the Technological Pedagogical Content Knowledge (TPACK) framework, the investigation aims to provide insights into how technology influences teaching practices and learning experiences, contributing to the discourse on education in Morocco and offering valuable insights for educators, policymakers, and researchers.

Shawn O'Neill, Bridgewater State University, USA

This chapter explores the innovative use of Artificial Intelligence (AI) to assist new science teachers in crafting engaging and effective lesson plans when formal curriculum resources are scarce or unavailable. Recognizing the challenges educators face in contexts where standard curriculum materials are limited, this paper aims to empower both pre-service and novice teachers through AI-driven tools designed to facilitate the creation of comprehensive, age-appropriate, standards-aligned science lessons. By integrating AI into teacher preparation programs, educators can access valuable insights, resources, and support to enhance their teaching practices and improve student learning outcomes. The theoretical and ethical implications of integrating AI, including fairness, privacy, and transparency, will also be addressed. The author ties in her experiences as both an elementary classroom teacher and a professor of a science methods class for pre-service teachers.

Chapter 7

ASSIA BENABID, *Faculty of Sciences, University Hassan II,*
   Casablanca
Imane EL IMADI, *Faculty of Sciences, University Hassan II,*
   Casablanca
Khalil Alqatawneh, *Tafila Technical University, Jordan*

This chapter investigates the importance of social variety in institutional frameworks, notably in higher education, in response to the urgent societal concerns of the twenty-first century. The goal is to foster an educational environment that values, respects, and includes all students, regardless of gender, race, or socioeconomic status. The main goal is to foster an environment in which students feel both academically engaged and empowered to reach their greatest potential. This involves an equitable and inclusive teaching strategy that recognizes student's different experiences, needs, and objectives, as well as collaborative efforts from all educational partners. The goal of this research is to investigate and propose solutions to improve equity in higher education, with the ultimate goal of creating educational settings that accommodate students; with different needs. The objectives include identifying critical areas for change in present educational practices, investigating the influence of inclusive teaching methods on student success, and recommending concrete ways for institutions to implement them. The methodology used in this study is a thorough evaluation of the existing literature on diversity, equity, and inclusion in higher education. It also includes case studies and examples of how inclusive approaches have been successfully implemented in diverse educational contexts. The theoretical framework is based on social justice theories, emphasizing the significance of providing equal opportunity for all individuals in the educational system. To achieve inclusion and equity, a comprehensive approach is advocated. Strategies such as accessibility and equity initiatives, flexible and adaptable teaching methods, active student engagement, inclusive communication, diverse representation in faculty and staff, diversity training programs, fair assessment practices, and transparent admissions policies are critical. Furthermore, financial support mechanisms, mentorship and tutoring programs, diversity-sensitive orientation campaigns, and the creation of inclusive courses and programs all help to build an equal educational environment. Faculty training has been acknowledged as a critical component in ensuring that educators have the skills and understanding required to effectively implement inclusive teaching techniques. Emotional support services and accessible physical infrastructure are also critical components in meeting the different needs of students. Finally, this study calls for a comprehensive and collaborative strategy to create equitable educational settings in higher education. By implementing the recommended measures, institutions can demonstrate their commitment to promoting diversity, fairness, and social justice, thereby helping students prepare for the challenges and opportunities of the 21st century.

Section 3
Instructional Technologies' Global Impact

Chapter 8

Meryem Ouelfatmi, Sidi Mohamed Ben Abdellah University, Morocco
Sadik Madani Alaoui, Sidi Mohamed Ben Abdellah University, Morocco
Jacquelynne Anne Boivin, Bridgewater State University, USA

Women's education has a history on a global scale of being marked by struggle, strife, persistence, progress, and more. The Middle East and North Africa (MENA) countries are no exception. This chapter addresses the status of women's education varies by country, but and while "progress" can describe the status in each MENA country, each nation has areas that warrant attention for future improvement. Higher education, specifically, is a level that warrants attention due to its societal impact for women. This review of the literature provides an overview of the status of women's higher education in a variety of MENA countries and summarizes the major gains that each country has taken for women's post-secondary education and what areas of improvement need to be addressed. The role that technology has played and can play in the future will be emphasized. By exploring these ideas, the goal is for readers to consider future research that can help ignite next steps in policies and structures that can promote women's access to higher education and completion of post-secondary degrees.

Chapter 9

Understanding LMS Usage in Higher Education: Examining the Interplay of Demographic and Usage Factors in UTAUT 207

Juby Thomas, Kristu Jayanti College, India
Vishnu Achutha Menon, Institute for Educational and Developmental Studies, India
T. K. Sateesh Kumar, Kristu Jayanti College, India
Lijo P. Thomas, Kristu Jayanti College, India

This chapter employs a quantitative survey methodology utilizing the Unified Theory of Acceptance and Use of Technology (UTAUT) questionnaire as the primary research instrument. The questionnaire was administered to 363 students in higher education institutions across Karnataka, India, representing diverse demographic backgrounds. Purposive sampling was employed to ensure the inclusion of students from various geographic settings within Karnataka. Data collection took place over five months, from January 2023 to May 2023, using online surveys administered through Google Forms. It examines the mediating role of psychological, socio-demographic (gender, location, education), and economic/behavioural (pattern of use and purpose of use) variables. Independent variables, including Performance Expectancy (PE), Effort Expectancy (EE), Social Influence (SI), and Facilitating Conditions (FC), were tested for their impact on dependent variables, Behavioural Intention (BI), and Attitude toward using technology (AT).

Chapter 10

Nadia Mohammed Nasser Abubaker, University of Aden, Yemen
SeyedMohammad Kashani, Iowa State University, USA
Awad M. Alshalwy, Omar Al-Mukhtar University, Libya
Ali Garib, Rice University, USA

The appearance of generative artificial intelligence (AI) has led to a paradigm shift in education worldwide, positioning the Middle East and North Africa (MENA) region between traditional pedagogy and technological innovations. To further explore this region's educational practices with generative AI, this chapter conducted a systematic review of research articles published between 2022 and 2024 on the MENA's integration of generative AI in higher education. Using qualitative thematic analysis, four major themes emerged: positive perceptions despite the lack of training, AI-assisted pedagogy, inevitable innovation reshaping educational norms, and challenges identified for successful generative AI integration. Despite the generative AI adoption in the MENA region, these implementations, still in the early stage, face several challenges that reflect the complexities of integrating generative AI in a region fraught with contextual hurdles and accustomed to traditional pedagogical practices, especially in under-resourced contexts. The chapter concludes with pedagogical implications.

Chapter 11

Aránzazu Gil Casadomet, Autonomous University of Madrid, Spain
Imane El Imadi, University of Hassan II Casablanca, Morocco
Mohamed Radid, University of Hassan II Casablanca, Morocco

This chapter describes a cooperative study that looked at the effects of online international collaboration on intercultural and academic development, conducted by universities in Morocco and Spain. It is designed to determine how cross-cultural initiatives affect students' academic development and intercultural competency. It involved 200 students and examined issues including time zones and technological differences while assessing the efficacy of online cooperation through a mixed-methods approach that includes questionnaires, interviews, and content analysis. The theoretical framework emphasizes mutual understanding and the role of technology in removing obstacles. It borrows from theories of collaborative learning and intercultural communication. Initial results demonstrate beneficial effects on communication and cultural understanding, highlighting the need of cross-cultural education in developing globally competent pupils in the face of growing digital interconnection.

Chapter 12
Enhancing Undergraduate Skills Through Interdisciplinary Data Projects and
Technologies 275
    Wanchunzi Yu, Bridgewater State University, USA
    Xiangrong Liu, Bridgewater State University, USA

In response to the fast-growing demand for data manipulation skills, it is crucial that the undergraduate curriculum evolves to integrate various technologies. This chapter delves into the authors' initiatives to incorporate data visualization, analysis tools, and artificial intelligence (AI) into the interdisciplinary undergraduate curriculum, Statistical Consulting, and Data Visualization undergraduate courses cross-listed by the Department of Mathematics and Department of Management. Two projects serve as examples of this integration: a survey data analysis project from participants of Collaborative University Business Experiences (CUBEs) at Bridgewater State University (BSU), and a Chinese Solar Photovoltaic Rooftop (PV) Adoption project, undertaken by a BSU interdisciplinary faculty-student research team in China. The results, findings, and presentations of students showcased in this paper underscore the significance of incorporating technologies into the teaching process, especially in the interdisciplinary curriculum.

Foreword

In **"Emerging Technologies Transforming Higher Education: Instructional Design and Student Success,"** editors Jacquelynne Boivin, Jabbar A. Al-Obaidi, and Madhusudana N. Rao present a timely and essential exploration of how cutting-edge technologies are redefining the landscape of higher education. This book provides a thorough examination of the intersection between technological advancements and educational practices, offering invaluable insights for educators, administrators, and policymakers alike.

As a seasoned professional in the field of higher education, I have observed the profound impact of technological innovations on teaching and learning. The rapid evolution of digital tools and platforms has brought about transformative changes, offering unprecedented opportunities to enhance educational experiences and outcomes. However, these advancements also come with challenges that necessitate careful consideration and strategic implementation.

The book opens with an in-depth analysis of Artificial Intelligence (AI) and its integration into higher education. AI has the potential to revolutionize how we approach teaching, learning, and academic administration. The authors explore the various applications of AI, from personalized learning platforms to automated administrative processes. They also address the ethical considerations and practical challenges associated with AI, emphasizing the importance of using these technologies responsibly and with a clear understanding of their limitations and implications.

One of the key strengths of this book is its examination of AI chatbots and their role in enhancing student support and engagement. Through a meta-synthesis of recent research, the authors highlight the benefits of AI chatbots in providing personalized assistance, improving efficiency, and increasing student engagement. They also discuss the practical and ethical issues that arise with the use of these tools, offering a balanced perspective on their potential and limitations.

The book also explores the use of AI in developing instructional materials, particularly in the field of science education. By addressing the gaps in science instruction at the elementary level, the authors demonstrate how AI can provide valuable resources and support for teachers, helping to bridge the divide in science education and improve student outcomes.

In addition to AI, the book covers a wide range of emerging technologies and their impact on higher education. For instance, it recounts the experience of a small college that adapted to the challenges of remote learning by establishing a Teaching and Learning Innovation Center. This case study illustrates the importance of institutional support in fostering innovative teaching practices and adapting to new educational paradigms.

The book also offers a global perspective, examining technological advancements in different regions, including the Middle East and North Africa(MENA) region. These chapters shed light on the diverse challenges and opportunities faced by higher education institutions around the world, highlighting the varying levels of technological adoption and the impact on educational access and quality.

The role of Learning Management Systems (LMS) in Indian education is another significant focus of the book. The authors discuss how LMS are transforming instructional practices, improving access to educational resources, and addressing geographical disparities. This section underscores the potential of technology to democratize education and enhance learning opportunities for marginalized communities.

Furthermore, the book explores how pedagogical approaches can be adapted to incorporate technology effectively. By examining the integration of explicit instruction with inclusive practices, the authors provide valuable insights into creating supportive and equitable learning environments that foster student success.

Ultimately, "Emerging Technologies Transforming Higher Education" serves as a crucial resource for anyone involved in the field of education. The thoughtful analysis and practical recommendations presented in this book offer a roadmap for navigating the complexities of technological integration and underscore the importance of a student-centered approach to educational innovation. I am confident that this book will serve as a valuable guide for educators, administrators, and researchers seeking to understand and harness the power of technology to enhance instructional design and promote student success. The contributions of the editors and authors provide a comprehensive and engaging exploration of how emerging technologies can shape the future of higher education.

I would like to express my deepest appreciation to Dr. Jacquelynne Boivin, Assistant Professor of Elementary and Early Childhood Education, Bridgewater State University, Dr. Jabbar A. Al-Obaidi, Professor of Communication, Bridgewater State University, and Dr. Madhusudana N. Rao, Professor of Geography, Director of MENA Studies Program, Bridgewater State University for their outstanding contributions and for offering this valuable book. Their collective expertise and unwavering dedication to advancing the field of higher education are evident throughout the pages of this work. Their insightful analyses, thorough research, and thoughtful recommendations provide a rich resource for educators, administrators, and policymakers navigating the rapidly evolving landscape of educational technology. Their commitment to enhancing instructional design and promoting student success through the integration of emerging technologies is truly commendable and will undoubtedly inspire and guide countless professionals in the field.

B.K. Ravi

Koppal University, India

Preface

INTRODUCTION

As we near the second half of the 2020's, it is an opportunity to consider how much life has changed since this decade began. Reflecting back on 2020, when Covid-19 was ravaging the planet, technology took on a whole new level of importance for people personally and professionally. Consider, for example, how common it is to have a Zoom call nowadays. In 2019, many of us either never heard of Zoom, or maybe used it a handful of times. Being at the office five days per week was the norm for many and the thought of "work from home days" seemed futuristic or borderline utopian. Fast-forward to 2024 and life is inherently different. Video-conferencing is routine and work location flexibility has reached new heights. Technology made all of this possible within a drastically fast period of time and what's both promising and scary, is that the tempo shows no signs of slowing.

Yes, this is an optimistic lens on technology to start and it is true that there is another side to the story. Technology, for example, has enabled hackers to gain access to private information in huge data breaches. Social media has been linked with anxiety and depression for people of all ages, especially adolescents. With every great tool comes its prices and it is paramount that we look at technological advances within higher education with a balanced perspective as well.

Higher education has historically been the venue for the "new." Whether it be in new research findings, or new social movements causing a stir amongst students, colleges and universities have been where the masses look to get a gauge on where a given nation or the world could be heading. We, as editors, saw a need in academic literature to help summarize and explore innovative technologies in higher education. We had questions about Artificial Intelligence, new assessment tools, and software that seems beyond the 2020s and as scholars, knew that an international lens would be the most effective way to learn about these technologies, how they are being used, their caveats and challenges, and more.

This edited book will serve as a culminating resource of scholarship from authors globally that unpacks the ways in which technologies of all kinds are actively influencing and impacting post-secondary education internationally. As editors, we were fortunate to have had a myriad of scholars from various countries contributed to this text. Their varied voices articulate an understanding of the status of technology in higher education and provide insights that lend themselves to foresight of how technology will benefit and guide higher education in the future. The obstacles and challenges are also delineated to better prepare readers, too.

This book is designed to offer modern international perspectives on higher education that are based on global learning and teaching engagement. The main impetus highlights the role of technology as a change-agent and conveyor for change on local, regional, and global arenas. This book addressed the following objectives:

- Provide insights regarding the current status of technology in higher education.
- Consider the trajectory of technology in higher education.
- Investigate the benefits and caveats of technologies in higher education.

In essence, this book balances case studies, original research, and literature reviews from a variety of discipline areas. In academia, scholarship can oftentimes feel siloed by domain. For instance, those in the "Hard Sciences" may only read papers that reflect Chemistry and Biology, but disregard work in the Humanities and social sciences. However, there is great value in learning from outside our disciplines.As scholars working in higher education, we share a common interest and thoughtfulness about our students' learning. We all strive for students to leave our classes with new skills and ideas to apply in their careers, and society's future. With this shared objective, our approaches, tools, insights, and warnings, can help us all, regardless of our field of study.

ORGANIZATION OF THE BOOK

Section 1: Defining and Exploring Instructional Technologies

Chapter 1: *Embracing How AI Responsibly Empowers Students and Faculty in Higher Education: Theoretical Perspectives*

The remarkably fast growth of educational technology has led to a myriad of teaching tools and approaches for both educators and students to learn and understand. This powerful chapter summarizes the current climate surrounding AI in higher education, including perspectives of organizations that support its usage, critical questions to examine, and cautions to consider. This chapter succinctly identifies some of the most effective AI teaching tools and softwares by explaining their formats and outlines their applications. A balance to theory and application is threaded throughout this chapter and serves as a useful overview to anyone in higher education.

Chapter 2: *Navigating the Role of Artificial Intelligence in Post-Secondary Educational Spaces*

In this review of the literature, the author looks closely at Artificial Intelligence (AI) as a tool in English and teacher preparation departments. Specifically, AI as a tool for teaching essay writing is explored with the intention of the reader leaving with ideas of effective AI usage with students in higher education.

Chapter 3: *AI Chatbots in Higher Education: A Meta-Synthesis*

Chatbots are an important tool that people are using for everyday life nowadays, so it is important for higher education to grasp how the tool affects post-secondary education. Learning experience considerations and practical/ethical issues are delineated in this review of qualitative studies.

Chapter 4: *A Holistic Approach to Improving Students' University Experience: Exploring Philosophical Orientation, Transformational Teaching Methods, and Flexible Learning*

In this phenomenological transcendental study, the researcher learned about faculty are responsive to the dynamic nature of teaching by committing to professional development. Technology-influenced collaborative environments, this chapter posits, are shown to be an effective means for acquiring new skills and improving older skills.

Section 2: Improving Instruction and Learning with Technology

Chapter 5: *The Impact of Instruction Technology on Class and Time Management in Moroccan Higher Education: The Case of Sidi Mohamed Ben Abdellah University*

Over the past 20 years, Morocco has been making major strides in integrating technology into higher education to broaden access and improve learning. This study employs the Technological Pedagogical Content Knowledge (TPACK) framework to explore how technology is impacting student learning and teaching methods at a particular university in Morocco.

Chapter 6: *AI-Enabled Science Lesson Development for Pre-service and Novice Teachers*

Teacher preparation programs in the US are largely discussing and starting to us Artificial Intelligence to improve their abilities to prepare pre-service teachers, but to also reflect what real-life teaching is like. Public schools in the US are starting to use AI with young students from having students use it themselves, to teachers using it to plan their lessons, AI is here to stay and education preparation needs to not shy away from it. This chapter explores these ideas within the context of Science education specifically, and uses a mixture of personal experiences with a review of the literature to paint a vivid picture of the changing nature of science education and teacher preparation.

Chapter 7: *Encouraging Quality: Approaches for Increasing Student Achievement in Higher Education via Involvement and Assistance*

Inclusivity is of paramount importance in higher education and for an institution to truly embody inclusivity, people of all sorts of backgrounds and lifestyles need to not only feel welcomed, but embraced. Ensuring quality higher education feels accessible to everyone is a worthy goal on a globally scale, and this chapters emphasizes its importance and provides practical insights on how it could be possible via innovative approaches.

Section 3: Instructional Technologies' Global Impact

Chapter 8: *Technology's Role in Enhancing Female Higher Education Access and Experience Across the MENA Region*

This review of the literature offers a powerful overview of the current status of women's opportunities in higher education in the Middle East and North Africa. Technology continues to serve as a tool to leverage women's access to post-secondary education and aid in women's ability to climb the professional-ladder within academia.

Chapter 9: *Understanding LMS Usage in Higher Education: Examining the Interplay of Demographic and Usage Factors in Utaut*

This chapter shares how the Unified Theory of Acceptance and Use of Technology (UTAUT) questionnaire was a key tool in learning more about students in Karnataka, India. Specifically, this study collected information regarding students' demographic information and paired it with performance and effort expectancy, social influence, and facilitating conditions. These background elements then led to insights from the survey regarding students' behavioral intentions and attitudes toward technology.

Chapter 10: *Reshaping Higher Education in MENA with Generative AI: A Systematic Review*

By conducting a systematic review of very recent literature (2022-2024), this chapter explores generative AI as an example of an innovative technology that is changing the landscape of higher education globally. The authors specifically investigate how the Middle East and North Africa are responding to these new technologies and depicts that juxtaposition between the region's determination to be prevalent and modern and the desire to uphold traditional teaching methodologies.

Chapter 11: *Crossing Boundaries: An Interactive Study of International Online Collaboration Between Spanish and Moroccan Universities*

Technology can serve as a powerful tool to enable global partnerships and collaborations. This chapter explains a mixed methods approach to investigate how technology can address obstacles to intercultural learning and international relations in higher education. This chapter captures the main ethos of this book, which is that there is great value in learning from those who are from outside our own cultures.

Chapter 12: *Bridging the Gap: Enhancing Understanding Skills Through Interdisciplinary Data Projects and Technologies*

This chapter exposes students to the cultural factors, Hofstedes's culture's consequences, and environmental factors. While this topic might be familiar to humanities, social sciences, management and business students, it likely presents a new and intriguing line of knowledge for students in the hard sciences majors.

CLOSING THOUGHTS

We hope that higher education faculty, administration, and researchers, all find value in this text to guide their work, evoke conversations and spur new questions. We aim for this text to be a unique resource for researchers, education policy makers, study abroad coordinators, undergraduate research, and global engagement organizations and offices. This book represents an international authorship that provides a powerful opportunity for faculty, students, administrators, researchers, and educators in general to learn about how AI and other innovative technologies are being used to inform their professional practices, their research, and ways to avoid or address the challenges.

As addressed in this book, technology offers creative ways to enable and enhance global partnerships and collaborations between higher education institutions. Technology in education can overcome linguistic barriers, strengthen international relationships, enrich intercultural learning, lessen the financial burden, and broaden global inclusion opportunities. The published chapters represent an up-to-date analysis of pedagogies, instructional technologies, academic modules, the best academic practices, and strategies for employing artificial (AI) intelligence ethically and responsibly in classrooms, laboratories, research, and academic assessments. This book can be adopted in its entirety or partially as a textbook for both graduate and undergraduate classes.

Jacquelynne Anne Boivin
Bridgewater State University, USA

Jabbar A. Al-Obaidi
Bridgewater State University, USA

Madhusudana N. Rao

Bridgewater State University, USA

Acknowledgement

Co-Editor's Shared Acknowledgement:

We would like to express our deep gratitude to Bridgewater State University (BSU) community for supporting our global engagement and the goals for internationalizing academic programs. Special Thanks to Dr. B.K. Ravi, Vice Chancellor, Koppal University, India for writing the Foreword for this book.

Dr. Boivin's Acknowledgement:

The word "appreciation" does not even come close to the fullness in my heart that I feel for all those that made this work possible. From colleagues close and from afar, I have learned so much from the contributors of this text, and I truly look forward to continuing to learn from them in the future, as with many I now have established relationships.

This text would not have been possible had I not had the unrelenting effort, inspiration, and insightfulness of my dear co-editors, Dr. Jabbar A. Al-Obaidi and Dr. Madhu N. Rao. With this being our second text together, we certainly are a "well-oiled machine" and our friendship and mutual academic admiration for each other made this experience one marked with laughs and learning. I am confident that we have more projects and adventures ahead of us, my friends!

Finally, I want to thank those closest to me: My husband, Craig Boivin, and my father, Gregson Chase. These two men are my "rocks" who keep me grounded, encourage me to never stop pursuing my goals, lift me when I'm down, and never cease to make me laugh. I'd be remiss if I did not also mention my cat, Remi. Her sassiness always keeps me in line and her relaxed way of life gets me to reflect on the fact that sometimes, we all just need to "do less." I'm so lucky to have so much support in my life.

Dr. Al-Obaidi's Acknowledgement:

I am grateful to my incredible and fearless co-editors, Dr. Jackie Boivin and Dr. Madhu N. Rao for their wisdom and dedication to learning and teaching and for sharing knowledge among different global communities. Jackie and Madhu, you are true scholars in every sense of the word, and I truly treasure your friendship and your high standards of professionalism.

I am (we are) deeply thankful to all contributors for this collective educational and intellectual volume. They displayed patience, understanding, and mutual respect throughout the meticulous process and up to the finish line of publishing this book.

My deepest gratitude and appreciation go to my wife Wafaa Al-Hassan. Her love and unwavering support are what keeps me going. To my beloved family Sarah, Ghayath, Erika, Reggie, and precious granddaughters Ayah-Nooriah, Amani, and our new beautiful addition "batboota" Gravity Alaia, thanks for keeping me smiling, optimistic, and energized.

Dr. Rao's Acknowledgement:

It is with a deep sense of pride and admiration that I acknowledge the relentless efforts put forward by my esteemed colleagues in this endeavor, Dr. Jackie Boivin and Dr. Jabbar Al-Obaidi. Without their combined sincere efforts this would not have come to fruition. This marks as our second book following the success of "The Role of Educators as Agents and Conveyors for Positive Change in Global Education", which was published by the *IGIGlobal* in 2023. Finally, we are a team and our collaborative efforts continue to drive us forward, and hope to accomplish much more in the realm of education ad infinitum.

Without saying, I am deeply grateful to my wife, Indira Devi, for her unwavering support and encouragement which have been crucial to my academic journey. Her steadfast belief in me has been a source of strength and freedom in my academic endeavors. I also thank my family -- Siddhartha, Anusha, and Pooja for their continuous good wishes. Our newest addition to the family, Uma Nannapaneni, is a beauty of joy with her growing day-to-day nuances and smiles. Finally, my heartfelt love goes to my late parents, Nannapaneni Subba Rao and Venkata Subbamma, who instilled the value of education as we were growing up and shaped my path and aspirations.

Section 1
Defining and Exploring Instructional Technologies

Chapter 1
Embracing How AI Responsibly Empowers Students and Faculty in Higher Education:
Theoretical Perspectives

Madhusudana N. Rao
https://orcid.org/0000-0002-5845-4561
Bridgewater State University, USA

Jabbar A. Al-Obaidi
https://orcid.org/0009-0008-9588-7535
Bridgewater State University, USA

ABSTRACT

The rapid advancement of artificial intelligence (AI) is reforming various sectors, and higher education is no exception. AI tools are increasingly being integrated into classrooms and learning environments, offering a range of opportunities for students and faculty alike. This chapter explores the various AI-powered tools that are being used in education today. These tools can potentially revolutionize how faculty teach and how students learn and engage. Providing personalized learning experiences, automating tasks, and making learning more engaging and effective. The literature review illustrates that AI enhances education by offering efficiency, personalization, and accessibility, catering to diverse learning styles. It enables adaptive learning, addressing individual needs and creating a more engaging and effective learning environment. his chapter discusses the benefits of building into a learning management system like Blackboard and other systems. Students can benefit

DOI: 10.4018/979-8-3693-3904-6.ch001

from AI if faculty build it into their syllabus and teaching pedagogy.

INTRODUCTION

The rapid advancement of AI technology has ushered in a new era of innovation, reshaping various aspects of our lives, including the realm of higher education. The integration of Artificial Intelligence (AI) tools in higher education has gained significant traction, offering innovative solutions to enhance the learning experience and streamline academic processes. As AI tools become increasingly sophisticated, they offer unprecedented opportunities to streamline academic processes, enhance learning experiences, and foster creativity. This research aims to provide an in-depth analysis of the various AI tools employed in higher education, their functionalities, benefits, drawbacks, and the ethical sensitivities surrounding their implementation.

Artificial intelligence tools "use machine learning to generate responses or perform basic tasks based on the criteria" user's input or what's known as prompt (clickup. com, para 8). It is not a stretch of the imagination to say that users including faculty and students are already using some features of Artificial Intelligence (AI) to augment their teaching and learning experiences. Information provided by various websites demonstrates that "Translation apps, mapping software, streaming services, email, e-commerce sites, and social media platforms were already using some form of AI to enrich our experiences with curated feeds, ads, and suggestions" (clickup.com, para 9). Embarrassing AI responsibly means understanding the features of AI and its positive and wide range potential along with its limitations. AI literate means being aware of its positive and negative consequences. Hence, the call for using AI responsibly is fundamental as it could enable and empower the faculty and students to enrich their higher education experience.

The U.S. Department of Education supports the use of AI to improve teaching, learning, and innovation at all levels of education. The Department recognizes that "Educators use AI-powered services in their everyday lives, such as voice assistants in their homes; tools that can correct grammar, complete sentences, and write essays; and automated trip planning on their phones" (Office of Educational Technology, May 2023, p.1). According to the Walton Family Foundation press release on March 1, 2023, "Within two months of its introduction, a 51% majority of teachers reported using ChatGPT, with 40% using it at least once a week, and 53% expecting to use it more this year. Just 22% of students said they use the technology weekly or more" (Walton Family Foundation, para 2). Other estimations suggested that ChatGPT has reached 100 million users just two months after launching on November 30, 2022.

Artificial intelligence-based approaches have become an integral component of teaching and learning in education. These approaches include learner models, pedagogical models, and learning domain models, which create an individualized, inclusive, and more welcoming learning environment for students (Luckin et al. 2016; Pham et al. 2022). The underlying argument is that advanced OpenAI provides opportunities for students and faculty to use the technology for specific purposes, which could be broadly helpful for enhancing teaching and learning. It also highlights the exaggerated concerns among some higher education institutions about students using technology to cheat and not do the required work themselves. Additionally, Professors benefit from AI assistants by streamlining administrative duties, managing student information, and facilitating scheduling tasks. This enables them to focus on what truly matters: imparting knowledge and fostering academic growth. Operational staff can also optimize their workflows for a more efficient educational environment.

AI AND HIGHER EDUCATION

This section highlights the ongoing conversation about generative artificial intelligence tools and their positive and negative impact on teaching and learning. It underlines faculty reactions to this technology, the administration's role in providing support, funds for training, and software, applying policies and regulations, and students' use of the technology. Therefore, some scientists prefer the term "augmented intelligence" instead of artificial intelligence. However, this designation continues to perceive the human brain as the source of actual intelligence. However, it also describes computers and computer programs with intelligent functions that people can use to develop or extend their intellectual capabilities" (Annuš, 2024, p.404; Holmes et al., 2019). Further, many research studies verify that personalization in education has become a mark for e-learning over the last decade (Annuš, 2024; Prokofyev et al., (2019).

Currently, faculty members are faced with the challenge of determining the appropriate use of technology in teaching and learning. They must also acknowledge that many students already use these tools, and it isn't easy to detect their use. Meanwhile, administrators are trying to figure out their role in establishing and enforcing institutional policies on issues like ethics, copyright, and code of conduct. College administrators aim to strike a balance between when it is necessary and beneficial to act and when it is seen as an unwelcome interference with the autonomy of faculty and students (The Chronicle of Higher Education Report, 2024). In "The Chronicle's" online survey, 826 people responded between April 16 and April 29,

2024. The following two questions were among the primary questions posed in the survey of The Chronicle of Higher Education (pp.30-31):

1. Where do you see the biggest potential for generative AI to negatively impact teaching and learning?
2. In the next five years, how likely are you to embrace generative-AI technology in your teaching practices?

In response to question number 1, 75% of administrators and 63% of faculty believe in the spread of false information as a concern while 62% and 59% of administrators and faculty respectively worry about the threats to academic integrity. This concern is legitimate and understandable as it allows both sides to be proactive in mitigating the negative features and applications of generative AI. From a futuristic perspective as per question number 2, more than 70% of administrators and faculty are likely to embrace the integration of generative AI technology in teaching practices over the next five years (The Chronicle of Higher Education Report, 2024, p. 31).

The responses from both the administrators and faculty to questions 1 and 2 may look inconsistent. However, logically, they are not. The responses of 70% of administrators and faculty represent the future of generative AI technology in teaching and learning. At the same time, they are not dismissing the potential challenges it brings to classrooms, coursework, or how students may misuse it. Simply put, they are embracing AI technology, but also, they are acknowledging its risks. Norbert Annus (2024) and other researchers argued that educators whether in general education or higher education have started exploring some of the learning opportunities that come with AI (Borasi et al (2024); Beck & Levine, 2023; Volante, DeLuca, & Klinger, 2023). Robert Annuš's study in 2024 showed about 70% of primary school teachers, 55% of high school teachers, and 63% of university employees foresee adopting any of the AI-based technologies (p. 411). Annuš concluded, "Machine learning and data analytics will enable education systems to understand better the individual needs of students" (p.412).

A survey of recent literature refers to the advantages and disadvantages of using AI tools in education whether in sciences, applied sciences, social sciences, businesses, or humanities. However, it should be noted that the groupings of pros and cons of AI do not necessarily fit all areas of specialties in education or the teaching and learning processes. However, Table 1 exhibits some of these advantages and disadvantages for discussion. This Table is an example but not an all-inclusive or comprehensive one.

Table 1. Advantages and Disadvantages of AI Tools

Potential Advantages	Potential Disadvantages
Expand personalized learning	Compromise ethics & Legal problems
Free up faculty time for more high-level tasks	Job loss
Enable leaners to be collaborative	Lack of experience with real cases in sciences
Encourage learners to become independent	AI systems exhibit superior skills compared to a learner
Provide automated assessment systems	Inaccurate analysis
Assemble data to make informed decisions	Hallucination
Eliminate stigmas and discrimination	Algorithm outputs include biases and discriminations
Interact autonomously and freely	Confidentiality and privacy
Enhance remote proctoring	Lack of empathy
Offer fair and understandable natural language processing (NLP)	Spread of fake news, misinformation, hate speech, and social polarization

The ultimate decisions and choices, however, are in the hands of humans. Several studies emphasized that authority, responsibility, and approvals are the duties of the human expert (Doraiswamy et al., 2020, as cited in Gültekin p. 148).

METHODOLOGICAL APPROACH

By conducting an extensive literature review and desk research, this chapter applied a thorough analysis and categorization of the development of technology and Artificial intelligence (AI) of the available data, computer software, Internet accessibility, faculty access, and the responsibilities that come with it. Guided by the descriptive and comparative methodology, this chapter introduced and comparatively described the most popular artificial intelligence tools for educational use cases, including image generation, coding, summarizing, content writing, note-taking, interpretation, video editing, audio transcribing, and time management. The descriptive methodology is deployed to examine AI assistants like ChatGPT, QuillBot, Copilot (formerly Bing Chat), Gemini, Consensus, Resume Worded, Tome, and Easy AI Checker. We aim to provide a comprehensive understanding of their applications in learning, writing, research, and pedagogy. This chapter's research question is whether AI (ChatGPT in particular) is an ally or a threat to higher education.

OBJECTIVES

The objectives of this chapter are:

1. Examine the academic perspectives on ChatGPT and others, such as QuillBot, Copilot (formerly Bing Chat), Gemini, Consensus, Resume Worded, Tome, Grammarly, and Easy AI Checker.
2. Explore the cutting-edge features and capabilities of AI technology and its integration into classroom and research.
3. Compare and discuss the theoretical perspectives on AI.

LITERATURE REVIEW

The significant technological development in the last ten years (2014-2024) has exceeded expectations and the power of imagination. Certainly, the artificial intelligence (AI) is the most noticeable. Regarding this technological advancement, in her article, Editor's Note *Bye-Bye, Smoke and Mirrors,* Cindy Davis (2024) wrote: "We are only just pulling up the launch pad of understanding the far-reaching impact it will have on every aspect of life. One could argue that the Wide World Web, CRISPR, and other revolutionary innovations will reach new and unimaginable heights with AI" (AVTechnology Guide, 2024, para 1).

According to Cindy Davis, AI, and the cloud emerged from behind the smoke and mirrors and were on display in a significant number of booths during the InfoComm event held in early June 2024. Shure's CEO, Chris Schyvinck, shared with Cindy Davis that "The whole AI terminology burst onto the scene when ChatGPT entered the mainstream thought process" (Davis, 2024, para 2). In her conversation with Cindy Davis, Chris Schyvinck elaborated: "Now AI is in everybody's consciousness, and I think that's good because there are a lot of conversations that have to be had around the right way to use it, and where people are doing some more nefarious things, and what has to be managed and figured out and taken care of"(Davis, 2024, para 4). Theresa Benson, Vice President of Product Management and Marketing at Mersive Technology, pointed out (AI is poised to revolutionize the AV field, making experiences more personalized, efficient, and immersive" (Davis, 2024, para 9).

Whether teaching in elementary, high school, a community college, or a university, these critical technologies, including AI quantum computing and advances in biotechnology, are changing and intersecting with one another so rapidly. Institutions of higher education are exploring creative ways to ethically leverage AI to empower students, faculty, and staff. Scholars and educators alike argue that AI is here to stay. Therefore, it is more productive to approach it and may adopt some of its aspects with a critical eye on its weaknesses or hallucinations associated with the large language models (LLMs), including ChatGPT, Bing, and Google's Bard.

Robert Blanck and David E. Balch (2024) cautioned that there are three types of hallucinations in LLMS:

1. Contradictions: LLMs can provide information that contradicts each other and is inconsistent.
2. False facts: LLMs can provide inaccurate data, and factually incorrect information, and create fabricated dates and frameworks.
3. Lack of nuance and context: LLMs "can fabricate information, citing made-up sources and statistics, and fail fact-checking exercises. This raises concerns about the potential impact on issues like election disinformation" (Blanck& Balch, May 15, 2024).

Beneficiaries of AI are required to understand critical media literacy, as well as information and technology literacy. Media and information literacy can help educators ensure the accuracy of information and data produced by AI before presenting it to their students or the public. Media and information literacy is based on the ability to dismiss the state of automaticity (or the ability to act without really thinking) that is, mindless acceptance of information generated by the media for example, or today's AI-powered information.

Students and learners in general may fall victim to this behavior and adopt the information prompted by AI without paying attention to its contradictions, faulty facts, and lack of consistency. AI is similar to media literacy, it is a continuum, not a category (Porter, 2005). Media, information, and technology literacy evolves around five important aspects, identify, evaluate, apply, analyze, and integrate the needed information. Fortune article (2024) stated: *"The potential for hallucinations in AI-powered applications can have detrimental consequences for student learning, assessment, and overall educational outcomes. Inaccurate or fabricated information generated by these systems can reinforce misconceptions, spread misinformation, and undermine the development of critical thinking skills among community college students" (para 3).*

Hallucinations occur when AI systems generate nonsensical, factually incorrect, or unfaithful content. Hence, the faculty members must bring this issue to their classes and discuss its precarious consequences. The CNET article illustrated how "a hallucination can include generative AI producing answers that are incorrect but stated with confidence as if correct" (2024, April 11, para 3)

According to the CNET article, a hallucination can include generative AI producing answers that are incorrect but stated with confidence as if correct. CNET article showed an example of how an AI chatbot responded that "Leonardo da Vinci painted the Mona Lisa in 1815," which is 300 years after it was painted (CNET, 2024, para 4). Testilo, 2024, and Google Cloud, 2024 pointed out that the reasons behind these AI system hallucinations are not entirely known. However, they are likely linked to biases in the training data, limitations of the language models (LLMs), and a lack of contextual understanding (para 4). For example, S. Li et al. (2024) explain: "a multi-feature fuzzy evaluation model based on artificial intelligence (AI) to streamline the evaluation process and provide an efficient framework for accessing teaching methods" (pg.1). The AI multi-feature fuzzy evaluation model offers a solution to the challenges encountered by the Physical Education Teaching Methods in Colleges and Universities in the world. The two biggest challenges are having an "excess of evaluating elements and a lack of assessment framework" (pg.1). In the same vein, S. Li et al. (2024) proposed:

"The multi-feature fuzzy evaluation model based on artificial intelligence to streamline the evaluation process and provide an efficient framework for accessing teaching methods. The framework integrates natural/human language using fuzzy instructions considering three evaluation perspectives, including the management stage, instructors, and students and employs the enhanced cuckoo search optimization algorithm"(p..1).

Along this line, J. Haung (2021) envisioned another approach for the use of IoT technology to gather and evaluate current student conduct and achievement information, resulting in a more precise and effective evaluation of teaching quality. The results show that the proposed strategy could enhance the effectiveness and precision of assessing the quality of instruction and empowering students and faculty (J. Haung, 2021; Li, S et al; 2024).

Further, S. Li et al. (2024) described that the conventional method for evaluating the quality of teaching consists of two categories, 1) comprehensive understanding of the subject matter and 2) comprehensive student achievement in school, to establish the instructing index and assessment index (para 33). Indeed, AI could be a reliable ally to the profession of teaching and learning and provide real-time data.

Norbert Annuš (2024) argues that teachers' job is to help students learn how to be independent and information seekers (pg. 405). Annus explained, "Self-reliance in the digital age is essential, and this includes the ability to search for, find, and use information appropriately" (pg.405). Further, Annuš (2024), Panigrahi & Joshi (2020), and Annuš & Paksi, 2023, outlined the advantages of using AI in education:

1. Reduction of paper-based tests. Tests do not need to be printed but can be distributed and made available to students via various online platforms.
2. Facilitate the assessment process and make it much easier to "produce, reproduce, and access tests" (pg. 406).

3. The system allows users to complete a test from a random bank of questions at any time during a specified day and indicates limits on the number of attempts and the test duration.
4. IA can also monitor the rhythm of typing by using key combinations and the paste function to eliminate cheating.
5. AI's existing platform enables teachers to proctor online exams remotely.
6. Students can take tests and write their essays from anywhere.

In a robust survey and analytical study, Norbert Annuš (2024) concluded by following applicable analysis, which enforces the premise of our current research. Annuš's study (2024) showed the top preferred technology for educational institutions: "*Nearly 70% of those working in primary schools, 55% of those teaching in high schools, and 63% of those working in universities envision implementing this technology as their primary AI tool. The use of automated assessment systems is seen as important mainly by university teachers, which could also mean automated improvement of dissertations. For primary school teachers, chatbots and predictive models have taken a back seat. However, they ranked higher for secondary school and university teachers*" (p. 411).

According to a study by Miriam Sullivan et al. (2023), "Academic Perspectives on ChatGPT, however, have not unanimously declared AI tools as a monumental threat to higher education" (p. 32). Furthermore, Miriam Sullivan et al., (2023) observed, "Other responses have been nuanced, pointing out that while ChatGPT can contain factual inaccuracies and biases, it can enhance student learning" (p. 32).

BACKGROUND AI TOOLS AND SOFTWARE

The Stanford Institute for Human-Centered AI (2023) showed "a notable acceleration of investment in AI as well as the increase of research in ethics, including issues of fairness and transparency" (Maslej et al., 2023 p 3). The following AI tools illustrate that AI is not one thing but an "umbrella for a growing set of modeling capabilities" (U.S. Department of Education, 2023, p 11).

Please be aware that the insertion of any of the AI software, description of any AI tools, or hypertext links for various organizations in this research does not imply any endorsement or promotion of these services by the authors of this chapter. This section describes some of the recent popular tools and software. However, it is expected that more AI tools will be launched.

ChatGPT: The AI Study Companion, https://chatgpt.com.

The ChatGPT, an AI was launched on November 30, 2022, by San Francisco-based Open AI. Historically, one of the first ChatGPTs, ELIZA, was created by computer scientist Joseph Weizenbaum at MIT AI's laboratory. According to UNESCO's annual report of 2023, "ChatGPT is a language model that allows people to interact with a computer more naturally and conversationally. GPT stands for "Generative Pre-Trained Transformer" and is the name given to. A family of natural language models developed by open Artificial Intelligence (AI)" (p. 5).

ChatGPT, an AI chatbot developed by OpenAI, began its journey with a demo release on November 30, 2022, quickly gaining viral popularity on social media.

OpenAI, founded in December 2015, spearheaded ChatGPT's development, with subsequent iterations like GPT-1 in June 2018, GPT-2 in February 2019, and GPT-3 in June 2020 showcasing significant advancements in text generation capabilities. The latest iteration, GPT-4, continues to enhance model alignment, reduce offensive content generation, and improve factual accuracy. Throughout its evolution, ChatGPT has revolutionized natural language understanding and generation, paving the way for transformative applications across various industries.

ChatGPT has emerged as a powerful learning companion. This conversational AI chatbot can summarize texts, paraphrase complex materials, assist with research, generate flashcards and quizzes, and even provide grammar guidance and note-taking assistance. While ChatGPT offers numerous benefits, it is crucial to acknowledge its potential drawbacks, such as accuracy limitations, biases present in the training data, and ethical concerns regarding misuse and manipulation (Marr, Bernard 2023).

QuillBot: The AI Writing Assistant, https://quillbot.com.

QuillBot, developed in 2017 by Rohan Gupta, Anil Jason, and David Silin, is an AI-powered text rewriting and paraphrasing software initially designed as a full-sentence thesaurus. QuillBot's journey began with a simple tool posted on Reddit, and it has evolved into a powerful writing assistant, benefiting students, professionals, and language enthusiasts worldwide. QuillBot's team continuously refines and enhances its features to meet user needs.

QuillBot, an AI-powered writing tool, serves as a valuable sidekick for students and academics. Its core functionalities include paraphrasing text to avoid plagiarism, summarizing long passages, checking grammar, generating citations, and offering a comprehensive writing environment (Singh, Jagjit 2023). QuillBot helps avoid plagiarism, enhances clarity and fluency, saves time, and boosts creativity. However, it may struggle with capturing the full meaning of complex texts, face contextual challenges, and require a stable internet connection or paid subscription for full access (Sangwan, Sujata 2021).

Copilot (Formerly Bing Chat): The Multifaceted AI Assistant, https://copilot.microsoft.com.

Announced on Feb 7, 2023, as Bing Chat, powered by Microsoft's Azure OpenAI Service and based on GPT-4, which also developed ChatGPT, has evolved into a versatile AI assistant and is now termed Copilot. It is a multifaceted AI assistant with applications for both casual users and business professionals. It offers engaging conversations, task completion, secure data handling, productivity boosting, and accessibility across various platforms (Conway, Adam 2014). Copilot's adaptability makes it a valuable asset for both personal and professional applications in higher education (Brue, Melody 2023). While Copilot provides versatility, efficiency, and valuable insights, it may have potential inaccuracies, require a subscription cost for advanced features, and necessitate continuous adaptation to its evolving capabilities (Beatman, Andy 2023, Roose, Kevin 2023).

Gemini (Formerly known as Bard): Google's versatile AI Chatbot for Research and Writing, https://gemini.google.com.

May 2023 marked a significant moment for AI advancements during Google's I/O event. Google announced Bard and on February 8, 2024, officially renamed it to Gemini while integrating it with Google products/apps like Gmail, Maps, and YouTube. Gemini with access to all these apps gained momentum in its usage.

Google's Gemini serves as a versatile AI chatbot with strengths in question-answering, drafting, summarizing, translating, and providing information (Alston, Elena 2024). Powered by Google's Pathways Language Model (PaLM 2), Gemini offers a user-friendly interface for conducting research, generating text, and seeking clarification on various subjects (Metz, Cade 2023). While it provides natural language interaction and text generation capabilities, its accuracy may vary depending on the complexity of the topic or question.

Consensus: The AI-Powered Research Tool, https://consensus.app.

Eric Olson and Christian Salem, who come from a consumer tech background, created the Consensus app with a total funding of $4.25 million, including reinvestment from pre-seed round backer, Winklevoss Capital. In May 2019, Consensus released its official app, designed for secure polling and real-time government feedback in South Burlington, Vermont, USA.

Consensus is an AI-powered research tool and scientific literature search engine that enables users to search and retrieve relevant scientific research papers, answer questions based on research findings, generate comprehensive summaries, and filter results based on specific criteria (Diprose, Leigh 2019). Its capabilities include retrieving relevant research papers, answering questions based on findings, generating comprehensive summaries, filtering results, and providing access to full texts (Plumb, Taryn 2024). Consensus streamlines literature reviews and research exploration, saving time and effort for scholars (Ibrahimov, Vugar 2023). While it saves time and effort, eliminates bias, and simplifies literature reviews, it may have accuracy limitations, require a paid subscription for full access, and raise concerns about its overreliance on AI.

Resume Worded: The AI Resume Optimizer, https://resumeworded.com.

Rohan Mahtani was the founder and lead architect. Resume Worded is an AI-powered resume-writing tool that helps users create resumes tailored to specific job descriptions. It generates AI-powered summaries, provides feedback and suggestions, offers resume templates, analyzes job descriptions, and checks for formatting and grammatical errors (Njuguna, Samuel 2023). It offers features like resume optimization, keyword analysis, and tailored recommendations based on job descriptions. By leveraging AI, Resume Worded helps students and recent graduates present their qualifications effectively to potential employers. While it improves resume quality and increases the chances of landing interviews, it may have limited customization options compared to dedicated resume writing services (Alsakkaf, Roqaia, 2023).

Tome: The AI Presentation Partner, https://tome.app.

Tome was started in 2020 by Keith Peiris and Henri Liriani, a team of engineers who came out of META, San Francisco, California. In December 2022, Tome Introduced generative storytelling. This innovative feature allows creators to generate entire narratives from scratch using AI. Within just five months of its launch, the platform amassed a staggering one million users, surpassing the user base of popular tools such as Dropbox and Slack.

Tome AI is a powerful tool for creating visually appealing and engaging presentations. It utilizes AI and natural language processing to generate slides and narratives swiftly, either from scratch or existing content (Maina, Alphan 2023).

Tome's collaborative capabilities and design enhancement features make it an asset for students and educators alike (Jones, Sarah 2024).

Easy AI Checker: Ensuring Academic Integrity or Promoting Ethical AI Practices, https://easyaichecker.com.

The Easy AI Checker is a product developed by CompanionLink Software, Inc., which has a long-standing history. Founded in 1978, CompanionLink primarily focuses on creating products that facilitate synchronization between personal computers (PCs) and mobile phones. As for the Easy AI Checker app itself, development began in March 2023. By mid-April, over half of the content evaluated and tested using the app showed evidence of substantial AI generation. The creators recognized the need for a faster and more efficient plagiarism-checking solution, leading to the birth of this service.

Easy AI Checker is a free app that detects plagiarism and AI-written content using GPT Zero, promoting ethical AI practices in academia (Presswire, Ein 2023). By leveraging GPT Zero's AI smarts and natural language processing, it generates quick reports to ensure the originality of written work (Bruns, Wayland 2023). While it ensures originality and saves time, it may have accuracy limitations, a limited scope, and raise ethical concerns about ownership and creativity. This tool helps maintain academic integrity in an era where AI-generated content is becoming increasingly prevalent.

GradeScope: AI-Assisted Grading and Feedback, https://www.gradescope.com/.

GradeScope, an American ed-tech company, founded in 2014 by Pieter Abbeel, Arjun Singh, and Ibrahim Awwal. In 2018, Gradescope was acquired by Turnitin, a significant milestone in its journey. During the COVID-19 pandemic, Gradescope responded to the shift in education by releasing a LockDown Browser to ensure secure online exams for students who are studying remotely.

GradeScope is an ed-tech platform that incorporates AI to streamline grading and provide personalized feedback. Its AI-grading feature analyzes student submissions, identifies patterns, and offers targeted feedback. GradeScope's AI capabilities not only save time for educators but also enhance the learning experience for students.

Grammarly: The AI Grammar and Writing Assistant, https://www.grammarly.com.

Grammarly was founded in 2009 by Max Lytvyn, Alex Shevchenko, and Dmytro Lider. These visionary creators were behind MY Dropbox, an app that checks essays for plagiarism. Initially, Grammarly was designed as an educational app to help university students improve their English skills. It later expanded its reach to end customers who use English in everyday life. They launched an online editor as a paid subscription product, focusing primarily on grammatical error correction (GEC) to assist students with their writing. The company quickly became cash-flow positive, and they rebranded their venture as Grammarly.

Grammarly is a widely used AI-powered writing assistant that offers grammar checking, plagiarism detection, and concise writing suggestions. It helps improve writing quality, ensures originality, and saves time. However, it may have accuracy limitations, raise ethical concerns about ownership and creativity, and lack transparency regarding its inner workings (Sullivan, Shelby 2023).

Comparison of selected AI Tools:

While these selective AI tools share the common goal of enhancing academic pursuits, they differ in their specific functionalities and areas of focus. Different AI tools are relentlessly evolving from several parts of the world and there will be others added in the near future catering to a different purpose for the public that is not already available. Table 2 provides a comparative overview of their key features and applications.

Table 2. An Overview of the Selected AI Tools in Higher Education

AI Tool	Primary Function	Key Features	Academic Application
ChatGPT	Conversational AI	Text generation, summarization, research assistance	Learning, writing, note-taking
QuillBot	Writing Assistance	Paraphrasing, grammar checking, citation generation	Academic writing, plagiarism avoidance
Copilot	Multifaceted Assistant	Task completion, data handling, productivity boost	Personal and professional tasks

continued on following page

14

Table 2. Continued

AI Tool	Primary Function	Key Features	Academic Application
Gemini	Research and Writing	Question answering, text generation, information retrieval	Research, writing, translation
Consensus	Research synthesis	Literature search, summarization, question answering	Literature reviews, research exploration
Resume Worded	Resume Building	Resume optimization, keyword analysis, job matching	Career development, job applications
Tome	Presentation Creation	Slide generation, design enhancement, collaboration	Presentations, visual communication
Easy AI Checker	Plagiarism Detection	AI content detection, originality checking	Academic integrity, ethical AI practices
GradeScope	Grading and feedback	AI-assisted grading, personalized feedback	Grading efficiency, learning enhancement
Grammarly	Writing assistant	AI powered grammar correction, writing suggestions	Grammar checking, accuracy limitations

THEORETICAL FRAMEWORK

For decades, there has been ongoing discussion regarding the relationship between education and technology, influencing both theory and practice in the use of instructional technology. However, among the most prominent learning theories, "behaviorism, cognitivism, connectionism, constructivism, and humanism", two theories, constructivism, and behaviorism, appeared to be closely applicable to integrating education and technology.

Behaviorism theory in education assumes a "learner is essentially passive, responding to environmental stimuli. The learner starts as a blank slate (i.e., tabula rasa), and behavior is constructed through positive or negative reinforcement (Nalliah & Idris 2014, p. 51). Behaviorism theory emphasizes observable behaviors and the reaction to external stimuli as the primary factors influencing learning. In this case, YI tools represent the "external stimuli" that students pay attention to and interact with. Therefore, technology in education significantly influences the behavior of students. For instance, technology, such as ChatGPT, educational games, and adaptive learning systems, has been designed to provide immediate feedback and reinforcement, aligning with the goals of the curriculum. Overall, AI in higher education provides a platform that supports and enhances teaching and learning. Additionally, education behaviorism theory offers a theoretical framework for the process of learning and teaching and educational assessment. According to behaviorism theory, AI applications in higher education involve five elements: student, teacher, curriculum, technology, and learning outcomes assessment.

On the other hand, constructivist theory in education emphasizes that learning is an active process for students. This principle is crucial because it focuses on the learner and acknowledges the important role of the mind, involving various elements and measurable attributes (Nalliah & Idris 2014, p. 51). When learners actively engage with information, they start the process of construction. AI tools can be instructed to provide lessons with visual images and other illustrative materials to stimulate learners and activate the process of learning.

ETHICAL CONSIDERATIONS & DETRIMENTS

While AI tools offer numerous benefits, it is crucial to address their potential drawbacks and ethical implications:

1. Accuracy and Bias Concerns: AI models may exhibit biases present in their training data or produce inaccurate results, potentially leading to unfair assessments or misinformation. This highlights the need for critical evaluation and fact-checking.
2. Overreliance and Potential for Misuse: Excessive dependence on AI tools could hinder critical thinking and creativity, and there is a risk of misusing these tools for unethical purposes, such as plagiarism or cheating.
3. Privacy and Data Security Risks: The use of AI tools may raise concerns about data privacy and security concerns, particularly when handling sensitive student information or internal institutional data.
4. Ethical Implications: The integration of AI in education raises ethical questions regarding authorship, ownership, and the potential impact on human creativity and intellectual development.
5. Accessibility and Affordability: While some AI tools are free or offer student discounts, others may have subscription fees, potentially limiting access for some students or institutions.
6. Academic Integrity: The availability of AI writing assistants and plagiarism detection tools could potentially discourage students from developing critical thinking and writing skills, leading to an over-reliance on technology.
7. Ownership and Creativity: The use of AI-generated content raises questions about ownership, authorship, and the future of creative expression.

8. Transparency and Accountability: The inner workings of AI algorithms may lack transparency, making it difficult to understand how decisions are made and to ensure accountability.

THE APPLE BASKET ANALOGY: STRATEGIES FOR AI IN HIGHER EDUCATION

Institutions of higher education in the U.S. and worldwide have recognized and understood the cyclical effects of AI on education. To describe the status of AI and its fast growth, the authors of this chapter use the apple basket analogy to describe the status of AI and its rapid advancement They compare the majority of apples being fine while a few are spoiled to the current state of AI. This suggests that effort is needed to distinguish the good aspects of AI from the problematic ones. Therefore, on one hand, entrepreneur and governance expert Amit Jaitly (2024) encouraged educators to *explore "the potential of artificial intelligence (AI) in the field of education holds many exciting possibilities. Learners and teachers alike can benefit from the many platforms that offer interactive simulations and personalized learning paths, among other features. Learners and teachers alike can benefit from the many platforms that offer interactive simulations and personalized learning paths, among other features"* (para 3). On the other hand, Danial Schwartz, Dean of the Graduate School of Education, Stanford University, cushioned, "Technology offers the prospect of universal access to fundamentally new ways of teaching. A lot of AI is also going to automate really bad ways of teaching. So, think about it as a way of creating new types of teaching" (Chen, para 5, 2023). So, the consumers of the apple basket would never discard all the apples, but only the rotten ones. Then, the question becomes: Can higher education institutions develop effective policies to maintain the "new ways of teaching" that AI offers and encircle the "really bad ways"?

The Secretary of Education Miguel A. Cardona and thoughtful colleagues (2023) discussed a comprehensive answer to the above question in an extensive report. Secretary Cardona made the case for addressing AI in education now. The following reasons were compiled from Secretary Cardona's report.

1. AI may enhance educational services by enabling better achievement of educational priorities on a notable scale, lowering costs, providing teachers with more support, and allowing teachers to extend the support they offer to individual students when they need it. Examples include, but are not limited to, voice as-

sistants, mapping tools, shopping recommendations, essay-writing capabilities, and other familiar applications (Cardona et al., 2023).

2. The option of "Developing resources that are responsive to the knowledge and experiences students bring to their learning—their community and cultural assets—is a priority" (Cardona et al; 2023, p. 2).

3. The fear of "system-level risks and anxiety about potential future risks" includes a greater level of surveillance of students, risk of data privacy, replacement of teachers by AI, algorithmic discrimination and bias, and systematic unfairness in the learning opportunities or resources (Cardona et al; 2023, p. 2).

4. The level of vulnerability arises because of the scale of conceivable unintended or unanticipated consequences caused for example by instructional decisions to be automated at scale, educators may uncover unwanted consequences that have a direct impact on some students. These issues of scale and the influence of AI required a well-thought approach to harvest its benefits "while mitigating unintended consequences that may exacerbate educational disparities" (TechEd Maven Consulting, para 6, 2024).

Given the urgency of addressing AI immediately (now), Bridgewater State University (BSU) in Massachusetts, U.S., for example, organized the Inaugural Artificial Intelligence Summit on Monday, April 29th, 2024. The Summit Committee invited experts, practitioners, and enthusiasts in the field of artificial intelligence to the summit. The keynote speaker was Abran Maldonado, the Leading AI expert, OpenAI ambassador, and co-founder of Create Labs. As co-founder of Create Labs, a Black and Brown-founded startup, Abran is leading the charge in the AI and metaverse design space, bringing his unique perspective to an industry that has historically been dominated by a narrow set of voices (Artificial Intelligence Summit Program, 2024). BSU website stated, "As a Gates Millennium Scholar with a background in Hip-Hop, digital media, and youth culture, Maldonado has always been passionate about expanding access to technology and empowering those who have been underrepresented in the field" (para 3).

The authors of this chapter attended the summit and took notes. During his presentation, Abran Maldonado stated, "Technology has the power to unlock a brighter future for all, and I want to make sure that everyone has the opportunity to benefit from it." The BSU Artificial Intelligence Advisory Board is striving to put in place a plan and policies to facilitate the use of AI. Abran Maldonado introduced the first Afro-Latina and Bilingual C.L.Ai.R.A. Maldonado stated, "C.L.Ai.R. A. is more than just an AI. She's an ambassador for humanity, bridging the gap between technology and understanding. Unlike traditional AI chatbots, C.L.Ai.R. A. offers opinionated, thoughtful, insights, reflecting her unique perspectives and extensive interactions with diverse audiences" (Artificial Intelligence Summit Program, 2024).

BSU Artificial Intelligence Summit offered a variety of workshops for faculty, students, and staff. During discussions, attendees recognized that AI tools have both strengths and weaknesses. Participants from BSU were informed that if privacy is a concern, they can use their BSU credentials to log into and use Google Gemini and Microsoft Office. Additionally, Microsoft offers reliable data and privacy protections when using a commercial account such as the one associated with their BSU user account (Lepage, 2024). By introducing these kinds of preliminary approaches, BSU prepares its community to work together and develop a strategy. The literature review reveals several strategies that perfectly respond to the concerns raised by higher education institutions (HEIs) regarding AI and its fast-paced development.

Here are some viable components for HEIs to adopt:

First: Considering AI and its Tools as an Integrated Part of Institution Cybersecurity

The traditional separation between the departments of information technology, instructional design, computer science, and cybersecurity should end. AI is influencing all these departments and units. Therefore, integrating it with the institution's cybersecurity will benefit every member of the campus community. The integration could also reduce cost, increase awareness among campus members, and save time.

Second: Strengthening Institutional Governance for Cybersecurity

The higher education institutions (HEIs) need to prioritize cybersecurity by involving institutional senior administrators, including deans and chairs of departments, and gaining their commitment. Leadership should understand that cybersecurity is not just the responsibility of IT departments but a focus for the entire institution. Just as digital technologies are aligned with business strategy, cybersecurity should receive the same level of attention (Cheng and Wang, 2022; Johnston and Hale, 2009; Wilkin and Chenhall, 2010; Ferguson; Green; Vaswani and Wu, 2013; Chong.; Tan and Felix, 2012; Nolan and McFarlan, 2005; Rothrock; Kaplan and Van Der Oord, 2018; Spremić and Šimunic, 2018). Further, researchers argue that the formation of a new and comprehensive institutional structure and applying a policy of checks and balances could effectively enhance institution governance for cybersecurity (Huang et al., 2010).

Third: Revisiting Existing Regulations, Policies, and Practices

In the view of Baskerville and Siponen (2002); and Cheng and Wang (2022) policies for cybersecurity are official high-level declarations that represent an organization's course of action regarding the use and protection of information and digital assets (p. 7). The regulations and policies need to be updated to respond to new technological advancements, such as AI, information and data, and cybersecurity.

Fourth: Promote AI Literacy, Ethics, and Code of Conduct

Promoting artificial intelligence culture in higher education institutions (HEIs) could be accomplished by organizing workshops and through other training venues for faculty, students, and staff. There is an emphasis on individual responsibility and accountability, ethics, and professional conduct in dealing with and evaluating information and data made available by AI. Educating faculty, students, and staff about the ethical considerations regarding AI technology use is crucial for responsible integration in teaching and learning. Promoting AI literacy could benefit both students and faculty by showing them how to avoid AI hallucinations, unfounded citations, made-up stories, and unreliable data.

Fifth: Ask AI to Propose a Strategy

Repudiation: As an exercise to demonstrate the efficiency of AI when explicit instructions are given, on July 13, 2024, the authors asked AI to generate a strategy for AI in higher education. Here it is:

1. Integration of AI-powered personalized learning: Implementing AI-powered tools and platforms that offer personalized learning experiences can help cater to individual student needs, learning styles, and pace of learning. These tools can adapt to students' strengths and weaknesses, providing tailored educational content and feedback.
2. Automation of administrative and repetitive tasks: Leveraging AI for automating administrative tasks such as grading, scheduling, and basic inquiries can free up valuable time for educators, allowing them to focus more on teaching and mentoring students. Additionally, automating routine tasks can lead to more efficient academic operations.
3. Ethical implementation and governance of AI: It is crucial to develop clear ethical guidelines and governance structures for the use of AI in higher education. Institutions should prioritize transparency, fairness, accountability, and privacy when implementing AI in educational settings. Educating faculty and students

about the ethical considerations surrounding AI technology is also essential for responsible integration.

Interestingly, the third component of the AI proposed strategy talks about developing "clear ethical guidelines" which is compatible with what is brought up by the authors in the fourth point "Promote AI Literacy, Ethics, and Code of Conduct".

DISCUSSION AND ANALYSIS

A. Discussion of Objectives

Guided by the methodological approach, this research reviewed and discussed the most recent studies on AI and its tools. It examined and described AI assistants like ChatGPT, QuillBot, Copilot (formerly Bing Chat), Gemini, Consensus, Resume Worded, Tome, and Easy AI Checker. It offered a description of their applications relevant to the classroom, writing, research, and methodology.

In the section "Background AI Tools and Software", the chapter offered a description of the available AI tools as the literature revealed a notable increase in investment in AI and an accelerating interest of researchers to investigate issues of ethics, fairness, equity, privacy, and transparency. Objective 1 in this chapter is to "Examine the academic perspectives on ChatGPT and others like QuillBot, Copilot (formerly Bing Chat), Gemini, Consensus, Resume Worded, Tome, and Easy AI Checker" met. Nine AI generative tools were discussed. The literature review on AI illustrated that most users have a basic level of literacy and to how these tools work (Sullivan et al. 2023, p. 32). Media coverage of AI has been patchy with sensationalistic portrayals "(Sullivan et al. 2023).

Objective 2 "Explore the cutting-edge features and capabilities of AI technology and its integration into classroom and research" still needs more investigative and in-depth research. However, the chapter discussed a valuable experiment by Professor Ethan Mollick, Associate Professor at the Wharton School of the University of Pennsylvania, (February 17, 2023). Mollick wrote: "I fully embraced AI in my classes this semester (spring), requiring students to use AI tools in a number of ways" across three separate undergraduate and masters-level classes. (Mollick, 2023, para 1).

Mollick's (2023) experimental work with classes is based on the. following procedures Mollick explained: all classes had the same AI policy with a guide on how to use AI, write with ChatGPT, and generate ideas with ChatGPT (para 3 and para 4).

1. One class was designed around an expansive AI utilization to help students generate ideas and produce written materials.
2. A second class had assignments with AI required, while AY was optional to use to complete another set of class assignments.
3. Students enrolled in the third class were introduced to AY tools and how to use them but the instructor did not provide certain assignments.

The lessons learned from this experiment include A.) without AI-appropriate training students will get it wrong, B.) adhering to certain policies is essential, C.) having an open discussion with students will enhance their self-confidence, D.) understanding the issue of ethics becomes paramount for students, and finally, E.) students appreciate the conversation regarding issues of accuracy, biases, academic integrity, and limitations.

The discussion and literature review provided positive support for the research question of whether AI (particularly ChatGPT) is an ally (asset) or a threat to higher education. It should be acknowledged that AI has its advocates and adversaries, but still, AI offers opportunities to enrich student learning and success and provides alternatives to faculty to cut back on some managerial issues related to classroom management, assignments, and scheduling.

Relevant to AY applications, the report of the U.S. Department of Education (2023) highlighted two critical aspects: Advanced educational applications can converse and interact with students and teachers. There is the concept of the "human hand" that is built into the AI similar to C.L.Ai.R. A. which was introduced by Abran Maldonado (BSU Artificial Intelligence Summit Program, 2024).

B. Advantages of AI Tools in Higher Education

The integration of AI tools in higher education offers numerous advantages, including:

1. Enhanced Learning Experiences: AI assistants like ChatGPT and Gemini provide personalized learning support, offering explanations, summaries, and interactive learning materials, catering to diverse learning styles and needs.
2. Improved Writing and Research Capabilities: Tools like QuillBot, Consensus, and Gemini assist students and researchers in paraphrasing, grammar checking, citation generation, literature search, and research synthesis, fostering academic integrity and streamlining the research process.
3. Increased Productivity and Efficiency: AI tools such as Copilot, Tome, and GradeScope automate tasks, streamline workflows, and provide timely feedback, saving time and effort for both students and educators.

4. Accessibility and Personalization: Many AI tools offer user-friendly interfaces, accessibility across multiple platforms, and personalized recommendations, making them inclusive and adaptable to individual needs.
5. Career Development Support: Tools like Resume Worded assist students and recent graduates in crafting compelling resumes, optimizing them for specific job descriptions, and increasing their chances of securing employment opportunities.

C. Commonalities of AI Tools

- Free Limited Versions: All AI tools are free to use up to a limited version. Use of Premium features requires payment.
- Developed with Machine Learning: These AIs are built using machine learning techniques.
- Quick Response Time: AI tools provide quick responses to queries.
- Not 100% Perfect: The tools are not entirely robust and need verification for accuracy.
- Still Evolving: AI tools are in a continuous growth stage.

FINDINGS

The literature review illustrated the positive and negative dimensions regarding the utilization of AI in higher education. The positivity in adopting AI in teaching and learning includes providing students with opportunities to figure out and understand the accuracy of data and information and not accept everything ChatGPT produced for them. It also helps students to improve their writing quality, secure originality, and save time.

The negative side, however, may appear in accuracy limitations, ethical problems concerning ownership and creativity, and the lack of transparency, unfairness, and intended or unintended discriminatory issues and unwanted consequences.

Faculty members could benefit from AI capabilities not only because it saves time but also enhances the pedagogical approach to teaching and enriches the learning experience for students. Professors and teachers benefit from AI assistants by streamlining administrative tasks and administering student information, and it could also handle class scheduling. Freeing faculty from these daunting tasks gives them more time to focus on teaching, conveying knowledge, and nurturing an inclusive environment to ensure academic growth.

Another leading finding indicates that higher education institutions (HEIs) are in critical need of upgrading existing regulations and introducing new policies to manage and integrate AI and its open sources in classes, management, scheduling, creating syllabi, and the whole operation of teaching and learning.

There are concerns about ethical problems, AI trustworthiness, fact checks, privacy, contradictions, and even hallucinations. Miguel A. Cardona, Secretary, U.S. Department of Education et al. (2023) emphasized the central role of humans in this technology: "A top policy priority must be establishing human in the loop as a requirement in educational applications, despite contrary pressures to use AI as an alternative to human decision making" (p.9). The literature review in this chapter highlighted this point.

CONCLUSION

AI pushed educational and instructional technology to the cutting edge. Any miscalculated move could cut off connectivity between AI technology and the massive body of learners and teachers. AI is being used by both students and faculty. Students use it to generate ideas and images, create apps, draw maps, facilitate group work, and provide data and needed information. Faculty members turn to AI to assist them with class management, design assignments, and the potential of interactive simulations.

The chapter outlines a strategy for implementing AI in higher education and links practical components to the strategy. The integration of departments of information technology, instructional design, computer science, and cybersecurity is a feasible idea that higher education institutions (HEIs) should consider. While there are many speculations about AI, the literature review demonstrated that there are opportunities for faculty and students to adopt some AI tools to enhance teaching and learning and to increase student success.

The integration of AI tools in higher education presents both opportunities and challenges. These tools have the potential to revolutionize learning, writing, research, and productivity by offering personalized support, streamlining processes, and fostering creativity. However, it is crucial to address the potential drawbacks, such as accuracy concerns, overreliance, and ethical implications. As AI technology continues to evolve, educational institutions, educators, and students need to embrace these tools responsibly and ethically. By fostering a balanced approach that combines AI assistance with critical thinking, fact-checking, and academic integrity, we can harness the power of AI to enhance the educational experience while preserving the core values of higher education.

Ongoing research, open dialogue, and collaboration among stakeholders are vital to navigating the ethical and practical considerations surrounding AI in higher education. By doing so, we can unlock the transformative potential of these tools while ensuring that they serve as catalysts for intellectual growth, innovation, and the pursuit of knowledge. The integration of AI tools in higher education offers numerous benefits, including enhanced learning experiences, streamlined academic processes, and improved productivity. However, it is crucial to address the potential drawbacks and ethical considerations surrounding their implementation. Institutions must strike a balance between leveraging the advantages of AI tools and ensuring academic integrity, privacy, and ethical practices. Continuous research, open dialogue, and responsible implementation strategies are essential to harness the full potential of AI in higher education while mitigating its risks and challenges.

In conclusion, AI discussion in higher education institutions (HEIs) will continue and the voices of faculty, students, and staff must be included as they represent the heart and soul of teaching and learning, knowledge introduction, and sharing.

LIMITATIONS

The discussion, analysis, findings, recommendations, and conclusion of this study are limited by the data and literature review. The proposed strategies are derived from previous studies and the ways that we envision moving AI forward. Thus, it is limited by our interpretation and approach. Further, AI tools are consistently changing and so are the benefits and the challenges.

FUTURE RESEARCH

There is still a great need to further investigate AI and cybersecurity best practices and to conduct empirical studies to assess the impact of AI on student learning. AI is a complicated topic and comes with various issues that need further research to resolve problems and manage rising issues. Another area of research is needed to study whether AI enhances learning for students with disadvantaged backgrounds and different abilities.

ACKNOWLEDGMENTS

We thank our graduate student, Chetana Musunuru, at Bridgewater State University, Massachusetts, for her assistance.

REFERENCES

Alsakkaf, R. (Sept 29, 2023) https://medium.com/lampshade-of-illumination/resume-worded-ccd8331158f3

Alshaikh, M. (2020). Developing cybersecurity culture to influence employee behavior: A practice perspective. [CrossRef]. *Computers & Security*, 98, 102003. DOI: 10.1016/j.cose.2020.102003

Alston, E. (Feb 28, 2024) https://zapier.com/blog/how-to-use-google-bard/

Alzahrani, L. (2023). Analyzing Students' Attitude and Behavior Toward Artificial Intelligence Technologies in Higher Education. [IJRTE]. *International Journal of Recent Technology and Engineering*, 11(6), 65–73. DOI: 10.35940/ijrte.F7475.0311623

Annuš, N. (2024). Education in the Age of Artificial Intelligence. *TEM Journal*, 13(1), 404–413.

Annuš, N., Csóka, M., & Paksi, D. (2023). Learning Management Systems and Their Possibilities in Education - Case of Slovakia. 17th International Technology, *Education and Development Conference*, 6981-6986. Doi: DOI: 10.21125/inted.2023.1896

Artificial Intelligence Blog https://www.artificial-intelligence.blog/ai-news/from-bard-to-gemini-a-look-at-the-evolution-of-googles-ai-assistant. Accessed on July 16, 2024.

Awa-abuon, J. (2023). How to Reduce AI Hallucination With These 6 Prompting Techniques. https://www.makeuseof.com/how-to-reduce-ai-hallucination/

Baskerville, R., & Siponen, M. (2002). An information security meta-policy for emergent organisations. [Google Scholar] [CrossRef] [Green Version]. *Logistics Information Management*, 15(5/6), 337–346. DOI: 10.1108/09576050210447019

Beatman, A. (Dec 14, 2023) https://azure.microsoft.com/en-us/blog/azure-openai-service-powers-the-microsoft-copilot-ecosystem/#:~:text=Copilot—powered%20by%20Microsoft%20Azure,infrastructure%20from%20cloud%20to%20edge

Blanck, R., & Balch, D. E. (2024). Mitigating Hallucinations in LLMs for Community College Classrooms: Strategies to Ensure Reliable and Trustworthy Ai-Powered Learning Tools. Faculty Focus Daily, May 15, 2024._https://www.facultyfocus.com/articles/teaching-with-technology-articles/mitigating-hallucinations-in-llms-for-community-college-classrooms-strategies-to-ensure-reliable-and-trustworthy-ai-powered-learning-tools/?st=FFdaily;sc=FF240515;utm_term=FF240515&mailingID=6501&utm_source=ActiveCampaign&utm_medium=email&utm_content=Mitigating%20Hallucinations%20in%20LLMs%20for%20Community%20College%20Classrooms%3A%20Strategies%20to%20Ensure%20Reliable%20and%20Trustworthy%20AI-Powered%20Learning%20Tools&utm_campaign=FF240515 Accessed: May 15, 2024.

Borasi, R. Miller, E. David; Vaughan-Brogan, Patricia; DeAngelis, Karen; Han, Yu. Jung & Sharon, Mason. (2024). *An AI Wishlist from School Leaders*. Phi Delta Kappa, May 1, 2024, 47-58. https://web-p-ebscohost-com.libserv-prd.bridgew.edu/ehost/pdfviewer/pdfviewer?vid=3&sid=e4171dce-a14d-40f5-97f4-303c18f16832%40redis

Brue, M. (July 20, 2023). https://www.forbes.com/sites/moorinsights/2023/07/20/microsoft-puts-ai-chat-to-work-with-bing-chat-enterprise/?sh=1a8eb6a219b1

Bruns, W. (Oct 26, 2023). https://easyaichecker.com/blog/2023/10/the-ethics-of-ai-detection-and-humanizing-a-comprehensive-analysis/

Chen, C. (2023). *AI Will Transform Teaching and Learning. Let's Get it Right*. (March 9, 2023), Stanford University, Human-Centered Artificial Intelligence_https://hai.stanford.edu/news/ai-will-transform-teaching-and-learning-lets-get-it-right

Cheng, E., & Wang, T. (2022). C.K.; Wang, Tianchong. (2022). Institutional Strategies for Cybersecurity in Higher Education Institutions. *Information (Basel)*, 13(4), 192. DOI: 10.3390/info13040192

Chong, J. L., Tan, P., & Felix, B. (2012). IT governance in collaborative networks: A socio-technical perspective. Pac. Asia J. Assoc. Inf. Syst. 4, 31–48. [Google Scholar] [CrossRef] [Green Version CNET. (2024, April 11). ChatGPT Glossary: 42 AI Terms That Everyone Should Know. https://www.cnet.com/tech/computing/chatgpt-glossary-42-ai-terms-that-everyone-should-know/

Conway, A. (May 07, 2024). https://www.xda-developers.com/microsoft-copilot/#:~:text=Copilot%20was%20developed%20by%20Microsoft,you%20can%20use%20it%20freely

Davis, C. (2024). Artificial Intelligence is the Most. AVTechnology Guide, 2024. https://issuu.com/futurepublishing/docs/avtechnology_june_guide_2024_0035?fr =sYWZmOTc0ODQ2NDY

Diprose, L. (May 09, 2019) https://medium.com/consensus-ai/consensus-update-5 -the-consensus-app-dff638b21eac

Doraiswamy, P. M., Blease, C., & Bodner, K. (2020). Artificial intelligence and the future of psychiatry: Insights from a global physician survey. *Artificial Intelligence in Medicine*, 102, 101753. DOI: 10.1016/j.artmed.2019.101753 PMID: 31980092

Ferguson, C., Green, P., Vaswani, R., & Wu, G. (2013). Determinants of effective information technology governance. [Google Scholar] [CrossRef]. *International Journal of Auditing*, 17(1), 75–99. DOI: 10.1111/j.1099-1123.2012.00458.x

Fortune (April 11, 2024). Hallucinations are the bane of AI-driven insights. Here's what search can teach us about trustworthy responses, according to Snowflake's.

Guhanarayan, V. (2023). 4 Ways to Prevent AI Hallucinations. https://www.makeuseof .com/prevent-ai-hallucination/

Mücahit, G. (2022). *The Advantages and Disadvantages of Using Artificial Intelligence in Mental Health Services.* Journal of Human & Society / İnsannsan ve Toplum. September 1, 2022

Han, J. (2020). Changes in attitudes and efficacy of AI learners according to the level of programming skill and project interest in AI project. *Journal of The Korean Association of Information Education.*, 24(4), 391–400. DOI: 10.14352/ jkaie.2020.24.4.391

Holmes, W., Bialik, M., & Fadel, C. (2019). Artificial Intelligence. In *Education Promises and Implications for Teaching and Learning*. The Center for Curriculum Redesign.

Huang, J. (2021). An Internet of Things evaluation Algorithm for Quality Assessment of Computer-Based Teaching. *Mobile Information Systems*, 2021, 9919399. DOI: 10.1155/2021/9919399

Huang, R., Zmud, R. W., & Price, R. L. (2010). Influencing the effectiveness of IT governance practices through steering committees and communication policies. [Google Scholar] [CrossRef]. *European Journal of Information Systems*, 19(3), 288–302. DOI: 10.1057/ejis.2010.16

Ibrahimov, V. (Sept 14, 2023) https://medium.com/@aiVugar/consensus-ask-ai -questions-and-obtain-conclusions-from-research-papers-48f80a8c717

Jaitly, A. (2024). *Engaging Minds, Empowering Futures: How AI is Revolutionizing Education and Keeping Students Hooked*. LinkedIn. March 22, 2024. https://www.linkedin.com/pulse/engaging-minds-empowering-futures-how-ai-education-keeping-jaitly-2oplc/

Johnston, A. C., & Hale, R. (2009). Improved security through information security governance. [Google Scholar] [CrossRef]. *Communications of the ACM*, 52(1), 126–129. DOI: 10.1145/1435417.1435446

Jones, S. (July 02, 2024) https://edrawmind.wondershare.com/ai-features/tome-ai-review.html

Kim, S., & Lee, Y. (2021). Basic study for the development of artificial intelligence literacy instrument. *Proceedings of the Korean Association for Computer Education Conference, 25*(2(A)), 59–60.

Lacy, L. (2023). Hallucinations: Why AI Makes Stuff Up and What's Being Done About It.

Li, S., Wang, C., & Wang, Y. (2024). Fuzzy evaluation model for physical education teaching methods in colleges and universities using artificial intelligence. *Scientific Reports*, 14(1), 4788. DOI: 10.1038/s41598-024-53177-y PMID: 38413670

Lin, C., Yu, C., Shih, K., & Wu, Y. (2021). STEM based Artificial Intelligence Learning in General Education for Non-Engineering Undergraduate Students. *Journal of Educational Technology & Society*, 24(3), 224–237.

Luckin, R., Holmes, W., Griffiths, M., & Forcier, L. B. (2016). *Intelligence unleashed. An argument for AI in education*. Pearson.

Maina, A. (Oct 26, 2023) https://alphanmaina.medium.com/tome-ai-use-ai-to-transform-your-ideas-into-appealing-visuals-131c7dade7f4

Maldonado, A. (April 29, 2024). https://studentbridgew.sharepoint.com/SitePages/Artificial-Intelligence-Summit.aspx

Marr, B. (March 19, 2023). https://www.forbes.com/sites/bernardmarr/2023/05/19/a-short-history-of-chatgpt-how-we-got-to-where-we-are-today/?sh=633d8a14674f#open-web-0

Maslej, N; Fattorini, L; Brynjolfsson, F; Etchemendy, J; Ligett, K; Lyons, T; Manyika, J; Ngo, H; Niebles, J.C; Paril, V; Shoham, Y; Wald, R; Clark, J. and Perrault, R. (2023). The AI Index 2023 Annual Report. Stanford University: AI Index Steering Committee, Institute for Human-Centered-AI.

Metz, C. (March 21, 2023). https://www.nytimes.com/2023/03/21/technology/google-bard-guide-test.html

Mollick, E. (2023). My Class Required AI. Here's What I've Learned so Far. https://www.oneusefulthing.org/p/my-class-required-ai-heres-what-ive

Nalliah, S., & Idris, N. (2014). Applying the learning theories to medical education: A commentary. International E-Journal of Science. *Medical Education*, 8(1), 50–57.

Njuguna, S. (July 24, 2023). https://www.linkedin.com/pulse/how-i-use-resume-worded-make-my-winning-one-samuel-njuguna/

Nolan, R.; McFarlan, F.W. (2005). Information technology and the board of directors. Harv. Bus. Rev. 2 83, 96. [Google Scholar]

Panigrahi, A., & Joshi, V. (2020). Use of Artificial Intelligence in Education. *The Management Accountant Journal.*, 55(5), 64–67. DOI: 10.33516/maj.v55i5.64-67p

Park, W., & Kwon, H. (2024). Implementing artificial intelligence education for middle school technology education in Republic of Korea.(2023). *International Journal of Technology and Design Education*, 34(1), 109–135. DOI: 10.1007/s10798-023-09812-2 PMID: 36844448

Pham, S. T. H., & Sampson, P. M. (2022). The development of artificial intelligence in education: A review in context. *Journal of Computer Assisted Learning*, 38(5), 1408–1421. DOI: 10.1111/jcal.12687

Porter, J. (2005). *Media Literacy* (3rd ed.). Sage Publications, Inc.

Presswire, E. (June 9, 2023) https://www.wate.com/business/press-releases/ein-presswire/638444700/easy-ai-checker-launches-free-app-to-quickly-flag-plagiarism-and-ai-generated-content/

Prokofyev, K. G., Zmyzgova, T. R., Polyakova, E. N., & Chelovechkova, A. V. (2019). Transformation of the education system in a digital economics. *Proceedings of the 1st International Scientific Modern Management Trends and the Digital Economy: From Regional Development to Global Economic Growth*, Yekaterinburg, 614-619. Doi: DOI: 10.2991/mtde-19.2019.123

Roose, K. (Feb 16, 2023) https://www.nytimes.com/2023/02/16/technology/bing-chatbot-microsoft-chatgpt.html

Rothrock, R. A., Kaplan, J., & Van Der Oord, F. (2018). The board's role in managing cybersecurity risks. [Google Scholar]. *MIT Sloan Management Review*, 59, 12–15.

Sangwan, S. (July 14, 2021). https://yourstory.com/2021/07/chicago-jaipur-ai-startup-quillbot-one-stop-writing-platform

Singh, J. (July 12, 2023). https://cointelegraph.com/news/what-is-quillbot

Spremić, M., & Šimunic, A. (2018). Cyber security challenges in digital economy. In *Proceedings of the World Congress on Engineering*, London, UK, 4–6 July 2018; International Association of Engineers: Hong Kong, China, pp. 341–346. [Google Scholar]

Sullivan, M., Kelly, A., & McLaughlan, P. (2023). ChatGPT in Higher Education: Consideration for Academic Integrity and Student Learning. *Journal of Applied Learning & Teaching*, 6(1), 31–40.

Sullivan, S. (April 03, 2023). https://sulliwrites.medium.com/grammarly-can-slightly-change-your-articles-a-i-content-score-aff21b30271e

TechEd Maven Consulting. (2024). Embracing AI in Education: Understanding Its Impact. https://www.linkedin.com/posts/teched-maven-consulting_ai-future-of-teaching-and-learning-reportpdf-activity-7097776305177317376-Q6SG/

UNESCO. (2023). ChatGPT and Artificial Intelligence in Higher Education, Quick Start Guide. Document Code: ED/HE/IESALC/IP/2023/12. 1-14.

Vyse, G. (2024). *How Generative AI is Changing the Classroom.* This report is underwritten by Amazon Web Services (AWS). The Chronicle of Higher Education Inc. https://www.chronicle.com/featured/digital-higher-ed/how-generative-ai-is-changing-the-classroom?utm_campaign=che-ci-cnt-ci-aws-generativeai&utm_medium=em&utm_source=mkto&utm_content=24-06-30-v2&mkt_tok=OTMxLUVLQS0yMTgAAAGUZL5SQT7fpYZvjlqt6F-0qquU3syDw4TKw1Elm-GTQBmZNvmNgONH5y2AEQqJR8DBSngqD1_mpIa6nn5qWX4PY8B9wevYUO1ZZIlL4YNiE1Rn5Uo

Walton Family Foundation. (March 1, 2023). Teachers and Students Embrace ChatGPT for Education, New Survey from Walton Family Foundation Finds. https://www.waltonfamilyfoundation.org/chatgpt-used-by-teachers-more-than-students-new-survey-from-walton-family-foundation-finds

Wilkin, C. L., & Chenhall, R. H. (2010). A review of IT governance: A taxonomy to inform accounting information systems. [Google Scholar] [CrossRef]. *Journal of Information Systems*, 24(2), 107–146. DOI: 10.2308/jis.2010.24.2.107

KEY TERMS AND DEFINITIONS

AI Hallucinations: Hallucinations occur when AI systems generate irrational, misleading information and data, incorrect content, misplaced scientific and historical, and unreliable analysis.

Augment Intelligence: Some experts and researchers use the word augment instead of artificial to create a sense of reliability and confidence in AI. It also refers to the process of enhancement.

Behaviorism: This learning theory claims that learners inquire observe and react to external incentives (stimuli). AI tools provide a variety of audio and visual materials for learners to interact with and learn from.

C.L.Ai.R. A: It is the first Afro-Latina and Bilingual AI launched by Abran Maldonado. C.L.Ai.R.A. can offer opinionated and insightful perspectives

Constructivism: This educational and learning theory claims learners construct knowledge rather than only receive information. It emphasizes that learners construct their understanding of things, people, and the environment on prior knowledge. Constructively, AI can share both knowledge and information.

Educational Technology: The term refers to digital delivery tools teachers and learners use to present lessons. Educational technology includes, but is not limited to, computer hardware and software, audio, video, and AI tools.

Chapter 2
Navigating the Role of Artificial Intelligence in Post–Secondary Educational Spaces

Tatum Joy Sommer
https://orcid.org/0009-0001-9229-2025
Texas A&M University, USA

ABSTRACT

Within this chapter, the author will address the multifaceted nature of artificial intelligence (AI), a machine's ability to simulate the human mind. The author evaluates generative AI and its pros, cons, and reliability. First, the author examines AI's effect on essay writing in higher-level education. Then, the author explores how preservice teachers can be equipped to address and implement proper usage in the classroom. The author includes literature reviews of scholarly texts that help address the research question: How do English professors and teacher educators negotiate AI as a tool for essay writing and teaching? The author will evaluate data through a theoretical framework that analyzes and assesses emergent data and is supported by pedagogical anecdotes. This framework is designed to guide teachers in their own evaluation of AI in the writing process. The findings will help equip teacher educators with tools to implement AI within their classrooms and identify the proper usage of AI for essay writing in higher education. The findings are designed to assist university boards, teacher educators, and preservice teachers in making informed decisions regarding AI in postsecondary classrooms.

DOI: 10.4018/979-8-3693-3904-6.ch002

NAVIGATING THE ROLE OF ARTIFICIAL INTELLIGENCE

As artificial intelligence (AI) gains media attention and popular usage worldwide, faculty and students are on the precipice of something that could alter the future of writing in the educational setting. AI platforms such as ChatGPT and Grammarly can perform functions from the complex to the simple: Compose entire essays on a provided topic or simply elevate the vocabulary of an existing draft. These functions significantly affect how university professors manage expectations for essay writing and support students' writing development in their classes. The author aims to explore considerations of AI's power and limitations as a tool for engaging in the writing process while shedding light on steps that need to be taken to prepare preservice teachers (PSTs) best to integrate AI in their future classrooms.

METHODS

The author focused on identifying scholarly texts that address generative AI, its advantages, disadvantages, and reliability, specifically in the context of academic writing and teaching practices. The author's search strategy focused on scholarly work, with keywords such as "human intelligence," "artificial intelligence," "essay writing," "teacher education," "teacher education," and "AI-TPACK."

Then, the author gathered sources from peer-reviewed journals, Humanities, and Social Science Communications. The author identified relevant studies and then organized the data into a matrix. The matrix organized the 20 articles by title, methodology, and results. The author conducted a mixed method review and the extraction of data focused on key themes: The effectiveness of AI in enhancing student writing skills and concerns regarding AI's influence on ethicality, critical thinking, and creativity, while also exploring strategies for integrating AI tools into educational curricula to help cope with the increase in generative AI platforms.

The author included sources regarding AI published in the last decade, ensuring the relevancy of the findings. To further support the scholarly sources, the author conducted interviews with university faculty. The researcher gathered recent university AI statements from their public Web sites. These statements provide a firsthand account of how information on AI is affecting universities worldwide.

THEORETICAL FRAMEWORK

To properly inform literature reviews and personal experiences, the author will utilize the technological pedagogical knowledge (TPACK) framework (Celik, 2023) and the cognitive process theory of writing (Flower & Hayes, 1981) as lenses to examine the limitations and power of AI to support the writing process in classrooms. The cognitive process theory of writing helps with content knowledge and impacts the cognitive processes of planning, translating, and reviewing during the writing process. The TPACK framework focuses on managing technology integration in educational spaces—notably, the importance of technological, pedagogical, and content knowledge to inform teachers' decision-making. Additionally, the author will explore the multidimensionality of "intelligence" borrowing from Gardner's (2006) theory of multiple intelligences, which suggests the following eight different modes of intelligence: Linguistic, mathematical, spatial, musical, bodily-kinesthetic, naturalist, interpersonal, and intrapersonal intelligence. A holistic and multifaceted understanding of the complexity of intelligence aids understanding how closely AI can get to mimicking human intelligence.

LITERATURE REVIEW

AI's Pros, Cons, and Efficiency

Scientific innovation has brought up ethical concerns since its inception. Mary Shelley's 19th-century novel *Frankenstein* (Shelley, 1818) provides an accessible narrative through which to understand these concerns. Within the fictitious text, scientist Victor Frankenstein, drawing on scientific innovation, created a creature unlike any man. He produced a living human-like being made of dead animal parts. The creature came to life one day with a fully functioning body and mind, like a human being. While the novel is entertaining, Shelley aimed to explore the more pressing issues with scientific innovation and the moral implications that creators hold when producing new technology. The novel addresses concerns such as human interference with nature, the danger of ambition, and the problem with humans "playing God." The idea of these "Frankenstein issues" can be used as a blanket term to describe any idea or invention whose consequences are ill-considered. A modern-day Frankenstein issue is AI, which mirrors Shelley's concern with fabricated consciousness and intelligence as an invention that holds promise, but also spurs a fear of the unknown. This technology is constantly evolving and is unmanageable. AI has inspired many to evaluate the power of innovation and its dangers. We see this same questioning in Shelley's novel when the monster decides to kill the loved ones of its creator out of revenge. Contemporary AI threatens to kill off something we value culturally and love: Composition. It also promises to alleviate repetitive work and iterative communication. Like the creature in *Frankenstein,* AI holds promise of both positive and negative impacts on humanity, which must be addressed in the classroom to encourage the appropriate usage of AI.

To understand the implications of AI, it is vital to first look at its origins. When Dartmouth hosted a summer research workshop regarding AI in 1956, the term AI was formally coined. The workshop shared ideas about possible emergent technology in the future. The conversations sparked revolutionary thinking on what humans can do with the power of technology. The expansion of technology came from humans' ambition to innovate with the primary goal of making life more efficient. While these ideas held promise, they were not practicable at the time due to the cost and effectiveness of testing. It was not until 1980 that the ideas explored at the Dartmouth conference were revitalized. Innovators developed deep learning on computers and claimed the ability for computers to mimic the human thought process or "intelligence" (Cordeschi, 2017). Now, in 2024, there has been a massive jump from the early understanding of AI. AI appears everywhere, even if people do not actively seek out its use. Most people may recognize early incorporations of AI, such as Apple's Siri or Google's search engine, which can predict and autocomplete input text.

AI uses information gathered from the entirety of the Web to shape an answer to whatever prompt is given. AI Creators claim that AI then emulates human intelligence to produce a response tailored to the given input provided. Intelligence is best defined as "one's ability to learn from experience and to adapt to, shape, and select environments" (Sternberg, 2022, p. 19). A person's intelligence can be modified by unique experiences such as genetics, upbringing, and environment, creating a diverse spread of individuals worldwide. Many branches sprout from the tree of human intelligence, such as linguistic intelligence, emotional intelligence (EI), and interpersonal intelligence. Recognizing the complex dimensions of human brains explains the difficulty of mimicking human intelligence. Multiple modes of intelligence shape a person's thoughts and emotions. These are traits specific to humans that shape how minds work and the work they produce. Silveira and Lopes (2023) explain that "machine intelligence is the ability to replicate the human mental faculty and to perform human-like functions" (para. 29). The inclusion of the word "perform" indicates that these forms of computation are not organic in that these devices do not have the humanistic experiences to affect their intelligence, rather they perform or act as a human thought. Gardner's (2006) theory of Intelligence best explains the multifaceted nature of human intelligence. Figure 1 illustrates Gardner's eight modes of intelligence.

Figure 1. Gardner's Eight Modes of Intelligence (adapted fromSternberg, 2022)

EI falls under Gardener's inclusion of interpersonal and intrapersonal thinking. EI is best defined as the "ability to monitor one's and others' feelings and emotions, discriminate among them, and use this information to guide one's thinking and actions" (Salovey & Mayer, 1990, p. 433). Everyone's EI is unique to their life and experiences. Therefore, it is one aspect of intelligence that is found hardest to replicate within computational intelligence. Many studies regarding AI focus on the machine's technological abilities but do not address its abilities to replicate emotional human thought processes.

For example, childhood trauma can impact someone's EI and the way they view the world. If a student were asked to write a personal essay about their childhood, answers would vary depending on whether the subject has altered EI due to adverse childhood experiences. If the student placed the prompt into a generative AI platform and used whatever essay that emerged, they would have a very sterile and generalized output. This example proves individual experiences will uniquely shape a person's thoughts, directly influencing their written work. The question is: How can a computer mimic these thought processes, and can they accurately mimic the range of human response when asked a similar essay prompt to the one above?

This question is especially relevant to higher education, where essays written in various modes and discourses are a dominant way for students to portray their language skills and EI. The multidimensional nature of intelligence is challenging to reproduce mechanically. Bhattacharya (2022) took an alternative look at AI in hopes of evaluating AI's emotional qualities. Bhattacharya uncovered that "it lacks intuition and cultural sensitivity, which are human qualities" (p. 648), revealing that, although AI has come a long way, it does not properly replicate emotional learning. These findings are significant in essay writing because, when students are tasked with writing essays, their unique experiences inform their diction, writing style, and tones. Therefore, when students use AI to answer essay prompts and execute the work for them, it often emerges as "robotic" due to its lack of emotional input, which can harm the efficacy of students' writing, impacting the clarity of their writing and degrading their skills in gathering and assessing information on their own.

The emerging consensus between professors and researchers is that having students complete personal essays and analysis assignments using AI would generate robotic and impersonal tones. AI's inability to fully mimic human intelligence, specifically emotional intelligence, fuels English professor's critiques of AI in the context of essay writing. They claim that AI is not superior to human intelligence and that cultivating students' EI is more important now than ever.

On the other hand, AI has proven effective in essay instruction and development. AI can offer input on various measures, from correcting grammatical errors to initiating brainstorming. Moreover, AI can also provide information on the subject or topic a student plans to address. This is beneficial for the student to gather the information required to support their claims within their writing. Like a Google search engine, AI can provide a holistic view with a wide variety of information on a topic without having to manually scan through hundreds of articles. These abilities make AI appealing to busy students, as it streamlines processes in conventional writing. While speeding up the writing process is efficient, the result may be lackluster if writers entirely depend on AI to complete the process.

Processes for invention and composition have been innovated by teachers and researchers over many generations. For example, brainstorming can be introduced as early as first grade (in Texas) and used deep into a student's college experience. College students are trained to employ the steps of the writing process as follows: Prewriting, organizing, revising, editing, and proofreading. The steps aim to inspire and inform a person's desired outcome for their text. While no method fits everyone, this general writing process has been taught and replicated throughout schooling and gives students a strong foundation. As the writing process is utilized, it fosters a sense of naturally growing creativity as a person's thoughts and ideas progress.

Many concerns surround AI, its intrusiveness to the writing process, and its interruption to natural creativity. While some agree that AI could be beneficial in its ability to spark ideas that students can expand upon, three main concerns persist: AI reduces work ethic, AI will stall research/analysis skills, and AI does not provide the cognitive training inherent to the writing process. In other words, writing is itself a form of learning, rather than a mere output of learning. These concerns, if founded, indicate that AI interrupts some of the most crucial contributions of the educational process.

However, several researchers have pointed to the advantages of AI-assisted composition. Marzuki et al. (2023) investigated the impact of AI, such as ChatGPT and Quilbot, on the writing process. Unlike many claims that AI hindered the writing process, they found "unanimous agreement among the teachers about the positive role of AI writing tools in enhancing the clarity and logical progression of students' writing" (p. 15). The authors stated that AI can benefit university students' writing if they "do not become overly reliant on these tools, which could inhibit their critical thinking and problem-solving skills" (p. 15). Professors claim that there is a balance between AI's intrusiveness and its efficiency. Therefore, university staff emphasize that guidelines must be established to ensure students use AI to aid their work while continuing to teach and exercise the writing process to ensure that students cultivate these vital skills.

The cognitive process theory further supports the idea of a hierarchical process that writers routinely follow when constructing an essay. Flower and Hayes (1981) described the "distinctive thinking process" that can be best organized by prewriting, writing, and rewriting (Figure 2). Their model visualizes the "schematic representations of processes and elements that are often misleading. The arrows indicate that information flows from one box or process to another; that is, knowledge about the writing assignment or knowledge from memory can be transferred or used in the planning process, and information from planning can flow back the other way" (Flower & Hayes, 1981, p.386)

Figure 2. Identifying the Organization of Writing Processes (Flower & Hayes, 1981, p. 366)

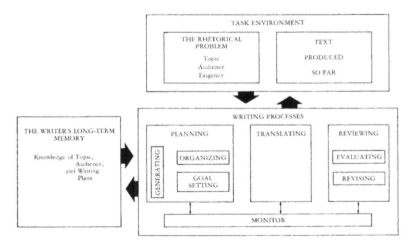

The prewriting stage requires planning, generating, organizing, and goal setting. This stage facilitates internal ideas coming to explicit articulation. By using experimental input for ChatGPT, Lingard (2023) revealed its strengths: Outlines, titles, and counterarguments. Lingard emphasized that supporting students who use AI in brainstorming for their papers could leave them with misconstrued ideas and falsified information. However, she did not discount AI entirely; she emphasized AI's benefits in helping with grammar, structure, and outlines in essay writing. She revealed that AI is beneficial when a writer is stuck and needs inspiration. Overall, Lingard (2023) encouraged students to use ChatGPT and similar instruments as supplemental tools while crediting its usage, which is most beneficial when writers infuse their unique tone and style into the text.

The translation stage is a more logistical phase, where writers must meet "a spectrum from generic and formal demands through syntactic and lexical ones down to the motor tasks of forming letters" (Flower & Hayes, 1981, p. 373). According to Flower and Hayes (1981), shifting one's "attention to demands such as spelling and grammar, the task of translating can interfere with the more global process of planning what one wants to say" (p. 373). This finding brings up a critical point concerning the benefits of student AI use for grammar and spelling-related concerns. Web sites such as Grammarly work to adjust language and grammar without masking students' original and unique ideas. Therefore, when students write without worry of grammar, they can better communicate their ideas. Lastly, the reviewing stage contains subsections of evaluating and revising. Reviewing can happen naturally as one writes or strategically once the text is finished. This is where platforms like Grammarly can be beneficial as students complete their work first, then throw it into Grammarly to correct grammar and spelling. Therefore, employing supplemental AI for these naturally occurring tasks could be beneficial in aiding a student's work without disrupting their thought process.

Researchers raise questions about the reliability of AI. AI generated responses can be outdated or even inaccurate. Numerous users report receiving fabricated citations and incorrect information. Lambert and Stevens (2023) found that bias, discrimination, and stereotyping cannot be eliminated from AI-generated responses because these opinions are culled from existing Internet materials. Similarly, it is impossible to eliminate misinformation, and the web contains articles and sources spanning a multitude of creators and viewpoints, not all of them creditable. When using AI, students need to be cognizant of the historical implications of racial injustices that the internet platforms may capitalize on. Addressing these injustices, PSTs can enhance their knowledge and conversations with students surrounding AI. Professors deem this as one of the most concerning aspects of AI. Emphasizing the importance that AI generated findings need to be verified by human users. Many professors exclaim that they teach their students to cross-reference their information and not treat AI as a one-size-fits-all source for any information provided.

In a fast-moving field such as AI research, publication may lag practice. The author, therefore, interviewed several instructors who are grappling with the implications of AI for writing. These practitioners provided vignettes that may assist in the practical application of research findings. Several instructors at Texas A&M helped shed light on how AI has affected writing instruction and outlined their personal ideas about where universities should go from here. The discussion focused on the question: What is your experience with AI? From there, the conversation naturally flourished, focusing on the bigger picture of AI.

The first issue raised was academic honesty. Within the data, cheating emerged as a common worry amongst university staff and researchers. Out of the 18 articles, excluding the syllabus statements, 8 addresses plagiarism as one of the main ethical quandaries caused by AI. The articles used varying words to describe this ethical dilemma such as integrity, plagiarism, and cheating. The Texas A&M Honor Council has been working with many AI reports, recently. If a professor suspects plagiarism or cheating, they first run it through a plagiarism detector, which can evaluate the work's percentage of originality. It is necessary to keep in mind that no plagiarism detector is 100% accurate. Nevertheless, if professors believe the flagged percentage of AI use is significant, they can turn the case over to the Honor Council. One instructor discussed a recent increase in AI-related reports. Adhering to Family Educational Rights and Privacy Act laws, they could not give exact details from any cases. However, the process through which the Honor Council addresses AI generated writing has evolved in the last several semesters. Any plagiarism suspected by instructors can be reported to the TAMU Honor Council. Then, the case is brought to the board, and they look at the multiple perspectives on the student artifact, often pinning the decision on "students' word vs. the teachers under the knowledge that detection often produces false positives" (personal interview, May 30, 2024). The council keeps this in mind to ensure they are relying on something other than an invalid source, and other considerations are necessary and have recently been identified. This could include document history or proof that the students created this work. A vital point the council addresses is the increase in unfair racial and psychological disparities and their correlation to false positives. The author urges honors councils to consider that second-language writers and people who are neurodivergent often get false positives on AI detection (personal interview, May 30, 2024). A writer's bilingual background can contribute to their work being wrongfully flagged as AI, because those students who have been learning proper English structures for a long time will routinely construct sentences and ideas that are more formal and assiduous, in the sense that they are set to match the appropriate grammar and textbook rules embedded in their English education. A syntactically formulaic way of writing may be evident in second-language expression; the adherence to strict rules of usage can come across to the reader as robotic and consequently be misidentified as AI-generated. In contrast, a native English speaker may write more loosely due to their comfort with the language. It is therefore necessary to understand the AI detector's biases. It becomes challenging when a professor swears a student utilized AI because AI itself rated the probability of machine generation highly. In contrast, bilingual students may be at a disadvantage when bringing up the biases of AI detection and the intricacies of dealing with these reports when using AI detecting tools.

Elkhatat et al. (2023) similarly investigated the capabilities of AI, its tailored responses to writing prompts, and the tools necessary to identify if a student's text is unique or AI-generated. Ironically, they studied an AI bot's ability to detect AI writing. They identified studies in which the Open AI classifier was utilized to determine if AI had written a text. The authors found the classifier accurately identifies 26% of true positives, while incorrectly labeling 9% as false positives (Elkhatat et al., 2023). Therefore, multiple AI checkers should be used to identify ratings. Elkhatat et al. (2023) concluded that, while AI detection tools can provide insight into the makings of a text, they perform inconsistently; therefore, a mix of manual review and technological review must be combined to holistically evaluate a student's paper for AI.

An increasing mistrust has developed between students and teachers since the emergence of AI, transiting relationships and creating paranoia surrounding cheating. Elkhatat et al. (2023) pointed out that it is necessary not to rely solely on AI to flag cheating or misconduct. Formulating a system of cross-references and examinations will protect students from false allegations. At the same time, these systems will provide professors with materials to identify plagiarism when it does occur. For example, pairing the AI detector's findings with document history and students' organic knowledge will give a holistic understanding of a student's cheating or lack thereof. These tools reduce uncertainty surrounding allegations and protect students against targeting. If institutions could implement a holistic evaluation to detect plagiarism, they could eliminate many false Honor Council meetings and nourish student and professor relationships with mutual trust.

Lambert and Stevens (2023) conducted multiple surveys to collect cohesive data. Two surveys that stood out were those given to over 1,000 college students in the United States. These surveys inquired if students used AI, on what assignments, how often, and how they felt about using these tools. Lambert and Stevens found that "30% of students had used ChatGPT on written homework. Of those, almost 60% had used it on more than half of their assignments" (p. 5), despite acknowledging that it is cheating. Statistics such as these often fuel professors' negative views of AI, as they argue it is expedient. Lambert and Stevens (2023) also addressed students who used ChatGPT to write their entire essays. Based on the students' unique responses, the authors concluded that they also knew that relying on AI to complete their work was morally incorrect and against the rules. However, most students explained that their reasoning relied on reducing the time spent on essays—and efficacy—resulting in the student receiving a better grade. These findings indicate that many students seek shortcuts to demanding assignments like essays. For most students, the promise of a quickly completed assignment outweighs regard for possible consequences or moral implications. Academic integrity has suffered as reliance on technology escalates. One way to mitigate integrity issues in academic writing is to encourage to cite AI as a source, thus enabling students to consult AI to aid their writing rather than relying on it to complete their assignments. Students should credit the AI origins of any material as if it were parallel to any other source, if AI is a supplemental aid for their writing it should be cited in their work.

This mutual sense of trust can be harnessed through the citing of AI. When a student uses AI but does not claim its work as their own, it is like getting information from a textbook or a Web site. By allowing the usage and citation of AI, professors are acknowledging AI's benefits in addition to its disadvantages.

Instructors will want to work with those benefits. One emergent theme in Lambert and Steven's research is that "95% of students said their grades had improved since studying with ChatGPT" (2023, p. 5). Also, using practical AI systems such as Grammarly can help students refine their original work. The emergence of AI as a tool for study and revision shows that AI can be helpful for students; however, they must use it ethically and abide by the rules set by their institution. Overall, professors recognize that AI can be helpful as a tool for students to refine their skills when used as supporting material to their work and giving credit to where they received their information. Providing a guide to students to cite AI will minimize confusion surrounding correctly giving credit to one's sources.

To equip students with proper tools for how to utilize AI, effectively and morally, universities have sent out AI statements to inform proper usage. Texas A&M University, for example, has supplied its student body with AI statements. The Texas A&M Center for Teaching Excellence states that the possible modes of action should be to produce a syllabus statement to identify the university-wide acceptable use of generative AI and offer guidance while allowing individual instructors to determine their syllabus statement. This statement explains that the university does not block the use of AI, but instead, suggests ways to harness its power (Texas A&M University, 2024). Trinity University, to use another example, explains that all AI-aided submissions will be considered plagiarism (Trinity University, 2023). Texas A&M is a large public university whereas Trinity is a smaller private university. Therefore, it is vital to keep in mind that differing university characteristics, such as school size, location, and whether it is private or public, will affect the university's approach to AI.

AI'S EFFECT ON PSTS

While the logistics of AI are debated, there is one truth to the matter: AI will affect future generations' learning and capabilities. Therefore, it is necessary to analyze the opportunities for AI in the classroom, especially looking at both risks and benefits, to create a holistic understanding of its classroom impact (Byrd et al., 2023). To successfully incorporate AI curriculum into classrooms, implementing guidance and logistics must be taught to future generations of teachers. For PSTs to successfully integrate AI technology in their classroom, universities must include it in the PST curriculum, requiring an alteration in coursework to better align with TPACK values. These steps and strategies are helpful guidelines for teacher educators to walk PSTs through navigating AI. By furthering PST education on AI, they will feel more confident and able to incorporate machine-assisted learning in a classroom setting. Research has pointed to a new strand of TPACK's framework, namely, AI-TPACK. This framework consists of the previously explored TPACK foundation, such as pedagogical knowledge (PK), content knowledge (CK), and pedagogical content knowledge (PCK) (Ning et al., 2024). This new framework consists in the integration of knowledge-based understanding of AI within each focus, expanding TPACK to AI-TPACK, which focuses on PK, CK, PCK, AI-Technological Pedagogical Knowledge (AI-TCK), AI-Technological Content Knowledge (AI-TPK), and AI-TPACK itself (Ning et al., 2024). The inclusion of AI in the TPACK framework will provide a "specialized form of knowledge that emerges from the intersection of three distinct areas: Disciplinary knowledge (content expertise), pedagogical knowledge (teaching methods and strategies), and AI technological knowledge" (Ning et al., 2024, p.3). Adding AI to The TPACK framework will help PSTs modify their pedagogical approaches to include AI, which will prepare them and their students with essential skills for a digitally driven society (Ning et al., 2024).

To successfully incorporate AI into the TPACK framework, it is vital that school boards prepare practicing teachers with additional AI training and courses that will close knowledge gaps surrounding AI and create a unified teaching staff within a district. Infusing AI across classrooms will create an interdisciplinary understanding of AI. Teacher educators can provide PSTs with lesson ideas to incorporate AI into their students' learning. For example, PSTs could be taught how to complete a text set—a collection of multiple texts across different genres that focus on a central theme. Supportive texts often follow one main text to inspire prior learning or create depth to the focus text. A text set would be an essential tool for teaching and expanding upon the idea of AI in the literary sense, formulating a text set with books that explore technological innovation in diverse ways. Partnering fiction, nonfiction, poetry, and videos allows for an inclusive assessment of technology and how it impacts the world.

To get AI-TPACK successfully implemented among universities, schools must destigmatize the proper use of AI. Increased discussion regarding AI will enhance the support provided for PSTs. Teacher educators are now tasked with continuing student-centered instruction while offering materials such as guidelines and best practices. This means they are not facing this new discussion alone (Byrd et al., 2023). AI can be used for many creative abilities and significantly aid students' brainstorming ability. Therefore, a balance between using AI as supplemental material and copying AI's outputs is vital to breaking the stigma around AI. A way to do this is to increase collaboration between students and teachers. Teachers should not immediately reprimand or become suspicious when a student asks about AI as this will inspire fear and secrecy surrounding the usage of AI. Creating an inclusive and open environment to discuss concerns or benefits of AI allows for more insightful discussion and boundaries to the topic and its usages. This will allow students to be less fearful of technology. Allowing for a class-wide experimentation with AI where students can input prompts and evaluate the effectiveness of the AI-generated response will help students analyze AI's strengths and weaknesses. This exercise will give students a real-world understanding that this tech is assistive not all-capable, and it is still in a developmental phase. Therefore, students will be less likely to entirely depend on AI, when they understand that their work can be strengthened by help from AI, whether this is brainstorming or looking up a fact. In addition, students will know that AI has a complicated relationship with the truth and that copying AI will not only be plagiarism, but often is weaker work than their years of education can earn them.

An instructor who works holistically with AI in his writing classes made a crucial point: "if you are engaging with the software, you are making a deal with the devil in one capacity" (personal interview, May 30, 2024). This is due to AI's biases, its impact on the learning environment, and its disregard for privacy. For example, AI gathers data from a wide variety of Web sources, but not every Web site can be monitored and removed for hateful speech or biases. Therefore, when AI gathers data from the Internet, there is always a chance that the information it presents is biased (Akgun & Greenhow, 2022). The creators of AI platforms have not fully resolved these issues, yet; therefore, PSTs must be equipped to address these issues to reduce misinformation and increase students' autonomy when using AI. One way to do so would be for universities to follow in the steps of The MIT Media Lab team, who "offers an open-access curriculum on AI and ethics for middle school students and teachers," spanning from AI Bingo and to resources for teachers such as AI and Data Privacy workshops (Akgun & Greenhow, 2022, p.436).

Using AI, as the MIT's example indicates, is not cheating or plagiarism because, as one instructor observed, "writing is always engaging with the world in these complicated ways; it is a tool available for you [his students]" (personal interview,

May 30, 2024) However, you are still accountable for the information you provide rather than trying to block it, which I think is an arms race we will lose as teachers," (personal interview, May 30, 2024). A teacher's duty, in this instance, is to inform their class on AI's societal and ethical impacts and ensure their students know how to use AI effectively and ethically, recognizing its impact on the world around them.

Thus, PSTs' knowledge of AI is not just "technical, but also pedagogical and ethical knowledge and skills" (Celik, 2023, p. 9). The TPACK framework is vital for effective teaching with the state of the current technology. Ethicality must come to the forefront of current discussion, as AI will help further enhance the TPACK framework (Karina & Kastuhandani, 2024). Integrating the conversation surrounding ethicality in preservice teaching classrooms could look something like a debate of the moral implications of AI or evaluating research to see where AI is lacking, therefore taking the knowledge they learned through these classes and carrying it into the field with them, so they can ensure the modes of technology provided to their students are helping them, not harming.

In contrast, AI's ability to quickly provide information can combat PSTs' time and energy spent on lesson planning. PSTs can integrate AI to offer practical demonstrations, provide models of written prose, offer new processes for students to develop multimodal writing, quickly generate different response models, and stimulate discussion about various approaches to a writing prompt. These technologies allow instructors to "show" and "tell" what different writing strategies look like (Byrd et al., 2023, p. 9). AI offers practical usages and guidance for PSTs, as they are often tasked with creating complete lesson plans for their first years of teaching. This is why many educators are arguing AI as an impactful tool for PSTs to harness. Partnering the information, they gain from their student teaching experiences with AI can help create unique and efficient lesson planning. The collaboration of one's personal and technological knowledge allows the PSTs to "customize their lesson plans and teaching strategies to be the most suitable for students," allowing PSTs to quickly form lessons or work that can cater to multiple learning approaches and capacities (Karina & Kastuhandani, 2024, p. 560).

A connection between Karina and Kastuhandani's data and Gardener's Theory of Intelligence later emerged when synthesizing the data. Gardner's theory "is based upon a variety of sources of evidence, among them neuropsychological as well as psychometric evidence" and is vital to educational research, as he suggests that a student's strengths and weaknesses in terms of intelligence vary (Sternberg, 2022, p. 21). This theory supports the idea that learning is most successful when instruction and assessment cater to different learning styles and modes of intelligence. Gardener (as cited in Miller, 2002) stated that, "if teachers operate according to the verbal and computational model of intelligence alone, then so many people are going to be left out," thus emphasizing the need for unique incorporation of assignments to cater to a variety of students' needs (p. 123). Gardener's theory supports contemporary recent research on varied learning styles. Both sources emphasize that students need activities that cater to different learning styles to understand a concept holistically. Karina and Kastuandani emphasize this point and conclude that AI is an effective tool for doing so. When instructed to do so, AI can provide PSTs with numerous strategies to adapt a lesson activity to kinesthetic learning, auditory learning, etc. Therefore, a teacher can effectively and efficiently place their lesson plans and goals into a generative AI such as ChatGPT, and they will be given varied ways to present a lesson. Both teacher instruction and student retention will benefit. However, the PST curriculum must be revised by universities to incorporate AI-related training and information.

The risks associated with AI for PSTs and teachers are mostly the vast amount of work it will take to integrate AI fully and adequately into classrooms. Increased training for teachers requires a more extensive study of both AI usage and training processes. To increase comfort and minimize confusion, PSTs can benefit from learning about AI integration before they are placed in the field. Integrating AI curriculum in lesson plans and PST education will require more work for both the PST and the teacher educators; however, it will create wide-spread AI knowledge and inform guidelines for the upcoming wave of certified teachers. They are leaving supplemental training up to the discretion of the school boards, employing PSTs. Nevertheless, to reduce the knowledge gap between veteran teachers and PSTs, training should be implemented to create a baseline knowledge of AI and its usage amongst school staff. Akgun and Greenhow (2022) suggested that AI would require more professional development for both preservice and in-service teachers. The authors placed emphasis on the importance of school districts providing professional development experiences. More data should be found on the impact of these professional development seminars and how many teachers and PSTs implement the tools they learn (Akgun & Greenhow, 2022). However, these suggestions have financial and time implications as "not all learning institutions, especially those located in remote areas, have sufficient Internet access or a reachable budget," which can further produce inequities in education (Karina & Kastuhandani, 2024, p. 561).

The increase in energy devoted to AI curriculum and integration "will divert PSTs' attention away from other teaching practices and course content, unless adequate resources are given to build it into the curriculum" (Byrd et al., 2023, p. 7). Therefore, supporting PSTs within their college educator prep classes is vital. Universities must work with core state standards, such as Texas's Essentials Knowledge and Skills (TEKS), to inspire a curriculum standard to be added for AI. Currently, there is not a TEKS standard for AI. However, there are TEKS regarding digital citizenship, plagiarism, and media literacy. Finding a way to incorporate the teaching of AI and its boundaries would be a beneficial skill to add to these state requirements. This would aid PSTs immensely, as being educated on their required state standards and involving the usage of AI in teacher certification exams would create a generation of teachers prepared to face AI in the classroom.

CONCLUSION

The future of navigating AI rests with PSTs, motivated classroom veterans, and university researchers; all who engage with AI must use it appropriately. Current literature suggests that, as a general education community, much must be done to ensure AI is implemented and monitored to serve PSTs and students. The data of the above literature reviews help inform the question: How do English professors and teacher educators negotiate AI as a tool for essay writing and teaching? Ultimately, the research successfully proved that the academic community is divided in terms of using AI in essay writing. The literature review provided valuable arguments from both sides of the divide. These findings remain important to encourage further research on AI as well as challenge the discussion regarding AI as no advantage or disadvantage outweighs the other. The culmination of research unveiled that current English professors do primarily negotiate AI as a tool to enhance an in-dividual's writing. Through generative outlines and enhanced writing assistance through programs such as Grammarly, students can rely on AI to check their work or help create a base for an assignment. Professors argue that, given AI's ability to answer questions almost instantly, students can use it as a supportive tool for quick brainstorming. However, individuals must educate themselves via research and first-hand experiences of the possible mistakes resulting from uncritical reliance on technology. Utilizing AI for an outline can help increase writing efficiency, and many teachers do not see the harm in using AI as a helper tool if students do not directly plagiarize AI material. However, writing instructors argue that using AI to write full essays will negatively affect students' ability to be creative and generate original ideas. As a result, many scholars conclude that AI is not perfect: It often makes mistakes, can be unethical, further promotes educational inequality, and can be misused by students. AI offers significant benefits, but challenges must be ad-dressed. AI's abilities are ever-growing; therefore, educating students and teachers on correct usage will help mitigate these problems. The research yielded straight-forward conclusions regarding PSTs. The data unveiled that AI is both helpful and effective for PSTs to use for their own teaching material. AI's innovative tools can equip PSTs with various lesson plans that cater to many learning styles and increase efficiency in lesson planning. Researchers suggest that teacher education should teach PSTs how to approach logistics of AI such as enforcing plagiarism rules and teaching students AI limitations. Continued research is vital to better inform PSTs, university students, and staff on the best practices for AI so that its potential can be harnessed. The review of the literature indicates further studies will need to be conducted on the gaps in AI detection tools and AI-TPACK's effectiveness when integrated into the PST curriculum. Holistically, addressing the concept of AI starts with universities producing best practices, destigmatizing conversations surrounding AI, and increasing support for PSTs regarding AI curriculum, allowing all AI users to harness the powers and innovation that come with AI in the most responsible way possible. In navigating the role of AI in higher-level English courses and PST education, it is crucial to consider the evolving landscape of AI technology, its potential benefits in enhancing teaching practices, and the importance of maintaining a balance between AI assistance and human involvement in education. In depth comparisons of specific types of AI could enhance professors' understanding of its capabilities. The author suggests further studies on AI involvement in PST setting will demonstrate AI's prominence in classrooms. A beneficial study might involve providing a self-reflection analysis or survey. Surveying PSTs currently in the field regarding their incorporation or troubles with AI. The available informs many professors' stances that while AI can offer valuable support in various educational aspects, human teachers remain essential in the teaching process, emphasizing the need for thoughtful integration of AI to complement traditional teaching methods. AI usage is deemed most impactful in preparing PST material and classroom integration, encouraging teacher educators to inform their PSTs with tools and knowledge of best practices for their future classrooms.

Implications and Limitations

This chapter relies on an emerging research base, rather than unique data collection. However, the existing research supports the author's unique positions in education to help guide the conversation about AI's use for writing in classrooms. The author also understands that one problem is finding unbiased sources, as AI research can be addressed as a gray political or moral area, in terms of AI within the government's policy creation, data protection, and regulation of AI. AI challenges moral questions and ideologies. The author acknowledges these concerns throughout the chapter to ensure their data are factual by evaluating source ethicality and reliability. Additionally, the author analyzed PST regulations relative to their position in Texas. Identifying curriculum outside of Texas will allow further evaluation of differences or similarities that could inform the understanding of AI integration in the statewide curriculum. Lastly, there is a need for additional longitudinal studies on the long-term effects of AI integration in education and comparative analyses of different AI tools and platforms.

REFERENCES

Adisa, K., Byrd, A., Flores, L., Gibson, A., Green, D., Hassel, H., Johnson, S., Kirschenbuam, M., Lockett, A., Mathews, E., & Mills, A. (2023). MLA-CCCC joint task force on writing and AI working paper: Overview of the issues, statement of principles, and recommendations. *Humanities Commons.*https://hcommons.org/app/uploads/sites/1003160/2023/07/MLA-CCCC-Joint-Task-Force-on-Writing-and-AI-Working-Paper-1.pdf

Ahmad, S. F., Han, H., Alam, M. M., Rehmat, M., Irshad, M., Arrano-Munoz, M., & Ariza-Montez, A. (2023). Impact of artificial intelligence on human loss in decision making, laziness and safety in education. *Humanities & Social Sciences Communications*, 10(1), 1–14. DOI: 10.1057/s41599-023-01787-8 PMID: 37325188

Akgun, S., & Greenhow, C. (2022). Artificial intelligence in education: Addressing ethical challenges in K-12 settings. *AI and Ethics*, 2(3), 431–440. DOI: 10.1007/s43681-021-00096-7 PMID: 34790956

Bhattacharya, S. (2022). Artificial intelligence, human intelligence, and the future of public health. *AIMS Public Health*, 9(4), 644–650. DOI: 10.3934/publichealth.2022045 PMID: 36636147

Celik, I. (2023). Emotional intelligence. *Computers in Human Behavior*, 138. Advance online publication. DOI: 10.1016/j.chb.2022.107468

Cordeschi, R. (2017). AI turns fifty: Revisiting its origins. *Applied Artificial Intelligence*, 21(4-5), 259–279. DOI: 10.1080/08839510701252304

Elkhatat, A. M., Elsaid, K., & Almeer, S. (2023). Evaluating the efficacy of AI content detection tools in differentiating between human and AI-generated text. *International Journal for Educational Integrity*, 19(17), 17. Advance online publication. DOI: 10.1007/s40979-023-00140-5

Flower, L., & Hayes, J. R. (1981). A cognitive process theory of writing. [REMOVED HYPERLINK50FIELD]. *College Composition and Communication*, 32(4), 365–387. DOI: 10.58680/ccc198115885

Gardner, H. (2006). "Multiple Intelligences: New Horizons in Theory and Practice." *Basic Books,*https://a.co/d/hkd8AP2

Gravel, J., Gravel, M. D., & Osmanlliu, E. (2023). Learning to fake it: Limited responses and fabricated references provided by ChatGPT. *Mayo Clinic Proceedings. Digital Health*, 1(3), 226–234. Advance online publication. DOI: 10.1016/j.mcpdig.2023.05.004

Karina, B., & Kastuhandani, F. (2024). Preservice English teachers' lived experience in using AI in teaching preparation. *Journal Ilmiah Pendidikan*, 5(1), 550–568. Advance online publication. DOI: 10.51276/edu.v5i1.767

Lambert, J., & Stevens, M. (2023). Chat GPT and generative AI technologies: A mixed bag of concerns and new opportunities. *Computers in the Schools*, 1—25. https://doi.org/DOI: 10.1080/07380569.2023.2256710

Lingard, L. (2023). Writing with ChatGPT: An illustration of its capacity, limitations & implications for academic writers. *Perspectives on Medical Education*, 12(1), 261–270. Advance online publication. DOI: 10.5334/pme.1072 PMID: 37397181

Marzuki, W., Widiati, U., Rusdin, D., Darwin, , & Indrawati, I. (2023). The impact of AI writing tools on the content and organization of students' writing: EFL teachers' perspective. *Cogent Education*, 10(2), 2236469. Advance online publication. DOI: 10.1080/2331186X.2023.2236469

Miller, G. D. (2002). *Peace, value, and wisdom*. Brill Rodopi., DOI: 10.1163/9789004496071

Ning, Y., Zhang, C., Xu, B., Zhou, Y., & Wijaya, T. (2024). AI-TPACK: Exploring the relationship between knowledge elements. *Sustainability (Basel)*, 16(3), 978. Advance online publication. DOI: 10.3390/su16030978

Salovey, P., & Mayer, J. D. (1990). Emotional intelligence. Emotion, Cognition, and Personality, 9(3), *Science Direct,* 185—211. DOI: 10.1016/0160-2896(93)90010-3

Shelley, M. (2017). *Frankenstein; the Modern Prometheus. Amazon Classics*. Kindle Edition.

Silviera, T., & Lopes, H. (2023). Intelligence across humans and machines: A joint perspective. *Frontiers in Psychology*, 14, 1209761. Advance online publication. DOI: 10.3389/fpsyg.2023.1209761 PMID: 37663348

Sternberg, R. (2022). Intelligence. *Dialogues in Clinical Neuroscience*, 14(1), 19–27. DOI: 10.31887/DCNS.2012.14.1/rsternberg PMID: 22577301

Texas &M University, & the Center for Teaching Excellence. (2024). *Generative AI syllabus statement considerations*. https://cte.tamu.edu/getmedia/1d5e4ef6-97f1 -4065-987f-3c9dfecbb7bd/TAMU-CTE_GenAI-SyllabusStatementConsiderations .pdf

Trinity College. (2023). *Sample syllabus statement*. https://www.trincoll.edu/ctl/wp -content/uploads/sites/110/2023/09/Sample-Syllabus-Statements-on-AI.pdf

Chapter 3
AI Chatbots in Higher Education:
A Meta–Synthesis

Fate Jacaban Bolambao
https://orcid.org/0000-0003-4245-5911
Cebu Normal University, Philippines

Angeline M. Pogoy
Cebu Normal University, Philippines

Michel Plaisent
University of Quebec at Montreal, Canada

ABSTRACT

This chapter evaluates the qualitative studies on how AI chatbots impact HE, specifically their benefits and challenges. A systematic search was conducted across academic databases resulting in the inclusion of 27 research papers published between 2018 and 2023. The research in this involved utilizing the Critical Appraisal Skills Programme (CASP) checklist for Systematic Review to evaluate the quality and relevance of each study followed by a thematic analysis of the data using Braun and Clarke's approach to identify key themes. The first theme, " Improved Learning Experience," explores the benefits of including personalized support, increased engagement, user-friendliness, skills development, and efficiency. The second theme, ": Practical and Ethical Issues," delves into the practical and ethical issues, such as ethical concerns, pedagogical limitations, information accuracy, and technical challenges. A balanced approach to integrate AI chatbots in HE, addressing ethical and technical concerns while maximizing its benefits were given emphasis on the studies reviewed and evaluated.

DOI: 10.4018/979-8-3693-3904-6.ch003

INTRODUCTION

The implementation of AI-driven chatbots in higher education has brought about a substantial revolution, offering a means to accomplish UNESCO's Sustainable Development Goal 4 by 2023. This innovative technology has the capacity to transform the teaching and learning process in colleges and universities, resulting in a more streamlined and impactful educational framework. The incorporation of AI chatbots into higher education institutions has initiated conversations regarding their advantages, challenges, and ideal implementation strategies. However, there exists a lack of meta-synthesis research about the experiences of both students and instructors while interacting with AI chatbots in the college environment. This study attempts to bridge this gap by examining the impact of chatbots on promoting academic literacies in higher education institutions. Employing a meta-synthesis, the research explored the potential incorporation of chatbots in the instruction and acquisition of academic literacies in higher education.

The widespread adoption of Artificial Intelligence chatbots, especially with the introduction of ChatGPT in late 2022, has grown more and more apparent. In the field of higher education, chatbots employ artificial intelligence and natural language processing to imitate human interaction, providing customized learning experiences to students in colleges and universities. Through data analysis, they provide tailored recommendations and comments, offer 24/7 support, and reduce the strain of instructors (Khan & Khan, 2023). As of 2016, universities have already incorporated chatbots, which utilize artificial intelligence to support students, according to Viano (2023). One of the main benefits of AI technology is its ability to improve research efficiency and accuracy. Khan and Khan (2023) emphasized the several advantages of using AI chatbots into education, such as uninterrupted availability, tailored learning experiences, prompt feedback, cost efficiency, enhanced accessibility, stress alleviation, and increased student involvement. Furthermore, the use of chatbots in higher education has greatly improved the quality of education. These chatbots are employed to encourage communication and collaboration between students and teachers, administer exams and provide feedback, as well as address student inquiries (Ilieva et al., 2023). These customized instructional methods address the specific needs of students, offering a smooth learning process that promotes academic literacy. Chatbots provide students with the necessary resources to efficiently pursue their academic goals and thrive in their chosen fields (Kooli, 2023).

Nevertheless, the growing presence of AI chatbots in higher education gives rise to a number of concerns. Lately, there has been growing concern within the education sector regarding the rise of Artificial Intelligence (AI), specifically AI generative tools. Ensuring accuracy and reliability is an important concern when it comes to integrating AI chatbots into higher education. The possibility of deliberately providing students with incorrect or misleading information is a significant challenge that needs to be addressed (Andrew, 2023). Lewandowski (2023) highlighted the potential impact on interpersonal relationships and empathy within academic settings due to the lack of human interaction and emotional intelligence. Considering data privacy and security is of utmost importance when implementing chatbots, as they involve the sharing of student information. In their study, King (2023) examines the misuse of AI and chatbots in universities, specifically addressing the growing issue of plagiarism. Developing chatbots presents various challenges, including limited training data, usability heuristics, ethical concerns, evaluation methods, user opinions, programming complexities, and data integration obstacles (Labadze et al., 2023). In addition, an overreliance on chatbots may impede the development of critical thinking skills among university students.

Higher Education in the Philippines

Within the realm of higher education in the Philippines, educators are growing more apprehensive about academic integrity as students increasingly rely on ChatGPT and other AI tools to fulfill their academic obligations (Banzuelo, 2023). Nevertheless, the incorporation of artificial intelligence (AI) into educational settings currently faces a lack of clear direction from governmental entities like the Commission on Higher Education. Legislative efforts within the country primarily prioritize economic opportunities, with minimal consideration given to the potential effects on educational integrity and teaching methodologies (Chi, 2023). Considering the potential of AI to revolutionize various industries, it is important to closely examine its implications for academia. The University of the Philippines acknowledges the various impacts of AI in higher education, including addressing concerns about bias and privacy, while also recognizing its potential to advance societal welfare and promote inclusive economic growth (Sj, 2023).It is important to recognize that AI will not replace professors or students in the educational setting. Education is a profound experience that extends beyond the use of technological tools (Adeva, 2023). The importance of thoroughly examining the implications of AI tools such as ChatGPT in the field of education cannot be overstated. It is essential to grasp the ever-changing nature of AI in academic settings and how it impacts teaching methods, academic honesty, and the overall educational experience. AI chatbots have become increasingly popular among students in higher education because of their user-friendly interface and their ability to provide timely feedback on academic tasks. However, the growing dependence on AI chatbots has resulted in a surge in academic dishonesty and a decrease in students' critical thinking abilities.

The studies above provide valuable insights into the benefits and challenges of utilizing AI chatbots in higher education and their impact on students' academic literacy. However, a comprehensive synthesis of this knowledge is currently lacking. The isolated nature of research findings across studies makes it difficult for university professors and instructors, students and other researchers to understand the topic comprehensively. Hence, a meta-synthesis will be conducted to answer the following questions: (a) What are the advantages of using AI chatbots in educational processes in higher education? and, (b) What are the disadvantages of using AI chatbots in educational processes in higher education? This research on chatbots in higher education will help stakeholders understand their potential value in enhancing educational experiences.

METHODOLOGY

Research Design

The authors employed the Meta-synthesis which is a methodological approach utilized in the synthesis of primary qualitative research (Sim & Mengshoel, 2022). The objective was to acquire a broader perspective, enhanced generalizability, conceptual advancement, or increased practical applicability, the objective is to obtain insights beyond the limitations of any singular primary study (Campbell et al., 2003; Thorne et al. 2004; Malterud 2019). This approach entailed the integration of discrete findings derived from qualitatively oriented research investigations that are thematically connected, as well as qualitative outcomes focusing on AI Chatbots in higher education.

Search Strategy

A systematic search was performed on academic internet sources to identify published research articles in English language journals that focus on AI Chatbots in the field of education. The researcher utilized the academic databases Google Scholar, Scopus, Semantic and PubMed in order to determine pertinent published study. The present study encompassed the retrieval and combination of scholarly literature concerning the implications of AI Chatbots in the field of education, with a specific emphasis on papers published from 2020 to 2023. The following keywords was used to select the studies: (a) Artificial Intelligence (AI), (b) chatbots, (c) qualitative study, (d) higher education. The researchers employed the Critical

Appraisal Skills Programme (CASP) checklist for Systematic Review to assess the remaining studies. The data collected was organized following the guidelines outlined in the Preferred Reporting Items for Systematic Reviews and Meta-Analyses (PRISMA) flow diagram.

Inclusion and Exclusion Criteria

Included studies in this review was selected based on the following criteria: (1)AI chatbots, (2) in the context of Higher Education, (3) qualitative research outputs, (4) published article, (5) peer-reviewed, (6) 2018-2023 studies, (7) English language, (8) must qualify for the quality assessment using Critical Appraisal Skills Programme (CASP) Checklist, and (9) at least cited once.

Data Analysis:

Thematic data analysis was employed to identify the fundamental or recurring themes of AI Chatbtos in higher education. Thematic analysis is a qualitative research method that identifies, analyzes, and interprets patterns of themes within data. It helps researchers explore complex phenomena, identify significant trends, and generate insights. The method is flexible and rigorous and can be applied to various research questions (Windle et.al., 2020).The data that was chosen for study underwent Thematic analysis, using the technique developed by Clarke and Braune (2017). This thematic analysis methodology is an iterative and structured process that comprises six distinct steps. The initial stage is to become acquainted with the available data, then generate codes, create themes, review themes, define and name themes, and locate exemplars. This method is widely used in business and academic settings to analyze qualitative data and identify recurring patterns and themes. By following this methodology, analysts can systematically and rigorously examine data and extract meaningful insights that can inform decision-making and drive future research.

RESULTS AND DISCUSSION

Search Result

Figure 1 shows the search result in identifying themes included in the meta-synthesis and organized using the PRISMA 2020 Flow Diagram.

Figure 1. PRISMA flow diagram in the inclusion of studies

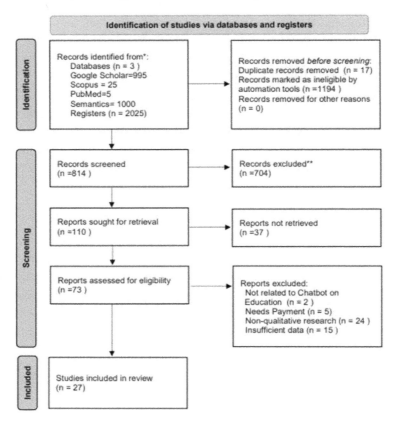

The study used four scholarly databases: Google Scholar, Scopus, PubMed, and Semantics, provided by Publish or Perish Software, to collect data. A total of 2025 studies were gathered from these databases. Google Scholar yielded 999 studies, Scopus yielded 25, Semantics yielded 1000, and PubMed yielded 5 studies. During the identification phase, an automated technique determined that 1211 studies were ineligible due to duplication. The researches undertook robust screening, and as a result, 704 manuscripts were removed during the screening phase. A number of these research provided little information, were not easily accessible online, were non-qualitative, and had no bearing on the topics of AI chatbots or in higher education. Fifteen (15) studies were included in the studies.

Table 1. Included studies

Number	Author/s	Year	Setting/s	Title
1	Lidén and Nilros (2020)	2020	Sweden	Perceived benefits and limitations of chatbots in higher education
2	Slepankova, Marta	2021	Sweden	Possibilities of Artificial Intelligence in Education: *An Assessment of the role of AI chatbots as a communication medium in higher education*
3	Terrance Lopez and Meer Qamber	2022	Sweden	The benefits and drawbacks of implementing chatbots in higher education: A case study for international students at Jönköping University
4	Nayab Iqbal, et.al	2022	Pakistan and Malaysia	Exploring teachers' attitudes towards using chatgpt
5	Sambhav Gupta and Yu Chen	2022	California	Supporting inclusive learning using chatbots? A chatbot-led interview study
6	Woithe, J., & Filipec, O.	2023	Sweden	Understanding the Adoption, Perception, and Learning Impact of ChatGPT in Higher Education: A qualitative exploratory case study analyzing students' perspectives and experiences with the AI-based large language model
7	Oksana Stepanechko and Liubov Kozub	2023	Ukraine	English Teachers'concerns About The Ethical Use Of Chatgpt By University Students
8	Micheal M. van Wyk, Michael Agyemang Adarkwah, and Samuel Amponsah	2023	Africa	Why All the Hype about ChatGPT? Academics' Views of a Chat-based Conversational Learning Strategy at an Open Distance e-Learning Institution
9	Aqdas Malik, M. Laeeq Khan and KhaLID huSSAIN	2023	Michigan and Oman	How is ChatGPT transforming academia? Examining its impact on teaching, research, assessment, and learning
10	Blanka Klimova and Prodhan Mahbub Ibnan Seraj	2023	Czech Republic and Bangladesh	The use of chatbots in university EFL settings: Research trends and pedagogical implications
11	Iffat Sabir Chaudry, et.al.	2023	United Arab Emirates	Time to Revisit Existing Student's Performance Evaluation Approach in Higher Education Sector in a New Era of ChatGPT—A Case Study
12	Yousef Wardat, et.al.	2023	United Arab Emirates, Oman, Saudi Arabia, Abu Dhabi	ChatGPT: A revolutionary tool for teaching and learning mathematics
13	Mehmet Firat	2023	Turkey, Sweden, Canada and Australia	What ChatGPT means for universities: Perceptions of scholars and students
14	Chokri Kooli	2023	Canada	Chatbots in education and research: A critical examination of ethical implications and solutions

continued on following page

Table 1. Continued

Number	Author/s	Year	Setting/s	Title
1	Jurgen Rudolph, Samson Tan and Shannon Tan	2023	Singapore	ChatGPT: Bullshit spewer or the end of traditional assessments in higher education?

Theme 1: Improved Learning Experience through AI Chatbots

In today's ever-evolving realm of higher education, the conventional teaching methods, which relied on standardized approaches, are gradually giving way to more personalized and engaging learning experiences (Exploring the Impact of AI Bots on Educational Institutions - LiveChatAI.com, 2023). Several chatbot development platforms have been introduced to create educational bots that can effectively engage with students and provide them with valuable information in a concise manner (Kumar, 2021). Nitirajsingh and Gide (2019) highlight the use of advanced technology in innovative educational tools to tackle the specific challenges faced in higher education.

The research in this chapter has shown that the use of AI chatbots in education can have a positive impact on academic literacy, critical thinking skills, and knowledge retention. Additionally, they can help improve productivity, facilitate effective communication, and increase student engagement in the learning process (Labadze et al., 2023; Sandu, 2020). In addition, AI chatbots provide valuable assistance to educators by handling various tasks like scheduling, grading, and sharing information. This enables instructors to focus on teaching and engaging with students, enhancing the overall learning experience (Labadze et al., 2023). As a result, the incorporation of AI chatbots into educational settings has great potential to improve the learning journey of college students.

The first theme of this research focuses on the advantages of using AI chatbots in higher education, which can lead to an improvement in the learning experiences of students. Out of fifteen researches from different countries, twelve of them presented the benefits of AI chatbots in education. During the analysis of the literature, five sub-themes emerged.

Sub-theme 1: Personalized Learning Support and Feedback

The integration of AI-powered chatbots into higher education holds great promise for research, as it has the potential to greatly enhance personalized learning initiatives. Advanced chatbot technologies, such as ChatGPT, have proven their capability to provide timely, captivating, and responsive interactions that cater to the unique requirements of students (Okonkwo & Ibijola, 2021). Through the removal of barriers like shyness or hesitation in seeking clarification, chatbots facilitate personalized learning experiences that can cater to the specific needs of every student (Firat, 2023). Research conducted by Iqbal et al. (2022) and Chaudhry et al. (2023) emphasizes the ability of AI chatbots to provide customized educational material and prompt feedback on assignments and tests, accessible at all times (Lo, 2023).

Sub-theme 2: Increased Learning Engagement and Interaction

Chatbots have the potential to revolutionize the learning experience in higher education settings, according to Montenegro-Rueda et al. (2023). Through promoting more interaction between students and instructors, chatbots encourage social engagement and help learners align their focus with their learning objectives by providing direct communication channels. In addition, chatbots enhance the acquisition of knowledge and skills by encouraging experiential learning and experimentation, which promotes active engagement in the learning process (Rudolph et al., 2023). Encouraging cooperation and collective effort among students, chatbots play a significant role in nurturing essential interpersonal and problem-solving abilities that are necessary for achieving success in academic and professional domains within higher education.

Sub-theme 3: User-Friendly and Accessible

AI chatbots are a versatile technical tool that blends simplicity and complexity, providing many advantages in the field of higher education. As emphasized by Ross (2018), these entities function independently, offering prompt educational support to consumers. This cutting-edge technology guarantees uninterrupted availability of verified data for a wide array of consumers, as highlighted by Okonkwo & Ibijola (2021). Slepankova (2021) found that students in higher education find AI Chatbots acceptable due to their user-friendly nature, fairness, and 24/7 availability. These chatbots serve as convenient solutions for basic instructional, informational, and support duties. Moreover, the prompt release of information has a good effect on students emotional state by removing negative feelings linked to waiting. In addition, the AI chatbots have a user-friendly interface that does not require any specialist technological expertise (Klimova et al., 2023;Iqbal et al., 2022), thus making it accessible to a broad spectrum of users.

AI chatbots are essential in promoting inclusion and fairness in higher education by ensuring that students from varied backgrounds have equitable access to educational opportunities (Kooli, 2023).

Sub-theme 4: Skills Development and Enhancement

Integrating chatbots into higher education settings provides a means to develop crucial 21st-century competencies, such as critical thinking, problem-solving, cooperation, computer literacy, and data literacy, among others. Klímová and Ibna Seraj (2023) present empirical evidence demonstrating the beneficial effects of incorporating chatbots on the development of critical thinking abilities in University English as a Foreign Language (EFL) students. Their methodology has resulted in measurable enhancements in students' capacity for critical thinking, hence eliminating barriers related to language acquisition and boosting self-assurance in speaking the desired language. Chatbots provide personalized support and guidance to college students, allowing them to explore complex subjects, assess information critically, and engage in significant dialogues. This provides them with the fundamental abilities necessary to flourish in an increasingly interconnected and ever-evolving global community.

Sub-theme 5: Increase Efficiency and Foster Innovation

Chatbots serve as virtual teaching assistants for the teachers and students in higher education, enhancing and optimizing numerous facets of the learning experience. The swift progression of technology has provided opportunities for educators to adopt novel pedagogical approaches (Rudolph et al., 2023). Furthermore, chatbots enable the consolidation and preservation of various forms of information into a centralized entity (Okonkwo & Ibijola, 2021. In addition, chatbots have the capacity to execute mathematical computations and resolve problems, thereby augmenting the educational experience (Wardat et al., 2023). Chatbots provide immediate and individualized assistance, enabling both students and instructors to effectively navigate complex concepts, resolve inquiries, and improve overall learning outcomes in higher education.

Theme 2: Practical and Ethical Issues of AI Chatbots in Education

AI chatbots are of significant importance in higher education as they provide individualized learning experiences, enhanced accessibility, and increased student engagement. These resources are highly beneficial for educators who aim to cultivate learning environments that are both efficient and open to all. However, in addition to these favorable benefits, substantial obstacles emerge. Lewandowski (2023), chatbots may provide inaccurate or incomplete information, lack human interaction and emotional intelligence, and pose threats to data privacy. The presence of errors in AI recommendations, as emphasized by Greene (2023), may exert an adverse influence on educational achievements. Concerns regarding the introduction of bias by AI algorithms and the apprehension that instructors will be laid off from their jobs further complicate their implementation. In addition, the implementation of AI-generated educational materials poses further obstacles, (AIContentfy, 2023). These challenges encompass apprehensions regarding accuracy, reliability, potential partialities, constraints on innovation, reliance on technology, and the imperative for stringent quality assurance. These challenges highlight the necessity for thorough implementation and supervision in order to guarantee that AI-enhanced education truly provides advantages for tertiary students.

The challenges and concerns related to the incorporation of AI chatbots in higher education are also explored in the present research, which is evident in the second theme identified in this investigation. Eleven of the fifteen researches hailing from different countries contributed their insights regarding the obstacles faced when implementing AI chatbots in the field of education. Four sub-themes surfaced from an exhaustive literature review, providing insight into the challenges and apprehensions associated with the implementation of AI chatbots in higher education.

Sub-theme 1: Ethical Implications and User Misuse

In higher education, chatbots represent a form of AI technology utilized for communication via natural language. As an example, their incorporation gives rise to remarkable ethical concerns, specifically with regard to the privacy of users (Firat, 2023). It is imperative to comply with privacy regulations and guidelines, which consider variables such as socioeconomic status, gender, age, and ethnicity, all of which impact the chatbot's persona (Okonkwo & Ade-Ibijola, 2021). Van Wyk et al. (2023) have expressed apprehensions regarding the possible introduction of biases into the results and the erosion of user privacy via the use of user data) Furthermore, Malik et al. (2023) emphasize the ethical considerations associated with artificial intelligence (AI), highlighting the potential for it to promote superficial understanding of concepts and generate complications pertaining to scholarly integrity. Concerns regarding academic dishonesty and plagiarism, which spread false information and compromise academic integrity, are also raised in relation to the implementation of AI in higher beducation (Rudolph et al., 2023; Malik et al., 2023; Lo, 2023; Van Wyk et al., 2023). Moreover, it has been emphasized by Kooli (2023) that the utilization of chatbots or other artificial intelligence (AI) tools to respond to examination queries may amount to academic dishonesty and plagiarism,thereby contradicting the core tenets of scholarship and academic honesty. Potential ethical dilemmas could arise as a result, and students' critical thinking, creativity, and ability to apply acquired knowledge to real-world scenarios could be impeded, thus **impeding their academic progress.**

In addition, the implementation of chatbots could potentially impede the capacity of university instructors to precisely evaluate the unique abilities of each pupil (Van Wyk et al., 2023). The existing approaches to authorship verification are inadequate in detecting texts generated by artificial intelligence and do not deliver the level of accuracy required to assess the work of students (Chaudhry et al., 2023). The aforementioned ethical considerations underscore the criticality of exercising caution when incorporating AI technology into higher education in order to preserve academic integrity and guarantee equitable assessment procedures.

Sub-theme 2: Lack of Pedagogical Focus

Beyond technological implementation, the integration of AI chatbots into higher education presents challenges such as ensuring that chatbot functionalities are aligned with curricular objectives and instructional methodologies. According to Wollney et al. (2021), technological considerations are frequently given precedence in the development of chatbots for educational purposes, rather than their potential to effectively support and enhance learning within a well-defined pedagogical framework. A methodology preoccupied with technology may fail to consider critical components that are indispensable for the smooth integration of chatbots into educational practices. At present, there exists a scarcity of scholarly investigations pertaining to the precise information requirements that chatbots can fulfill and their efficacy in doing so. Assessing the pedagogical effectiveness of chatbots is a critical undertaking (Nee, 2023). As a result, it is critical that higher education institutions and educators conduct exhaustive evaluations of the educational efficacy of chatbots in order to comprehend their complete potential as valuable educational tools.

Sub-theme 3: Limitations in Information Accuracy and Credibility

The implementation of AI chatbots in higher education environments has presented a number of difficulties, specifically to their precision, reliability, and capacity to efficiently process intricate data. These limits encompass factors such as inconsistent reliability, inaccurate referencing, repetitive and redundant output from the instrument. (Woithe & Filipec, 2023). The issue of information reliability presented by chatbots is of considerable importance, given that errors that persist in perpetuating the spread of false or erroneous data could compromise academic integrity (Lo, 2023). Furthermore, it is imperative to acknowledge that chatbots might possess certain limitations when it comes to precisely resolving mathematical problems. This underscores the significance of comprehending the precise capabilities and constraints of these systems prior to integrating them into educational methodologies. Therefore, it is not recommended to exclusively depend on chatbots for mathematical problem-solving duties. Due to their inherent limitations in effectively addressing intricate mathematical concepts, their application for such purposes should be approached with caution. Moreover, although AI chatbots possess the capability to produce prose at a rapid pace, their output consists solely of simple replicas of pre-existing material, devoid of the complexity and subtlety inherent in text generated by humans (Rudolph, 2023). This highlights the significance of recognizing the basic constraints of AI chatbots and enhancing their implementation in higher education settings with human proficiency and analytical abilities.

Sub-theme 4: Technical Challenges

The seamless integration of chatbots into higher education settings presents a number of technical challenges such as operational constraints like unavailability of the chatbots caused by traffic (Woithe & Filipec, 2023) this require meticulous consideration and specialized knowledge to overcome. Okonkwo et al. (2021) emphasize that the aforementioned challenges may be complex in nature and necessitate a high level of technical expertise to ensure efficient maintenance and monitoring. Furthermore, Van Wyk et al. (2023) highlight a significant drawback linked to chatbots: the exorbitant expense associated with acquiring premium accounts, which are required to partake in their complete array of advantages. The presence of this financial barrier could potentially impede the extensive implementation and application of chatbots within educational settings.

CONCLUSION AND RECOMMENDATION

In this chapter, various advantages and drawbacks of incorporating chatbots into higher education have been uncovered. A number of benefits and challenges associated with the integration of chatbots into higher education have been revealed in this research. It is imperative to overcome these challenges in order to completely actualize the advantages of chatbots. As one promotes personalized learning, heightened student engagement, and improved pedagogical efficacy, ethical concerns concerning data security, academic integrity, and privacy come to the forefront. Hence, it is critical to establish precise ethical principles and regulatory frameworks to oversee the utilization of AI chatbots in tertiary education, thereby guaranteeing a beneficial influence on the scholastic progress of students. It is imperative that these guidelines explicitly cover privacy, data security, and academic integrity in order to ensure the protection of students' welfare and maintain the integrity of the educational journey. It is imperative that educators, developers, and researchers work together to ensure that chatbots improve learning outcomes and are consistent with educational objectives. Stakeholders must navigate this complex terrain and embrace the opportunities while recognizing ethical and pedagogical complexities. Successful integration of this tool depends on a balance between innovation and responsibility, empowering both educators and learners in their pursuit of knowledge.

LIMITATIONS

The study of AI chatbots in higher education has been limited in its exploration of student perspectives. The scope of chapter was limited to examine the benefits and challenges from the educators' perspectives and experiences only. Hence, the direct experiences and feedback from students have not been adequately explored when they are using AI chatbots in their classes.

FUTURE RESEARCH

It is suggested that gathering in-depth insights from students on their experiences with AI chatbots would be explored and determine its effectiveness. This would provide a more comprehensive understanding of the impact of these technologies on the learning process, student engagement, and academic outcomes. The students' direct experiences are crucial to fully evaluate the effectiveness and implications of integrating AI chatbots into higher education. By prioritizing the collection of student feedback, future studies can shed light on how students perceive the usefulness of chatbots, any concerns they may have regarding privacy or academic integrity, and how these tools influence their learning behaviors and critical thinking skills. This student-centered approach will enable the researchers to develop a more holistic understanding of the role of AI chatbots in enhancing or hindering the educational experience from the learner's perspective.

REFERENCES

Adeva, P. K. (2023, April 5). *Will AI chatbots take over education?* Philippine Collegian. https://phkule.org/article/813/will-ai-chatbots-take-over-education

Ali, F., Choy, D., Divaharan, S., Tay, H. Y., & Chen, W. (2023). Supporting self-directed learning and self-assessment using TeacherGAIA, a generative AI chatbot application: Learning approaches and prompt engineering. *Learning: Research and Practice*, 1–13. https://doi.org/DOI: 10.1080/23735082.2023.2258886

Artificial intelligence in education. (2023). *UNESCO*. https://www.unesco.org/en/digital-education/artificial-intelligence

Banzuelo, N. (2023). What Filipino students are saying about ChatGPT. *BusinessWorld Online*. https://www.bworldonline.com/technology/2023/04/19/517952/what-filipino-students-are-saying-about-chatgpt/

Chaudhry, I. S., Sarwary, S. M., Refae, G. E., & Chabchoub, H. (2023). Time to Revisit Existing Student's Performance Evaluation Approach in Higher Education Sector in a New Era of ChatGPT — A Case Study. *Cogent Education*, 10(1), 2210461. Advance online publication. DOI: 10.1080/2331186X.2023.2210461

Chi, C. (2023, July 19). Should ChatGPT be banned in schools? UP crafts 'responsible' AI use guidelines. *Philstar.com*. https://www.philstar.com/headlines/2023/07/19/2282226/should-chatgpt-be-banned-schools-crafts-responsible-ai-use-guidelines

Dimitriadis, G. (2020). Evolution in Education: Chatbots. *Homo Virtualis*, 3(1), 47–54. DOI: 10.12681/homvir.23456

Exploring the Trend and Potential Distribution of Chatbot in Education: A Systematic Review - Volume 13 Number 3 (Mar. 2023) - ijiet. (n.d.). https://www.ijiet.org/show-186-2428-1.html

Firat, M. (2023). What ChatGPT means for universities: Perceptions of scholars and students. *Journal of Applied Learning and Teaching*, 6(1).

Greene, R. T. (2023, April 24). *The pros and cons of using AI in learning: Is ChatGPT helping or hindering learning outcomes?* eLearning Industry. https://elearningindustry.com/pros-and-cons-of-using-ai-in-learning-chatgpt-helping-or-hindering-learning-outcomes

Gupta, S., & Chen, Y. (2022) "Supporting Inclusive Learning Using Chatbots? A Chatbot-Led Interview Study," *Journal of Information Systems Education*: Vol. 33: Iss. 1, 98-108.*arXiv (Cornell University)*. https://doi.org//arxiv.2306.03823DOI: 10.48550

Ilieva, G., Yankova, T., Dimitrov, A., Bratkov, M., & Angelov, D. (2023). Effects of Generative Chatbots in Higher Education. *Information (Basel)*, 14(9), 492. DOI: 10.3390/info14090492

Iqbal, N., Ahmed, H., & Azhar, K. (2023). Exploring Teachers' Attitudes towards Using Chat GPT. *Global Journal for Management and Administrative Sciences.*, 3(4), 97–111. Advance online publication. DOI: 10.46568/gjmas.v3i4.163

Khan, S., & Khan, S. (2023, April 17). AI Chatbots for Education: How They are Supporting Students and Teachers? - EdTechReview. *EdTechReview*. https://www.edtechreview.in/trends-insights/trends/ai-chatbots-for-education-how-they-are-supporting-students-and-teachers/

King, M. R. (2023). A conversation on artificial intelligence, chatbots, and plagiarism in higher education. *Cellular and Molecular Bioengineering*, 16(1), 1–2. DOI: 10.1007/s12195-022-00754-8 PMID: 36660590

Klímová, B., & Seraj, P. M. I. (2023). The use of chatbots in university EFL settings: Research trends and pedagogical implications. *Frontiers in Psychology*, 14, 1131506. Advance online publication. DOI: 10.3389/fpsyg.2023.1131506 PMID: 37034959

Kooli, C. (2023). Chatbots in Education and Research: A Critical Examination of ethical implications and solutions. *Sustainability (Basel)*, 15(7), 5614. DOI: 10.3390/su15075614

Kumar, J. A. (2021). Educational chatbots for project-based learning: Investigating learning outcomes for a team-based design course. *International Journal of Educational Technology in Higher Education*, 18(1), 65. Advance online publication. DOI: 10.1186/s41239-021-00302-w PMID: 34926790

Labadze, L., Grigolia, M., & Machaidze, L. (2023). Role of AI chatbots in education: Systematic literature review. *International Journal of Educational Technology in Higher Education*, 20(1), 56. Advance online publication. DOI: 10.1186/s41239-023-00426-1

Lewandowski, J. (2023). The applications and challenges of chatbots in education. *TS2 SPACE*. https://ts2.space/en/the-applications-and-challenges-of-chatbots-in-education

Lidén, A., & Nilros, K. (2020). *Percieved benefits and limitations of chatbots in higher education.* DIVA. https://www.diva-portal.org/smash/record.jsf?pid=diva2%3A1442044&dswid=1887

Lo, C. K. (2023). What Is the Impact of ChatGPT on Education? A Rapid Review of the Literature. *Education Sciences*, 13(4), 410. DOI: 10.3390/educsci13040410

Lopez, T., & Qamber, M. (2022). The benefits and drawbacks of implementing chatbots in higher education : A case study for international students at Jönköping University (Dissertation).https://urn.kb.se/resolve?urn=urn:nbn:se:hj:diva-57482

Okonkwo, C. W., & Ade-Ibijola, A. (2020). Chatbots applications in education: A systematic review. *Computers and Education: Artificial Intelligence*, 2, 100033. DOI: 10.1016/j.caeai.2021.100033

Rudolph, J., Tan, S., & Tan, S. (2023). ChatGPT: Bullshit spewer or the end of traditional assessments in higher education? *Journal of Applied Learning and Teaching*, 6(1). Advance online publication. DOI: 10.37074/jalt.2023.6.1.9

Sandu, R. (2020). Adoption of AI-Chatbots to enhance student learning experience in higher education in India. *ResearchGate*. https://www.researchgate.net/publication/338868551_Adoption_of_AI-Chatbots_to_Enhance_Student_Learning_Experience_in_Higher_Education_in_India

Sim, J., & Mengshoel, A. M. (2022). Metasynthesis: Issues of empirical and theoretical context. *Quality & Quantity*, 57(4), 3339–3361. DOI: 10.1007/s11135-022-01502-w

Sj. (2023, August 30). ChatGPT in the Philippines: A revolution in AI and education - TechSergy. *TechSergy*. https://techsergy.com/chatgpt-in-the-philippines/

Slepankova, M. (2021). *Possibilities of Artificial Intelligence in Education : An Assessment of the role of AI chatbots as a communication medium in higher education.* DIVA. https://www.diva-portal.org/smash/record.jsf?pid=diva2%3A1617720&dswid=6364

Stepanechko, O., & Kozub, L. (2023). English Teachers' Concerns About the Ethical Use of Chatgpt by University Students. *Grail of Science*, 25(25), 297–302. DOI: 10.36074/grail-of-science.17.03.2023.051

Van Wyk, M. M., Adarkwah, M. A., & Amponsah, S. (2023). Why All the Hype about ChatGPT? Academics' Views of a Chat-based Conversational Learning Strategy at an Open Distance e-Learning Institution. *Open Praxis*, 15(3), 214–225. DOI: 10.55982/openpraxis.15.3.563

Viano, A. (2023, April 28). How Universities Can Use AI Chatbots to Connect with Students and Drive Success. *Technology Solutions That Drive Education*. https://edtechmagazine.com/higher/article/2023/02/how-universities-can-use-ai-chatbots-connect-students-and-drive-success

Wardat, Y., Tashtoush, M. A., AlAli, R., & Jarrah, A. M. (2023). ChatGPT: A revolutionary tool for teaching and learning mathematics. *Eurasia Journal of Mathematics, Science and Technology Education*, 19(7), em2286. Advance online publication. DOI: 10.29333/ejmste/13272

Woithe, J., & Filipec, O. (2023). *Understanding the Adoption, Perception, and Learning Impact of ChatGPT in Higher Education : A qualitative exploratory case study analyzing students' perspectives and experiences with the AI-based large language model*. DIVA. https://www.diva-portal.org/smash/record.jsf?pid=diva2%3A1762617&dswid=-6729

Wollny, S., Schneider, J., Di Mitri, D., Weidlich, J., Rittberger, M., & Drachsler, H. (2021). Are We There Yet? - A Systematic Literature Review on Chatbots in Education. *Frontiers in Artificial Intelligence*, 4, 654924. DOI: 10.3389/frai.2021.654924 PMID: 34337392

Zhang, J., Oh, Y. J., Lange, P., Yu, Z., & Fukuoka, Y. (2020). Artificial intelligence Chatbot Behavior change model for designing artificial intelligence chatbots to promote physical activity and a healthy diet: Viewpoint. *Journal of Medical Internet Research*, 22(9), e22845. DOI: 10.2196/22845 PMID: 32996892

ADDITIONAL READINGS

Aloqayli, A., & Abdelhafez, H. (2023). Intelligent Chatbot for Admission in Higher Education. *International Journal of Information and Education Technology (IJIET)*, 13(9), 1348–1357. DOI: 10.18178/ijiet.2023.13.9.1937

Ayanwale, M. A., & Ndlovu, M. (2024). Investigating factors of students' behavioral intentions to adopt chatbot technologies in higher education: Perspective from expanded diffusion theory of innovation. *Computers in Human Behavior Reports*, 14, 100396. DOI: 10.1016/j.chbr.2024.100396

Chatterjee, S., & Bhattacharjee, K. K. (2020). Adoption of artificial intelligence in higher education: A quantitative analysis using structural equation modelling. *Education and Information Technologies*, 25(5), 3443–3463. DOI: 10.1007/s10639-020-10159-7

Crompton, H., & Burke, D. (2023). Artificial intelligence in higher education: The state of the field. *International Journal of Educational Technology in Higher Education*, 20(1), 22. DOI: 10.1186/s41239-023-00392-8

Essel, H. B., Vlachopoulos, D., Tachie-Menson, A., Johnson, E. E., & Baah, P. K. (2022). The impact of a virtual teaching assistant (chatbot) on students' learning in Ghanaian higher education. *International Journal of Educational Technology in Higher Education*, 19(1), 57. DOI: 10.1186/s41239-022-00362-6

Heryandi, A. (2020, July). Developing chatbot for academic record monitoring in higher education institution. [). IOP Publishing.]. *IOP Conference Series. Materials Science and Engineering*, 879(1), 012049. DOI: 10.1088/1757-899X/879/1/012049

Khalil, M., & Rambech, M. (2022, June). Eduino: A telegram learning-based platform and chatbot in higher education. In *International Conference on Human-Computer Interaction* (pp. 188-204). Cham: Springer International Publishing. DOI: 10.1007/978-3-031-05675-8_15

Kumar, V. R., & Raman, R. (2022, March). Student Perceptions on Artificial Intelligence (AI) in higher education. In *2022 IEEE Integrated STEM Education Conference (ISEC)* (pp. 450-454). IEEE.

Liu, L., Subbareddy, R., & Raghavendra, C. G. (2022). AI intelligence Chatbot to improve students learning in the higher education platform. *Journal of Interconnection Networks*, 22(Supp02), 2143032. DOI: 10.1142/S0219265921430325

Neumann, M., Rauschenberger, M., & Schön, E. M. (2023, May). "We need to talk about ChatGPT": The future of AI and higher education. In *2023 IEEE/ACM 5th International Workshop on Software Engineering Education for the Next Generation (SEENG)* (pp. 29-32). IEEE.

Ouyang, F., Zheng, L., & Jiao, P. (2022). Artificial intelligence in online higher education: A systematic review of empirical research from 2011 to 2020. *Education and Information Technologies*, 27(6), 7893–7925. DOI: 10.1007/s10639-022-10925-9

Ragheb, M. A., Tantawi, P., Farouk, N., & Hatata, A. (2022). Investigating the acceptance of applying chat-bot (Artificial intelligence) technology among higher education students in Egypt. *International Journal of Higher Education Management*, 8(2). Advance online publication. DOI: 10.24052/IJHEM/V08N02/ART-1

Saaida, M. B. (2023). AI-Driven transformations in higher education: Opportunities and challenges. *International Journal of Educational Research and Studies*, 5(1), 29–36.

Vargas-Murillo, A. R., de la Asuncion, I. N. M., & de Jesús Guevara-Soto, F. (2023). Challenges and opportunities of AI-assisted learning: A systematic literature review on the impact of ChatGPT usage in higher education. *International Journal of Learning. Teaching and Educational Research*, 22(7), 122–135.

Wang, Y., Liu, C., & Tu, Y. F. (2021). Factors affecting the adoption of AI-based applications in higher education. *Journal of Educational Technology & Society*, 24(3), 116–129.

Yang, S., & Evans, C. (2019, November). Opportunities and challenges in using AI chatbots in higher education. In *Proceedings of the 2019 3rd International Conference on Education and E-Learning* (pp. 79-83). DOI: 10.1145/3371647.3371659

KEY TERMS AND DEFINITIONS

Chatbot: chatbots are computer applications capable of simulating the conversation of a human either by using a series of manipulations from the decomposition of sentences, data collection on the Internet, sorting and appreciating its relevance, and finally organizing the content as a short answer to continue an ongoing dialogue.

Engagement: refers to the level of interest, attention, and participation of students while interacting with the AI chatbots during learning activities. It encompasses the degree to which students are actively involved, motivated, and invested in the learning process facilitated by the AI chatbots.

Information accuracy: refers to the degree of quality and correctness of the responses generated by AI chatbots. It encompasses the chatbot's ability to provide precise and truthful information that aligns with established facts and knowledge to ensure that students receive valid and trustworthy content during their learning interactions.

Information credibility: refers to the trustworthiness and reliability of the content generated by AI chatbots, which influence students' perceptions of the information's accuracy and validity.

Meta-synthesis: is an approach to make a systematic review of selected and qualified qualitative research related to AI chatbots. It observes rigor in the selection of studies for inclusion and effectively combines their findings to provide meaningful insights. This qualitative research design is similar to meta-analysis which is used to combine quantitative results.

Pedagogical focus: is the specific teaching methods, strategies, and approaches used by instructors or professors or AI chatbots to facilitate learning based on lesson objectives. This involves instructional innovation, assessment, and feedback that are employed to help students learn effectively. The pedagogical focus can vary from teacher-centered approaches to student-centered approaches using technology, such as AI chatbots, to enhance the learning experience and personalize instruction.

Skills enhancement: refers to the improvement or development of various skills, such as writing, problem-solving, critical thinking, and communication through the use of AI chatbots in education

User misuse: refers to illegitimate or improper use of AI chatbots by individuals who are not authorized to use them or who use them for purposes other than those intended by the developers or educators. This can include using AI chatbots for malicious activities, such as spreading misinformation, engaging in cyberbullying or using them in ways that are not aligned with the intended educational goals.

Chapter 4
A Holistic Approach to Improving Students' University Experience:
Exploring Philosophical Orientation, Transformational Teaching Methods, and Flexible Learning

Jherwin Pagkaliwagan Hermosa
https://orcid.org/0000-0001-8562-3028
Laguna State Polytechnic University, Philippines

Edilberto Z. Andal
https://orcid.org/0000-0002-9095-4734
Laguna State Polytechnic University, Philippines

ABSTRACT

This chapter explored the philosophical orientation, transformational instruction practices, flexible learning, and students' university experience. It utilized a phenomenological transcendental design with ten participants. The various sections in this chapter reveal that to stay competitive and relevant in the ever-evolving field of education, it is imperative that our faculty continually acquire new skills, upgrade existing ones, and engage in professional development. An effective approach to achieve this is by fostering a technology-infused collaborative environment, as such environments have been proven to enhance student learning. For our teachers' philosophical orientation, a particular focus can be placed on existentialism as a philosophy for study. By utilizing a qualitative phenomenological method, we can

DOI: 10.4018/979-8-3693-3904-6.ch004

delve into the personal and profound experiences of learners, thereby uncovering humanism and exploring the perspective of the respondents in-depth.

INTRODUCTION

In response to the global pandemic, schools have undergone significant changes in management and teaching methods. Along with these changes, leadership styles such as transactional, charismatic, transformational, and interactive have gained prominence in educational management worldwide. Embracing this shift, Laguna State Polytechnic University has implemented the Flexible Teaching and Learning Model. This model aims to deliver quality and equitable education during these challenging times. The LSPU Learning Continuity Plan, approved by the Board of Regents, guides the university in the opening of classes for the First Semester AY 2020-2021.

Moreover, it is crucial to value the experience and perspectives of students, as they are the ones directly affected by the abrupt changes in the learning environment (Hijazi, 2020). Both universities and students recognize the significance of student experience and satisfaction. It is the ethical responsibility of universities to deliver education and research of the highest quality and standards, meeting the needs of society (Sahin, 2015). Students, being the primary stakeholders of universities, hold the authority in shaping their own experience and understanding of higher education. It is their voices and judgments that define their personal encounters. Hence, students assume a pivotal role in the management of universities by offering feedback on the aspects they deem most essential and their overall satisfaction.

By fostering and promoting engaged partnerships with students, institutions can improve teaching, course design, assessments, and quality processes which produce the best outcomes for students (Alexander, 2020).

Thus, in this chapter, the researcher prioritized how transformational instructional practices, and the instructor's philosophical orientation, influence students' university experiences. Universities and stakeholders care about student satisfaction and experience. Therefore, we can say that flexibility is of special significance and has become the core of university reform: 1) Focus on greater accessibility: Universities must be flexible enough to attract and recruit more new student groups; 2) Focus on individual students so that they can learn when they want it, what they want, and the way they want it. Shifting the focus from teachers to students is believed to help meet these needs, thereby improving teaching for a wider range of students. But despite these milestones, the students' experiences in the conduct of flexible learning were not given enough emphasis. Although they were able to learn effectively and efficiency despite of the sudden migration to flexible learning, their human experience as a student studying in a university, their aspirations, motivations, struggles, communication and real life experience were not given enough considerations.

Hence, the authors have tried to explore the mediating effect of teachers' philosophical orientation, and transformational instructional practices to the implementation of flexible learning at Laguna State Polytechnic University. Studying and understanding these factors could allow refinement of programs, better communications, better engagement, interest, and motivation among students of the university. Further, the findings of the study could be an input to academic rules and policies in the revised LSPU's Learning Continuity and Contingency Plans as a response to the implementation of face-to-face classes and hybrid setup in the educational sector. A student's university experience primer for a bridge program is desired to be developed to sustain the cognitive learning outcomes, student engagement and motivation, and student's self-assessed academic performance.

SIGNIFICANCE OF THE STUDY

We have attempted to determine the importance of a holistic approach to improving students' university experience by exploring philosophical orientation, transformational teaching methods, and integration of flexible Learning thus, the study is likewise important for the following:

Students. This study may help to sustain students' cognitive and affective well-being, allowing them to actively participate in a blended learning environment.

Teaching Personnel. This study could make the LSPU Faculty more aware on the role of the orientations and leadership practices to have a better implementation of the Flexible Learning in the University. It will also raise their awareness about the value of constants recalibrations of skills related to teachings and learning.

Administrations. This study may help them to determine the level of the faculty performance on the implementations of the flexibe learning in the university. The result of the study could provide them a solid basis for the creation of faculty development program.

Academic community. The educational community may find this study useful for improving current guidleines and framework on the implementations of the Flexible learning. They may also conduct recalibration and capabalitiy programs on the recent trends in the new normal.

LIMITATION OF THE STUDY

The scope of this chapter was limited to the understanding of a holistic approach to improving students' university experience by *exploring philosophical orientation, transformational teaching methods, and integration of flexible learning* This study concentrated LSPU San Pablo Campus only. The respondents of this study were only limited to the third and fourth year students of LSPU across four campuses who has experienced flexible learning modality for more than two (2) years. The researchers conducted the data gathering via Google form from February to April 2023 using modified research instruments on philosophical orientation, transformational instruction practices, and implementation of flexible learning and students' university experience. Semi-structured survey instrument and FDG were utilized for the qualitative transcendental phenomenology to know the qualitative part of the study.

LITERATURE REVIEW

Transformational leadership

Anderson (2013) sees that transformational leadership is a popular topic among scholars around the world. Research on this topic has appeared in the literature used in the United States in educational research, as well as in practice. In Latin American countries, transformational leadership has been studied as an instructional practice more than as a leadership management practice. Leadership practices encourage leaders to work toward achieving specific goals to improve the quality of organizations through the ideals of equality, fairness, and justice. Transformational leaders understand the importance of motivating followers to go beyond their self-interests and to attend to their necessities (Hammad & Hallinger, 2017). This style of leadership is often associated with vision, the establishment of guidelines for the restructuring and realigning of an organization, development of working staff, and involvement with the external community via publicity and networking actions. Aldridge, (2015) suggested that an effective form of leadership that seems to promote in an optimal way digital innovation is transformational leadership. The leader of transformational leadership aims to motivate followers, seek to meet their highest needs, and commit their full commitment. Transformational leadership, which is associated with charisma and vision, emerges as the most appropriate model, as it by definition focuses on issues of change and transformation (Cortellazzo et al., 2019). Much of what has been discovered about such leadership in this body of research reinforces the validity of some core sets of leadership practices. The creation of vision and the establishment of guidelines and goal directions can motivate leaders' colleagues in a way that they have a shared purpose as a vital stimulant for their work. Shared vision via the implementation of group goals is correlated with high-performance expectations.

The aspect of the development of staff has a significant contribution to motivation and the principal purpose of this is not only to promote the skills and the knowledge of academics and other staff in order to accomplish organizational goals but also the predisposition to persist in fulfilling these goals as personal traits such as commitment, capacity, and resilience (Nyakan et al., 2018).

Flexible Learning

In the study of Aliazas & Callo (2019) flexible learning is a pedagogical approach allowing flexibility of time, time place and aiudience including, but not solely focused on the used of technology although it commonly uses the delivery methods of distance learning education and facilities of education technology, this may vary depending on the levels of technology, availability of devices, internet connectivity, level of digital literacy and approaches. Moreover, Bates (2017) stated that flexible learning is not a new concept and has been a core issue in distance education for some time. A central element of flexible learning is the provision of choice to learners. Instead of the instructor or the institution making key decisions about learning dimensions, the learner has a range of options from which to choose (Brooks & Grajek, 2020).

Philosophical orientation

The quality of the education depends directly upon the quality of the educators. It is no longer acceptable for educators to possess only skills and knowledge necessary to teach. It is also a need to have the dispositions to become effective teachers during teaching practices. (Stephens, 2019) It is a fact today that the goal of teacher education programs is to train future educators in such a way to produce highly qualified individuals so that they have the knowledge, skills and dispositions to become effective teachers to fostering growth and learning for their students (Bryd & Alexander, 2020)

In the study of Rideout (2016) mentioned that the basic determinant of individuals' educational dispositions is their educational philosophies. Because, educational dispositions are formed based on educational philosophy. A personal educational philosophy is an essential and active element of a teacher. It was also noted by Soccorsi (2018) that acquiring a philosophy is powerful, in that it directs and guides a teacher's teaching practices in the classroom as well as how they perceive teaching and learning and the students around them. Educational philosophy is a discipline or thinking method that provides a point of view for educators. Indeed, an educator's philosophy impacts perceptions, beliefs, understanding and values to the point where all decisions can be traced back to their educational philosophy. Hence, becoming aware of and making sense of a philosophical stance is important in teacher education. Educational philosophy is arranged into branches of philosophy which can be viewed and recognized as orientations to teaching and education. In the context of this study, the main five educational philosophies were taken into account (Ryan, 2018).

MATERIALS AND METHODS

We employed a transcendental phenomenological design to explore and gain a deep understanding of the lived experiences of individuals who have encountered their teacher's Transformational Instruction Practices and the Implementation of Flexible Learning at the university level. The data collection occurred at the Laguna State Polytechnic University, San Pablo City Campus during the second semester of the academic year 2022-2023. To ensure a diverse and qualified pool of participants, two methods were utilized. Firstly, notifications were posted on Instagram and Facebook to inform interested individuals about the study and encourage them to contact the researcher through an online screening survey. Secondly, the researcher reached out to their network of contacts.

In this investigation, a purposeful sampling technique was employed to select 10 participants (Creswell, 2015). These participants were specifically chosen among third-year and fourth-year students attending LSPU, who had been exposed to flexible learning for a minimum of two years. The majority of the respondents fell within the age range of 21-23 years, with a total of 6 participants, while 4 participants were aged 24 or above. The female respondents outnumbered the male respondents, with 7 females and 3 males. In terms of their academic track, 4 participants were enrolled in the ABM program, 2 in HUMSS, 2 in TV, 1 in STEM, and 1 in GAS.

The authors incorporated a series of semi-structured interview questions. These questions formed the interview protocol, which included the research inquiries. The initial in-depth interview took place for about an hour, accommodating the respondents' availability. Alongside the interview notes, audio recordings of the interviews were made. Prior to commencing data collection, the interview questions received validation from external experts. The data collection process began with an initial screening, during which the study's purpose and the participants' expectations for the interview were discussed. The participants were provided with an informed-consent form, comprehensive study details, and asked to schedule their first interview.

The interviews were conducted either over video-conferencing or in-person, based on mutual agreement between the interviewer and participants. Pseudonyms were employed to safeguard their identities. The interview transcripts were carefully examined for codes and themes using a modified version of the methodologies outlined by Stevick (1971), Colaizzi (1973), and Keen (1975), as described by Moustakas (1994). The chosen research methodology for this study was transcendental phenomenology, as it aimed to comprehend the significance of the participants' experiences. Furthermore, the systematic procedures and detailed data analysis steps outlined by Moustakas (1994) prove particularly valuable for novice researchers. The adoption of a transcendental approach with systematic procedures aligns with the philosophical perspective of striking a balance between objective and subjective approaches to knowledge while ensuring meticulous and rigorous data analysis.

RESULTS

Following radical changes in school management and teaching methods as a result of the global pandemic, as well as changes in leadership styles as a function of management, contemporary approaches to leadership: transactional, charismatic, transformational, and interactive have become more frequently the focus in educational management around the world.

However, the researchers prioritized how transformational instructional practices, mediated by the instructor's philosophical orientation, influence students' university experiences. Universities and stakeholders care about student satisfaction and experience. A university's moral purpose is to provide high-quality education and research to meet society's needs. Because students are the most important customers of universities, their experiences, knowledge, and understanding of higher education must be based on their voices.

Table. 1. Summary Table of the Emerging Themes

VARIABLE	QUESTION	RECURRENT ANSWERS
PHILOSOPHICAL ORIENTATION	1. How do your actions as a student reflect your beliefs about teaching and learning?	- The way students act reflects their attitudes toward education and learning. For instance, a student is more likely to study hard and persevere when encountering challenges if they believe they are capable of acquiring something if they dedicate enough effort. - I believe that learning, so as, teaching was a vital part of a student. My actions were the reflections of what I have learned from school. - My actions reflect my belief about teaching and learning by listening to the topic so that it will benefit me as a student. - And having a habit of setting high standards on things also affects my belief in teaching and learning; for example, if I like the class then I give my full attention to it and vice versa.
TRANSFORMATIONAL INSTRUCTION PRACTICES	1. What would it mean to transform education?	- It is a must for that the objectives of the school must be specific and based on the needs of society to achieve transformative education. - The teacher should also invest in preparation, and develop creative lesson plans, and must always be on the lookout for materials and ways to continuously improve the lesson. - It is one of the most important things a leader should do. Education will be improved and of better quality as a result of transformation. It will certainly help many students because improved education will inspire them. - It would mean a lot if it is transformed into a better environment for everyone they would provide a more sustainable development and empowerment for students.
EFFECTIVENESS OF IMPLEMENTATION OF FLEXIBLE LEARNING	1. What opportunities in learning were unraveled in the students' journey in flexible learning?	- It is the opportunity to adapt to the environment we have and be flexible on the new setup for us to be able to learn. - Their journey inspires confidence and lets them feel comfortable expressing themselves regardless of their level of ability. - The importance of learning the new opportunity. Yes, it has been a very important thing for a student but upon experiencing the "flexible learning", the way the tasks were given was different from before, and sometimes it was time-consuming and demanding. - It promotes individualized learning, which can help us students reach their maximum potential.

continued on following page

Table. Continued

VARIABLE	QUESTION	RECURRENT ANSWERS
STUDENTS' UNIVERSITY EXPERIENCE	1. Why creating better experiences for students is a worthwhile but challenging endeavor that will take years to accomplish, along with the cooperation of many people?	- Our teaching staff normally give me helpful feedback on how I am doing. - In conclusion, creating better experiences for students is an important and valuable goal because it holds the power to shape their futures and unlock their full potential. - Creating better and more creative with the cooperation of many People experiences for students is indeed hard work but through this process learners' engagement peaks to the top resulting to a better academic performance and building more effective learners for everyone - I feel confident in dealing with a wide range of people.

Table 1 displays the recurring responses of the participants regarding the implementation of Transformational Instruction Practices and Flexible Learning to the Level of Students' University Experience in specific areas of interest. These areas include: (1) *students' perspectives on teaching and learning, (2) understanding of transformative education, (3) experiences with flexible learning, and (4) enhancements to university experiences for students.*

Through this new experiences, faculty members bring with them a diversity of life experiences, educational experiences, personalities, learning preferences, and uniqueness in their teaching approaches. This shapes their perspectives on their teaching practices, influences how they will teach in the future, and even influences their students to participate in learning process.

The outcomes confirm four thematic: (1) students' belief about teaching and learning. In this, teachers enable learners to make adaptive attributions for 'success' and 'failure' in learning, who include opportunity for the mastery of curriculum content, and who incorporate meaningful choice and involvement in learning activities are promoting positive self-beliefs and thereby supporting the development of healthy self-concept. (2), understanding of transformative education. It encourage learners to reach their full potential and goes beyond cognitive knowledge to impart core values, attitudes and skills that promote respect for human rights, justice, diversity, equality and a sustainable future. Meanwhile, the thematic (3) Students' journey in flexible learning suggest that they also took an affective stance towards the flexible learning course due to their need for communication. On the other hand the thematic (4) creating better learning experiences for students. They argue that one of the main drivers of flexible learning is to provide helpful feedback to learners. Feedback allows learners to see aspects of their learning, their status, progress, improvements. They observe that flexible learning has a moral dimension, given its development can enable the advancement of outcomes related to social justice and equity from an educational perspective. They have also noted that the importance of collaborative learning which leads to active participation and interaction on the part of both students and instructors.

1. Students' beliefs about teaching and learning.

The significance of researching beliefs stems from their strong influence on individuals' decisions and actions (Fives et al., 2015). Notably, teacher beliefs play an essential role in shaping perceptions and intentions within learning environments and teacher professional development. Consequently, there is growing recognition of the need for qualitative research on teacher beliefs. The purpose of the study was to investigate the opinions of third and fourth-year students from LSPU SPC regarding the teaching and learning of critical educational concepts. The researcher utilized open-ended focus group interviews as a means to gather insights on learning, teaching, and teacher knowledge. The participants, including LSPU faculty members, generally displayed a highly positive stance towards teaching and learning. A participant from the study noted that teaching and learning instilled confidence among students, enabling them to communicate their thoughts effectively regardless of their level of proficiency (Participant 1, Transcript 1). These statements signify a belief that students acquire knowledge in diverse ways, with certain methods being more effective than others, commonly referred to as the "learning styles" belief. It is crucial for educators to comprehend that learner self-perception encompasses both academic and non-academic aspects.

A crucial aspect to consider is that self-concept can have an impact on academic achievement, but it is also greatly influenced by contextual and environmental factors. Teachers play a crucial role in fostering positive self-beliefs by allowing students to attribute their successes and 'failures' in learning to adaptability, providing opportunities for content mastery, and incorporating meaningful choice and engagement in learning activities. This, in turn, supports the development of a healthy self-concept (Zevalsiz, 2014). Hence, it is vital for teachers aiming to enhance learner self-confidence to prioritize the support and development of self-concept, as it significantly contributes to increasing competence (Callo and Yazon, 2020). To promote gender equity within schools, teachers serve as the primary agents of change. Research has demonstrated that teachers' beliefs and practices rooted in gender stereotypes have a substantial impact on gender differences observed among students (Hung et al., 2020). One of the study participants expressed the importance of treating all students equally, regardless of various factors such as age, gender, nationality, intellectual ability, or personal attractiveness, in the context of teaching and learning (Participant 4, Transcript 1). It is interesting to note that Lüftenegger et al. (2020) discovered a correlation between teachers promoting individualization and autonomy in the classroom and a reduction in gender differences in motivation.

Teachers who prioritize equality, autonomy, and individualization seem to be less influenced by unconscious gender biases and more attentive to the unique abilities and needs of their students. By allowing students to choose tasks or learning settings that align with their interests and abilities, promoting equality, autonomy, and individualization creates a positive motivational environment where diversity among students is embraced as a natural occurrence, acknowledged by the teacher, and effectively addressed.

Motivational support is widely recognized as a crucial approach to lessen gender disparities in the classroom (Yue et al., 2019). In a related context, one participant emphasized the significance of teachers incorporating their personal life experiences to enhance classroom discussions (Participant 8, Transcript 2). The involvement of social interaction in learning has been found to increase learner engagement (Tengi et al., 2017). According to Redding and Courbett (2018), students benefit from their teachers sharing personal experiences, as it fosters active dialogue and interactions. Leveraging experiences for social learning is a proven and preferred method of learning that respects learners' natural preferences, devoid of coercion.

2. Understanding the Significance of Transformative Education

Within the realm of education, transformative teaching practices emphasize the importance of altering the conditions of schools and classrooms to enhance learning. Whether it is teachers or principals, the leaders in educational institutions focus on restructuring the physical and social aspects of the school environment to create better conditions for students.

To elaborate on this concept, one of the participants shared their perspective, stating that "schools must have specific objectives that align with the needs of society to achieve transformative education" (Participant 10, Transcript 2). Education must provide individuals with clear objectives that equip them with the knowledge, skills, and values necessary to address the interconnected challenges of the 21st century (UN Secretary-General, 2015).

It is no longer sufficient for education to solely focus on teaching fundamental literacy and numeracy skills. Nowadays, education must go beyond that and empower individuals to become catalysts for sustainable change. They need to be equipped with the ability to effectively address global challenges. Such awareness and capacity can only come to fruition if educational institutions set clear objectives based on the needs of learners in the 21st century. Merely ensuring universal access to education is insufficient to tackle persistent issues like poverty, inequalities, racism, and climate change. What we truly require is a transformative education system that enables learners to reach their utmost potential. This system must surpass the acquisition of cognitive knowledge and also instill core values, attitudes, and skills that foster respect for human rights, justice, diversity, equality, and a sustainable future.

Participant 15, in addition, emphasizes the importance for teachers to invest in preparation, develop innovative lesson plans, and constantly seek out new materials and methods to enhance the quality of their teaching (Transcript 3). According to Jenkins (2020), teaching is the dynamic process of transferring knowledge and skills from a teacher to a learner. This encompasses the actions involved in educating and instructing individuals. It is a transformative practice that shapes one's mind, character, and physical abilities. Teaching demands a genuine passion for learning and is a profession that only those truly dedicated can thrive in. It involves a developmental journey where students progressively advance from simpler to more sophisticated ideas and abilities. As a teacher, an integral aspect of your role is to guide, motivate, and support your students throughout their educational growth.

Students must acknowledge the limitations of their existing skills, knowledge, and perspectives. It is equally important for them to have opportunities to test and apply new skills and attitudes (Kabilan et al., 2020). Furthermore, a participant emphasized the significance of a strong school administration that brings together teachers, staff, students, and parents (Participant 18, Transcript 4). Recent studies indicate that administrative support plays a vital role in fostering effective educators and establishing problem-solving teams that lead the way in transforming educational institutions (Floweret al., 2017). School administrators have the responsibility of providing teachers with access to professional development and resources to effectively address student needs, including behavior and disciplinary issues. Effective transformative education in educational institutions relies heavily on a robust foundation (Fortune et al., 2021). Thus, to ensure the success of both your school and students, it is essential to prioritize support for teachers. If you are contemplating how administrators can assist teachers, the crucial steps involve offering guidance, fostering opportunities for collaboration among peers, conducting meaningful evaluations, and recognizing them as esteemed professionals.

3. Exploring the Students' Experience in Flexible Learning

The Philippine higher education sector has recognized the necessity of adopting alternative learning methods, moving away from traditional teaching approaches towards flexible strategies. Although there has been extensive research on flexible learning, limited studies have focused on understanding the significance of students' familiarity with inflexible knowledge as an effective learning approach.

In this regard, participant 2 conveyed that their educational journey instilled confidence in them and provided a platform to freely express themselves, regardless of their skill level (Participant 2, Transcript 1). Learners who possess attributes such as self-supervision, self-regulation, a penchant for self-exploration, and open-mindedness, among others, have a notable impact on the effectiveness of flexible learning (Francisco& Barcelona, 2020). "They must possess the inclination for spontaneous learning to pursue independent study. Consequently, learners must possess a greater capacity for self-directed learning to complete the course. By adopting a flexible learning approach that empowers learners to take responsibility for their own choices, numerous opportunities can arise.

In addition, one participant noted a significant communication gap between students and instructors. There were instances where further clarification was needed regarding certain lecture content, but these points were left unexplained by the instructors (Participant 6, Transcript 2). The participants also expressed a desire for communication, which affected their perception of the flexible learning course. They compared face-to-face classes with their virtual learning environment and were critical of the latter for not meeting their need for socializing with friends. According to Gedera, et al., (2015), motivation plays a key role in self-regulated learning for learners utilizing technology. The primary features of motivations include specific motivations, success goals, confidence, self-efficacy, and power confidence. In one instance during the course, a participant emphasized the importance of utilizing technology, such as virtual classrooms, to effectively share resources, materials, and communicate with students (Participant 8, Transcript 3). The challenges faced by participants regarding technology are discussed within the second main theme, which encompasses crucial technical aspects like internet connectivity and online tools. When examining the broader narratives on flexible learning, students consistently mention the role of information technology, particularly internet connection, as a significant factor impacting their effectiveness (Boamah et al., 2018). Furthermore, students' familiarity with relevant online tools to support learning in flexible learning environments directly influences their self-efficacy. The majority of respondents are considered beginners when it comes to using learning management systems, online communication tools, storage devices, creating and packaging video materials, and uploading and managing web content.

4. Enhancing Student Learning Experiences.

Educational institutions are increasingly prioritizing the tracking and improvement of the overall student experience. They recognize that the quality of this experience directly impacts an institution's reputation and its ability to attract new students. About this matter, one participant highlighted the significance of receiving "helpful feedback from their teaching staff regarding their progress" (Participant 1, Transcript 1). Jackson (2020) contend that offering informative feedback to learners is a key driver of flexible learning. Feedback enables learners to gain insights into their learning process, current status, progress, and areas for improvement. There is evidence supporting the claim that feedback does not diminish the quality of a student's learning experience and performance. It may even improve or be on par with traditional learning methods.

According to Serkan et al. (2019), positive feedback from teachers indicates that learners effectively utilized flexibility and achieved better learning outcomes. Understanding the various ways in which flexibility can be incorporated into personalized learning design can enhance student collaboration, particularly among students with similar characteristics. Furthermore, a participant in flexible learning shared their experience of developing the ability to consider alternative perspectives (Participant 7, Transcript 2). This highlights the importance of exploring and adopting diverse forms of flexible learning, as emphasized in a study by Asma et al., (2021) According to their observations, they support this claim by pointing out the increasing diversity in the student population, spanning all age groups, social segments, and individual needs. They also note a moral aspect to flexible learning, as its implementation can foster social justice and equitable outcomes within the educational context. In fact, Jeffrey et al. (2021) further highlight that flexible learning could inadvertently align with the socially oriented objectives that most universities strive for as part of their strategies. Bas and Senturk (2019) argue that flexible learning brings numerous benefits to both students and Higher Education Institutions (HEIs), and these advantages should not be disregarded. As the adoption of flexible learning continues to rise, HEIs have come to realize that it entails substantial investment, not only in terms of technology but also in training and reconfiguring staff and structures.

Bas and Senturk (2019) discuss how the current technology available to Higher Education Institutions (HEIs) allows for more open, personalized, and flexible provisions. This trend is expected to continue growing. An important lesson for HEIs is the need to have policies and capabilities that enable them to take advantage of technologies. These actions facilitate the achievement of socially oriented goals, such as expanding access to HEIs.

Continuing on this subject, a participant (Participant 10, Transcript 2) expressed confidence in dealing with diverse individuals. Whether the learning environment is online or not, creating a sense of community among learners is a challenging task in any classroom setting. However, the benefits of belonging to a community, especially a virtual one, should outweigh any associated costs. Llanes et al., (2020) highlights the benefits of collaborative learning, referred to as "collective goods" including knowledge capital, social capital, and communion. The success of the community relies on these benefits outweighing technical difficulties, time and monetary costs. Collaborative learning, as evidenced by Irwin et al., (2017), is considered an effective pedagogical approach that easily adapts to online learning environments. This approach emphasizes group and cooperative efforts among both students and instructors, with active participation and interaction being key elements. The members of the learning environment must engage in social interaction, cooperation, and evaluation of actions, which collectively contribute to the development of the group's knowledge base. Moreover, these interactions can be facilitated irrespective of physical location or other limitations through the use of telecommunications and electronic networks.

CONCLUSION

Faculty members bring a range of diverse life experiences, educational backgrounds, personalities, learning preferences, and unique perspectives to their teaching approaches. These factors shape their viewpoints on teaching practices, influence their future teaching methods, and have an impact on their students' engagement in the learning process. The results of the study validate two key themes: (1) students' beliefs about teaching and learning and (2) understanding of transformative education. Teachers who promote adaptive attributions for success and "failure" in education, offer opportunities for curriculum content mastery, and incorporate meaningful choice and involvement in learning activities foster positive self-beliefs, thus supporting the development of a healthy self-concept. It is widely acknowledged that transformative education, extending beyond mere cognitive knowledge, is necessary to instill fundamental values, attitudes, and skills that foster respect for human rights, justice, diversity, equality, and a sustainable future. The third theme, titled "Students' Journey in Flexible Learning," asserts that students developed an emotional connection to the flexible learning course due to their communication requirements. On the contrary, the fourth theme enhances the learning experiences of students. The proponents argue that providing constructive feedback to learners is one of the primary catalysts for flexible learning. Feedback enables students to gauge their knowledge, standing, progress, and areas that can be further improved.

To ensure seamless teaching and learning during and beyond the pandemic, higher education institutions must empower tech-savvy students who are increasingly seeking more innovative and captivating educational materials. By creating an enticing online learning environment, these institutions can cater to the interests and requirements of students. Simultaneously, our faculty members are acknowledging the rise of new digital skills in this era and recognizing the indispensable need for continuous reskilling, upskilling, and professional development to remain competitive and relevant in the new normal of education. Promoting a technology-enhanced collaborative environment would be beneficial as collaborative learning settings foster students' growth and success. The pandemic has taught educators the importance of social discourse and collaboration, which are crucial for students' cognitive development across all age groups and are imperative for education in the new normal society. In the meantime, upcoming researchers can carry out a concurrent investigation to examine the impact of philosophical orientation on the implementation of transformational instructional practices and flexible learning techniques in university students' academic journey. When examining teachers' philosophical orientation, the study could specifically concentrate on existentialism as a philosophical framework. This choice is based on its ability to reveal humanistic values and the personal experiences of individuals. To delve into the learners' perspectives more comprehensively, a qualitative phenomenological approach can be employed.

Declaration of Conflict

The authors declare that they have no known competing financial interests or personal relationships that could have appeared to influence the work reported in this paper.

ACKNOWLEDGMENTS

The researchers would like to acknowledge the Laguna State Polytechnic University Academic Community for always inspiring us to be the agents of innovation, progress, and quality education.

REFERENCES

Abenes, R., & Malibiran, A. L. (2020). Filipino diaspora in the light of Louis Althusser's concept of ideology. *The URSP Research Journal*, 6(1), 21–30.

Acar, H., Akar, M., & Acar, B. (2016). Value orientations of social workers. *Kastamonu Education Journal.*, 24(1), 97–118.

Afsar, B. S., Asad, S., & Syed, I. A. (2019). The mediating role of transformational leadership in the relationship between cultural intelligence and employee voice behavior: A case of hotel employees. *International Journal of Intercultural Relations*, 69, 66–75. DOI: 10.1016/j.ijintrel.2019.01.001

Aldridge, M. (2015). Modelling mindful practice. Reflective Practice. *International and Multidisciplinary Perspectives.* DOI: 10.1080/14623943.2015.1023278

Alexander, S. (2020). Flexible Learning in Higher Education. *International Encyclopedia of Education. 441–447.* DOI: 10.1016/B978-0-08-044894-7.00868-X

Alsalem, A. S. (2018). Curriculum orientations and educational philosophies of high school Arabic teachers. *International Education Studies*, 11(4), 92–95. DOI: 10.5539/ies.v11n4p92

Asma U.l., Hosna, L., & Mahmud Hamid, T. (2021). A Review of the relationship of Idealized Influence, Inspirational Motivation, Intellectual Stimulation, and Individual Consideration with Sustainable Employees Performance. *International Journal of Progressive Sciences and Technologies*

Barret, L., & Long, V. (2012). *The Moore Method and the Constructivist Theory of Learning: Was R. L. Moore a Constructivist?* Taylor and Francis., DOI: 10.1080/10511970.2010.493548

Barton, G. M., & Ryan, M. (2014). Multimodal approaches to reflective teaching and assessment in higher education: A cross disciplinary approach in creative industries. Higher Education Research & Development, 33, 409–424. *International Studies on Educational Management.*.DOI: 10.1080/07294360.2013.841650

Bates, T. (2017). *The 2017 national survey of online learning in Canadian post-secondary education: methodology and results*. International Journal of Education and Technology., DOI: 10.1186/s41239-018-0112-3

Boamah, S., Spence, K., Wong, C., & Clarke, S. (2018). Effect of transformational leadership on job satisfaction and patient safety outcomes. *Nursing Outlook*, 66(2), 180–189. Advance online publication. DOI: 10.1016/j.outlook.2017.10.004 PMID: 29174629

Braidotti, R. (2019). A Theoretical Framework for the Critical Post-humanities. *Theory, Culture & Society*, 36(6), 31–61. DOI: 10.1177/0263276418771486

Brooks, C., & Grajek, S. (2020). Faculty Readiness to Begin Fully Remote Teaching. er.educause.edu/blogs/2020 /3/faculty-readiness-to-begin-fully-remote-teaching

Bryd, D., & Alexander, M. (2020). Investigating special education teachers' knowledge and skills: Preparing general teacher preparation for professional development. *Journal of Pedagogical Research*. https://doi.org/.DOI: 10.33902/JPR.2020059790

Callo, E., & Yazon, A. (2020). Exploring the Factors Influencing Faculty and Students' Readiness on Online Teaching and Learning as an Alternative Delivery Model for the New Normal. https://www.hrpub.org/journals/article_info.php?aid=9556

Callo, E., Yazon, A., & Briones, M. (2020). *LSPU Primer on Facilitation Flexible Learning: Migrating to the New Normal*. LSPU Board Resolution No. 061 Series of 2020.

Colebook, C. (2017). *What Is This Thing Called Education?* Sage Journal., DOI: 10.1177/1077800417725357

Coleman, R., & Ringrose, J. (2013). *Deleuze and Research Methodologies*. Taylor and Francis. DOI: 10.1515/9780748644124

Cortellazzo, L., Bruni, E., & Zampieri, R. (2019). The Role of Leadership in a Digitalized World. *A Review.Frontiers in Psychology*, 10, 1938. Advance online publication. DOI: 10.3389/fpsyg.2019.01938 PMID: 31507494

Creswell, J. W. (2015). *Qualitative inquiry & research design: Choosing among five approaches*. Sage Journal.

Dixon-Román, E. (2021). *Social epistemology and the pragmatics of assessment*. Sage Journal.

Dziuban, C. (2018). Blended learning: the new normal and emerging technologies. Front. *Education. Educational technology journal. /*.DOI: 10.1186/s41239-017-0087-5

Emmanuel, W. (2020). Online learning in the time of COVID-19: A Computer Science Educator's Point of View. https://arete.ateneo.edu/connect/online-learning -in-the-time-*of-covid19-a-computer-science-educators-point-ofview? -4kG hBbzL-5wp8vCiczqCnqX4*

Fives, H., Lacatena, N., & Gerard, L. (2015). *Teachers' beliefs about teaching (and learning)*. Routledge.

Flower, A., McKenna, J. W., & Haring, C. D. (2017). Behavior and classroom management: Are teacher preparation programs preparing our teachers? *Preventing School Failure*, 61(2), 163–169. DOI: 10.1080/1045988X.2016.1231109

Fortune, M.F., Spielman, M., & Pangelinan, D.T. (2021). Students' Perceptions of Online or Face-to-Face Learning and Social Media in Hospitality, Recreation and Tourism. *Journal of Tourism and Management.*

Francisco, C., & Barcelona, M. (2020). Effectiveness of an Online Classroom for Flexible Learning. *International Journal of Academic Multidisciplinary Research.*

Gedera, D., Williams, J., & Wright, N. (2015). Identifying factors influencing students' motivation and engagement in online courses. In Koh, C. (Ed.), *Motivation, leadership and curriculum design*. Springer., DOI: 10.1007/978-981-287-230-2_2

Hammad, W., & Hallinger, P. (2017). *A systematic review of conceptual models and methods used in research on educational leadership and management in Arab societies*. Taylor and Francis., DOI: 10.1080/13632434.2017.1366441

Hijazi, S. (2020). *International Outreach for university post-crisis*. QS Intelligence Unit.

Hung, M., Chou, C., Chen, C., & Own, Z. (2020). Learner readiness for online learning: Scale development and student perceptions. *Elsevier. 3 (55).*https://www .sciencedirect.com/science/article/abs/pii/S0360131510001260?via% *3Dihub*

Illanes, P., Law, J., Sarakatsannis, J., Sanghvi, S., and Mendy, *A. (2020). Coronavirus and the Campus: How Can US Higher Education Organize to Respond?* McKinsey and Company.

Iqbal, U., & Ralf, B. (2013). *Textbook of Educational Philosophy*. Kanishka Publishers.

Irwin, C., Ball, L., Desbrow, B., & Leveritt, M. (2017). Students' perceptions of using Facebook as an interactive learning resource at university. *Australasian Journal of Educational Technology*, 28(7), 1221–1232.

Irwin, C., Ball, L., Desbrow, B., & Leveritt, M. (2017). Students' perceptions of using Facebook as an interactive learning resource at university. *Australasian Journal of Educational Technology*, 28(7), 1221–1232.

Jackson, C. J. (2020). Transformational leadership and gravitas: 2000 years of no development? *Personality and Individual Differences*, 156, 109760. DOI: 10.1016/j.paid.2019.109760

Jenkins, K. (2020). *Towards impactful energy justice research: Transforming the power of academic engagement.* PLOS Journal., DOI: 10.1016/j.erss.2020.101510

Kabilan, M. K., Ahmad, N., & Abidin, M. J. Z. (2020). Facebook: An online environment for learning of English in institutions of higher education? *The Internet and Higher Education*, 13(4), 179–187. DOI: 10.1016/j.iheduc.2010.07.003

Lone, A. A (2015). Reconstruction of Islamic Education: with special reference to AllamaIqbal's Educational philosophy. FUNOON. *International Journal of Multidisplinary Research- Vol. I, Issue 2.*

Lone, S. (2015). *Impact of childlessness on life and attitudes towards continuation of medically assisted reproduction and/or adoption.* Taylor and Francis., DOI: 10.3109/14647273.2015.1006691

Lüftenegger, M. (2020). Multiple Social and Academic Achievement Goals: Students' Goal Profiles and Their Linkages. *Journal of Experimental Education.* Advance online publication. DOI: 10.1080/00220973.2022.2081959

Mahdi, M. (2015). *IbnKhaldun's Philosophy of History: A Study in the Philosophic Foundation of the Science of Culture.* Routledge.

Mark, B. (2018) Benefits and challenges of doing research: Experiences from Philippine public school teachers. *Issues in Educational Research*https://www.iier.org.au/iier28/ullaabs.html

Martin, F., Budhrani, K., & Wang, C. (2019). *Examining Faculty Perception of Their Readiness to Teach Online.* Online Learning Journal. DOI: 10.24059/olj.v23i3.1555

Naldoza, N. (2020, April). Online Teaching and Learning Preparedness. *Survey.* https://docs.google.com/forms/d/e/1FAIpQLSfU_i57h19jgASOby9PeWZtrpNeYw FIc8ApdBkhFAcOxj5uA/viewform

Nguyen, M. H., & Nguyen, T. H. (2014). The Influence of Leadership Behaviors on Employee Performance in the Context of Software Companies in Vietnam. *Advances in Management & Applied Economics*, 4(3), 157–171.

Nyakan, B. A., Getange, K. N., & Onchera, P. O. (2018). Influence of principals' management competencies on supervision of instruction in public secondary schools in Homabay County, Kenya. *International Journal of Novel Research in Education and Learning*, 5(3), 1–6. www.noveltyjournals.com

Rashid, M., & Mamunar, R. (2018). Social Media Advertising Response and its Effectiveness: Case of South Asian Teenage Customers. Social Media Advertising Response and its Effectiveness: Case of South Asian Teenage Customers. *Global Journal of Management and Business Research*, 18(4), 9–16. https://journalofbusiness.org/index.php/GJMBR/article/view/249

Rauf, M., Ahmad, M., & Iqbal, Z. (2013). Al-Farabi's Philosophy of Education. http://muslimheritage.com/article/al-farabis-doctrine-education-betweenphilosophy-and-sociological-theory?page=1clxxvii

Redding, S., & Corbett, J. (2018). *Shifting school culture to spark rapid improvement: A quick start guide for principals and their teams*. WestEd.

Rideout, V. (2016). Measuring time spent with media: The Common Sense census of media use by US 8- to 18-year-olds. *Journal of Children and Media*, 10(1), 138–144. Advance online publication. DOI: 10.1080/17482798.2016.1129808

Ryan, G. (2018). Introduction to positivism, interpretivism, and critical theory. *Nurse Researcher*, 25(4), 14–20. Advance online publication. DOI: 10.7748/nr.2018.e1466 PMID: 29546962

Ryan, G. (2018). Introduction to positivism, interpretivism and critical theory. *Nurse Researcher*, 25(4), 14–20. Advance online publication. DOI: 10.7748/nr.2018.e1466 PMID: 29546962

Saeverot, H., Reindal, S., & Wivestad, S. (2013). *Introduction: Reconnecting with Existentialism in an Age of Human Capital*. Philpapers.

Sahin, M. (2015). Essentialism in philosophy, psychology, education, social and scientific scopes. *Journal of Innovation in Psychology, Education and Didactics*.

Serkan, Ü., Reyhan, A., & Korkmaz, F. (2017). Exploring Teaching Profession from a Sociological Perspective: Evidence from Turkey. Universal. *The Journal of Educational Research*, 5(5), 874–880. DOI: 10.13189/ujer.2017.050519

Soccorsi, L. (2013). Instilling a personal teaching philosophy in preservice teachers: Vitally important but not always easy to achieve. *Journal of Student Engagement: Education Matters*, 3(1), 21–28.

Stephens, K. (2019). *Teacher Dispositions and Their Impact on Implementation Practices for the Gifted.* Sage Journal. DOI: 10.1177/1076217519862330

Tengi, M. L., Mansor, M., & Hashim, S. (2017). A Review Theory of Transformational Leadership for School. *International Journal of Academic Research in Business & Social Sciences*, 7(3). Advance online publication. DOI: 10.6007/IJARBSS/v7-i3/2847

Yasin, F., Firdaus, R., & Jani, M. (2013). *Islamic Education.* The Philosophy, Aim, and Main Features.

Yılmaz, K., Altınkurt, Y., & Çokluk, Ö. (2014). Developing the educational belief scale: The validity and reliability study. *Educational Sciences: Theory & Practice*, 11(1), 343–350.

Yue, C., Men, A., Rita, L., & Ferguson, M. (2019). Bridging transformational leadership, transparent communication, and employee openness to change: The mediating role of trust. *Public Relations Review*, 45(3), 101779. DOI: 10.1016/j.pubrev.2019.04.012

Zabala, A. (2014). Q method: A Package to Explore the Human Perspective Using Q Methodology. *The R Journal*, 6(2), 163–173. DOI: 10.32614/RJ-2014-032

Zevalsiz, S. (2014). Value Perception of University Students. *International Periodical for Languages. Literature and History of Turkish or Turkic*, 9(2), 1739–1762.

Section 2
Improving Instruction and Learning With Technology

Chapter 5
The Impact of Instruction Technology on Class and Time Management in Moroccan Higher Education:
The Case of Sidi Mohamed Ben Abdellah University

Youssef Laaraj

Faculty of Sciences and Techniques, Sidi Mohamed Ben Abdellah University, Morocco

ABSTRACT

Morocco has been actively attempting to modernize its education system by embracing and promoting the use of information and communication technology (ICT), as outlined in official documents such as The National Charter and Loi Cadre 51-17. Initiatives like integrating digital tools and e-learning platforms have aimed to improve access to quality education for over two decades. This chapter investigates the innovative technology integration in Moroccan university classrooms at Sidi Mohamed Ben Abdellah University, and particularly examines its effects on class and time management. Using a mixed-methods approach, the research investigates university teachers' experiences with the use of modern technologies in their classes. Within the Technological Pedagogical Content Knowledge (TPACK) framework, the investigation aims to provide insights into how technology influences teaching practices and learning experiences, contributing to the discourse on education in Morocco and offering valuable insights for educators, policymakers, and researchers.

DOI: 10.4018/979-8-3693-3904-6.ch005

INTRODUCTION

In the contemporary landscape of education, the integration of technology has emerged as a crucial facet in the pursuit of educational advancement and adaptation to the demands of the 21st century. Following the COVID-19 pandemic, which has transformed the nature of teaching and learning, modern technologies have become indispensable tools for both teachers and students in and beyond the classroom. This chapter embarks on an exploration of the profound influence of technology integration within Moroccan university classrooms, with a particular focus on its implications for class and time management. Grounded in official educational reforms such as The National Charter, The Strategic Vision 2015-2030, and *Loi Cadre* 51-17, Morocco's commitment to leveraging digital tools and e-learning platforms underscores its dedication to enhancing access to quality education. Yet, critiques (CSEFRS, 2021) have questioned the efficacy of integrating technology in education. These critiques touched upon varied issues such as teacher training, resources, connectivity, socioeconomic disparities, and the like. The chapter unravels the intricate interplay between technological, pedagogical, and content knowledge and the correlation between adopting modern teaching technologies and time as well as class management. It also endeavors to contribute meaningful insights to the discourse on technology integration in education, offering valuable perspectives for educators, policymakers, and researchers invested in shaping the future of Moroccan education.

DEFINITION OF CONCEPTS

The intersection of technology and education necessitates an intelligible definition of key concepts, which became indivisible features in the description of this timely popular topic. Despite assumed academics' familiarity with these topics, illustrating the scope of use of some key concepts for a larger audience of readers is indispensable to establishing and maintaining a common ground of understanding between the authors and the readership.

INFORMATION AND COMMUNICATION TECHNOLOGIES:

Information and communication technologies (ICT) refers to technologies that give access to information through Telecommunication. (Singh, 2021). Thanks to ICT, people can communicate in real-time with others at a distance through means such as instant messaging, voice and video conferencing, and social networking websites. In education, ICT encompasses tools and platforms that facilitate learning and teaching processes, such as educational software, digital resources, online communication platforms, and multimedia applications. These technologies are integrated into educational settings to enhance access to information, foster collaboration among students and educators, personalize learning experiences and prepare learners for the digital challenges of the modern world.

MODERN TECHNOLOGIES:

Modern technology is an umbrella term. Yet, as the term is self-evident in its general use, it is, here, used to designate technologies that can aid in education. In this sense, the rem encompasses a wide variety of digital tools and platforms, which transcended the boundaries of brick-and-mortar classrooms, bringing learning to the fingertips of students and educators alike. (Kumar et al, 2024). Berkeshchuk, et al (2020) highlight that modern technologies have come to make up for the increasing demand on education from afar due to evolving global conditions such as the impossibility of personal face-to-face communication and quarantine conditions.

EDUCATION TECHNOLOGIES:

While modern technologies, in their general use, designate all types and sorts of technologies that serve a variety of purposes, including education, education technology refers firsthand to its educational purposes. According to Dron (2022), education technologies are the tools that are used 'pedagogically'. That is to say, the software and hardware teachers use purposefully and deliberately to achieve educational objectives and outcomes in the most efficient ways. The term, thus, includes "learning management systems, textbooks, electronic whiteboards, courses, etc. – almost any technology (from a factory to a word processor)" which can "be used to support or engender learning" (Dron,22, p. 6).

The essence of education technology refers to tools intentionally used for educational purposes. These tools are employed by teachers to achieve educational goals efficiently. The emphasis is on how these technologies support and enhance learning processes through deliberate integration into educational practices.

Regardless of their meticulous differences, the terms modern technology, education technology, instruction technology, and innovation technology are used somewhat interchangeably in this article. The distinction lies primarily in how the first word of each phrase underscores the nature or purpose of the technology involved. However, readers need not overly concern themselves with detailed differences between these terms. Instead, the overarching goal is to emphasize the integration of various beneficial technologies into educational practices, focusing on how these tools can enhance and enrich the learning experience

TPACK FRAMEWORK:

To set out a simple but comprehensive scope of this research, the study is conducted within the TPACK framework. TPACK is a framework or model which illustrates the relationships and the complexities between three basic components: technology, pedagogy, and content (Schmidt, 2009). "The belief that effective technology integration depends on content and pedagogy suggests that teachers' experiences with technology must be specific to different content areas" (p. 128). TPACK prescribes the essential knowledge teachers need to effectively incorporate technology into their teaching practices and how they can acquire this knowledge.

BACKGROUND

Modern technologies, education technologies, innovation technologies, information and communication technologies are novel terms that have gone very popular over the last decade across the realm of education. With COVID-19, the compulsory shift to using technology in teaching and learning has eventually led to these tools becoming typical of education nowadays and no longer icing on the cake as they were envisioned before, at least by developing countries. The different terms may hold some tiny nuanced distinctions, yet they have been broadly used to designate the same thing.

In their book *Integrating Educational Technology into Teaching*, Roblyer and Doering (2013) define educational technology as "a combination of the processes and tools involved in addressing educational needs and problems, with an emphasis on applying the most current digital and information tools" (p, 16). To avoid unnecessarily detailed nuances of the term, this study adopts the said definition. The study explores how teachers' use of education technology impacts their time as well as their class management.

In their article, *The Impact of Time Management on the Students' Academic Achievements,* Nasrullah and Saqib Khan (2015) examine the importance of time as a precious commodity that all people possess equally. "The secret to achieving success in life is effectively managing this resource"(p, 66). This implies that in education, like most other jobs, tasks, missions, etc., time management involves the practice of effectively organizing and prioritizing tasks and activities to optimize productivity and achieve goals.

Managing time efficiently may not lead to optimal learning outcomes and does not necessarily involve effective management of the class. Hence, to not only boost education outcomes but also ensure smooth undemanding procedures, effective classroom management is key. According to Marzano and Marzano (2003) in their book *Classroom Management That Works* classroom management encompasses the strategies and techniques employed by educators to create and maintain a conducive learning environment, including maintaining discipline, fostering student engagement, and promoting positive interactions.

To highlight the significance of classroom management in the process of teaching and the outcomes of learning Tracey Garrett, in her work *Effective Classroom Management The Essentials,* draws attention to several facets that make managing class a veritable issue for novice as well as experienced teachers. "Despite the importance of classroom management, the majority of teacher education programs still do not require or even offer a course with an explicit focus on classroom management. Because of this lack of training, many educators begin (and continue) teaching with numerous misconceptions about what constitutes effective classroom management" (Garrett, 2014, p, 1).

The integration of technology into teaching is in essence not meant for its sake. Before instruction technology know-how, teachers are supposed to have a robust knowledge of both their subject matters and the teaching methodologies and approaches. The goal is to carry out their instruction with the assistance of modern technologies only to yield better and time- and effort-saving outcomes. Hence, the TPACK Framework is an educational framework that integrates Technological, Pedagogical, and Content Knowledge, emphasizing the interplay between these three domains to guide effective technology integration in teaching and learning contexts. (Mishra & Koehler, 2006). This framework underscores the significance of teachers' ability to effectively combine these domains to enhance teaching and learning experiences. Ultimately, the TPACK framework not only informs research endeavors but also offers practical insights for educators striving to optimize technology integration for improved student learning outcomes.

METHODOLOGY

The study for this chapter addresses the question of the impact of innovation technology on time and class management. To this end, it employs a mixed-methods approach in addressing this question, which is split into the following sub-questions: 1) Are instructors at USMBA proficient and skilled in employing digital teaching technologies? 2) To what extent do instructors at USMBA integrate innovative teaching technologies into their pedagogical practices? 3) How does the utilization of educational technologies by instructors impact their management of class sessions and time allocation? 4) What are the primary obstacles encountered by instructors at USMBA in the adoption of teaching technologies, and how do these hurdles affect their effectiveness in teaching and the dynamics within their classrooms? The overarching aim of this investigation is to explore and evaluate the ramifications of technology implementation by university instructors on their management of time and classes.

Instruments and Analysis

The questionnaire, disseminated electronically to all faculty members across the diverse schools within USMA University, comprises both closed- and open-ended questions. The closed-ended questions are structured to quantify the level of instructors' training and proficiency in leveraging digital teaching technologies, their frequency of employing innovative teaching methodologies, and their perceptions regarding the influence of technology on class management and time allocation. Meanwhile, the open-ended inquiries are designed to solicit nuanced qualitative insights into the challenges encountered by instructors in integrating technology into their instructional practices and the perceived impacts on their effectiveness in teaching and classroom dynamics. Subsequently, the data garnered through the questionnaire are analysed using descriptive statistics, inferential analysis, and thematic analysis.

Participants

The participants in this academic research comprise a diverse cohort of professors belonging to Sidi Mohamed Ben Abdellah University of Fez, Morocco. 76 male and female teachers representing of different age groups participated in the survey, giving their intake on the value of innovation technologies in education, according to their experiences. Participants range from novice educators to seasoned veterans, across all faculties and schools within USMBA. They instruct a myriad of majors and disciplines. Through their participation, this study endeavors to glean insights into the multifaceted dynamics of teaching and learning within the academic milieu of USMBA University, offering a comprehensive understanding of pedagogical practices across disciplines

Figure 1. Participants' genders

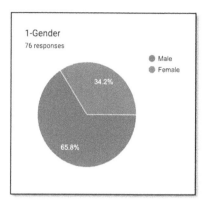

Despite the will to ensure a fair gender parity, the randomized data collection yielded a slight disparity in gender representation. This may not suggest that male professors are more willing to take part in the study but may reflect faculty proportions where males outnumber their female counterparts in the teacher population of the USMBA. According to Bouchara (2022), despite huge efforts and abundant official backing through multiple texts and documents, female professors still constitute a mere minority among university faculty nationwide. Her study revealed that until the year 2021, less than 29% are females compared to more than 71% male professors.

Figure 2. Participants' age categories

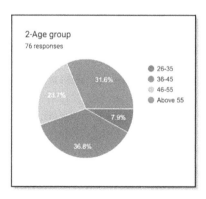

The age distribution of university professors participating in the study shows a balanced parity of different age categories of professors. A smaller proportion, however, comprising 10%, are between 26 and 35, which can be ascribed to the fact that most university professors get recruited after having spent many years in research or work. A significant concentration of professors in the middle to later stages of their careers, potentially reflecting the typical trajectory within academia where individuals tend to attain tenure and advance in their positions as they age.

Figure 3. Participants' years of experience

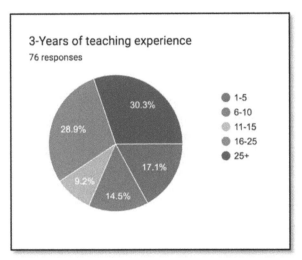

As for the years of professional experience, Figure 3 shows that most participants are experienced teachers. Nearly one-third of the participants possess an extensive teaching experience of more than 25 years, reflecting a significant segment of seasoned educators. A comparably large number falls within the range of 16 to 25 years of experience, making up a substantial group of mid-career professionals. 14.5% % have between 6 and 10 years of experience, indicating a notable representation of early-career educators. Moreover, 17% fall into the categories of 1 to 5 years, while 9.2% have 11 to 15 years of experience. This distribution underscores a diverse landscape within the academic community, characterized by a blend of seasoned and early to mid-career professors. Connecting these findings to the previous text, the chart corroborates the notion of a substantial concentration of professors in the middle to later stages of their careers.

Figure 4. Participants' areas of teaching

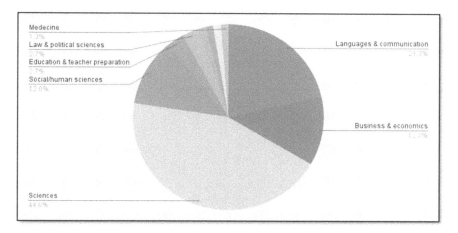

To ensure valid generalizable findings, the survey is conducted across the different disciplines and majors in higher education. Notably, though, the largest proportion, comprising more than 40%, are professors of sciences, which encompasses mathematics, physics, medicine, chemistry, and the like. Additionally, more than one-fifth of participants teach languages and communication. Moreover, nearly 12% are professors of social or human sciences, reflecting a noteworthy but comparatively smaller representation in areas such as sociology, psychology, philosophy, and theology. Furthermore, 8% are professors of business and economics, representing a specialized subset within the surveyed population.

In conclusion, the methodology employed for this study adopts quantitative and qualitative data collection and analysis. By using open and closed-ended questions, the survey tailored specifically for university teachers representing diverse age groups, levels of experience, and academic specialties, was meant to capture participants' perspectives in regards to the use of technology in teaching.

RESULTS AND DISCUSSION

Faculty Training and Proficiency

Understanding the proficiency of teachers in utilizing technology within educational settings is an essential part of this study. The survey is partly set to investigate the extent to which teachers have adequately benefited from in-service training on the use of technology as a pedagogical instrument. By examining the nature and scope of the training programs teachers have completed, this study seeks to shed light set the context for understanding and processing the extent to which innovation technologies are used within higher education in Morocco.

Figure 5. Teacher training on innovation technologies

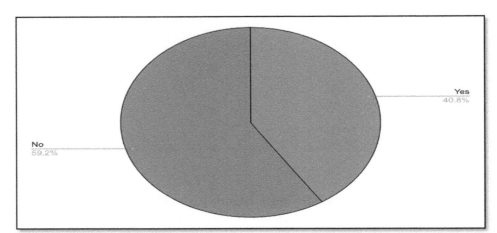

The results of the question of whether university teachers have had in-service training on the use of digital teaching technology over the past four years. The findings reveal a notable disparity among respondents. Nearly 60% reported no benefit from such training in contrast to about 40% denying having benefited from any training. The proportion demonstrates a vast dichotomy in teachers' development in this regard as almost the pie is divided into two halves of disparately qualified teachers. These findings underscore the need for addressing barriers to effective training in digital teaching technology integration. To further dig into teacher training components, the following question is an open-ended query eliciting what the subject or the matter of the training teachers have had.

One-fifth of the total number of respondents reported having been trained on the *Moodle* platform. This is the vast majority of university professors having written similar answers to the open question about what training they had over the last four years. A second majority of respondents reported that they have been trained on various trainings on the use of online technologies in teaching and learning. These include the effective use of different education platforms, the adaptation and utilization of digital resources, online course design, interactive whiteboards, and the like.

Focusing on the last four years emanates from the fact that COVID-19 constituted a milestone, if not a starting point, in the integration of technology in education due to the status of contingency. Thus, since the notorious pandemic, it has been around four years of massive public debate over the promotion and use of modern technologies in teaching and learning. Interestingly, however, not all the training has been carried out by universities or education institutions according to some participants. Several organizations have dispatched personal development and capacity-building programs in favor of educators such as the US embassy or ITEC India. Overall, the responses suggest a mix of formal and informal training experiences.

The majority of teachers did not have substantial benefits from pedagogical digital training. Even with mediocre training, significant focus has been placed on navigating the *Moodle* platform, exploiting digital resources, and crafting effective online courses. Interestingly, it is concerning that a considerable portion of this training was not administered by educational institutions or local authorities but rather by international agencies and bodies through some embassies such as the United States, France, and India. The palpable shortage in training opportunities is doomed to affect teachers' proficiency and use of technology in their daily teaching practices.

Figure 6. Level of proficiency at innovation technologies

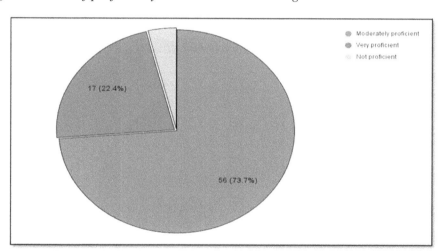

The chart provides a comprehensive overview of the proficiency levels among USMBA University's teachers in the use of innovation technologies for teaching purposes. Among "very proficient", "moderately proficient", and "not proficient", the largest segment comprises nearly three quarters report to be moderately proficient, indicating a basic grasp of innovation technologies, which requires further development and mastery. Meanwhile, almost one in four teachers present themselves as being very proficient in utilizing technology effectively in actual teaching. However, despite being a tiny portion, the number of teachers categorized as not proficient raises concerns regarding the barriers hindering their proficiency and know-how.

Factors such as lack of training, limited access to resources, or resistance to change may contribute to this disparity in proficiency levels among university teachers all over the country. Thus, addressing these challenges through targeted professional development programs, resource allocation, and institutional support is crucial to bridge the gap and ensure all educators can harness the full potential of innovation technologies in enriching the learning experience. This gap is doomed to yield an eventual gap in the use of innovation technologies among the three groups.

Teachers' use of Innovation Technologies

Within this context, exploring teachers' use of education technologies is a key objective of this study. Obtaining an insight into the frequency of teachers' use of technology allows for a delimitation of the status quo and an understanding of the efforts that still need to be made to promote education to meet today's globalizing digital world.

Figure 7. Frequency of using innovation technologies

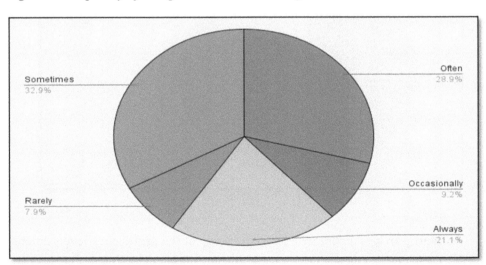

The findings represented in the chart above offer an insightful glimpse into the varying degrees of teachers' technology integration within the teaching practices. With 60% of teachers reporting an overall frequent use of technology (sometimes/often), in addition to a considerable portion of one-fifth stating that they always incorporate technology, it becomes apparent that a significant number of teachers are actively engaging with technological tools to enhance their teaching. Conversely, the 8% of teachers who rarely incorporate technology and the 10% who do so occasionally suggest that this segment may either face challenges in integrating technology effectively or hold reservations regarding its utility in their teaching contexts. Such findings underscore the importance of providing targeted support and resources to address barriers to technology integration, whether they stem from technical constraints, pedagogical concerns, or attitudinal barriers.

The diversity in teachers' levels of proficiency mirrors an interesting reality of a faculty population characterized by significant variation in skill levels. This heterogeneity poses both challenges and opportunities within educational settings. While some educators seem to possess significant know-how in the matter of teaching technologies, others surely require professional development and motivation to enhance and update their skills. Recognizing and addressing this diversity is crucial for fostering an innovative and latter-day learning environment.

To further check the rates and scope of technology use, an open-ended question was addressed to elicit what technologies and tools USMBA teachers employ in their teaching. The investigation reveals a multifaceted landscape characterized by the integration of various platforms and applications by teachers of different schools and faculties belonging to USMBA. A considerable number of answers converge on the widespread use of engaging and interactive platforms in teaching practices. Teachers exhibit a strong reliance on platforms such as Mentimeter, Answer Garden, Quizizz, Kahoot, Moodle, Google Classroom, and Canvas LMS. These platforms are instrumental in fostering student engagement and interaction as they target not only interactivity, class dynamics, and assessment, nut also autonomous learning. By leveraging these tools, educators aim to create dynamic learning environments conducive to collaborative learning experiences.

Complementing the use of interactive platforms are online meeting tools, notably Google Meet and Zoom, which have been very popular in Morocco since the outbreak of Covid-19 in 2020. The prevalence of these tools underscores the shift towards remote teaching modalities, particularly in response to the challenges posed by the COVID-19 pandemic. Yet, despite having returned to actual classes, teachers kept relying on these platforms to facilitate synchronous sessions and virtual classrooms, emphasizing the importance of real-time communication and collaboration in remote learning contexts.

In addition to facilitating engagement and communication, teachers reported that they employ accessible and abundant digital content and applications in their teaching practices. Experiment simulations, videos, and podcasts are among the digital resources teachers use to enhance student understanding and cater to different learning styles and areas. This integration reflects an awareness of the value of multimedia resources in enriching learning experiences and promoting deeper conceptual understanding. Through the strategic use of these applications, educators aim to optimize instructional efficiency and foster meaningful interactions with students within and beyond the classroom.

Having said this, the findings reveal a preponderance of the use of presentation tools to create visually engaging and interactive learning materials. Prezi, Canva, Active Inspire, interactive boards, Google Forms, Google Sheets, and SlideShare are among the most cited tools by teachers to deliver content and assess student learning effectively. The integration of these tools reflects a commitment to innovative teaching methods that prioritize student engagement and participation, in contrast to conventional teaching tools and practices that prevailed in Moroccan education for decades.

In conclusion, the qualitative analysis elucidates the diverse array of educational tools utilized by university teachers to enhance their teaching practices. From engaging and interactive platforms to multimedia content integration and specialized applications, educators demonstrate a commitment to innovation in their instructive missions. The adoption of these tools reflects a broader shift towards technology-enhanced teaching methods aimed at fostering meaningful learning experiences in Moroccan higher education.

Innovation Technology and Class dynamics

Understanding the correlation between the use of innovation technology in teaching and class dynamics is essential for to optimize learning environments. This section explores this relationship, as it attempts to uncover how technology influences the teaching and learning experiences and overall classroom atmosphere.

Figure 8. Impact of technology on classroom dynamics and learning experience

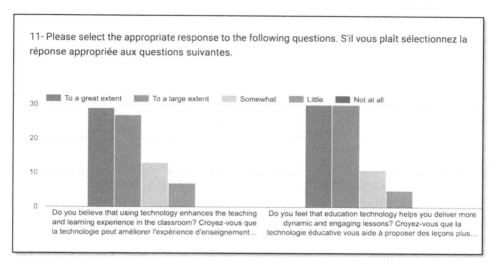

The chart depicts the distribution of university professors' perceptions regarding the impact of innovative technologies on the teaching and learning experience from the teachers' perspective. On a five-points scale, nearly three quarters of the total number of respondents perceive these technologies to impact the teaching and learning experience to a *great* or *large extent*. On the other hand, around one fifth of professors consider the impact to be *somewhat* significant, while less than 10% indicate a more reserved stance, suggesting that the impact is "*little*." Remarkably, no respondents dismiss the impact entirely, with no one opting for "*not at all*."

To ensure that technology usage impacts on teaching and learning, the questionnaire enquires about professors' perspectives regarding the role of innovative technologies in delivering dynamic and engaging lessons. Notably, around 80% of respondents believe that these technologies contribute to dynamic teaching to a *great* or *large extent*. Moreover, less than 15% endorse the view that innovative technologies *somewhat* enhance lesson dynamism. However, an insignificant portion of respondents express more reserved opinions, indicating that the impact is *little*. Strikingly, none of the respondents dismiss the contribution entirely, with no one opting for "*not at all*." This distribution underscores a widespread teachers' acknowledgment of the potential of innovative technologies to forge engaging education activities.

These findings reflect a significant recognition among university professors of the influence of innovative technologies on teaching and learning. They indicate a clear consensus among respondents regarding the impact of innovative technologies on the teaching and learning experience at a typical Moroccan university. A vast majority of almost three-quarters of the total respondents perceive these technologies to have a substantial positive impact on the teaching and learning experiences. Importantly, a negligible proportion of respondents express reserved opinions about the impact. Remarkably, none of the respondents dismiss the impact entirely, underscoring a widespread recognition of the role of innovative technologies in education. These findings collectively highlight the widespread acknowledgment among teachers of the potential of innovative technologies to create engaging educational activities, emphasizing their importance in contemporary teaching practices

Participant professors have attempted to account for their mainstream endorsement of the tight connection between the use of innovation technologies and effective classroom management and learning quality. A professor of Communication at the Faculty of Sciences and Techniques (FST) states, in this regard, that "Using technology makes students more intrigued to participate and engage in the lessons because they enjoy using their smartphones to facilitate learning and explore how beneficial they are for the learning process". The statement suggests that incorporating technology into lessons can increase student engagement. Students' affinity for using smartphones implies that leveraging smartphones in educational activities can enhance their (students) motivation and participation.

What makes the learning activities intriguing, according to a professor at the National School of Applied Sciences (ENSA) is their ability to promote interaction. She states that

L'utilisation des ressources éducatives numériques rend le cours attractif. Toutefois, dans un tel contexte, le professeur et l'étudiant œuvrent dans un esprit de complémentarité des rôles des uns et des autres. L'objectif escompté est de motiver les étudiants et de les booster afin qu'il deviennent acteurs dans leur propre apprentissage.

This statement emphasizes the role of digital educational resources in making classes attractive. Yet, it highlights the importance of collaboration between teachers and students get along and reach common educational objectives. Hence, a shift towards a student-centered approach, along with a collaborative spirit, renders learners more motivated and autonomous

To further corroborate this stance, a female Business English professor at the National School of Commerce Management (ENCG) relates her personal experience as she states:

As a language instructor, when I invite my students to use tech tools in their different learning tasks and projects, I feel that they seem more enthusiastic and engaged because these gadgets provide them with a different learning experience, a

learning experience that they should call many of their senses, skills, and abilities; they watch, listen, analyse, evaluate, interpret... .

The participant observes heightened enthusiasm and engagement among students when they use technological equipment. She feels that her students are prompted to engage different senses and make use of varied skills and abilities. Ultimately, this fosters a dynamic and interactive learning environment, encouraging active participation and empowering students to take a more proactive role in their language acquisition journey

Another faction of respondents expressed a more reserved stance regarding the utility of technology in the classroom. In this regard, a professor at the Faculty of Letters of Dhar El Mehraz campus (FLDM) states:

I believe that while technology can enhance teaching and learning experiences by providing additional resources and interactive elements, it's not necessarily key to the success of a lesson. Excessive dependence on technology can sometimes negatively impact the development of content and skills. Additionally, some university students of FLDM may not be familiar with the use of technology in teaching, which could hinder their engagement with educational technology.

While digital knowledge and competency may be lacking among several students, which certainly affects their technology-facilitated learning, the idea of excessive dependence on technology may admittedly be counterproductive.

A professor of Sciences at the National Faculty of Education (ENS) alludes to the importance of resorting to technology only in cases when the latter serves a purpose that cannot be met otherwise. *"Si on utilise des ressources interactives et surtout pour les phénomènes ou l'expérience est difficile à réaliser, très couteuse ou impossible. Dans ce cas une simulation est très enrichissante"*. In scientific disciplines, where experimentation is fundamental to learning, the use of technology can be a much more efficient substitute for traditional methods and the absence of tools.

Still, a tiny minority of respondents reject the idea of integrating technology into the teaching of some disciplines, which they consider to be uniquely intertwined with conventional chalk-and-talk methodology. In this regard, a professor states: *"Je pense que la meilleur façon pour enseigner les Mathématiques est la méthode classique avec la craie et loin de toute technologie"*. Overall, teachers' views concerning the impact of technology on managing classes and facilitating effective learning procedures are massively in convergence. Apart from minor exceptions of teachers still clinging to traditional teaching, most teachers maintain that innovation technologies promote learning engagement and alleviate teaching loads.

Innovation Technology and Time and Class Management

Technology is certainly a catalyst in the evolution of teaching and learning. Among its myriad implications is its presumed impact on time and class management. With the integration of digital tools and platforms, educators are presented with unprecedented tools to integrate into their daily teaching practices. This section delves into the multifaceted ways in which technology is set to reshape notions of time and class management, offering insights into its benefits, challenges, and implications for modern pedagogy.

Figure 9 . The impact of innovation technologies on time and class management

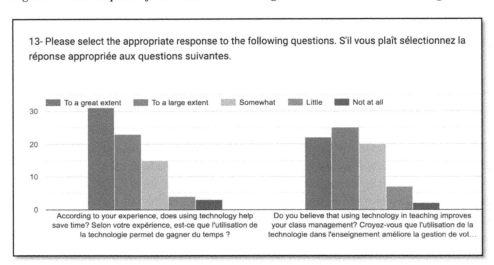

The survey reveals intriguing insights into the perceptions of university teachers regarding the impact of technology on time management in teaching. In response to the question about the influence of employing technology on time management, one-third of the respondents indicated that technology contributes "*to a great extent*" to saving time in their teaching practices. Moreover, approximately one-quarter of the participants report that technology aids in saving time "*to a large extent*". Around 15% of the respondents seem neutral and they express that technology contributes "*somewhat*" to time savings in teaching. This group may have experienced moderate benefits from technology integration but might also encounter challenges or inefficiencies that limit its full potential. A minority of respondents, comprising a small fraction of the sample, comprising less than 10% indicated that technology contributes "*a little*" or "*not at all*" to saving time. These individuals may face barriers such as technological complexity, resistance to change, or inadequate training and support.

The findings mirror a mainstream positive perception among university teachers regarding the role of technology in the effective management of time within their teaching practices. However, there exists variability in the extent to which technology is perceived to contribute to time management, reflecting diverse experiences and contexts. While a substantial portion of teachers acknowledge the time-saving potential of technology, there seems to be a dire need to address the challenges encountered by educators who perceive limited time-saving impacts.

Similarly, the findings reveal diverse but positive perceptions among educators regarding the extent to which technology impacts class management. Approximately 22% of the respondents indicate that technology contributes "*to a great extent*" to class management. Furthermore, one in four participants reports that technology facilitates class management "*to a large extent*". Around one in five of the surveyed teachers express that technology *somewhat* contributes to efficient class management. This segment may perceive moderate benefits from technology integration, experiencing improvements in certain aspects of class management while encountering challenges or limitations in others. In contrast, less than 7% of the respondents see that technology has minimal impact in their teaching practices. Interestingly, only two participants indicate that technology has no impact on class management. Overall, the results underscore a tight relationship between technology integration and class management.

Participants have attempted to account for their options regarding the point in question through a plethora of reasons. Mainstream statements presented arguments regarding the positive perceptions and linkage between innovation technologies and effective management of time and class. In this regard, a professor at the Faculty of Sciences and Techniques (FST) states: "It saves time as it exempts teachers from xeroxing, distributing handouts, correcting, etc. It is quick and accessible. As for managing class, it may not be very efficient as some students would be easily distracted by other features such as social media".

Another professor at the National School of Applied Sciences (ENSA) corroborates this stance and emphasizes the particularity of technology not only in reducing time but also in increasing efficiency and enhancing productivity.

Sans nul doute (…) cela lui permet de gagner en efficacité et en productivité. Au lieu de perdre le temps à écrire, les étudiants s'impliquent et interagissent puisqu'ils recevront la version ppt du cours. Donc, le temps précieux de la séance est consacré aux échanges constructifs et non à l'écriture du contenu

Productivity and efficiency are intertwined with time saving, as the latter allows for refining and learning and additional reinforcement and remedial activities. Contents are presented in no time, which exempts teachers and students alike from tiring and tedious writing. In its simplest images, PowerPoint -as a technology-facilitated tool- helps teachers devise and cover ample learning points in a short lapse of time.

In this same respect, a professor of social sciences at the Faculty of Letters of Sais (FLS) reports that "the use of PPT already gives the professor an idea of the amount of time allocated to each slide, making sure the professor covers all aspects of the lessons for every session". A tiny visual illustration not only substitutes huge waste of chalk-and-talk time but even ensures that the prepared content is all covered, which leaves no room for eclipsing any activity or exercise.

The second mass of respondents went for a neutral stance as they reported that the use of innovation technologies *somewhat* impacts on time or class management. In an attempt to account for this ambivalent opinion, teachers insist that technology has both advantages and drawbacks. In this respect, a language professor at the Faculty of Letters and Human Sciences of Dhar El Mehraz (FLDM) states:

In fact, using technology in the classroom can save time through task automation but may also require additional time for preparation and troubleshooting. Sometimes some technical issues can disrupt the lesson flow, and some students always need extra support in using technology, affecting class management.

Using technology offers the potential to expedite various educational tasks through automation, thereby saving valuable time for both educators and students alike. However, this efficiency gain is counterbalanced by the necessity for additional time investments in preparation and troubleshooting. While technology can enhance teaching methodologies and content delivery, its effective utilization often demands meticulous preparation to ensure seamless integration into lesson plans. Moreover, the dynamic nature of technology means that technical issues occur, which disrupts the natural flow of the lesson and consumes precious instructional time.

To support this view, another teacher of sciences at the Faculty of Sciences and Techniques (FST) questions the significance of innovation technologies in class management as he states that *"La gestion de la classe, pas toujours puisque parfois les étudiants sont dissipés quand ils savent qu'ils vont récupérer le cours"*. Class management can be challenging as students become distracted and inattentive since they anticipate the possibility of catching up on the lesson later. When students perceive they will have a second chance to grasp the content, they may be less inclined to fully engage during the class, which affects classroom dynamics and management.

The insignificant minority of participants who do not approve of technology seem to crave arguments that belittle its importance in teaching. An experienced professor of Sciences at the Faculty of Education (ENS) reports *"Difficulté de gérer le temps en cas de plusieurs classes et un effectif élevé"*. The testimony highlights the difficulty of managing time effectively when dealing with multiple classes and a high number of students. Large classes do not allow for attending to individual student needs and maintaining classroom discipline, especially with the use of technology.

Challenges Facing Teachers' Adoption of Innovation Technologies

Apparently, in the ever-evolving landscape of education, integrating technology into teaching has become a necessity nowadays. Most teachers have confirmed its significance and embraced its use for a rewarding educational journey. However, a considerable part of the teachers' population highlights that the transition to modern technology-based instruction is not without its hurdles. In this section, we delve into the complexities that teachers encounter when incorporating technology into their classrooms and the apprehensions those who do not use it have, and which shapes their negative attitudes. Understanding these challenges is paramount, as it not only sheds light on the intricacies of modern education but also paves the way for informed solutions and enhancements in pedagogical approaches. By exploring these challenges, we aim to provide valuable insights that can empower educators to harness the full potential of technology in their teaching endeavors

Figure 10. Challenges encountered by teachers integrating IT

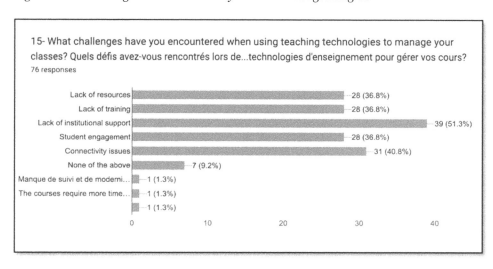

The results expose participants perspectives over common challenges encountered when using teaching technologies. The fact that over 50% of respondents opt for *"lack of institutional support"* as a primary challenge underscores a systemic issue within educational institutions. Without sufficient backing from administration and education authorities, educators may struggle to effectively implement and sustain technology-enhanced teaching methods. Issues of school culture, instructional leadership, management, and philosophy come into question in fostering innovative and creative educational practices among teachers in the digital age.

The second significant percentage of more than 40% identify *"connectivity issues"* as a practical obstacle faced in leveraging digital tools. Institutions and classrooms with unreliable internet access or infrastructure pose a real challenge for integrating technology into learning and teaching.

This stark reality points to significant infrastructure challenges within the Moroccan higher education system, where a lack of reliable internet access hampers the incorporation of digital tools in university classrooms. This state of affairs underscores the urgent need for targeted interventions to address its causes and implications. Governments need to invest in infrastructure upgrades and policy measures aimed at ensuring access to free reliable internet connection for educators and students alike. Without such initiatives, the potential of technology to enhance teaching and learning experiences in Moroccan universities will remain unrealized, perpetuating inequities and hindering progress in the digital age

Furthermore, the findings reveal that substantial portions of educators perceive *"lack of resources,"* *"lack of training,"* and *"student engagement"* as significant challenges. The results show that there is a crying need for professional development opportunities and tailored support in both technical proficiency and pedagogical strategies. The fact that over 70% of respondents agreed on these challenges presents a clear idea of customary mainstream constraints. The findings are tantamount to a recognition of resource constraints, an emphasis on the importance of ongoing professional development to empower teachers with the necessary skills for effective technology integration, and a call for effective student engagement measures. Tackling these challenges demands a comprehensive approach that encompasses investment in resources, provision of training opportunities, and implementation of engagement strategies, ultimately enabling educators to harness the full potential of technology to enhance learning experiences for all students

Only around 10% of respondents report facing no major obstacle in integrating and employing technologies in teaching. These results align with the official CSE-FRS report in 2021 has addressed issues that accompany online or hybrid education during COVID-19. This suggests that the majority of educators encounter at least one of the aforementioned obstacles when utilizing teaching technologies, emphasizing the multifaceted nature of the challenges inherent in digital education. This result underscores the widespread recognition of the challenges reported in this study. It suggests that the vast majority perceive multiple barriers that put spoke in the wheel of technology integration in education. Addressing these challenges is critical for educational institutions and policymakers particularly, necessitating joint targeted efforts for and fostering a culture of technology adoption in education.

The findings leave no shadow of doubt about the persistence of pressing issues and constraints in the way of modernizing and upgrading education practices at Moroccan University. Addressing these challenges requires a holistic approach that combines institutional support, technological infrastructure improvements, targeted training initiatives, and strategies to enhance student engagement, ultimately fostering a more conducive environment for effective teaching and learning in the digital age. Yet, the mainstream positive attitudes and actual adoption of technology amongst teachers is a veritable barometer for a promising digitalized education.

CONCLUSION

This chapter investigated the correlation between the employment of innovation technologies in teaching and the teachers' management of both time and class. Through an opinion poll of teachers of various disciplines at Sidi Mohamed Ben Abdellah University of Fez, Morocco, the paper presents an insight into the benefits and downsides of technology integration and dependence in Moroccan higher education. The study underscores a prevailing inclination among educators to embrace innovative technologies within their pedagogical frameworks, attributing this inclination primarily to the perceived advantages of time optimization and the creation of dynamic engaging instructional modalities. This mainstream tendency among teachers signals a promising shift in the educational practice over the years to come. The results underscore educators' recognition of technology's potential not only to enrich and facilitate teaching and learning experiences but also yield optimal education outcomes. The survey unveiled a wide range of tools and platforms deployed by teachers, underlining their significance and practicality to promoting educational practices. Nonetheless, the inquiry also identifies substantial impediments, including insufficient institutional support, connectivity issues, deficient professional development opportunities, resource scarcity, and concerns regarding student engagement. In developing Morocco, and a post-covid19 era, when technology is part and parcel of education, it is imperative to address these barriers comprehensively to harness the full potential of technological integration in education. This necessitates the establishment of robust support infrastructures, training initiatives, and sustained resource provisioning to cultivate an environment conducive to the seamless amalgamation of technology and pedagogy.

RECOMMENDATIONS

While mainstream teachers' approval is encouraging, teachers' attitudes and perspectives also highlight the importance of the dire need for support and professional development to effectively integrate technology into their classrooms. By capitalizing on this widespread approval and investing in continuous training and support, educational institutions can harness the full potential of technology to create dynamic and transformative learning environments that prepare students for success in an increasingly digital world.

A comprehensive approach to integrating technology in education is required. This approach should envisage teachers' and student's proficiency and readiness. Moving forward, there is a pressing need for greater collaboration between local educational bodies and international entities to ensure that teacher training programs are tailored to meet the specific requirements and challenges of the education landscape, ultimately fostering more meaningful and impactful professional development opportunities for educators. An FST professor states in this vein:

Je pense qu'il faut introduire progressivement la technologie dans l'enseignement et s'assurer que ces outils sont à la fois acceptés et assimilés par les usagers. C'est une vraie culture que les enseignants et leurs apprenants doivent s'approprier en douceur, et non, de manière brusque

As technology continues to evolve and permeate every facet of teaching and learning, it is evident that education stakeholders, especially teachers, and students, should embrace a new culture for teaching and learning where technology is used when it is more practical and fruitful than classical ways. Moreover, such training initiatives should not only focus on technical proficiency but also emphasize pedagogical integration, ensuring that teachers can harness technology to its fullest potential in fostering meaningful and impactful learning experiences for all students.

Still, an important point is to be kept in mind: technology should be used for its sake. In the words of a Communication teacher at the Faculty of Letters and Human Sciences Dhar El Mehraz (FLDM), "Educators should always remember that the use of technology is not an end in itself, rather it's one way to facilitate the teaching/learning". Integrating technology into the teaching and learning process should only be meant to enhance the experience. This means that the significance of traditional teaching approaches and human interaction is beyond question. Moreover, continuous training and support for both educators and students are essential to ensure the effective utilization of technology both inside and outside the classroom.

REFERENCES

Berkeshchuk, I. S., Shcherbak, I. V., Shkvorchenko, N. M., Masytska T. E. & Chornyi, I. V. (2020). Modern Technologies and Applications of ICT in the Training Process of Teachers-Philologists. *International Journal of Higher Education*. Vol. 9, No. 7; 2020 URL: https://doi.org/.DOI: 10.5430/ijhe.v9n7p84

Bouchara, A. (2022). Les femmes à l'université marocaine: des trajectoires fractures. Observatoire Francophone pour le developpement inclusif par le genre. Cahiers de recherche OFDIG, no 02-2022. ISBN: 978-2-9821216-1-4.

de l'Éducation, C. S. de la Formation et de la Recherche Scientifique (CSEFRS). (2021). Enseignement au temps de covid au maroc. Rapport thématique. ISBN : 978-9920-785-37-2.

Dron, J. (2022). Educational technology: What it is and how it works. *AI & Society*, 37(1), 155–166. Advance online publication. DOI: 10.1007/s00146-021-01195-z

Kumar, L., Singh, P., & Tiwari, D. (2024). Use and Utility of Modern Technology in Learning and Teaching. *Atharv Publication, Bhopal* (M.P.) ISBN: 978-93-94945-60-9

Marzano, R., & Marzano, J. (2003a). *Classroom management that works: Research based strategies for every teacher*. Association for Supervision and Curriculum Development.

Mishra, P., & Koehler, M. J. (2006). Technological Pedagogical Content Knowledge: A Framework for Teacher Knowledge. *Teachers College Record*, 108(6), 1017–1054. DOI: 10.1111/j.1467-9620.2006.00684.x

Nasrullah, S., & Saqib Khan, M. (2015). The Impact of Time Management on the Students' Academic Achievements. *Journal of Literature, Languages and Linguistics*. ISSN 2422-8435 An International Peer-reviewed Journal Vol.11, 2015.

Roblyer, M. D., & Doering, A. H. (2014). Integrating Educational Technology into Teaching. Pearson. Allyn and Bacon. ISBN. 0135130638, 9780135130636. M Rose, G. (January, 2015). Innovation and Information Technology. DOI:. In book: Wiley Encyclopedia of ManagementDOI: 10.1002/9781118785317.weom070007

Schmidt, D. A., Baran, E., Thompson, A. D., Mishra, P., Koehler, M. J., & Shin, T. S. (2009). Technological Pedagogical Content Knowledge (TPACK): The Development and Validation of an Assessment Instrument for Preservice Teachers. *International Society for Technology in Education (ISTE)*, 800.336.5191. *JRTE*, 42(2), 123–149.

Singh, R. (2021). Information Communication Technology. https://www
.researchgate.net/publication/350087090_INFORMATION_COMMUNICATION
_TECHNOLOGY

Chapter 6
AI–Enabled Science Lesson Development for Pre–Service and Novice Teachers

Shawn O'Neill

Bridgewater State University, USA

ABSTRACT

This chapter explores the innovative use of Artificial Intelligence (AI) to assist new science teachers in crafting engaging and effective lesson plans when formal curriculum resources are scarce or unavailable. Recognizing the challenges educators face in contexts where standard curriculum materials are limited, this paper aims to empower both pre-service and novice teachers through AI-driven tools designed to facilitate the creation of comprehensive, age-appropriate, standards-aligned science lessons. By integrating AI into teacher preparation programs, educators can access valuable insights, resources, and support to enhance their teaching practices and improve student learning outcomes. The theoretical and ethical implications of integrating AI, including fairness, privacy, and transparency, will also be addressed. The author ties in her experiences as both an elementary classroom teacher and a professor of a science methods class for pre-service teachers.

INTRODUCTION

As a former elementary school teacher with over two decades spent in the early elementary classroom, I was always well-prepared and well-practiced when teaching reading, writing, and mathematics. The "other" subjects, science and social stud-

DOI: 10.4018/979-8-3693-3904-6.ch006

ies were addressed sporadically and often mentioned in other core subjects, such as English Language Arts (ELA) in students' anthology books, which seemed to qualify as instruction. Weekly classroom magazine subscriptions included science and social studies content and were incorporated if and when there was time. What was missing was a formal curriculum.

In Massachusetts, students are formally tested on their science knowledge in grade 5. Because of this, many school districts do not purchase a science curriculum until grade 3. The result is that students in grades K-2 are often not taught science. Then, in Grade 5, they are tested by the state and cannot correctly answer curriculum questions based on science standards from grades K-22. Many students are only exposed to science and hands-on activities in the older elementary school grades.

Teachers either spent hours upon hours finding their own science materials and lessons that were hopefully standards-aligned or, in some cases, would forgo teaching science altogether. This was often the easier choice since many teachers, both novices and experienced, felt their knowledge of science content was lacking. That, coupled with a lack of curriculum, materials, and professional development, meant that science was not made an instructional priority in the early elementary grades.

Existing research highlights a significant concern regarding the lack of science instruction in elementary grades. Numerous studies have documented that science receives considerably less instructional time compared to subjects like mathematics and reading. For instance, a study by Blank (2013) revealed that on average, elementary school teachers spend only 19 minutes per day on science in grades K-3 and 24 minutes in grades 4-6. This limited exposure is compounded by findings from the 2018 National Survey of Science and Mathematics Education, which reported that only 20% of K-3 teachers teach science daily, compared to 36% for mathematics and 28% for reading/language arts (Banilower et al., 2018). Furthermore, teacher preparedness is a critical issue; the same survey indicated that only 39% of elementary teachers felt well-prepared to teach science, in stark contrast to the 77% who felt prepared to teach reading/language arts (Banilower et al., 2018). The National Academies of Sciences, Engineering, and Medicine (2021) also found that only 30% of K-5 teachers reported having access to high-quality instructional materials for science. These deficiencies in instructional time, teacher preparedness, and resources contribute to suboptimal student performance in science, as evidenced by the National Assessment of Educational Progress (NAEP) 2015 Science Assessment, where only 37% of fourth-grade students performed at or above the proficient level (National Center for Education Statistics, 2016). This body of research underscores the urgent need for increased focus and investment in science education at the elementary level to foster early interest and competency in scientific disciplines.

FOCUS OF THE CHAPTER

This chapter examins the challenges that pre-service and novice teachers face when creating science lessons. Pre-service teachers often deal with their own personal feelings regarding their ability to learn science and how to teach it. Novice teachers, again, often possessing feelings of low self-efficacy, may struggle with finding or creating quality, standards-based lessons that they can feel confident in teaching. We will look at the introduction of Artificial Intelligence platforms and how they can help our teachers find the confidence they might lack.

CHALLENGES IN SCIENCE LESSON DEVELOPMENT

Both pre-service and novice teachers face multiple challenges when tasked with creating quality science lessons. These challenges may include low teacher self-efficacy, lack of teacher science content knowledge, inadequate pre-service teacher preparation, and the absence of formal curriculum and related science materials.

Research focusing on elementary science teachers suggests that novice teachers demonstrate anxiety and lack confidence when teaching science. A 2018 NSSME+ report indicated that only 39% of elementary teachers felt well-prepared to teach science, compared to 77% who felt well-prepared to teach reading/language arts. Teachers often report low self-efficacy, consider themselves lacking in knowledge and practices, and experience motivational frustration (Brown, 2017). Teachers recognize the importance of the National Science Teachers Association (NSTA), Next Generation Science Standards (NGSS), or their own state standards but often are unsure how to incorporate these in their lesson planning. This lack of confidence can also lead to feelings of inadequacy and reluctance to explore innovative teaching strategies, such as AI, further hindering the development of engaging and effective science lessons.

Knowledge and experience play an essential role in teaching science and developing scientific content that fosters a learning environment rich with scientific inquiry. Another significant challenge is pre-service and novice teachers' limited science content knowledge. Johnson (2018) highlights the impact of this deficiency on lesson planning and delivery, noting that teachers who lack a strong grasp of science concepts may struggle to explain complex ideas in a way that is accessible and engaging to students. This can result in inaccurate or incomplete explanations, leading to misconceptions and gaps in student understanding. Without a solid foundation in science content, teachers may find it challenging to develop meaningful and engaging lesson plans that align with curriculum standards and learning objectives. This low self-efficacy may also lead to a lack of enthusiasm for teaching the content. This enthusiasm and confidence are crucial to engage our students and foster lifelong learning, especially in the early elementary years.

Often, teacher education programs fail to prepare teachers for effective science instruction. Pre-service teachers may receive limited exposure to science content and pedagogy, resulting in a lack of confidence and competence in teaching science. This inadequate preparation can leave teachers feeling ill-equipped to address their students' diverse learning needs and adapt to the dynamic nature of science education. Pre-service teachers may struggle to develop the skills and knowledge necessary to create engaging and effective science lessons without comprehensive training and support.

The absence of standardized curriculum guidelines and related science materials poses another challenge for pre-service and novice teachers. The National Research Council (2012) highlights teachers' difficulties in developing science lessons without a clear framework or set of resources to guide their instruction. Without formal curriculum guidelines, teachers may struggle to identify appropriate learning objectives, select relevant instructional materials, and design engaging learning activities. This can result in inconsistent, incomplete, and poor science instruction that fails to provide students with a comprehensive understanding of scientific concepts.

Another hurdle that teachers face is a lack of time. This challenge with time may relate to time dedicated to instruction, preparation of curriculum, and confidence in the content area. Due to those discrepancies, elementary educators may dedicate far less time to science instruction or entirely omit science from their curriculum. The National Science Teaching Association (NSTA) states that allocating dedicated time each school day for young learners to participate in rigorous and enriching science instruction is imperative. According to the NSTA (2018), this commitment ensures students receive the foundational knowledge and skills necessary for scientific literacy and critical thinking development. By integrating science lessons into the academic day, students can develop a deeper understanding of scientific concepts from an early age, fostering curiosity, exploration, and hands-on learning. However, according to the research, this science integration does not occur on the same regularity as other elementary subjects.

Forty percent of elementary teachers say they spend just 60 minutes or less teaching science each week. Just one-third of elementary teachers say they feel prepared to teach science, but 85 percent of teachers say they have not received any professional development in science during the last three years. And while nine in ten principals say science education is very important and should start early, less than half of principals (44%) believe it is likely that a student would receive high-quality science instruction in his or her school (Lawrence Hall of Science Press Release, 2011).

Teachers often feel pressured to spend more time in other content areas, particularly math and reading, as students are tested in these subjects. Time limitations often decrease teachers' willingness to include science in the classroom. Low teacher self-efficacy/beliefs in their ability to be effective science teachers have also been identified as a significant barrier to teaching science in elementary school. Prior research indicates that the amount of science coursework completed in college significantly predicts teacher efficacy. Thus, if teacher preparation programs are lacking in science methods courses, it makes sense that our pre-service teachers will graduate feeling unprepared and lacking. An obvious method to help address these concerns is to require additional science courses for preservice teachers. Other deliberate interventions can also be implemented before and during the preservice experience to help teacher candidates build their science teacher efficacy.

The lack of science education in elementary schools is a concern from an educational, economic, cultural, and public health standpoint (L. Ferguson, 2022). In most communities, young children are curious about natural phenomena and are naturally inclined to dig in and engage in hands-on learning activities. By the time these students reach middle or high school, there often is decreased interest and engagement in science (Riegle-Crumb et al., 2023). Although much attention has been paid to middle and high school science education, elementary schools often have limited time and resources dedicated to science, and teachers are less likely to feel knowledgeable and confident in teaching science (M. Pompea and Russo, 2023).

While novice teachers may be able to partake in curriculum creation experiences and/or professional development, novice and pre-service teachers often are not. What is the best way to prepare these teachers to create engaging, rigorous, and standards-based science curriculum materials in such situations? The educational technology world would argue that this is where new Artificial Intelligence (AI) tools for educators come into play. As AI and AI platforms boom, many AI tools have been created with classroom teachers in mind. These tools help teachers develop curricula specific to their classroom needs and can do so in a fraction of the time.

Looking back on my many years as an elementary school teacher, I vividly recall the countless hours I dedicated to crafting meaningful science lessons for my students. No curriculum was available, and science professional development was not offered to teachers. The district's focus was reading and math, the areas that students were tested on repeatedly throughout the school year. Each science lesson I created was a labor of love, meticulously designed to meet grade-level standards while fostering curiosity, critical thinking, and a love for learning. From selecting engaging topics to planning hands-on experiments and activities, every aspect of lesson preparation was thoughtful and time-consuming, one that I worked through alone as I was one of the only teachers adamant about teaching science regularly. I strived to ensure that each lesson was aligned with the standards and rigorous enough to challenge my students and promote a deep understanding of scientific concepts. Reflecting on those experiences, I realize now the immense amount of time, effort, and dedication that went into creating those science lessons. Having the benefit of an AI platform to craft these lessons for me would have been a tremendous help.

AI-DRIVEN TOOLS FOR LESSON PLANNING

As teachers navigate the world of AI in search of lesson-planning technology for their classrooms, they are faced with the question of where to begin. Artificial Intelligence and its many platforms have made great strides in education. AI-driven tools have been developed for various education processes, such as adaptive and personalized learning, real-time formative feedback, assessment creation, intelligent tutors, chatbots, etc. Today, the primary need in elementary grades is AI-driven tools for lesson planning. The new AI-driven tools, fed with good information, could solve the problems teachers have mentioned, like stress, anxiety, lack of time, effort, and preparation, controlling students, giving rewards, and making school joyful for both students and teachers.

There is also a range of tools focusing especially on increasing student-teacher efficiency and, therefore, helping educators to address students' individual performance or motivation. For example, by providing teachers with insights for understanding their students, enabling them to provide helpful feedback, or suggest appropriate intervention strategies, AI-based platforms promise to help teachers focus more on strategic issues and decrease the time spent on laborious activities like correcting tests, reports, or providing students' support based on available material. Therefore, AI could alleviate practical workload constraints that reduce confidence and contentious professional practices, such as 'teaching to the test' behaviors, by enabling more directive responses to what teachers perceive as immediate problems. In addition, AI offers the potential to deliver insight that reduces cognitive overload created by the large number of students that teachers might need to interact with by providing educators with access to whole-class and individual student data.

BENEFITS OF AI IN LESSON PLAN CREATION

In today's changing field of education, incorporating technology has become increasingly crucial to enrich learning experiences and equip students for the world's challenges. Among the advancements, AI is a powerful tool with vast potential to transform teaching and learning methods. For veteran educators and pre-service teachers alike, proficiency in AI is incredibly beneficial, especially when crafting science lessons for elementary school students. Not only are these AI sites allowing teachers to create standards-based aligned units and lessons, generate specific and actionable feedback, and personalize learning, but they also give teachers the ability to create these lessons in any language, thus helping to foster the all-inclusive environment that our students need and deserve.

Using AI to augment or potentially replace teacher instruction is an ongoing debate in artificial intelligence and education (Pelaez et al., 2022). However, there is a consensus that AI can still play a valuable role in amplifying and extending human teaching (L. Owoc et al., 2021). Over the last decade, there has been an increased effort by both academics and industry practitioners to develop AI-enhanced educational platforms, many of which are, or have been, explicitly applied to the K-12 domain. AI-driven tools for lesson planning are now being developed and are taking the education community by storm. The idea behind such tools is to provide teachers with educated predictions about what will work best in their classroom based on information teachers input into the site. These tools are still in their initial phases but have the potential to save teachers time and energy by essentially outsourcing the creation of lesson plans.

One such tool, MagicSchool.ai, begins its mission statement with the declaration, "Teachers are overworked and burnt out." If that doesn't immediately draw the eye of veteran teachers, I don't know what will. The site goes on to tell the user about the ease of use of their platform and the many benefits designed to assist both teachers and their students. There are over 60 tools designed especially for teachers, such as "Lesson Plan," "Rubric Generator," "Report Card Comments," "IEP Generator," and many more. These tools are incredibly appealing to teachers, as many of us often feel that there is never enough time to do everything for our students that we would like to. When faced with teaching the science standards and not having the curriculum or materials, a platform that will create a lesson in seconds using the materials available in the classroom is invaluable.

A second AI platform targeting teachers is Eduaide.Ai. This platform, also geared toward educators, advertises that it will assist teachers in lesson planning, finding teaching resources, and planning. When users navigate through the homepage, they will see options such as "The Teacher's Assistant," "Personalization Tools," "Feedback Bot," "Assessment Builder," and "Language Preferences." Aside from creating lessons in seconds, the ability to generate lessons, feedback, and other tools in multiple languages is incredibly beneficial to teachers. We no longer teach in a classroom where students speak the same language at home. Instead, we are surrounded by an incredible group of students with various backgrounds, languages, and cultures. Communicating with our students and their families in their native language is a gift, and AI platforms are making it possible, allowing teachers to create equitable and inclusive classrooms.

When educators log on to Lessonplans.ai, they see, "Create amazing lesson plans 10X faster with AI. Use AI to instantly generate high-quality lesson plans in seconds." What more does an educator without a curriculum, materials, or extra time need to see? Lessonplans.ai allows teachers to generate lessons for any grade level, K-12, and was created by teachers for teachers. Similarly to other lesson-generating sites, users can also develop lesson plans. The site promises to increase productivity and ensures that the lessons created are relevant and current. Unlike the sites mentioned above, Lessonplans.ai is a paid site without a free option, a feature many may find unappealing with so many quality, free options.

Although one of the most prominent advantages teachers find when utilizing AI technology is saving time, another massive benefit is the ability to create a curriculum where none exists. Many elementary schools do not have a formal science curriculum. This absence of curriculum often leads to teachers creating their own, usually unaligned curriculum, purchasing curriculum, or, in many cases, eliminating science instruction altogether (Garcia et al., 2021). AI platforms allow teachers to develop grade-level appropriate, standards-aligned science lessons instantly. These lessons can be quickly tailored to fit within time parameters, material constraints, and other challenges teachers face. By harnessing the power of AI, educators can leverage innovative tools and approaches to create engaging, effective, and inclusive science learning experiences for all students.

Incorporating AI in education is a paradigm shift, fundamentally altering traditional teaching approaches. AI-driven tools offer personalized learning experiences, adaptively catering to individual student needs and learning styles (Bullock-Rest, 2020). For pre-service teachers, understanding how to harness AI technologies empowers them to create tailored lesson plans that resonate with the diverse cognitive profiles of elementary students. By leveraging AI, educators can address student abilities and preferences variability, fostering deeper engagement and comprehension in science education.

THE ROLE OF TEACHERS IN AI-ENHANCED LESSON PLANNING

Teachers play a crucial role in AI-enhanced lesson planning, as they bring their expertise in pedagogy, subject matter knowledge, and an understanding of their students' needs. When using AI tools, teachers can customize lesson plans based on their students' needs, abilities, and learning styles. This allows teachers to personalize the curriculum for their classrooms. AI tools can assist teachers in curating materials that align with their state or national standards. They can be used to find interactive simulations, videos, articles, and other multimedia resources to enhance learning experiences. Instead of a teacher spending hours using Google and searching through often unrelated resources online, AI tools can do the same work in a fraction of the time, yielding much more personalized results.

Teachers can also use AI tools to analyze student performance data, identify patterns, and gain insights into teaching effectiveness. By tracking student progress over time, teachers can adjust their lesson plans accordingly and intervene early if students struggle. Teachers might use AI tools to provide feedback to students, create and use rubrics, or grade assignments, thus giving teachers more time to interact with their students on a more personal level.

The role of the teacher in AI-enhanced lesson planning is crucial. Teachers are the designers of the learning content. They provide the contextual framework for learning and assess the learning activity and outcomes. Teachers hold expertise on how content must be taught for their particular students. Most importantly, teachers hold learning design as part of their professional responsibility. This act of design, of developing ways to enable the learners to achieve the learning outcomes, is at the heart of teaching. Although the benefits of using AI to create curriculum are huge, the use of AI in education should never replace the employment of teachers and the relationships they make with their students.

Incorporating AI tools into pre-service teacher education can revolutionize traditional teaching methodologies and prepare our future teachers for the classroom setting. Exposing our preservice teachers to these tools and the proper ways to implement them allows them to create dynamic lesson plans tailored to individual student needs, thus promoting an inclusive learning environment. Teaching pre-service teachers to become familiar with AI-driven analytics and how these can provide teachers with insights into student performance and identifying areas that require additional attention is also essential. This exposure ensures pre-service teachers are well-equipped with modern teaching aids, making them adaptable and effective educators.

Equipping pre-service teachers with these skills is crucial when they are expected to teach subjects that may lack a formal curriculum, such as science. Although many states provide specific grade-level science standards, elementary curriculum resources are often scarce, and professional development is not always provided. Familiarity with state or national science standards is an essential first step for pre-service teachers, followed by proficiency in lesson planning.

While these new AI platforms can certainly assist in lesson creation and other time consuming teacher tasks, they will never replace the role of the teacher. Teachers are the most essential part of the learning environment, bringing enthusiasm and empathy to the classroom in a way that AI technology will never be able to. When good teaching and AI is used together, a potentially powerful partnership may result, that benefits both teachers and students.

ENHANCING SCIENCE TEACHING PRACTICES
AND STUDENT LEARNING OUTCOMES

When schools lack a formal science curriculum and set of assessments, it isn't easy to assess whether or not students are meeting the state standards and expectations for their grade level. For years, teachers have spent countless hours scouring the internet or brick-and-mortar establishments for science-related curricula that were appropriate for their grade level and addressed their specific state standards.

Research has consistently demonstrated that robust science instruction in the elementary grades has a profound impact on student outcomes, fostering both academic achievement and long-term interest in scientific fields. Studies have shown that early exposure to science education enhances critical thinking and problem-solving skills, which are crucial across all subject areas (Cairns et al., 2011). According to a report by the National Research Council (2012), students who engage in hands-on, inquiry-based science activities are more likely to develop a deeper understanding of scientific concepts and retain this knowledge over time. Furthermore, Osborne and Dillon (2008) found that positive early experiences with science can shape students' attitudes toward the subject, increasing their likelihood of pursuing science-related careers. Additionally, a study by Tai et al. (2006) revealed that students who express interest in science by eighth grade are three times more likely to earn a degree in a scientific field compared to their peers. These findings underscore the critical role of early science education in laying the foundation for future academic and career success.

AI technologies offer many creative possibilities for designing engaging and interactive learning experiences. Pre-service teachers with AI proficiency can leverage these tools to develop innovative science lessons that captivate students' interests and imaginations without the stress and time investment. From interactive simulations and virtual laboratories to educational games and multimedia presentations, AI opens up new avenues for experiential learning in elementary science education (Wang et al., 2020).

New AI platforms allow for the creating of interactive simulations, virtual laboratories, educational games, and multimedia presentations that can enhance the science learning experience (Chen et al., 2020) and meet students where they are academically. For example, AI-powered simulations allow students to explore scientific phenomena, conduct virtual experiments, and observe the outcomes in a safe and controlled environment (Nkisi-Orji et al., 2019). AI-driven educational games can gamify the learning process, making it more engaging and fun for students while reinforcing scientific concepts and problem-solving skills. Additionally, AI-generated multimedia presentations can bring abstract scientific concepts to life through engaging visuals, animations, and interactive elements, making complex ideas more accessible and understandable for young learners. These platforms also allow for differentiation, making the curriculum accessible for students on IEPs and our multilingual learners. AI-driven adaptive learning systems can personalize the learning experience by tailoring content and activities based on individual students' strengths, weaknesses, and learning preferences, ensuring each child receives the support they need to thrive.

By incorporating AI-driven elements into their lessons, teachers can stimulate curiosity, spark creativity, and inspire a lifelong passion for scientific inquiry among elementary students.

SUPPORT FOR SPECIAL EDUCATION AND MULTILINGUAL LEARNERS

Utilizing AI technology empowers teachers to create lessons that address students' needs, creating an inclusive environment where all students benefit. Teachers can address diverse challenges, such as personalizing instruction for struggling students and lesson and activity translation for multilingual learners.

AI-based translation platforms allow lessons to be translated into an ever-increasing number of languages, allowing students and their families to access the content in ways they have been unable to. Over the years, I have witnessed many families unable to access the classroom content and help their children since they were non-English speakers. This often creates barriers between families and schools and may create an environment of inequality and unease. Aside from lesson and content creation, AI platforms now allow for real-time translation of lectures and meetings, another way to provide inclusivity in classrooms.

When creating lessons for students on Individualized Education Plans (IEPs), AI platforms can adapt the content, pace, and even the lesson delivery to match the needs of students. These platforms can provide various media formats, allowing students to access information in the most suitable ways for their learning styles. The difficulty level can be adjusted as well as additional practice and scaffolded lessons. AI can also be used to modify assessments and analyze student performance.

By utilizing AI's different capabilities, elementary science lessons can be tailored to meet the diverse needs of special education students and multilingual learners. This promotes greater engagement, understanding, and overall academic achievement.

PREPARATION FOR PRE-SERVICE TEACHERS

As someone who used to teach elementary school and now instructs pre-service teachers in science methods, I understand how vital it is to equip educators with the skills and knowledge to use Artificial Intelligence (AI) to create science lessons when there's no formal curriculum available. Before I can begin to tackle that obstacle, however, I need to address the feelings of negativity surrounding science that my students often arrive at me with. My students rarely begin the semester feeling confident and excited about science and learning to craft science lessons for future elementary classrooms. After years of discussions with my pre-service teachers, I have found that, more often than not, this is a result of their own experiences or lack of experience in science. My university students often tell me they hated science or felt they were not good at it. They did not enjoy it as a student and dread teaching it. Most likely, they had a teacher who also did not enjoy teaching science or was not confident in their own science content knowledge, and that mindset transferred onto the students. The key to ending this cycle is to equip my pre-service teachers with the tools to create engaging, rigorous, and fun science lessons.

Pre-service teachers must have a foundational understanding of AI and its educational applications. This includes exploring the capabilities of AI algorithms, such as natural language processing, machine learning, and data analysis, and understanding how these technologies can support teaching and learning in science classrooms (Brom et al., 2020). Teachers should be given time to explore and experiment, crafting lessons with specific learning outcomes and goals in mind.

To effectively use AI in lesson planning, pre-service teachers require training in AI tools and platforms designed for education. This may involve becoming familiar with AI-driven learning management systems, curriculum development software, and adaptive learning platforms that offer personalized recommendations and resources based on student needs and learning objectives (Chen & Yu, 2021). AI technology's primary benefit is its ability to support teachers in curriculum design and adaptation. Pre-service teachers can learn how to use AI algorithms to analyze educational standards, identify learning objectives, and generate customized lesson plans and instructional materials that align with specific curriculum frameworks and grade-level standards. Training in AI technology should also emphasize collaboration and the sharing of best practices among pre-service teachers. By participating in professional learning communities and engaging with experienced educators and AI experts, pre-service teachers can gain valuable insights, exchange ideas, and collaborate on innovative approaches to AI-driven lesson planning and instruction (Williamson, 2019).

ETHICAL AND THEORETICAL CONSIDERATIONS

Integrating Artificial Intelligence into elementary science education marks a significant advancement in instructional practices, yet it introduces many ethical and theoretical considerations. While AI promises to revolutionize learning experiences and enrich educational outcomes, its implementation in the classroom raises complex questions surrounding equity, privacy, potential plagiarism, and the evolving role of human teachers in the educational process.

AI algorithms, while powerful, are not immune to bias and discrimination, and their use in educational settings can inadvertently disadvantage certain student groups. Research by Selwyn (2019) underscores the risk that AI algorithms may perpetuate societal biases, leading to unequal learning opportunities for students based on socioeconomic status, race, or gender. Educators must be vigilant in ensuring that AI-driven interventions in elementary science education are meticulously designed and implemented to promote equity and inclusivity for all students.

Training in ethical considerations ensures teachers use AI responsibly and ethically in their instructional practices. Educators must be acutely aware of the potential biases inherent in AI algorithms and take proactive measures to mitigate them. By acknowledging and addressing bias, educators can work towards fostering a learning environment that is fair and equitable for all students. Furthermore, teachers should be cognizant of the importance of safeguarding student privacy and data security when utilizing AI-driven technologies in the classroom. The sensitive nature of student data necessitates strict protocols to protect confidentiality and uphold ethical standards (Chen & Yu, 2021).

Integrating AI into elementary science education brings transformative opportunities for enhancing teaching and learning experiences. However, it presents complex ethical and theoretical challenges that must be navigated. By prioritizing equity, privacy, and ethical considerations in implementing AI-driven interventions, educators can harness the full potential of AI to create inclusive and empowering learning environments for all students.

CHALLENGES AND LIMITATIONS

While AI can greatly increase the generation of lesson content, there should be a concern regarding the content's accuracy and quality. AI platforms may not always have the contextual understanding or domain-specific knowledge necessary to develop high-quality science lessons (Wang et al., 2020). Technical limitations may also affect the ability to create quality lessons. These limitations could include challenges with natural language processing, understanding complex scientific concepts, or adapting to changes in educational standards and curriculum requirements (Brom et al., 2020).

AI-created content may lack the creativity and personalization teachers often bring to their lessons. This is an essential feature of the elementary lesson as it lends itself to increasing student engagement and learning outcomes. Additionally, AI may struggle to tailor lessons to individual students' diverse learning needs and preferences (Elias, 2021).

If pre-service and veteran teachers are expected to find or create standards-based aligned lessons, they must also be trained to use AI properly and efficiently. Teachers need a solid understanding of the fundamentals of AI, including its underlying principles, capabilities, and limitations. They need to know how to critically evaluate AI platforms and tools and maximize their uses in a way that benefits all of their students equally. By providing professional development and/or training that covers AI fundamentals, ethical considerations, tool selection, integration into instructional design, data analysis, collaboration, and ongoing support, educators can effectively leverage AI technologies to enhance teaching and learning outcomes in the classroom.

RECOMMENDATIONS

Whether or not to integrate AI and instruct our pre-service teachers on using it is personal and potentially controversial. AI-generated lesson plans can help teachers create quality, engaging lessons in subjects such as science, where the curriculum in the early elementary grades is often lacking or missing altogether. Elementary and early childhood teachers should embrace this opportunity to tailor instruction to the unique needs of each student, fostering a more inclusive and student-centered learning environment.

Educators should be encouraged to utilize AI-generated lesson plans to differentiate instruction, providing targeted support and enrichment activities to meet the diverse needs of their students. Professional development must be provided so teachers of all experience levels can effectively integrate AI-generated lesson plans into their teaching practices. Teachers require comprehensive professional development opportunities, and as our digital world continues to expand, this should include training on the platforms made available for teachers. Professional development sessions should focus on familiarizing teachers with AI technologies, navigating AI platforms, and effectively empowering them to integrate AI-generated resources into lesson planning and delivery.

CONCLUSION

In summary, incorporating AI into elementary science education has the potential to revolutionize teaching and learning approaches. Teachers now have the opportunity to create lessons in seconds that can be personalized for their students. Standards-based lessons can easily be created with rubrics and aligned assessments. Considerations such as student learning goals, language translation, and other student and classroom needs can be easily incorporated.

For educators, understanding and utilizing AI are beneficial skills and crucial in today's classrooms. Through AI tools, teachers can develop customized, creative, and diverse science lessons that spark interest, encourage thinking, and equip students for the demands of a world driven by technological advancements. As educators continue to adapt to the changing educational landscape, embracing AI as a pedagogical tool will be essential in shaping the future of elementary science education for both teachers and students.

As educators strive for equity and inclusion, AI has presented itself as a promising tool for leveling the playing field and addressing disparities in learning outcomes. AI-powered adaptive learning systems can provide targeted support and resources to students from diverse backgrounds, including those with special educational needs or language barriers (Chen & Yu, 2021). For pre-service teachers, understanding how to incorporate and utilize AI for inclusive education is essential in creating learning environments that accommodate the diverse needs of all students. By integrating AI into science lessons, teachers can ensure equitable access to high-quality education, regardless of students' individual circumstances or learning challenges and/or a lack of provided curriculum, thus promoting academic success for all.

REFERENCES

Banilower, E. R., Smith, P. S., Malzahn, K. A., Plumley, C. L., Gordon, E. M., & Hayes, M. L. (2018). *Report of the 2018 NSSME*. Horizon Research, Inc.

Blank, R. K. (2013). *What is the impact of decline in science instructional time in elementary school?* Council of Chief State School Officers.

Brom, C., Cihon, T. M., & Buchtová, M. (2020). Ethical Considerations for Teachers Using AI Technologies in Education. *Journal of Information Technology Education*, 19, 209–241.

Brown, J. M. (2017). Novice elementary science teachers' experiences of self-efficacy, anxiety, and frustration. *Journal of Science Teacher Education*, 28(1), 65–86.

Bullock-Rest, N. E. (2020). Artificial Intelligence in Education: A Literature Review. *Journal of Research on Technology in Education*, 52(1), 88–112.

Cairns, D., Sears, J., & Rehmat, A. P. (2011). The effect of inquiry-based science instruction on student achievement. *Journal of Science Education and Technology*, 20(5), 602–608.

Chen, N. S., Clarebout, G., & Kim Chwee, D. N. (2020). AI meets AI: Exploring the applications of artificial intelligence for authentic assessment. *Computers & Education*, 157, 103982. DOI: 10.1016/j.compedu.2020.103982

Chen, Y., & Yu, S. (2021). Artificial Intelligence Applications in K-12 Education: A Systematic Review. *Journal of Educational Computing Research*, 59(1), 126–148.

Elias, T. (2021). Artificial Intelligence in Education: Theoretical and Practical Considerations. *Educational Technology Research and Development*, 69(1), 105–128.

Ferguson, L. (2022). The lack of science education in elementary schools: An interdisciplinary concern.

Garcia, R. A., & Rodriguez, M. S. (2021). Challenges in elementary science education: The absence of formal curriculum. *Elementary Education Journal*, 38(3), 301–315.

Johnson, A. (2018). The impact of deficient science content knowledge on lesson planning and delivery. *Journal of Teacher Education*, 69(3), 245–258.

Lawrence Hall of Science. (2011). Elementary school teachers' perceptions and practices in science education (Press release). Retrieved from https://www.lawrencehallofscience.org/press_releases/elementary_school_teachers_perceptions_and_practices_in_science_education

National Academies of Sciences, Engineering, and Medicine. (2021). Science and Engineering in Preschool Through Elementary Grades: The Brilliance of Children and the Strengths of Educators. Washington, DC: The National Academies Press.

National Center for Education Statistics. (2016). *The Nation's Report Card: 2015 Science*. U.S. Department of Education.

National Research Council. (2012). *A framework for K-12 science education: Practices, crosscutting concepts, and core ideas*. The National Academies Press.

National Science Teaching Association. (2018). Position statement: The Next Generation Science Standards (NGSS). Retrieved from https://www.nsta.org/position -statement-next-generation-science-standards-ngss

Nkisi-Orji, I., Naeem, U., Mbah, G. C. E., & Munshi, A. A. (2019). Intelligent evaluation of learners' interaction records in simulation-based computer science education. *International Journal of Information and Communication Technology Education*, 15(3), 1–13. DOI: 10.4018/IJICTE.2019070101

Osborne, J., & Dillon, J. (2008). *Science education in Europe: Critical reflections*. The Nuffield Foundation.

Owoc, L., Rodriguez, A., & Kim, S. (2021). The role of AI in amplifying and extending human teaching. *Journal of Educational Technology & Society*, 24(3), 112–129.

Pelaez, J., Smith, K., & Chen, L. (2022). The debate on using AI to augment or replace teacher instruction. *Artificial Intelligence in Education Journal*, 15(2), 87–104.

Pompea, M., & Russo, M. (2023). Challenges in elementary science education: Limited time, resources, and teacher confidence. *Elementary Science Journal*, 20(1), 45–62.

Riegle-Crumb, C., King, B., & Irizarry, Y. (2023). Decline in interest and engagement in science among middle and high school students. *Journal of Research in Science Teaching*, 50(3), 374–392.

Selwyn, N. (2019). What's the Problem with Learning Analytics? *Journal of Learning Analytics*, 6(3), 11–19. DOI: 10.18608/jla.2019.63.3

Smith, J. K., & Brown, L. M. (2020). The role of artificial intelligence in curriculum development in elementary science education. *Journal of Educational Technology*, 45(2), 201–215.

Tai, R. H., Liu, C. Q., Maltese, A. V., & Fan, X. (2006). Planning early for careers in science. *Science*, 312(5777), 1143–1144. DOI: 10.1126/science.1128690 PMID: 16728620

Wang, F., Hannafin, M. J., & Lin, H. (2020). Effects of Artificial Intelligence Integration in Elementary Science Instruction. *Journal of Educational Technology & Society*, 23(3), 174–187.

Williamson, B. (2019). The Hidden Architecture of Higher Education: Building a Big Data Infrastructure for the 'Smarter University'. *International Journal of Educational Technology in Higher Education*, 16(1), 39–57.

KEY TERMS AND DEFINITIONS

Artificial Intelligence (AI): Artificial Intelligence, or AI, refers to the simulation of human intelligence in machines programmed to mimic cognitive functions such as learning, problem-solving, and decision-making. AI can personalize learning experiences, analyze student data, and assist teachers in various educational tasks.

Content Knowledge: Content knowledge is teachers' deep understanding of their teaching subjects. With strong content knowledge, teachers can confidently guide students through their learning, answer questions, address misconceptions, and create a culture of joy and curiosity.

Ethical Implications: Ethical implications in education refer to the moral considerations and dilemmas arising from using technology, instructional methods, or policies. This includes fairness, privacy, equity, and accountability in educational practices. For example, when implementing AI technologies in the classroom, educators must consider the ethical implications of data privacy, algorithmic bias, and equitable access to educational resources.

Individualized Education Plan: Abbreviated as IEP, an individualized education plan or program is a unique plan written for a student that provides free special education services and related services to support that student's individualized needs.

Multilingual Learners: Often abbreviated as ML, a multilingual learner is a student whose primary language is not English.

Novice Teachers: Novice teachers are educators new to the profession and have limited teaching experience. They may be recent graduates from teacher preparation programs or individuals transitioning from other careers into teaching. Novice teachers typically require additional support and mentorship as they develop their instructional skills and classroom management strategies.

Pre-Service Teachers: Pre-service teachers are enrolled in teacher preparation programs or training to become certified educators. They have not yet begun their formal teaching careers but are gaining the knowledge, skills, and practical experiences necessary to enter the profession. Pre-service teachers engage in coursework, field experiences, and supervised teaching practicums as part of their preparation.

Science Curriculum: The science curriculum refers to the structured framework of learning objectives, content standards, and instructional materials designed to guide science education in elementary schools. It outlines the essential concepts, skills, and inquiry-based practices students are expected to learn at each grade level and provides a curriculum for science instruction and assessment.

Science Lesson Development: Science lesson development involves planning, designing, and implementing instructional activities and resources to facilitate student learning in science. This includes identifying learning objectives, selecting appropriate instructional strategies, developing hands-on experiments or investigations, and assessing student understanding of scientific concepts.

Self-efficacy: Self-efficacy is a teacher's belief in their ability to teach a subject or skill effectively. This confidence plays a huge role in how teachers approach their lessons and interact with their students.

Teacher Preparation Program: Teacher preparation programs encompass formal training and professional development programs designed to equip educators with the knowledge, skills, and dispositions needed to teach in their respective subject areas and grade levels effectively. Teacher preparation programs may include coursework, field experiences, mentorship, and ongoing professional learning opportunities to support educators throughout their careers.

Theoretical and Ethical Implications: Ethical implications refer to the philosophical and moral considerations stemming from integrating theoretical frameworks and ethical principles into educational practices. This involves examining the broader implications of educational theories and ethical frameworks on teaching and learning outcomes and addressing the moral dilemmas inherent in educational research, policy, and practice.

Chapter 7
Encouraging Quality:
Approaches for Increasing Student Achievement in Higher Education via Involvement and Assistance

ASSIA BENABID

Faculty of Sciences, University Hassan II, Casablanca

Imane EL IMADI
https://orcid.org/0000-0001-9076-5039
Faculty of Sciences, University Hassan II, Casablanca

Khalil Alqatawneh

Tafila Technical University, Jordan

ABSTRACT

This chapter investigates the importance of social variety in institutional frameworks, notably in higher education, in response to the urgent societal concerns of the twenty-first century. The goal is to foster an educational environment that values, respects, and includes all students, regardless of gender, race, or socioeconomic status. The main goal is to foster an environment in which students feel both academically engaged and empowered to reach their greatest potential. This involves an equitable and inclusive teaching strategy that recognizes student's different experiences, needs, and objectives, as well as collaborative efforts from all educational partners. The goal of this research is to investigate and propose solutions to improve equity in higher education, with the ultimate goal of creating educational settings that accommodate students; with different needs. The objectives include identifying critical areas for change in present educational practices, investigating the influence of inclusive teaching methods on student success, and recommending concrete ways for institutions to implement them. The methodology used in this study is a thorough

DOI: 10.4018/979-8-3693-3904-6.ch007

evaluation of the existing literature on diversity, equity, and inclusion in higher education. It also includes case studies and examples of how inclusive approaches have been successfully implemented in diverse educational contexts. The theoretical framework is based on social justice theories, emphasizing the significance of providing equal opportunity for all individuals in the educational system. To achieve inclusion and equity, a comprehensive approach is advocated. Strategies such as accessibility and equity initiatives, flexible and adaptable teaching methods, active student engagement, inclusive communication, diverse representation in faculty and staff, diversity training programs, fair assessment practices, and transparent admissions policies are critical. Furthermore, financial support mechanisms, mentorship and tutoring programs, diversity-sensitive orientation campaigns, and the creation of inclusive courses and programs all help to build an equal educational environment. Faculty training has been acknowledged as a critical component in ensuring that educators have the skills and understanding required to effectively implement inclusive teaching techniques. Emotional support services and accessible physical infrastructure are also critical components in meeting the different needs of students. Finally, this study calls for a comprehensive and collaborative strategy to create equitable educational settings in higher education. By implementing the recommended measures, institutions can demonstrate their commitment to promoting diversity, fairness, and social justice, thereby helping students prepare for the challenges and opportunities of the 21st century.

INTRODUCTION

In education, inclusion and explicit pedagogy are emerging as fundamental approaches to encouraging all students' achievement, regardless of diversity. Indeed, explicit pedagogy concentrates on the precise, organized transfer of knowledge, whereas inclusion seeks to establish a learning atmosphere in which each student feels appreciated, respected, and encouraged.

Although these two methods are frequently taken into consideration separately, their combination has a great deal of potential to increase teaching and learning efficacy. Through the integration of explicit pedagogy and the principles of inclusion, educators can establish a learning environment in which every student receives individualized instruction that meets their specific needs and expectations.

In this chapter, we will investigate how combining inclusion and explicit pedagogy affects student learning, specifically how these complementary methods can encourage improved academic performance, more involvement, and a sense of belonging among all learners. In order to optimize the advantages of this integrated approach, we will also examine instructional tactics and practices.

In the evolving landscape of education, inclusion and explicit pedagogy are gaining prominence as essential strategies for enhancing student achievement across diverse learning populations. Explicit pedagogy focuses on the clear, systematic delivery of knowledge, ensuring that instructional methods are direct, transparent, and structured. This approach emphasizes breaking down complex concepts into manageable components, providing students with a solid foundation for understanding and mastery.

Conversely, inclusion aims to create a learning environment where every student feels valued, respected, and supported. This approach recognizes and celebrates diversity in all its forms—whether cultural, socioeconomic, linguistic, or cognitive—and seeks to address the unique needs of each learner. By fostering a sense of belonging and respect, inclusion ensures that students from various backgrounds can fully engage with the curriculum and reach their potential.

While these two approaches are often considered separately, integrating explicit pedagogy with inclusive practices presents a powerful opportunity to enhance educational outcomes. The fusion of these methodologies offers a framework where systematic instruction and individualized support work in tandem, creating a more effective and equitable learning environment.

This chapter aims to explore the impact of combining explicit pedagogy with inclusion on student learning outcomes. Specifically, it will investigate how this integration can lead to improved academic performance, increased student engagement, and a stronger sense of belonging among all learners. By examining the interplay between these complementary approaches, we seek to identify effective instructional strategies and practices that maximize the benefits of this integrated approach.

In analyzing how explicit pedagogy and inclusion can be harmonized, we will delve into various instructional techniques and their implications for creating a supportive and effective learning environment. The goal is to provide insights into how educators can leverage both approaches to foster an educational setting where all students have the opportunity to thrive.

In addition to assessing the impact on student achievement and involvement, this research will also explore the practical implications for educators. It will provide insights into how instructional methods can be adapted to create a more inclusive and supportive learning environment, where every student has the opportunity to succeed. Through this examination, the study seeks to contribute valuable knowledge on how to enhance educational practices by harmonizing explicit pedagogy with principles of inclusion, ultimately fostering a more equitable and effective educational experience for all students.

SIGNIFICANCE OF STUDY

In the context of rapidly evolving societal norms and increasing diversity within student populations, this study holds significant relevance. Higher education institutions are not only places of academic instruction but also microcosms of broader societal structures. As such, they play a critical role in shaping the attitudes, beliefs, and future behaviors of students. By investigating the importance of social variety—encompassing gender, race, socioeconomic status, and more—this study seeks to understand how these factors influence the educational experiences and outcomes of students. The research underscores the need for educational environments that do not merely tolerate diversity but actively embrace and celebrate it. Such environments are essential for fostering a sense of belonging and empowerment among all students, which in turn can enhance their academic performance and personal growth.

The significance of this study also lies in its potential to influence policy and practice. By identifying gaps and challenges in current institutional frameworks, the research can inform the development of more inclusive policies that ensure equitable access to educational resources and opportunities. Furthermore, the study highlights the importance of faculty and staff training in recognizing and addressing diverse student needs. The insights gained from this research can guide institutions in designing comprehensive professional development programs that equip educators with the skills and knowledge necessary to implement inclusive teaching strategies. Ultimately, this study aims to contribute to the broader discourse on social justice in education, providing a foundation for ongoing efforts to create more equitable and inclusive learning environments.

OBJECTIVES

Analyze Institutional Policies and Practices: To conduct a thorough analysis of existing institutional policies and practices related to diversity, equity, and inclusion, with the aim of identifying strengths and areas for improvement.

Assess the Impact of Diversity on Student Outcomes: To evaluate how different aspects of diversity, such as race, gender, and socioeconomic status, impact student engagement, academic achievement, and overall well-being.

Explore Best Practices in Inclusive Education: To investigate and document best practices in inclusive education from a variety of higher education contexts, highlighting successful strategies and their outcomes.

Develop a Framework for Inclusive Teaching: To propose a comprehensive framework for inclusive teaching that incorporates flexible pedagogical approaches, culturally responsive curricula, and supportive learning environments.

Promote Collaborative Efforts Among Stakeholders: To facilitate dialogue and collaboration among students, faculty, administrators, and other stakeholders in the development and implementation of inclusive policies and practices.

Evaluate the Role of Faculty and Staff Training: To assess the effectiveness of existing training programs for faculty and staff on issues related to diversity and inclusion, and to recommend improvements for these programs.

Provide Recommendations for Policy and Practice: To offer concrete recommendations for higher education institutions on how to implement changes that promote greater equity and inclusion, based on the study's findings and analyses.

By achieving these objectives, the study aims to make a meaningful contribution to the ongoing efforts to create more equitable and inclusive educational environments, ensuring that all students have the opportunity to succeed and thrive in higher education.

RESEARCH DESIGN AND METHODOLOGY

To thoroughly examine the significance of socioeconomic diversity and equity in higher education, this Chapter employs a mixed-methods approach, integrating both qualitative and quantitative techniques. This approach allows for a comprehensive analysis of the complex and multifaceted nature of diversity and equity issues, providing a richer and more nuanced understanding of the phenomena under investigation.

Quantitative Methods

The quantitative component of the study involves the collection and analysis of numerical data to identify patterns, trends, and correlations. This data is primarily gathered through structured surveys and questionnaires distributed to a representative sample of students, faculty, and administrative staff across various higher education institutions. These instruments are designed to measure attitudes, perceptions, and experiences related to socioeconomic diversity, inclusive practices, and equity within the educational environment.

Key quantitative metrics include

Demographic Information: Data on students' socioeconomic status, race, gender, and other relevant factors.

Academic Performance: Statistics related to grades, retention rates, and graduation rates, analyzed in relation to socioeconomic diversity.

Perceptions of Inclusivity: Survey questions aimed at gauging participants' perceptions of inclusivity and fairness within their institutions.

The quantitative data is analyzed using statistical techniques such as regression analysis, factor analysis, and correlation analysis. These methods help identify significant relationships and trends, providing empirical evidence to support the study's findings.

Qualitative Methods

The qualitative component complements the quantitative data by exploring the deeper, more subjective experiences of individuals within the educational system. This is achieved through methods such as:

In-depth Interviews: Conducting semi-structured interviews with students, faculty, and administrators to gain insights into their personal experiences and perspectives on socioeconomic diversity and equity. These interviews allow for the exploration of nuanced issues that may not be fully captured by quantitative measures.

Focus Groups: Organizing focus group discussions with diverse groups of students and faculty to foster open dialogue about challenges, successes, and areas for improvement related to diversity and inclusion. These discussions provide a platform for participants to share their stories and suggest practical solutions.

Case Studies: Developing detailed case studies of specific higher education institutions that have implemented innovative practices to promote socioeconomic diversity and equity. These case studies provide contextualized examples of best practices and the challenges faced in creating inclusive educational environments.

DATA INTEGRATION AND ANALYSIS

The mixed-methods approach allows for the integration of quantitative and qualitative data, providing a more holistic view of the research problem. The data is analyzed in an iterative process, where quantitative findings inform the qualitative inquiry and vice versa. For example, statistical trends identified in the quantitative data may lead to more focused qualitative questions, while themes emerging from qualitative data may prompt further quantitative analysis.

The use of triangulation—comparing and contrasting data from different sources and methods—enhances the validity and reliability of the study's findings. This comprehensive analysis helps to uncover both broad patterns and individual experiences, offering a detailed understanding of the impact of socioeconomic diversity and equity in higher education.

In conclusion, the mixed-methods design of this study ensures a thorough and balanced examination of the research questions, providing valuable insights that can inform policy and practice in higher education.

COLLECTION OF DATA

The data collection process for this study involves both qualitative and quantitative methods, ensuring a well-rounded and thorough examination of the issues surrounding socioeconomic diversity and equity in higher education.

Qualitative Data Collection

For the qualitative aspect, a comprehensive analysis of existing literature and research is conducted, focusing on inclusion, equity, and diversity in higher education. This involves:

Literature Review: An extensive review of academic journals, books, policy reports, and other scholarly sources is undertaken to identify key theories, concepts, and findings related to diversity and inclusion in educational settings. This review provides a theoretical framework for the study and highlights gaps in current research that this study aims to address.

Case Studies: Detailed case studies of specific higher education institutions known for their innovative approaches to promoting inclusion and equity are developed. These case studies include:

Institutional Profiles: Background information about each institution, including size, location, student demographics, and institutional mission.

Initiatives and Programs: Descriptions of specific initiatives, programs, and policies implemented to enhance inclusivity, such as diversity training for faculty, scholarship programs for underrepresented students, and inclusive curricula.

Outcomes and Impact: Analysis of the outcomes and impacts of these initiatives on the student body and the broader institutional culture.

Interviews and Focus Groups:

In-depth Interviews: Semi-structured interviews are conducted with a diverse range of participants, including students, faculty, administrative staff, and policymakers. These interviews explore personal experiences, challenges, and perceptions related to diversity and inclusion within their institutions.

Focus Groups: Focus group discussions are organized with participants from different backgrounds to gather a variety of perspectives on the effectiveness of current inclusion practices and to brainstorm potential improvements. These discussions facilitate the exploration of shared experiences and collective ideas for enhancing equity.

Content Analysis: Analysis of institutional documents, such as mission statements, diversity policies, and strategic plans, to understand the formal commitments and approaches to inclusion and equity within different institutions.

Quantitative Data Collection

The quantitative component involves the systematic collection of numerical data to assess perceptions and experiences of inclusivity among students and faculty. This is primarily accomplished through:

1. **Surveys**:
    o   **Survey Design**: A set of structured questionnaires is developed, with questions designed to capture a range of information, including demographic data, personal experiences, perceptions of inclusivity, and satisfaction with institutional efforts towards diversity and equity.
    o   **Target Population**: The surveys are distributed to a representative sample of students, faculty, and administrative staff across multiple higher education institutions. Efforts are made to ensure the sample is diverse in terms of socioeconomic status, race, gender, and other relevant factors.
2. **Data Collection Process**:
    o   **Administration**: Surveys are administered both online and in paper format to maximize participation. Anonymity and confidentiality are assured to encourage honest and open responses.
    o   **Response Rate Optimization**: Strategies such as follow-up reminders and incentives (e.g., gift cards, and participation certificates) are employed to enhance response rates.
3. **Data Analysis**:
    o   **Statistical Methods**: The survey data is analyzed using various statistical techniques, including descriptive statistics to summarize the data, and inferential statistics to examine relationships between variables (e.g., the relationship between perceived inclusivity and student satisfaction). Advanced analyses, such as regression models and factor analysis, may also be used to identify key predictors of positive inclusivity outcomes and areas needing improvement.

By combining these qualitative and quantitative data collection methods, the study provides a robust and comprehensive understanding of the current state of socioeconomic diversity and equity in higher education. The integration of these methods enables the exploration of both broad patterns and individual experiences, offering valuable insights for policy and practice improvements.

DATA ANALYSIS

The data analysis process involves systematically examining both qualitative and quantitative data collected during the study to extract meaningful insights and draw conclusions about the state of socioeconomic diversity and equity in higher education.

Qualitative Data Analysis

For the qualitative data, thematic analysis is employed to identify key themes and insights from the case studies, literature reviews, interviews, and focus groups. The process involves several steps:

Data Familiarization:

All qualitative data, including interview transcripts, focus group discussions, and case study narratives, are thoroughly read and re-read to gain a comprehensive understanding of the content.

Notes and initial impressions are documented to capture emerging ideas and patterns.

Coding:

The data is systematically coded by categorizing segments of text that relate to specific topics or themes. This process involves assigning labels (codes) to different parts of the data, such as phrases, sentences, or paragraphs, that are relevant to the research questions.

Theme Identification:

After coding, the codes are reviewed and grouped into broader themes that represent significant patterns or concepts in the data. Themes might include topics like "institutional support for diversity," "barriers to inclusion," "student experiences of discrimination," and "successful inclusivity initiatives."

The relationships between themes are explored to understand how they interact and influence each other.

Reviewing and Refining Themes:

The identified themes are reviewed for coherence and relevance. Some themes may be merged, split, or refined to better capture the data's essence.

This step ensures that the themes accurately reflect the data and are comprehensive in covering the research topics.

Theme Definition and Description:

Each theme is defined clearly, and illustrative quotes from the data are selected to exemplify the themes. This helps in conveying the richness and depth of the qualitative findings.

Reporting:

The final themes are reported and discussed, highlighting key insights and how they relate to the study's objectives and research questions. The findings are presented in a narrative form, supported by quotes and examples from the data.

Quantitative Data Analysis

For the quantitative data, statistical methods are used to analyze the survey responses. The process involves:

Data Cleaning and Preparation:

Survey responses are cleaned to remove incomplete or inconsistent data entries. This includes checking for missing values, and outliers, and ensuring consistency in responses.

Descriptive Statistics:

Descriptive statistics, such as frequencies, percentages, means, and standard deviations, are calculated to summarize the data. These statistics provide a general overview of the respondents' demographics, perceptions of inclusivity, and satisfaction with institutional diversity efforts.

The data is presented in tables and charts, making it easier to visualize and interpret the findings. For instance, tables may show the distribution of responses to questions about perceived inclusivity, while charts may illustrate differences in satisfaction levels among different demographic groups.

Inferential Statistics:

Where applicable, inferential statistical methods, such as t-tests, chi-square tests, or ANOVA, are used to examine differences and relationships between groups. For example, these tests can explore whether there are significant differences in perceptions of inclusivity based on socioeconomic status, race, or gender.

Advanced statistical techniques, such as regression analysis, may be employed to identify predictors of positive outcomes related to inclusivity and equity, such as higher student satisfaction or academic performance.

Data Interpretation:

The results from the descriptive and inferential analyses are interpreted to draw conclusions about the current state of socioeconomic diversity and equity in the surveyed institutions. This includes identifying key trends, highlighting areas of strength, and pinpointing areas needing improvement.

Reporting:

The quantitative findings are presented in a structured format, with clear tables, graphs, and charts to illustrate key points. The results are discussed in the context of the study's research questions and objectives, providing a comprehensive understanding of the survey data.

By combining these qualitative and quantitative analysis methods, the study offers a robust and comprehensive view of the issues surrounding socioeconomic diversity and equity in higher education. The mixed-methods approach ensures that the findings are well-rounded and grounded in both numerical data and rich, narrative insights.

REVIEWING AND REFINING THEMES: REVIEW OF LITERATURE

Section 1: Explicit Pedagogy and Its Importance in Education

Explicit Pedagogy Defined

Explicit pedagogy involves clear and structured teaching where the teacher provides direct instruction, modeling, and guided practice to help students understand and master new concepts. This approach is characterized by a focus on clarity, gradual progression from simple to complex ideas, and the explicit teaching of skills and knowledge (Engelmann & Carnine, 1991).

Benefits of Explicit Pedagogy

Research has shown that explicit pedagogy is particularly effective in helping students acquire foundational skills and knowledge. By breaking down complex concepts into manageable steps, this approach minimizes cognitive overload and supports students' gradual understanding and mastery (Sweller, Ayres, & Kalyuga, 2011). Moreover, explicit teaching is beneficial for all students, including those who may struggle with self-directed learning or have diverse learning needs (Rosenshine, 2012).

Critical Considerations and Applications

Explicit pedagogy also emphasizes the importance of continuous assessment and feedback. This allows educators to gauge students' understanding, identify areas for improvement, and adjust instruction accordingly (Hattie, 2009). In practice, explicit pedagogy involves a variety of teaching methods, including direct instruction, worked examples, and systematic practice.

Section 2: Inclusion and Diversity in Educational Settings

Understanding Inclusion

Inclusion in education refers to the practice of providing all students, regardless of their diverse backgrounds and abilities, with equitable access to learning opportunities. This approach seeks to create a supportive and accepting environment where every student feels valued and respected (Florian & Black-Hawkins, 2011).

Incorporating Diversity into Pedagogy

Recognizing and embracing diversity in the classroom involves understanding students' socioeconomic, cultural, and linguistic differences and tailoring teaching methods accordingly (Banks, 2015). This includes using diverse instructional materials, fostering inclusive classroom discussions, and promoting representation in course content.

Strategies for Inclusive Education

Educators are encouraged to employ various strategies to foster an inclusive learning environment. These include differentiated instruction, culturally responsive teaching, and the use of multiple teaching aids to accommodate different learning styles (Gay, 2018). Additionally, promoting intercultural dialogue and encouraging the participation of all students are critical components of inclusive education (Nieto & Bode, 2018).

Challenges and Opportunities

While the implementation of inclusive practices can present challenges, such as addressing implicit biases and ensuring equitable access to resources, it also offers significant opportunities for enhancing student engagement and academic success. Research indicates that inclusive education not only benefits marginalized groups but also enriches the learning experience for all students (Ainscow, Booth, & Dyson, 2006).

Integration of Explicit Pedagogy and Inclusion

The synergy between explicit pedagogy and inclusion lies in their shared goal of promoting student success by providing clear, structured instruction within an equitable and supportive learning environment. By combining these approaches, educators can ensure that all students receive high-quality instruction tailored to their unique needs and are empowered to thrive academically and personally (Tomlinson, 2017).

DISCUSSION

The Value of Equity and Social Variety in Higher Education: The conclusion of this chapter highlights how crucial it is to encourage socioeconomic diversity and justice in higher education. Social equity refers to making sure all students have equitable access to educational opportunities and resources, whereas social variety includes diversity in gender, color, socioeconomic position, and other dimensions. Creating inclusive learning settings that promote student engagement, success, and general well-being requires embracing social difference and equality.

Inclusive teaching strategies' function: The importance of inclusive teaching strategies in higher education is emphasized in the literature data. Differentiated education and culturally responsive teaching are two examples of inclusive pedagogical techniques that acknowledge and accommodate the varied requirements, learning styles, and backgrounds of students. Institutions can encourage academic engagement, improve student learning, and contribute to a more supportive learning environment.

Possibilities and Difficulties: The value of social diversity and justice is becoming more widely acknowledged, but there are still difficulties in putting these ideas into practical laws and procedures. Advancement toward fairness and inclusivity may be hampered by systemic obstacles, unconscious prejudices, and resource limitations. Nonetheless, these difficulties offer chances for creativity, cooperation, and group effort to promote socioeconomic diversity and justice in higher education.

Institutional Leadership and Commitment: It is great to see the survey results show that the institution has a strong commitment to diversity and inclusion. Students from a variety of backgrounds might feel a feeling of belonging on campus thanks in large part to institutional ideals. Converting institutional commitment into significant change requires strong leadership, transparent values communication, and concrete initiatives to support diversity.

Suggestions for Upcoming Activity

To further enhance social equity and diversity in higher education, institutions can implement the following actions:

Strengthening Institutional Policies and Frameworks:

Develop and enforce comprehensive diversity and inclusion policies that outline clear expectations and goals. These policies should be revisited regularly to ensure they remain relevant and effective.

Establish dedicated offices or committees for diversity, equity, and inclusion (DEI) to oversee the implementation of policies and initiatives. These bodies should have the authority and resources necessary to effect change.

Curriculum Development and Pedagogical Innovation:

Integrate courses and modules that address issues of diversity, equity, and inclusion across all disciplines. Encourage faculty to incorporate diverse perspectives and case studies into their teaching materials.

Promote pedagogical training for faculty, focusing on inclusive teaching strategies such as culturally responsive pedagogy, differentiated instruction, and universal design for learning (UDL).

Faculty and Staff Development:

Offer regular professional development opportunities focused on diversity, equity, and inclusion. This can include workshops, seminars, and training sessions on topics like implicit bias, inclusive communication, and equitable assessment practices.

Foster a diverse and inclusive faculty by implementing equitable hiring practices, supporting underrepresented groups, and creating mentorship programs.

Student Support Services:

Expand student support services to include mental health resources, academic advising, tutoring, and financial aid tailored to the needs of diverse student populations.

Create safe spaces and support networks for students from marginalized backgrounds, such as cultural centers, LGBTQ+ resource centers, and disability services.

Community Engagement and Partnerships:

Build partnerships with local communities and organizations to support diverse student populations and promote social equity. This can include outreach programs, community service initiatives, and collaborations with local businesses and non-profits.

Encourage student and faculty involvement in community-based research and service-learning projects that address local social justice issues.

Monitoring and Accountability:

Implement regular assessments and evaluations of DEI initiatives to measure progress and identify areas for improvement. Use data-driven approaches to track student outcomes and experiences related to diversity and equity.

Establish accountability mechanisms, such as DEI reports and audits, to ensure that institutional commitments to diversity and inclusion are being met.

Student Engagement and Empowerment:

Encourage student organizations and clubs that promote diversity and inclusion on campus. Support these groups with resources and opportunities for leadership development.

Provide platforms for students to voice their concerns and experiences, such as diversity councils, forums, and town hall meetings. Incorporate student feedback into institutional planning and decision-making processes.

Awareness and Education Campaigns:

Launch awareness campaigns to educate the campus community about the importance of diversity, equity, and inclusion. This can include events, speakers, and workshops that highlight diverse cultures and perspectives.

Celebrate diversity through cultural events, heritage months, and other activities that foster an appreciation for different backgrounds and experiences.

Resource Allocation and Investment:

Allocate resources and funding specifically for DEI initiatives. This includes scholarships for underrepresented students, funding for diversity programs, and investments in inclusive infrastructure.

Ensure that campus facilities and technologies are accessible to all students, including those with disabilities.

By implementing these actions, higher education institutions can create a more inclusive and equitable environment that supports the success and well-being of all students. It is essential for institutions to not only commit to these goals in principle but also to take concrete steps to realize them, fostering a culture of continuous improvement and innovation in diversity and inclusion practices.

FINDINGS

Table 1. Key Themes from Literature Review

Theme	Description
Importance of Inclusive Teaching	Literature emphasizes adapting teaching methods to meet diverse student needs.
Equity Initiatives	Successful implementation examples of equity initiatives in higher education institutions.

Interpretation of the Importance of Inclusive Teaching: Research highlights the necessity of inclusive teaching strategies for meeting the requirements of a diverse student body. These strategies include differentiated instruction, culturally sensitive pedagogy, and universal design for learning. Higher education institutions can establish more fair and productive learning environments by modifying their teaching practices to fit a range of learning styles, backgrounds, and skills.

Consequences: Using inclusive teaching strategies can raise student participation, enhance academic performance, and foster a more welcoming and encouraging campus environment. For educators to be prepared to address the different needs of their students, inclusive pedagogy training and professional development are essential.

Interpretation of Equity Initiatives: Promising equity initiatives documented in the literature show institutions taking the initiative to remove structural obstacles and advance justice. Targeted recruitment and retention campaigns, chances for financial aid and scholarships for disadvantaged students, and the creation of a curriculum that is culturally appropriate are a few examples of these approaches.

Implications: Higher education institutions can encourage greater social mobility and academic performance among historically marginalized student populations by putting into practice and building upon effective equity programs. Collaborative alliances with stakeholders and community organizations can increase the effectiveness of these programs and advance more general societal fairness objectives.

Inclusive teaching is essential for addressing the diverse needs of today's student population. Research underscores that effective inclusive teaching strategies—such as differentiated instruction, culturally sensitive pedagogy, and universal learning design (UDL)—are critical for creating equitable educational opportunities. These strategies are designed to:

- **Accommodate Diverse Learning Styles**: Differentiated instruction allows educators to tailor their teaching methods to accommodate various learning styles and abilities, ensuring that each student can access and engage with the material in a way that suits their individual needs (Tomlinson, 2014).
- **Foster Cultural Sensitivity**: Culturally responsive pedagogy involves integrating students' cultural references into the learning environment. This approach helps students from diverse backgrounds feel valued and understood, which can enhance their academic motivation and engagement (Gay, 2018).
- **Implement Universal Design for Learning (UDL)**: UDL principles advocate for creating multiple means of representation, expression, and engagement to support diverse learners. By designing flexible learning environments, educators can meet the needs of all students, including those with disabilities and different learning preferences (CAST, 2018).

Consequences of Inclusive Teaching Strategies

The implementation of inclusive teaching strategies has several positive consequences for both students and educational institutions:

- **Increased Student Engagement**: Inclusive teaching methods actively involve students in their learning process, leading to higher levels of engagement and participation. Students are more likely to be motivated and invested in their education when their diverse needs are recognized and addressed (Booth & Ainscow, 2011).
- **Enhanced Academic Performance**: Research has shown that inclusive pedagogical practices can improve academic outcomes by providing all students with the tools and support needed to succeed. Tailoring instruction to individual needs helps to bridge learning gaps and boosts overall academic achievement (Hattie, 2009).

- **Promoted Campus Inclusivity**: Creating an inclusive classroom environment contributes to a broader campus culture of acceptance and support. When students feel included and respected, it fosters a positive and nurturing atmosphere that benefits the entire academic community (Banks, 2015).

To maximize these benefits, educators must receive ongoing training and professional development in inclusive pedagogy. This training equips them with the skills and knowledge needed to effectively implement inclusive teaching strategies and respond to the diverse needs of their students.

Interpretation of Equity Initiatives

Equity initiatives aim to address and rectify systemic barriers that impede equal access to educational opportunities. Effective equity initiatives documented in the literature include:

- **Targeted Recruitment and Retention**: Institutions have developed programs to attract and retain students from underrepresented backgrounds. These initiatives may involve outreach efforts, mentorship programs, and support networks designed to improve student retention and success (Gurin et al., 2002).
- **Financial Aid and Scholarships**: Providing financial support through scholarships, grants, and financial aid is a crucial component of equity initiatives. These resources help alleviate the financial burdens faced by disadvantaged students, making higher education more accessible (Perkins, 2020).
- **Culturally Relevant Curriculum**: Developing and implementing curricula that reflect diverse cultural perspectives ensures that all students see their experiences represented in their studies. This approach not only enhances educational relevance but also fosters a more inclusive learning environment (Ladson-Billings, 1995).

Implications of Equity Initiatives

By adopting and expanding effective equity programs, higher education institutions can achieve several significant outcomes:

- **Increased Social Mobility**: Equity initiatives can provide historically marginalized students with the opportunities and support needed to excel academically and advance socially. This contributes to greater social mobility and helps to level the playing field (Cohen & Brawer, 2008).

- **Enhanced Academic Achievement**: Targeted support and resources for disadvantaged students can improve academic performance and retention rates. By addressing the specific challenges faced by these students, institutions can help them achieve their full potential (Tinto, 1993).
- **Strengthened Community Partnerships**: Collaborating with community organizations and stakeholders can enhance the effectiveness of equity programs. These partnerships can provide additional resources, support, and opportunities for students, contributing to broader societal goals of fairness and inclusion (Kezar & Maxey, 2014).

In conclusion, the integration of inclusive teaching strategies and equity initiatives is vital for creating fair and effective educational environments. By embracing these practices, higher education institutions can support the diverse needs of their students, promote academic success, and contribute to a more equitable society.

Table 2. Survey Results on Inclusivity Perceptions

Statement	Agree (%)	Neutral (%)	Disagree (%)
The institution values diversity and inclusion.	85	10	5
Inclusive teaching methods enhance student engagement.	70	20	10

Interpretation of Institutional Values: The high percentage of respondents who agreed that "The institution values diversity and inclusion" points to an inclusive, equitable, and diverse culture inside the organization. This impression implies that the campus community acknowledges and supports initiatives aimed at fostering inclusivity.

Consequences: A strong institutional commitment to diversity and inclusion can support campus diversity programs, improve student recruitment and retention, and help students from a variety of backgrounds feel like they belong. These efforts can be strengthened further by maintaining an open discourse regarding diversity and by clearly communicating the institution's ideals.

Effects of Inclusive Teaching Techniques

Interpretation: The survey results highlight the potential advantages of pedagogical techniques that stress student diversity and equity since they reveal positive impressions of inclusive teaching methods among the respondents. It is believed that inclusive teaching methods improve student involvement, encourage academic performance, and foster a more friendly and encouraging learning atmosphere.

Implications: Through faculty development initiatives, curricular updates, and institutional regulations, higher education institutions should give top priority to the adoption and promotion of inclusive teaching practices. Encouraging academic staff members to adopt inclusive practices can enhance student performance and make learning more equal for all students.

The analysis of these findings, in summary, emphasizes the vital role that equity programs and inclusive practices play in advancing social variety and equity in higher education. The research emphasizes the value of innovative teaching strategies and institutional dedication to diversity, and survey data shows how inclusive teaching approaches are seen to affect student performance and engagement.

Institutions of higher learning should keep funding equity projects, inclusive practices, and continuous evaluation in the future to guarantee that all students have equal access to resources and learning opportunities. In higher education, institutions can support broader societal goals of equality and social justice by eliminating systemic impediments and promoting an inclusive atmosphere.

The survey results reveal a high percentage of respondents who agreed that "The institution values diversity and inclusion." This response highlights several key aspects of the institution's culture and its approach to diversity:

- **Acknowledgment of Diversity**: The positive perception suggests that the institution recognizes and supports diversity as a fundamental value. This acknowledgment likely reflects a commitment to fostering an inclusive environment where all students feel respected and valued.
- **Support for Inclusivity Initiatives**: The high agreement level implies that the institution's efforts to promote inclusivity are visible and appreciated within the campus community. This could include diversity training programs, multicultural events, and policies designed to support diverse student populations.
- **Inclusive Culture**: An institution that values diversity and inclusion typically cultivates a culture where diverse perspectives are integrated into the academic and social fabric of the campus. This cultural aspect can contribute to a more positive and engaging student experience.

Consequences of Strong Institutional Commitment

The strong institutional commitment to diversity and inclusion has several important consequences:

- **Enhanced Campus Diversity Programs**: A firm commitment to inclusivity supports the development and continuation of campus programs that celebrate and support diverse identities. This includes initiatives such as affinity groups, cultural centers, and diversity-focused extracurricular activities.

- **Improved Student Recruitment and Retention**: Institutions that are perceived as inclusive and supportive are more likely to attract and retain students from varied backgrounds. This positive reputation can make the institution more appealing to prospective students who seek an environment that values diversity.

- **Increased Sense of Belonging**: Students from diverse backgrounds are more likely to feel a sense of belonging and acceptance when they see that the institution values and actively promotes diversity. This sense of belonging can improve student satisfaction and academic success.

- **Ongoing Dialogue and Communication**: Maintaining open dialogue about diversity and clearly communicating institutional values are crucial for reinforcing the commitment to inclusivity. Transparency in these efforts helps to build trust and ensures that diversity and inclusion remain central to the institution's mission.

Interpretation of the Effects of Inclusive Teaching Techniques

The survey results indicating positive impressions of inclusive teaching techniques suggest several benefits:

- **Enhanced Student Engagement**: Inclusive teaching practices that accommodate diverse learning styles and backgrounds are associated with higher levels of student engagement. Students are more likely to participate actively in learning when they feel their needs and perspectives are considered.

- **Improved Academic Performance**: Inclusive pedagogical methods can lead to better academic outcomes by addressing individual learning needs and providing equitable support. These techniques help bridge learning gaps and ensure that all students have the opportunity to succeed.

- **Fostering a Supportive Learning Environment**: Inclusive teaching contributes to creating a classroom atmosphere where students feel supported and valued. This environment can enhance overall student well-being and academic motivation.

Implications for Higher Education Institutions

To fully leverage the benefits of inclusive teaching and institutional commitment to diversity, higher education institutions should focus on the following actions:

- **Faculty Development**: Invest in professional development programs that train faculty in inclusive teaching practices. This training can help educators understand how to effectively implement inclusive strategies and adapt their teaching to meet the needs of all students.
- **Curricular Updates**: Revise curricula to reflect diverse perspectives and include content that is relevant to students from various backgrounds. Ensuring that course materials and assignments are inclusive can enhance the learning experience for all students.
- **Institutional Policies**: Develop and enforce policies that support diversity and inclusion, such as equitable assessment practices, inclusive hiring practices, and support services for underrepresented students. Clear policies can institutionalize inclusivity and promote sustained progress.
- **Continuous Evaluation**: Regularly assess the effectiveness of diversity and inclusion initiatives to ensure they are meeting their goals. Feedback from students and faculty can provide valuable insights for improving programs and practices.

CONCLUSION

In summary, the findings emphasize the critical role of equity programs and inclusive teaching practices in promoting social diversity and equity in higher education. The research highlights the importance of institutional commitment to diversity and the positive impact of inclusive pedagogical techniques on student performance and engagement. To support broader societal goals of equality and social justice, higher education institutions should continue to invest in and refine their equity initiatives, inclusive practices, and ongoing evaluation efforts. By addressing systemic barriers and fostering an inclusive campus environment, institutions can contribute to a more equitable and just society

RECOMMENDATIONS

Several suggestions are made for promoting social diversity and justice in higher education in light of the research findings:

Faculty Development: Make investments in professional development courses and training that put an emphasis on inclusive teaching methods and cultural sensitivity.

Targeted equality activities should be implemented, such as inclusive curriculum development, financial aid support, and recruiting and retention campaigns.

Community Engagement: To overcome structural obstacles and advance social mobility, cultivate alliances with stakeholders and community organizations

Continuous Assessment: To support continued advancements in equity and inclusivity, evaluate the campus environment, student opinions, and academic results regularly.

In conclusion, it takes coordinated efforts by institutional leaders, teachers, students, and community stakeholders to promote social variation and equity in higher education. Higher education institutions may establish transformative learning environments where all students are empowered to thrive and realize their full potential by adopting inclusive practices, putting targeted equity initiatives into action, and cultivating a culture of diversity and inclusion.

To advance social variety and equity goals inside higher education and support broader society initiatives toward diversity, fairness, and social justice, continued collaboration, advocacy, and dedication to equity will be crucial.

Based on the research findings, several strategic recommendations are proposed to enhance social diversity and justice in higher education. These suggestions are designed to address the key areas identified as crucial for fostering inclusive and equitable educational environments.

1. FACULTY DEVELOPMENT

Investment in Professional Development:

- **Training Programs**: Implement comprehensive training programs focused on inclusive teaching practices, cultural sensitivity, and equity in education. These programs should be designed to equip faculty with the skills and knowledge required to effectively address the diverse needs of students.
- **Ongoing Education**: Encourage continuous professional growth through workshops, seminars, and courses that emphasize the latest research and best practices in inclusive education. This can help educators stay informed about new strategies and tools for supporting all students.

Promotion of Best Practices:

- **Sharing Resources**: Develop platforms for faculty to share successful inclusive teaching strategies and resources. This could include creating a repository of lesson plans, activities, and case studies that highlight effective approaches to teaching diverse student populations.

- **Peer Mentoring**: Establish peer mentoring programs where experienced faculty members provide guidance and support to newer or less experienced educators on implementing inclusive practices.

2. TARGETED EQUITY INITIATIVES

Inclusive Curriculum Development:

- **Curriculum Review**: Regularly review and update the curriculum to ensure it reflects diverse perspectives and is inclusive of various cultural, social, and historical contexts. This can help students from all backgrounds see themselves represented and valued in their coursework.
- **Collaborative Design**: Involve diverse stakeholders, including students, faculty, and community members, in the curriculum development process to ensure that multiple viewpoints are considered and incorporated.

Financial Aid and Support:

- **Scholarships and Grants**: Increase the availability of financial aid, scholarships, and grants specifically targeted at underrepresented and disadvantaged students. This can help reduce financial barriers to higher education and support greater diversity within the student body.
- **Support Services**: Provide additional support services such as tutoring, mentorship, and counseling to assist students from diverse backgrounds in overcoming academic and personal challenges.

Recruitment and Retention Campaigns:

- **Diverse Hiring Practices**: Implement strategies to recruit and retain a diverse faculty and staff. This can include developing partnerships with organizations that focus on supporting underrepresented groups in academia.
- **Retention Programs**: Create programs designed to support the retention of diverse students and faculty, such as professional development opportunities, networking events, and support networks.

3. COMMUNITY ENGAGEMENT

Building Alliances:

- **Stakeholder Partnerships**: Form alliances with community organizations, local businesses, and other stakeholders to support initiatives that promote social mobility and address structural barriers. These partnerships can provide additional resources and support for equity initiatives.
- **Community Involvement**: Engage community members in discussions about diversity and inclusion to ensure that educational practices and policies are responsive to the needs of the broader community.

Addressing Structural Barriers:

- **Collaborative Solutions**: Work with community organizations to identify and address systemic obstacles that impact access to education. This could involve joint efforts to advocate for policy changes or develop community-based support programs.

4. CONTINUOUS ASSESSMENT

Regular Evaluation:

- **Campus Environment**: Conduct regular assessments of the campus climate to gauge the effectiveness of diversity and inclusion efforts. This can include surveys, focus groups, and feedback mechanisms to collect input from students, faculty, and staff.
- **Student Feedback**: Gather and analyze student feedback on their experiences related to diversity and inclusion. Use this information to make data-driven decisions and improve campus practices.

Academic Outcomes:

- **Performance Metrics**: Track academic performance and success rates of students from diverse backgrounds to identify areas where additional support may be needed. Use this data to inform policy changes and resource allocation.

Institutional Reflection:

- **Policy Review**: Regularly review institutional policies and practices to ensure they align with the goals of equity and inclusion. Make necessary adjustments based on assessment findings and emerging best practices.

Promoting social diversity and justice in higher education requires a concerted effort from institutional leaders, faculty, students, and community stakeholders. By investing in faculty development, implementing targeted equity initiatives, engaging with the community, and conducting continuous assessments, higher education institutions can create transformative learning environments where all students are empowered to succeed.

Continued collaboration, advocacy, and commitment to equity are essential for advancing diversity and justice goals within higher education. Institutions that embrace these recommendations can contribute to broader societal efforts toward fairness and social justice, helping to build a more inclusive and equitable future for all.

Conclusion

Overall, we can fairly claim that the effective fusion of explicit pedagogy and inclusiveness presents a great deal of promise for improving students' academic performance and overall well-being. Teachers can create learning environments where every student feels valued, respected, and supported in their learning by fusing the rigorous methods of explicit pedagogy—which ensure a clear and structured transmission of knowledge—with the principles of inclusion, which aim to value diversity and provide support tailored to individual needs.

It's true that this integrated approach fosters greater academic performance by providing high-quality instruction tailored to each student's unique needs. Additionally, it promotes involvement and higher levels of engagement in the classroom, which supports students' emotional health and sense of belonging.

Additionally, teachers can establish learning settings where every student, regardless of individual characteristics, has the chance to achieve and develop by implementing both an explicit and inclusive approach. This benefits their academic growth as well as their personal satisfaction and readiness for success in a diverse, globalized, and ever-changing world.

Finally, this dynamic mix provides a powerful framework for improving learners' overall well-being and creating inclusive, vibrant educational communities.

The integration of explicit pedagogy with inclusive teaching practices offers a transformative approach to enhancing academic performance and overall student well-being. By combining the structured, methodical nature of explicit pedagogy with the principles of inclusion, educators can create learning environments that are both rigorous and supportive, catering to the diverse needs of all students.

Enhanced Academic Performance

Explicit pedagogy, with its emphasis on clear, structured instruction and step-by-step progression, ensures that complex concepts are conveyed in an accessible manner. This approach reduces cognitive overload and helps students build a solid foundation of knowledge. When paired with inclusive teaching practices, which adapt to students' varying backgrounds and learning styles, the result is a highly effective educational experience. Students receive the high-quality instruction they need while also benefiting from an environment that acknowledges and supports their unique needs. This combination not only improves academic outcomes but also fosters a deeper understanding of the material.

Increased Student Engagement and Well-Being

Inclusive teaching practices create a classroom atmosphere where students feel valued and respected. When students see their diverse identities reflected in the curriculum and feel supported in their learning, they are more likely to engage actively in their education. This increased engagement is closely linked to improved academic performance and a stronger sense of belonging. Students who feel emotionally supported and included are more motivated, resilient, and satisfied with their educational experience.

Development of a Supportive Learning Environment

The fusion of explicit pedagogy and inclusion helps establish learning environments where every student has the opportunity to thrive. Explicit teaching methods ensure that all students have access to clear and systematic instruction, while inclusive practices ensure that individual differences are acknowledged and accommodated. This dual approach helps create a classroom where diversity is not only recognized but celebrated, and where every student can reach their full potential.

Preparation for a Diverse World

By integrating explicit pedagogy with inclusiveness, educators prepare students for success in a diverse, globalized world. This approach equips students with the academic skills they need while also fostering intercultural understanding and empathy. As students navigate a world characterized by rapid change and increasing diversity, the combination of clear instruction and inclusive practices provides them with the tools to succeed both academically and personally.

CONCLUSION

The dynamic integration of explicit pedagogy and inclusive teaching practices presents a powerful framework for enhancing educational outcomes and fostering vibrant learning communities. By ensuring that instruction is both structured and responsive to individual needs, educators can support students' academic growth, emotional well-being, and readiness for success in a complex world. This comprehensive approach not only benefits students but also contributes to the creation of inclusive and equitable educational environments that support all learners.

In summary, the synergy between explicit pedagogy and inclusiveness holds great promise for advancing educational equity and excellence. Institutions and educators that embrace this integrated approach can significantly improve the quality of education and create a more supportive and engaging learning experience for all students.

1. Academic Achievement and Mastery

The effective fusion of explicit pedagogy and inclusiveness provides a robust framework for enhancing students' academic achievement. Explicit pedagogy's clear and systematic instructional methods ensure that students grasp fundamental concepts thoroughly. When these methods are implemented within an inclusive framework, they become even more effective. Tailoring instruction to diverse learning styles and needs allows each student to access and master the curriculum more effectively. This approach not only supports students in understanding complex material but also helps bridge gaps in knowledge, leading to higher academic performance and mastery of subjects.

2. Improved Student Retention and Success

Inclusive teaching practices, supported by explicit pedagogy, contribute significantly to student retention and success. Students who feel valued and supported in their learning environment are more likely to remain engaged and motivated throughout their educational journey. The combination of clear, structured instruction with inclusive practices addresses barriers to learning, reduces dropout rates, and enhances overall student persistence. By creating an environment where all students can thrive, institutions foster a culture of success that benefits both individual learners and the academic community as a whole.

3. Enhanced Social and Emotional Development

Incorporating explicit pedagogy with inclusive teaching practices supports not only academic growth but also social and emotional development. Students in inclusive classrooms are more likely to experience a sense of belonging and emotional security. This supportive environment helps build self-esteem, encourages positive peer interactions, and fosters a strong sense of community. As students navigate their educational experiences, they develop critical social skills, empathy, and resilience, which are essential for their overall well-being and future success.

4. Increased Diversity and Cultural Competence

An integrated approach that combines explicit pedagogy with inclusiveness actively promotes diversity and cultural competence within educational settings. Inclusive teaching practices ensure that diverse perspectives are represented and respected, while explicit pedagogy ensures that all students can access and engage with the curriculum. This approach not only enriches the learning experience but also prepares students to thrive in a multicultural world. By fostering an appreciation for diversity and developing cultural competence, educators help students build the skills necessary to navigate and contribute positively to an increasingly interconnected global society.

5. Strengthened Institutional Reputation and Commitment

Institutions that successfully implement the combination of explicit pedagogy and inclusive teaching practices enhance their reputation as leaders in educational equity and excellence. Demonstrating a commitment to providing high-quality, inclusive education not only attracts a diverse student body but also strengthens institutional relationships with stakeholders, including parents, community organizations, and funding bodies. This commitment to inclusivity and academic rigor reflects positively on the institution, contributing to its overall success and sustainability.

6. Foundation for Continuous Improvement

The integration of explicit pedagogy and inclusive practices provides a foundation for ongoing improvement and innovation in education. By regularly assessing and refining teaching methods and curricular approaches, institutions can stay responsive to evolving educational needs and societal changes. This continuous improvement process ensures that educational practices remain effective, relevant, and aligned with the principles of equity and inclusion. It also fosters a culture of reflection and growth among educators, leading to more dynamic and responsive teaching environments.

Conclusion: A Vision for Inclusive Educational Excellence

The integration of explicit pedagogy and inclusive teaching practices represents a forward-thinking approach to education that addresses the diverse needs of students while maintaining high standards of instructional clarity and effectiveness. This approach not only enhances academic achievement and personal development but also prepares students for success in a diverse and rapidly changing world.

By embracing this comprehensive framework, educators and institutions can create learning environments that are equitable, inclusive, and conducive to the success of all students. The synergy between explicit pedagogy and inclusiveness fosters a vibrant and supportive educational community, ultimately leading to a more just and effective education system. Continued dedication to these principles will ensure that educational institutions remain at the forefront of promoting equity, diversity, and excellence in education.

REFERENCES

Ainscow, M., Booth, T., & Dyson, A. (2006). *Improving schools, developing inclusion*. Routledge. DOI: 10.4324/9780203967157

Banks, J. A. (2015). *Cultural diversity and education: Foundations, curriculum, and teaching* (6th ed.). Routledge. DOI: 10.4324/9781315622255

Bohr, D., & Kearns, R. (2016). The role of faculty development in promoting inclusive teaching. *Journal of Higher Education Policy and Management*, 38(1), 57–70.

Booth, T., & Ainscow, M. (2011). *The index for inclusion: A guide to school development led by inclusive values*. Centre for Studies on Inclusive Education.

CAST. (2018). *Universal design for learning guidelines version 2.2*. CAST.

Cohen, A. M., & Brawer, F. B. (2008). *The American community college* (5th ed.). Jossey-Bass.

DeAngelo, L., & Franklin, J. (2020). Financial aid and student success: A comprehensive analysis. *Higher Education Research & Development*, 39(4), 673–689.

Engelmann, S., & Carnine, D. (1991). *Theory of instruction: Principles and applications*. ADI Press.

Florian, L., & Black-Hawkins, K. (2011). Exploring inclusive pedagogy. *British Educational Research Journal*, 37(5), 813–828. DOI: 10.1080/01411926.2010.501096

Gay, G. (2018). *Culturally responsive teaching: Theory, research, and practice* (3rd ed.). Teachers College Press.

Gurin, P., Dey, E. L., Hurtado, S., & Gurin, G. (2002). Diversity and higher education: Theory and impact on educational outcomes. *Harvard Educational Review*, 72(3), 330–367. DOI: 10.17763/haer.72.3.01151786u134n051

Hattie, J. (2009). *Visible learning: A synthesis of over 800 meta-analyses relating to achievement*. Routledge.

Kezar, A., & Maxey, D. (2014). *Understanding the role of organizational culture in change management*. Jossey-Bass.

Ladson-Billings, G. (1995). Toward a theory of culturally relevant pedagogy. *American Educational Research Journal*, 32(3), 465–491. DOI: 10.3102/00028312032003465

McClure, R. (2021). Community engagement in higher education: Bridging the gap. *Journal of Community Engagement and Higher Education at Indiana State University*, 13(2), 22–35.

Nieto, S., & Bode, P. (2018). *Affirming diversity: The sociopolitical context of multicultural education* (7th ed.). Pearson.

Perkins, R. (2020). *Higher education and social mobility: What does research tell us?* Routledge.

Rosenshine, B. (2012). Principles of instruction: Research-based strategies that all teachers should know. *American Educator*, 36(1), 12–19.

Sweller, J., Ayres, P., & Kalyuga, S. (2011). *Cognitive load theory*. Springer. DOI: 10.1007/978-1-4419-8126-4

Tinto, V. (1993). *Leaving college: Rethinking the causes and cures of student attrition*. University of Chicago Press.

Tomlinson, C. A. (2014). *The differentiated classroom: Responding to the needs of all learners* (2nd ed.). ASCD.

Tomlinson, C. A. (2017). *How to differentiate instruction in academically diverse classrooms* (3rd ed.). ASCD.

KEY TERMS AND DEFINITIONS

Inclusion: Inclusion refers to the practice of creating environments in educational settings where all individuals, regardless of their background, abilities, or differences, are welcomed, valued, and supported. It involves recognizing and addressing diverse needs, removing barriers to participation, and ensuring that every student has equal access to opportunities and resources.

Equity: Equity involves providing fair and just treatment to all individuals by recognizing and addressing disparities and differences in needs. Unlike equality, which implies treating everyone the same, equity focuses on providing varied levels of support based on individual needs to achieve fair outcomes and opportunities. In education, equity means adapting resources, support, and policies to ensure that all students have the opportunity to succeed.

Diversity: Diversity encompasses the range of differences among individuals within a group, including but not limited to race, ethnicity, gender, socioeconomic status, sexual orientation, disability, and cultural background. In educational contexts, diversity highlights the presence of varied perspectives and experiences within the student body and staff, contributing to a richer learning environment and promoting mutual understanding and respect.

Accessibility: Accessibility refers to the design and implementation of systems, resources, and environments that are usable by all individuals, including those with disabilities. In education, accessibility involves ensuring that physical spaces, digital content, and instructional materials are available and usable for students with a range of abilities and needs. This includes providing accommodations and support to facilitate equal participation in learning activities.

Empowerment: Empowerment is the process of enabling individuals to gain control over their own lives, make informed decisions, and take actions that lead to positive outcomes. In educational settings, empowerment involves fostering students' self-efficacy, confidence, and autonomy by providing them with the tools, resources, and support needed to achieve their goals and realize their full potential.

Section 3
Instructional Technologies' Global Impact

Chapter 8
Technology's Role in Enhancing Female Higher Education Access and Experience Across the MENA Region

Meryem Ouelfatmi
https://orcid.org/0000-0002-1180-9652
Sidi Mohamed Ben Abdellah University, Morocco

Sadik Madani Alaoui
Sidi Mohamed Ben Abdellah University, Morocco

Jacquelynne Anne Boivin
https://orcid.org/0000-0002-5763-5707
Bridgewater State University, USA

ABSTRACT

Women's education has a history on a global scale of being marked by struggle, strife, persistence, progress, and more. The Middle East and North Africa (MENA) countries are no exception. This chapter addresses the status of women's education varies by country, but and while "progress" can describe the status in each MENA country, each nation has areas that warrant attention for future improvement. Higher education, specifically, is a level that warrants attention due to its societal impact for women. This review of the literature provides an overview of the status of women's higher education in a variety of MENA countries and summarizes the major gains that each country has taken for women's post-secondary education

DOI: 10.4018/979-8-3693-3904-6.ch008

and what areas of improvement need to be addressed. The role that technology has played and can play in the future will be emphasized. By exploring these ideas, the goal is for readers to consider future research that can help ignite next steps in policies and structures that can promote women's access to higher education and completion of post-secondary degrees.

INTRODUCTION

Education, on a worldwide scale, is considered a tool toward "success" in many domains in life. It is common knowledge that education is a significant aspect of progress, whether on the international, national, or individual level. The world is witnessing rapid innovative advancements especially in terms of technology, affecting all the various sectors necessary for the development of countries including but not limited to healthcare, business, and most importantly education. However, in some countries, the implementation of such technological innovations is struggling to maintain the same pace. In recent decades, the MENA region has shifted focus to the digitalization of education, making efforts to implement technologies to enhance students' learning outcomes and prepare them for the job market. Despite these efforts, the process continues to face many challenges and barriers. The latter vary across countries, levels of education, infrastructure, and so on… In terms of higher education, Sherif (2014) notes that the most pertinent challenges facing higher education in the MENA region consist of the available funding allocated to this sector, the wide gap existing between countries, and the effectiveness of higher education concerning equipping students with the necessary skills to further their careers. The gap, in this case, refers to the varying levels of development; while some countries hold financial and political support, others continue to struggle to attain political stability, funds/infrastructure, and gender equality.

Equality in terms of technology access and use is one of the most pertinent issues on this matter, whether in the context of the MENA region or globally (Gillwald & Partridge, 2022). According to the authors, the digital gender gap remains a great concern and a barrier to the development of multiple countries, highlighting the lack of existing research data solely concerned with women's accessibility and use of technology.

This chapter, thus, aims to further investigate the current efforts made to reach equity in access to educational technology and resources available to support such implementation in the MENA region.

Through focusing on higher education, this chapter also bears in mind the gender disparities within the job market. The critical review of the literature on this account aims to provide insights and policy recommendations to further these efforts, in hopes of reaching an inclusive digitized education. With this, we aim to answer the following questions:

1. What are the current issues and challenges facing the implementation of technology in terms of bridging the gender gap in the MENA region?
2. How can technology be utilized effectively to further women's involvement and access to higher education?

LITERATURE REVIEW

Education in the MENA Region

The MENA region is a diverse area; culturally, historically, and economically; comprising 19 countries with high rates of gas and oil export (45% and 60%), this region holds great potential for development (O'Sullivan et al., 2011). The diversity in this region is essential to understanding the multiple factors affecting technology and access to higher education. Thus, providing insights into the existing challenges and potential recommendations for further development. This section provides an overview of the current state and reforms related to higher education across the MENA region.

The United Arab Emirates, founded in 1971, has experienced rapid progress over the past 50 years. Despite establishing its first university in 1976, which can be viewed as the start of formal education in the country, it holds various notable national and international schools. The country's adult literacy rate increased from 53.51% in 1975 to 98.29% in 2019 (United Arab Emirates - literacy rate, 2022).

The basic education consists of primary level (1-6), middle school (6-8), and high school (9-12). The UAE's educational growth can be categorized into quantitative and qualitative change, as the first solely consists of increasing enrollment rates, while the second focuses on the quality of education (Gallagher, 2019). With this in mind, the Mohammed Bin Rashid Smart Learning Program was launched in 2012, to provide technology access to students and teachers, followed by the introduction of new modules such as business management, innovation design, and life skills (Ridge et al., 2017). Such changes are not only limited to basic education but also include visions for higher education. In 2012, the government issued an iPad initiative that allowed 14000 students to access tablet computers (Miles, et al, 2021). Additionally, the 2017 Ministry initiative embodied in the National Strategy for Higher Education 2030 aims at "developing students, linking academia and the labor market, engaging the private sector in curricular development, promoting and expanding the production of research and increasing the global competitiveness of its higher education institutions by creating new and innovative academic programmes" (Ashour, 2020, p.1). Despite these efforts, the author highlights the various challenges facing higher education in the country, including institutional, cultural, language proficiency, and curriculum adaptability to the rapid change in the labor market.

Bahrain, consisting of 40 islands, is also an oil-rich country with a vision to decrease its dependence on oil. The country's formal educational system is one of the oldest in the Gulf Region as the first school was established in 1919 under the British Mandate. Bahrain's education system consists of primary and secondary stages, whereby the primary stage is constituted of two cycles (cycle 1: grade 1 to 3, cycle 2: grade 4 to 6) and the second stage consists of one cycle (grade 7 to 9). According to the Federal Reserve Bank of St Louis Open Data, the latest record (15 years and above) shows that Bahrain has a 97.87% literacy rate. Bahrain's interests in the development of education are also apparent in the Economic Vision 2030 for Bahrain, which aims at providing institutional support for teachers, assessing the educational system to ensure efficiency and quality, and investing in advanced skills and research in efforts to be a knowledge-based economy (Mosly, 2022). As a constituent of the GCC (Gulf Cooperation Council), the country prioritizes the integration and use of technology in education, intending to equip students with the necessary skills to not only integrate the dynamic national job market but also the international ((Wiseman & Anderson, 2012; Razzak, 2017).

In contrast, some countries in the MENA region struggle to provide basic education due to political and civil unrest. Such circumstances are a great barrier for the development and even sustainability of education. Countries experiencing such unrest deal with issues such as increased rates of school dropouts, unemployment, and mental health issues, which are consequently detrimental to education (Haraki & Drwish, 2023). For instance, in the case of Palestine, the number of student dropouts varies from one area to another, being the highest in Gaza as opposed to the West Bank (Chamdimba et al, 2022). Access to technology, in this case, depends on a variety of factors, including but not limited to socio-economic, gender and even political (Aburub & Assaf, 2022).

Similarly, Almasri, et al (2019) highlight the vulnerability of schools in the case of the Syrian conflict which has affected enrollment rates, equitable access to education, and the displacement of millions of people in search of safety. Alongside the economic crisis, priority is given to reaching stability and security, leaving the Syrian educational system to suffer (Dryden-Peterson, 2015). Thus, when dealing with a region as diverse as the Middle East, it is essential to keep in mind these varying factors.

Similar to the case of Syria and Palestine, Sudan is a country witnessing political unrest due to the military takeover in 2021. According to the UNICEF education annual report (2021), the country's basic education is suffering major barriers despite recent efforts to raise enrollment rates. The report highlights the inequity in terms of access to education, the inefficiency of institutional management, the lack of stable and safe learning environments, and insufficient funds and investment especially in terms of public education. Policymaking in this country is multifaceted and is considered one of the biggest barriers to the development of the educational system. On this account, Alamin et al. (2022) conclude that, based on qualitative evidence synthesis, there is an inconsistency in terms of an agent of policymaking, highlighting a lack of coordination and implementation. The authors also note that the existing educational policies are not designed or implemented based on the country's needs but rather based on external influence. Acknowledging the social, economic, political and even historical factors when designing an educational policy is crucial, as the efficiency of such policies depends on whether it aligns with and fulfills the specific needs of the educational system in question.

Although holding abundant natural gas and oil reserves, Libya is also a country with a history of political instability and transformation. After its independence, the government made many efforts to create a unified cultural identity that intertwined with education, as religious schools were reopened alongside other educational institutions. With these efforts, the number of schools and students (especially female students) significantly increased and the focus on education increased especially after the 1969 revolution (Appleton, 1993). The educational system struggled further with the Arab Spring in 2011 and the civil war that ensued in 2014, making the execution of educational reforms difficult to accomplish. Similar to the case of Sudan, Libya also lacks a curriculum that is specifically designed for it, especially in higher education. As Elabbar (2017) states "the education authority simply authorizes their national university managers to apply whatever policy they personally feel is most suitable; this point has caused differences between universities and even faculties" (p.16). This, consequently, creates a gap between the skill sets and qualifications available for students and the expectations of the job market both on the national and international level, especially considering the language bans enforced (Tamtam et al, 2010).

As in any other country, education is an important aspect of the Tunisian government. According to the UNICEF Education Budget Brief (2022), the Tunisian allocated budget for education increased from 4.2 billion Dinars in 2010 to 5.7 billion Dinars in 2020. Despite this, the educational system faces numerous challenges, mainly due to the fast-paced cultural, social, and economic changes. Since its independence in 1956, Tunisia has established many reforms to provide access and quality basic education to all citizens. The government's Arabization policy, also present in neighboring countries with a history of colonization, aimed to unify the Tunisian national identity and eliminate the colonialist influence, which remains latent but persistent (Ben Salah et al., 2022). Additionally, despite the high rate of enrollment, the unemployment rate remains high, highlighting the gap between the provided educational skills and the labor market (Flayols et al., 2019). This gap is also apparent in the reforms pertaining to higher education, as Ben-Khalifa (2024) discusses "One of the main problems manifests itself in the mismatch between theory and practice. This means that what had been planned for as theories to reform our higher education remained at the level of papers" (p. 9).

TECHNOLOGY AND HIGHER EDUCATION EXPERIENCE

Overview of Technology-Enhanced Learning

In this fast-paced innovative era, technology has become indispensable across various aspects of our lives. Since the onset of the pandemic, educational systems across the world, namely in the MENA region, have recognized the unexplored potential of technology incorporation. With the rise of demand for digital skills as a crucial part of 21st-century skills, technology has reshaped students' engagement with course material, academic networks, and access to resources. This has led to the implementation of technology-enhanced learning.

Kirkwood & Price (2013) regard Technology-Enhanced Learning (TEL) as "the application of information and communication technologies to teaching and learning" (p.1). TEL can also be defined as "'any online facility or system that directly supports learning and teaching" (Jenkins et al., 2011, p.448). This definition provides the main objective of TEL: using technologies to improve the learning and teaching experience. The effectiveness of the educational experience is dependent on the quality of the learning and thus, relies also on the quality of teaching.

According to The Higher Education Funding Council for England (2009), there are three main gains efficient technology-enhanced learning can provide: efficiency, enhancement, and transformation. Efficiency in this case is related to decreasing expenditure, while enhancement entails the improvement of the learning journey and consequently the learning outcomes. Finally, transformation denotes significant changes to implemented methods or the creation and implementation of new ones.

However, the process of technology implementation, especially in the case of some MENA countries, has been on a superficial level. Livingstone (2012) states that "schools proving slower to change their lesson plan than they were to fit computers in the classroom" (p.9). In other words, educational change tends to be difficult to achieve especially when there is a lack of institutional support and training. In this case, many confuse technology-enhanced learning with simply using technologies such as PowerPoint or YouTube videos in class (Swanwick, 2013).

Since the end of the 19th century, educational systems have attempted to employ various technologies to enhance the learning process. One of the earliest educational technologies was introduced by Sidney L. Pressey in the 1920s. The teaching machine aimed to individualize the learning experience by allowing the students to interact with the provided questions or tasks. Considering the historical context, the introduction of the automated teaching machine highlights the industrial revolution's impact on education. At the time, as Petrina (2004) "For progressive educators and psychologists in general, society was antagonistic to the individual; schooling threatened individuality and human nature. The Automatic Teacher would simultaneously normalize, socialize, and liberate" (p.307). Decades later and with the rise of the behaviorist school of thought in the 1950s, Skinner's teaching provided an immediate response to the students with a reward system. Through this, the teaching machine controls students' learning behavior. This view on the learning process faced various criticisms, including but not limited to, as discussed by Benjamin (1988), concerns regarding efficacy, dehumanizing nature, and lack of teacher-student interaction. Similar to any technology adoption process, the implementation of these teaching machines has faced reluctance. The behavior control aspect was criticized and resulted in the fear of losing human agency (Green, 1968), as well as the machine's inability to effectively and wholly instruct all subjects. Margolis (1963) gave the example of poetry, stating that poems can be taught by machines but their appreciation and interpretation cannot.

Even with the current high demand for technology in the educational context, especially after the pandemic, there remains a need for educational change (Di Stasio & Miotti, 2021). In relation to STEM education, Virtual Lab (VL) environment gained major interest by the scientific community. Virtual labs are defined as "simulation environments that give students the opportunity to safely conduct practical experiments at their own pace transcending the barriers of physical and material spaces" (Elmoazen et al., 2023, p.1). Hong & Ghanavati (2022) highlight three assets of virtual labs in engineering education. According to the authors, virtual labs can help decrease expenditure, allowing for fast development of prototypes. Additionally, particularly in the case of large-scale projects, virtual lab simulations provide the ability to creatively and comprehensively experiment with design. These benefits are not only limited to higher education but can also help middle school students apply their theoretical knowledge and individually enhance their scientific learning (Liu et al., 2015). Based on the literature, as discussed by the systematic review provided by Mercado & Picardal (2023), virtual labs are highly beneficial to scientific education, namely in terms of biotechnology, however are not capable of replacing traditional labs.

With Web 2.0 technologies becoming prevalent, which allow for user interaction and engagement, higher education institutions across the world showed great interest in their adoption (Escofet & Marimon, 2010). The need for active learning and collaboration within higher education has resulted in the development of learning management systems. The latter can be viewed as an "education hub that provides a large and indispensable set of features to support educational activities such as classroom learning, distance education, and continuing education" (Al Mansoori et al., 2023, p. 558). In other words, learning management systems attempt to move the educational process to the digital world, not only providing organizational features, but also allowing students to take charge of their learning progress. An effective learning management system, according to Rosário & Dias (2022), needs to adhere to web and instructional design criteria. Web design relates to accessibility, meaning that it is only accessible to users affiliated with its educational institution (Labus et al., 2012). Moreover, each login page is designed based on the user providing varying specific features (course material and assessment for students and managerial features for teachers and administration for example). The instructional design criteria, in this case, entails establishing relevance to the learning objectives and the overall institutional educational vision, which can also consider language use and assessment design among other features (Snae & Brückner, 2008).

Overall, the interest in the effective implementation of technology enhanced learning remains on the rise. To ensure this, educators need to consider five elements: consistency, frequency, focus, network, and training (Kennedy & Dunn, 2018). According to the authors, to enhance the learning process, the use of technology must be consistent and frequently implemented while adhering to the specific learning needs and objectives of students. Moreover, institutional support and training must be available for both teachers and students, creating a space for connectedness and networking.

Global Trends in Technology Adoption: Challenges and Opportunities

One of the newly developed and widely adopted tools in education are Massive Open Online Courses (MOOCs). The latter can be defined as "online courses for the purpose of education are characterized by being accessible and scalable in the sense that anyone can access them" (Al-Rahmi et al., 2019, p. 2197). Based on this definition, MOOCs are characterized by their ability to defy the physical and time restrictions of traditional education. MOOCs can be categorized into three groups based on their emergence and approach (Zawacki-Richter et al., 2018). The first generation of MOOCS adopted a learner-centered methodology, allowing students to be the focus of the learning experience and encouraging peer-to-peer interaction

(Connectivism and Connectedness Knowledge (CCK08) offered by the University of Manitoba). The second generation was characterized by a teacher-centered approach, providing instructional material for learners but lacking active student interaction (Introduction to AI provided by Stanford University). Finally, the third generation attempted to combine the previously mentioned approaches to optimize the learning experience (Learning how to learn offered by University of California, San Diego, and McMaster). Although MOOCS possess a wide range of educational resources, literature shows that there are still a few concerns to address. For students, the self-regulated learning provided by these courses may increase chances of dropouts as well as increased cases of cheating (Kennedy (2014); Conole (2015)). Additionally, due to the large scale of learners, technical support may not always be accessible or able to fulfill the demands of all the students. Similarly, educators also note barriers when utilizing MOOCS, including but not limited to evaluation and assessment, student feedback and resources (Hew & Cheung, 2014)

Recently, the concept of gamification, coined in the early 2000s by Nick Pelling, has re-emerged as a popular educational approach. As the term entails, gamification refers to "an informal umbrella term for the use of video game elements in non-gaming systems to improve user experience (UX) and user engagement" (Deterding et al., 2011, p. 1). This approach directly and positively influences students' learning and academic performance (Filsecker & Hickey, 2014). As the literature demonstrates, gamification can be beneficial in various contexts such as medical studies (Knight et al., 2010) and work productivity (Unger et al., 2013). Although some studies found no direct significant effect of gamification on learners' motivation (Thom et al., 2012), others provided evidence of the role of rewards in enhancing retention and overall learning. In order to achieve an efficient implementation of gamification within education, Karnad, A. (2014) discusses a few points to put into consideration. The latter can be summarized as internal and external. The internal factors relate to the design and structure of the game, meaning that an effective educational game needs to stimulate cognitive skills while limiting distractions. To achieve this the author highlights the need for outsourcing expertise. The external aspects correspond to the post-design stage and consists of establishing the educational objectives, strategy of implementation that adheres to the institution and students' need, as well as providing the necessary infrastructure and tech support.

Innovations within the world of technology have resulted in the rise of immersive technologies, which not only revolutionized the entertainment and business world but also education. Commonly used immersive technologies include Virtual Reality (VR) and Augmented Reality (AR) which aim to alter users' perception. According to Tuomi et al. (2023), VR refers to "a fully artificial environment that a user can interact with", while AR "involves super-imposing digital content onto the real world" (p.21). These virtual environments are characterized by their focus on visual representation, allowing for deeper and safer exploration of procedures and/or objects (Liubchak et al., 2022). AR and VR can be implemented to enhance the learning process across various fields of study and research (history (Kysela & Štorková, 2015), anatomy (Ahmad et al., 2022; Saputro & Saputra, 2015), chemistry (Kamelia, 2015). The immersive feature of these technologies enhances user engagement and concentration, thus, increasing learners' knowledge acquisition and effectiveness (Eutsler & Long, 2021). In relation to engineering education, Kaur et al. (2022) discuss the benefits and drawbacks of utilizing AR and VR technologies in education. According to the author both technologies allow for visual presentation of prototypes and the optimization of knowledge acquisition and recall. However, the implementation and maintenance of such technologies can be costly, especially when there is a lack of funding and investment.

With the emergence of Artificial Intelligence (AI), Generative AI technologies gained notoriety and interest from users across various fields. The latter refers to a "form of AI that can autonomously generate new content, such as text, images, audio, and video" (Lv, 2023, p.208). According to the author, the basis of generative AI is based on machine learning. The latter consists of, as its name entails, employing the learning process in the generation of data. In other words, machine learning is based on imitating human thought processes which allows the creation of original output (Ayodele, 2010). Similar to the previously discussed technologies, generative AI can be utilized across various fields. In terms of the professional world, such technologies allow time reduction, especially regarding repetitive tasks, facilitate the generation of ideas, decision-making, and IT development procedures (Nhavkar, 2023). Along similar lines, Chen et al. (2023) highlight the role of generative AI in facilitating the financial decision-making process through the ability to analyze and classify information from financial documents or various types and sources. Additionally, the authors also discuss the immense potential of AI technologies in risk management for investors and startups as well as service customization of service for both professionals and customers. Within the educational context, Hancock et al. (2023) discuss AI technologies' ability to assist both teachers and students. Based on their discussion, teachers can utilize such technologies to enhance the quality of course content, allowing for the innovative creation of course material. For students, they can provide personalized instruction and evaluation based on learners' styles and educational needs, ensuring equality and equity for those unable to afford private tutoring. Despite the benefits, the implementation of AI technologies in the educational setting raises a few concerns. One of the major issues raised in this respect related to ethics and research responsibility. Chan & Hu (2023) and Malik et al. (2023) highlight a significant influence of AI technology use on students' academic misconduct, namely in relation to plagiarism. Additionally, information provided by these systems is not always free from bias and misinformation. On this account,

Bala & Colvin (2023) state that "when asked to justify a nonsensical response, it will use the same techniques, resulting in a reasonable-sounding but false answer" (p. 4). Thus, the implementation of generative AI, whether by students or teachers, in education necessitates regulation and guidance.

Overall, the interest in technology adoption and use to enhance the learning journey continues to rise. Similar to any innovation adoption process, specialized strategies need to be put in place. Schneckenberg (2010) highlights the importance of developing competence, which, according to the author, highly depends on organizational support and change. Moreover, Kotrlik & Redmann (2009) note that barriers to technology adoption face various challenges, focusing on issues pertaining to technology-related anxiety, institutional support/training, and gender. The latter is a major concern, especially in the context of the MENA region, which will be further discussed in the following section.

GENDER DISPARITIES IN HIGHER EDUCATION IN THE MENA REGION

Review of Gender-Related Challenges in the MENA Region

Despite the cultural, technological, and ideological development the world has witnessed, gender equality remains a challenge. Ensuring gender equality is the basis of any successful developed modern state, especially in support of female inclusion in the labor market (Adler, 2004). In this respect, according to the World Bank, female participation in the labor market has significantly increased by 47% from the 60s to the 2000s (as cited in Metcalfe, 2006, p. 96).

According to the Human Development Report (2019), female students have a higher completion rate (78%) of secondary education. In terms of higher education, female students make up 77% of university students (Maier, 2013). Regardless, female students continue to struggle to prove their competencies and skills, namely in terms of STEM education, due to male push-back. In this respect, the systematic review of Alzaabi et al. (2021) demonstrates the existing gender gap and prejudice yielding lack of resource accessibility and opportunities, hindering female STEM education and, consequently, job market integration. As an emerging knowledge-based economy with a modernisation vision, the UAE has made efforts to encourage female inclusion across various sectors. In terms of business and entrepreneurship, Emirati women significantly contribute to the country's economy (3.6 billion dollars), the majority of which stems from female-owned businesses (Al-Ansari et al., 2013). With the country's interest in globalization, various efforts have been established to support female entrepreneurial endeavors, including but not limited to establishment of funding institutions (Goby & Erogul, 2011), female entrepreneurship continues to be challenged. In this respect, Tlaiss (2014) highlights the major barriers to female entrepreneurship, the most significant of which are social expectations. Women are expected to prioritize their household responsibilities at the expense of their career ambitions. This, according to the author, along with lack of accessibility to funds (higher interest rates and collateral share), affects women's confidence in their business capabilities. Additionally, the authors emphasize the detrimental impact of the lack of familial support. This is also supported by Al Marzouqi & Forster (2011) who discuss family support as one of the significant factors of lack of female inclusion in the IT industry. The authors argue that male-dominated industries such as IT, especially when merged with patriarchal ideologies, lack female representation. This, in turn, negatively influences women's attitudes, thus discouraging female students from pursuing such careers. On this account, Jabeen & Faisal (2018) recommend "designing specialized programs/courses in synergy with higher educational institutions in the UAE, which will help the female entrepreneurs in enhancing their management skills and competencies for further growth and development" (p. 248).

Due to geographical proximity and cultural similarity, Bahrain's government has also been making efforts to close the gender gap within education and the job market. With the establishment of the National Plan for the Advancement of Bahraini Women plan in 2013, the number of female graduates increased surpassing their counterpart's rate (Sinha, 2020). Additionally, female students show higher performance in terms of Mathematics as early as the 4th and 8th grades (Mullis et al., 2016). However, similar to the case of the UAE, women struggle to attain opportunities in leadership and management, especially those of high ranking, due to cultural and institutional barriers (Al-Alawi, 2016). Despite the legislative and non-governmental empowerment efforts, as Sinha (2020) states, "Societal expectations lead women to voluntarily or involuntarily opt out of the progression in her role as a worker or drop out of the formal employment sector to focus on domestic responsibilities" (p.52). As this perspective is widely held by the male population, female integration and flourishing within education and the labor market remain a challenge.

Preceding the economic crisis 2011, the Syrian government has reduced the gender gap by 93% (Zaatari, 2013). According to Ramadan et al. (2021), female enrollment rates within the context of basic education ranged between 94% (second cycle) and 98% (first cycle). The authors highlight that one of the major barriers, post-crisis, is the lack of security. As previously mentioned, education takes a secondary priority level in the absence of political stability. This, combined with the economic crisis, consequently limits the accessibility and affordability of pursuing education regardless of gender. Almelhem et al. (2022) emphasize the role of societal factors and religious ideologies in limiting Syrian female education enrollment and completion, which also affect their pursuit of higher education and post-graduate positions (Dalati, 2021). As previously mentioned, political instability, particularly in the case of armed conflict, not only affects the stability and development of the educational system but also hinders the psychological and welfare of students. Moreover, in times of crisis, women tend to take on additional burdens and responsibilities (El-Bushra et al., 2002). Armed conflict, in the case of Palestine, has led to dispersion of civilians and even the educational system, subjugating it to various curricula, which are not free from colonialism influence (Najim, 2023). Although the right to education is one of the basics of human rights, it has become more of a privilege due to the constant attacks, destruction of infrastructure, and lack of accessibility (Salem, 2023). Despite this, education remains a crucial aspect of Palestinian communities, as "For many Palestinian refugees, education provides a sense of hope that they will eventually be able to utilize educational skills in the rebuilding of their country" (Shalhoub-Kevorkian, 2008, p.183). Najim (2023) conducted a mixed methods study focusing on female leadership in higher education in order to investigate the perceived challenges. The findings highlight the significance of social, cultural, and political challenges, followed by organizational and management barriers, and family, psychological, and subjective restrictions ranking last. However, the overall restriction in the context appears to be male bias, which results in social pressure and lack of organizational support.

Similarly, as previously mentioned, Sudan is a country struggling with political conflict, rendering the female educational journey challenging to fulfill. In addition to crisis and gender-based violence, which are one of the leading causes of dropouts, a key barrier to female education in Sudan is child marriage (Maper, 2024). Furthermore, due to the economic state of the country and individuals, the affordability and quality of education is an additional concern, leading to the lack of infrastructure, teachers, and gender-aware curriculum (Onia, 2021). Similarly, the Libyan case highlights comparable concerns. Despite diminishing the gender gap after the 2011 revolution, women continue to struggle with gaining access to positions of power due to bias (Rashed, 2017). The author demonstrates an additional point to consider within the Libyan social fabric, which is tribalism. The study highlights that there are divergent attitudes attributed to each of these tribes, for example, staff pertaining to the Abou-Hmirah tribe tend to be trusted more in decision-making within the workplace. Thus, this has the potential to add additional bias and prejudice to women belonging to underrepresented and/or marginalized groups. Although legislatively speaking, no significant barrier was reported (Al-ghariani, 2024), social and cultural factors remain of influence on accessibility and completion of education, particularly in the case of female students in rural areas (Elazhari, 2021). This goes along with the context of Tunisia. While this country has made various efforts to diminish the gender gap within education, access to education across rural areas remains a concern (Fűrész et al., 2023). Additionally, despite being often characterized as a secular country, "the mass consciousness of Tunisians maintains a set of ideas and norms on gender inequality generated by Islamic tradition" (Kashina, 2021, p.15). Whether stemming from the mainstream uninformed Islamic perspectives on gender roles or not, discrimination against women in education and the workplace continues to be a major detrimental factor for the development of educational systems, economic growth, and social justice.

CONCLUSION

The literature discussed in this paper highlights the vast potential of technology in enhancing the educational journey for both students and teachers. Moreover, an efficient implementation of technology adoption can facilitate reducing the gender gap and sexism, while fostering equity. However, the literature has also highlighted various barriers facing female education in the MENA region. The latter can be summarized into four categories: cultural/ ideological, policymaking/design, economic, and institutional. The major issue that is widely shared across the MENA region is the pressure to confine to traditional patriarchal conceptions of gender roles. Although some constitutions of countries in this region explicitly prohibit discrimination against women and encourage gender equality, others do not. Even with legislative support, the social pressure for women to prioritize family over their careers remains one of the most significant detrimental factors in this respect. Additionally, the MENA region consists of countries of varying economic and political conditions which necessitates consideration, especially regarding program design and policy change. Regarding economically challenged and politically unstable states, as well as those considered stable, further efforts are required in terms of infrastructure, access to technology, and tech support. Countries within the MENA region have shown interest in encouraging female education; however, further efforts need to be established and reinforced in hopes of not only decreasing the gender gap but also enhancing the efficiency and equity of education.

RECOMMENDATIONS AND FUTURE RESEARCH

Based on previously discussed barriers to female education in the MENA region, it is imperative to highlight key recommendations that can aid in achieving an efficient inclusive education. On a large scale, designing a program or initiative that is generalizable to the MENA region would be inefficient and inapplicable due to the varying conditions among such countries. Thus, further research is needed and encouraged on a national and even regional level. Moreover, as traditional patriarchal perceptions are one of the most significantly influential factors in this respect, the focus of women empowerment initiatives should not only be consecrated to female students but also be inclusive of their male counterparts. Based on the overview provided in this paper, the following recommendations, which can be applicable on the national level, can be made.

· The establishment of legislative modification to explicitly prohibit discrimination against women is essential. However, the reinforcement and application of such laws and policies are of greater importance.
· The design of programs and initiatives allowing female empowerment must be based on the needs and resources of each country. This allows to shift focus on gender and regional disparities, thus, encouraging inclusion of minorities. It is also essential to consider the continuous evaluation of the efficiency of such initiatives to further design innovation and implementation.
· The use and adoption of technology, particularly in countries of challenging economic and political instability, requires external as well as national funding opportunities. Additionally, available media can be utilized to increase female representation.

REFERENCES

Aburub, I., & Assaf, D. (2022). *Digital Transformation of Higher Education in Palestine: Employment, Obstacles, and Trends*. Baltic Journal of Law & Politics., DOI: 10.2478/bjlp-2022-002041

Adler, N. (2004). Shaping history: Global Leadership in The Twenty-First Century. In Scullion, H., & Lineham, M. (Eds.), *International human resource management: A critical text* (pp. 281–297). Palgrave.

Ahmad, I., Samsugi, S., & Irawan, Y. (2022). Penerapan Augmented Reality Pada Anatomi Tubuh Manusia Untuk Mendukung Pembelajaran Titik Titik Bekam Pengobatan Alternatif. *Jurnal Teknoinfo*, 16(1), 46. Advance online publication. DOI: 10.33365/jti.v16i1.1521

Al-Alawi, A. I. l. (2016, July). Status of Bahraini Women in The Banking and Financial Sector: Challenges and Opportunities. *Journal of International Women's Studies*, 17(4), 210–228.

Al-Ansari, Y., Pervan, S. & Xu, J. (2013). Innovation and Business Performance of SMEs: The Case of Dubai. *Education, Business and Society: Contemporary Middle Eastern Issues*, Vol. 6Nos 3/4, pp. 162-180.

Al Mansoori, A., Ali, S., Pasha, S. A., Alghizzawi, M., Elareshi, M., Ziani, A., & Alsridi, H. (2023). Technology Enhanced Learning Through Learning Management System and Virtual Reality Googles: A Critical Review. *Studies in Systems, Decision and Control*, 557–564. DOI: 10.1007/978-3-031-28314-7_48

Al Marzouqi, H. A., & Forster, N. (2011). An Exploratory Study of the Underrepresentation of Emirate Women in The United Arab Emirates' Information Technology Sector. *Equality, Diversity and Inclusion*, 30(7), 544–562. DOI: 10.1108/02610151111167016

Al-Rahmi, W., Aldraiweesh, A., Yahaya, N., Bin Kamin, Y., & Zeki, A. M. (2019). Massive Open Online Courses (MOOCs): Data on Higher Education. *Data in Brief*, 22, 118–125. DOI: 10.1016/j.dib.2018.11.139 PMID: 30581914

Alamin, A., Muthanna, A., & Alduais, A. (2022). A Qualitative Evidence Synthesis of The K-12 Education Policy Making in Sudan and the Need for Reforms. *SAGE Open*, 12(1), 215824402110710. DOI: 10.1177/21582440211071081

Alghariani, M. (2024). Libyan Women: Examining Their Educational Reality and Contribution to Economic Development.

Almasri, N., Tahat, L., Skaf, S., & Masri, A. A. (2019). *A Digital Platform for Supervised Self-Directed Learning in Emergencies: The Case of The Syrian Crisis. Technology, Pedagogy and Education*, 28(1), 91–113. DOI: 10.1080/1475939X.2019.1568293

Almelhem, S., Almshhor, E., Alabdullah, S., Kadan, B., Alzoabi, M., & Jhar, A. (2022). Factors Affecting Gender Balance In Higher Education In Northwest Syria: Challenges And Potential Actions. *International Journal of Educational Research Open*, 3, 100164. DOI: 10.1016/j.ijedro.2022.100164

Alzaabi, I., Ramírez-García, A., & Moyano, M. (2021). Gendered STEM: A Systematic Review and Applied Analysis of Female Participation in STEM in The United Arab Emirates. *Education Sciences*, 11(10), 573. DOI: 10.3390/educsci11100573

Appleton, L. A. (1993). *Educational Development in Western Libya, 1942-1952: A Critical Assessment of the Aims.* Methods and Policies of the British Military Administration.

Ashour, S. (2020). Quality Higher Education is the Foundation of a Knowledge Society: Where Does the UAE Stand? *Quality in Higher Education*, 26(2), 209–223. Advance online publication. DOI: 10.1080/13538322.2020.1769263

Ayodele, T. (2010). Machine Learning Overview. .DOI: 10.5772/9374

Bala, K., & Colvin, A. (2023). *Generative Artificial Intelligence for Education and Pedagogy.*

Ben-Khalifa, T. (2024). A Critical Perspective to Higher Education in the 21st Century Tunisia: The Problems of the Present and the Challenges of the Future. Trends in Education and Educational Studies, 1(1), 1-13 ceiling or sticky floor? *Journal of North African Studies*, 28(4), 976–1005. DOI: 10.1080/13629387.2022.2113992

Ben Salah, M., Chambru, C., & Fourati, M. (2022). The colonial Legacy of Education: Evidence from Tunisia. SSRN *Electronic Journal*. https://doi.org/DOI: 10.2139/ssrn.4101795

Benjamin, L. T. (1988). A History of Teaching Machines. *The American Psychologist*, 43(9), 703–712. DOI: 10.1037/0003-066X.43.9.703

Chamdimba, P., Ahed-Ahmad, B., Ouedraogo, A., Mizunoya, S., Angieri, R., Amaro, D., Mishra, S., & Kelly, P. (2022). Palestine Education Fact Sheets https://data.unicef.org/wp-content/uploads/2022/12/2022Palestine-Education-Fact-Sheet-2022FINAL.pdf

Chan, C. K. Y., & Hu, W. (2023). Students' Voices on Generative AI: Perceptions, Benefits, and Challenges in Higher Education. *International Journal of Educational Technology in Higher Education*, 20(1), 43. Advance online publication. DOI: 10.1186/s41239-023-00411-8

Chen, B., Wu, Z., & Zhao, R. (2023). From Fiction to Fact: The Growing Role of Generative AI in Business and Finance. SSRN *Electronic Journal*. DOI: 10.2139/ssrn.4528225

Conole, G. (2015). Designing Effective MOOCs. Educational Media International, 52(4), 239–252. https://doi.org/. *Current Issues in Comparative Education*, 20(1), 45–67.DOI: 10.1080/09523987.2015.1125989

Dalati, S. (2021). Factors Affecting Syrian Female Researchers' Experience During Crisis: Inductive Approach. *Business. Management and Economics Engineering*, 19(01), 91–110. DOI: 10.3846/bmee.2021.13232

Deterding, S., Sicart, M., Nacke, L., O'Hara, K., & Dixon, D. (2011). Gamification: Using Game-Design Elements in Non-Gaming Contexts. In Proceedings of the 2011 Annual Conference Extended Abstracts on Human Factors In Computing Systems - CHI EA '11 (p. 2425). *New York, USA: ACM Press*. DOI: 10.1145/1979742.1979575

Di Stasio, M., & Miotti, B. (2021). Perspectives for School: Maker Approach, Educational Technologies and Laboratory Approach, New Learning Spaces. *Makers at School, Educational Robotics and Innovative Learning Environments*, 3–9. DOI: 10.1007/978-3-030-77040-2_1

Dryden-Peterson, S. (2015). *The Educational Experiences of Refugee Children in Countries of First Asylum*. Migration Policy Institute., Retrieved from https://www.migrationpolicy.org/sites/default/files/publications/FCD_Dryen-PetersonFINAL-WEB.pdf

El-Bushra, J., El-Karib, A., & Hadjipateras, A. (2002). *Gender-Sensitive Programme Design and Planning in Conflict-Affected Situations*. ACORD.

Elabbar, D.A. (2017). Libyan Political Conflict: Effects on Higher Education Development.

Elazhari, E. S. (2021). Cultural Impact on Social Position and Women's Education in Libya. [IJSRP]. *International Journal of Scientific and Research Publications*, 11(4), 425–427. DOI: 10.29322/IJSRP.11.04.2021.p11257

Elmoazen, Ramy & López-Pernas, Sonsoles & Misiejuk, Kamila & Khalil, Mohammad & Wasson, Barbara & Saqr, Mohammed. (2023). Reflections on Technology-enhanced Learning in Laboratories: Barriers and Opportunities.

Escofet, A., & Marimon, M. (2010). Web 2.0 and Collaborative Learning in Higher Education. *Web-Based Education*, 699–714. DOI: 10.4018/978-1-61520-963-7.ch047

Eutsler, L., & Long, C. S. (2021). Preservice Teachers' Acceptance of Virtual Reality to Plan Science Instruction. *Journal of Educational Technology & Society*, 24(2), 28–43. https://www.jstor.org/stable/27004929

Filsecker, M., & Hickey, D. T. (2014). A Multilevel Analysis of The Effects of External Rewards on Elementary Students' Motivation, Engagement and Learning in an Educational Game. *Computers &amp. Computers & Education*, 75, 136–148. DOI: 10.1016/j.compedu.2014.02.008

Flayols, A., Jongerius, D., & Bel-Air, F. (2019) Tunisia: Education, Labour Market, Migration. *The Dutch Ministry of Foreign Affairs*, 9 Apr. 2019.

Fűrész, E., Szabóné Tóth, É., Tóth, K., & Amariei, D. (2023). Adult Education's Role in Rural Development and Women's Empowerment in Tunisia and Hungary: Exploring Cross-Regional Collaboration, Growth Opportunities, and Gender-Inclusive Strategies. *Studia Mundi – Economica, 10*(1), 14–25. https://doi.org/DOI: 10.18531/sme.vol.10.no.1.pp.14-25

Gallagher, K. (2019). Challenges and Opportunities in Sourcing, Preparing and Developing a Teaching Force for the UAE. *Education in the United Arab Emirates*, 127–145. DOI: 10.1007/978-981-13-7736-5_8

Gillwald, A., & Partridge, A. (2022). Gendered Nature of Digital Inequality - UN Women. https://www.unwomen.org/sites/default/files/2022-12/BP.1_Alison%20Gillwald.pdf

Goby, V., & Erogul, M. (2011). Female Entrepreneurship in The United Arab Emirates: Legislative Encouragements and Cultural Constraints. *Women's Studies International Forum*, 34(4), 329–334. DOI: 10.1016/j.wsif.2011.04.006

Greene, M. (1968). Technology and the Human Person. *Teachers College Record*, 69(4), 385–393. DOI: 10.1177/016146816806900404

Hancock, R. S. B., Azhar, S., Mezei, S., Aas, M. B., & Gijsbertsen, B. (2023). Reconsidering Education Policy in the Era of Generative AI. Global Solutions. Retrieved from https://www.global-solutions-initiative.org/policy_brief/reconsidering-education-policy-in-the-era-of-generative-ai/

Haraki, O. A., & Drwish, D. H. (2023). The Impact of the Syrian Conflict on the Educational and Behavioral Development of Students: Insights from Intermediate School Teachers in Homs City. *PáGinas De EducacióN/Páginas De Educación, 16*(2), 85–110. DOI: 10.22235/pe.v16i2.3172

Hew, K. F., & Cheung, W. S. (2014). Students' and Instructors' Use of Massive Open Online Courses (MOOCs): Motivations and Challenges. *Educational Research Review*, 12, 45–58. DOI: 10.1016/j.edurev.2014.05.001

Hong, B., & Ghanavati, A. (2022). The Virtual Laboratory: A Natural Vehicle for Simulation in Engineering Education. *ASEE-NE 2022 Proceedings*. DOI: 10.18260/1-2--42213

Jabeen, F., & Faisal, M. N. (2018). Imperatives for Improving Entrepreneurial Behavior Among Females in the UAE. *Gender in Management*, 33(3), 234–252. DOI: 10.1108/GM-03-2016-0042

Jenkins, M., Browne, T., Walker, R., & Hewitt, R. (2011). The development of Technology Enhanced Learning: Findings from a 2008 Survey of UK Higher Education Institutions. *Interactive Learning Environments*, 19(5), 447–465. DOI: 10.1080/10494820903484429

Kamelia, L. (2015). Perkembangan Teknologi Augmented Reality Sebagai Media Pembelajaran Interaktif Pada Mata Kuliah Kimia Dasar. *JURNAL ISTEK*, 9(1). https://journal.uinsgd.ac.id/index.php/istek/artic le/view/184

Karnad, A. (2014). *Trends in educational technologies*. The London School of Economics and Political Science.

Kashina, A. (2021). "Gender Equality in Tunisia: Current Trends" JOSSTT 1(01):04. DOI: https://doi.org/DOI: 10.52459/josstt1140721

Kaur, D. P., Kumar, A., Dutta, R., & Malhotra, S. (2022). The Role of Interactive and Immersive Technologies in Higher Education: A Survey. *Journal of Engineering Education Transformations*, 36(2), 79–86. DOI: 10.16920/jeet/2022/v36i2/22156

Kennedy, M., & Dunn, T. J. (2018). Improving the Use of Technology Enhanced Learning Environments in Higher Education in the UK: A Qualitative Visualization of Students' Views. *Contemporary Educational Technology*, 9(1). Advance online publication. DOI: 10.30935/cedtech/6212

Kirkwood, A., & Price, L. (2013). Technology-enhanced Learning and Teaching in Higher Education: What is 'Enhanced' and How Do We Know? A Critical Literature Review. *Learning, Media and Technology*, 39(1), 6–36. Advance online publication. DOI: 10.1080/17439884.2013.770404

Knight, J. F., Carley, S., Tregunna, B., Jarvis, S., Smithies, R., de Freitas, S., Dunwell, I., & Mackway-Jones, K. (2010). Serious Gaming Technology in Major Incident Triage Training: A Pragmatic Controlled Trial. *Resuscitation*, 81(9), 1175–1179. DOI: 10.1016/j.resuscitation.2010.03.042 PMID: 20732609

Kotrlik, J. W., & Redmann, D. H. (2009). A trend study: Technology Adoption in The Teaching-Learning Process by Secondary Agriscience Teachers-2002 And 2007. *Journal of Agricultural Education*, 50(2), 62–74. DOI: 10.5032/jae.2009.02062

Kysela, J., & Štorková, P. (2015). Using Augmented Reality as a Medium for Teaching History and Tourism. *Procedia: Social and Behavioral Sciences*, 174, 926–931. DOI: 10.1016/j.sbspro.2015.01.713

Labus, A., Simić, K., Vulić, M., Despotović-Zrakić, M., & Bogdanović, Z. (2012). An Application of Social Media in E-learning 2.0. *25th Bled Econference - Edependability: Reliable And Trustworthy Estructures, Eprocesses, Eoperations And Eservices For The Future, Proceedings, 557-572.*

Literacy rate, Adult Total for Bahrain. *FRED*. (2024, June 4). https://fred.stlouisfed.org/series/SEADTLITRZSBHR

Liu, D., Valdiviezo-Díaz, P., Riofrio, G., Sun, Y.-M., & Barba, R. (2015). Integration of Virtual Labs into Science E-learning. *Procedia Computer Science*, 75, 95–102. DOI: 10.1016/j.procs.2015.12.224

Liubchak, V. O., Zuban, Y. O., & Artyukhov, A. E. (2022). Immersive Learning Technology for Ensuring Quality Education: Ukrainian University Case. *CTE Workshop Proceedings, 9*, 336–354. https://doi.org/DOI: 10.55056/cte.124

Livingstone, S. (2012). Critical Reflections on the Benefits of ICT in Education. *Oxford Review of Education*, 38(1), 9–24. DOI: 10.1080/03054985.2011.577938

Lv, Z. (2023). Generative Artificial Intelligence in the Metaverse Era. *Cognitive Robotics*, 3, 208–217. DOI: 10.1016/j.cogr.2023.06.001

Maier, S. (2013). *From the Classroom to the Boardroom: Enhancing Women's Participation in The GCC Workforce. Policy Note 4.* Mohammed Bin Rashid School of Government.

Malik, A. R., Pratiwi, Y., Andajani, K., Numertayasa, I. W., Suharti, S., Darwis, A., & Marzuki, . (2023). Exploring Artificial Intelligence in Academic Essay: Higher Education Student's Perspective. *International Journal of Educational Research Open*, 5, 100296. DOI: 10.1016/j.ijedro.2023.100296

Maper, S. (2024). Analysing Barriers to Girls' Education Outcomes in South Sudan. *Texila International Journal of Management*, 10(1), 1–7. DOI: 10.21522/TIJMG.2015.10.01.Art001

Margolis, R. J. (1963). *Do Teaching Machines Really Teach?* Redbook.

Mercado, J., & Picardal, J. P. (2023). Virtual Laboratory Simulations in Biotechnology: A Systematic Review. *Science Education International*, 34(1), 52–57. DOI: 10.33828/sei.v34.i1.6

Metcalfe, B. D. (2006). Exploring cultural dimensions of gender and management in the Middle East. *Thunderbird International Business Review*, 48(1), 93–107. DOI: 10.1002/tie.20087

Miles, R., Al-Ali, S., Charles, T., Hill, C., & Bligh, B. (2021). Technology Enhanced Learning in the MENA Region: Introduction to the Special Issue. *Studies in Technology Enhanced Learning*, 1(2). Advance online publication. DOI: 10.21428/8c225f6e. df527b9d

Mosly, A. (2022). *Education in the GCC: Developments and Trends*. Gulf Research Center.

Mullis, I. V. S., Martin, M. O., & Loveless, T. (2016). 20 Years of TIMSS International Trends in Mathematics and Science Achievement, Curriculum, and Instruction. Retrieved from http://timssandpirls.bc.edu/timss2015/international-results/timss2015/wpcontent/uploads/2016/T15-20-years-of-TIMSS.pd

Najim, D. M. (2023). Challenges Facing Palestinian Women in Assuming Leadership Positions in Higher Education Institutions: Glass Ceiling. *International Conference on Gender Research,* 6(1), 192–200. DOI: 10.34190/icgr.6.1.1136

Nhavkar, V. (2023). Impact of Generative AI on IT Professionals. *International Journal for Research in Applied Science and Engineering Technology*, 11(7), 15–18. Advance online publication. DOI: 10.22214/ijraset.2023.54515

O'Sullivan, A., Rey, M. E., and Mendez, J. G. (2011). Opportunities and Challenges in the MENA Region. *The Arab World Competitiveness Report, 2011-2012*.

Onia, S. I. (2021b). Girls' Education Policy in Sudan: Challenges and Prospects. *MANAGERE : Indonesian Journal of Educational Management*, 3(3), 196–210. DOI: 10.52627/ijeam.v3i3.175

Petrina, S. (2004). Sidney Pressey and the Automation of Education, 1924-1934. *Technology and Culture*, 45(2), 305–330. DOI: 10.1353/tech.2004.0085

Ramadan, M., Hwijeh, F., Hallaj, O. A., Salahieh, S., & Diab, M. (2021). The Status of Gender Equality and Women's Rights in Syria.

Rashed, R. (2017). *Structure*. Gender, Tribalism, And Workplace Power In Libya.

Razzak, N. A. (2017). E-Learning and National Innovation in Bahrain: Opportunities, Challenges, and Future Developments. (April 2-3, 2017).

Ridge, N., Kippels, S., & ElAsad, S. (2017). Fact Sheet: Education in the United Arab Emirates and Ras Al Khaimah. Sheikh Saud bin Saqr Al Qasimi Foundation for Policy Research.

Rosário, A. & Dias, J. (2022). Learning Management Systems in Education: Research and Challenges. .DOI: 10.4018/978-1-6684-4706-2.ch003

Salem, O. (2023). Education And Challenges in Palestine. (Gendered Impact within Women, Peace And Security). *MIFTAH*. http://www.miftah.org/Display.cfm?DocId =26830&CategoryId=13

Saputro, R. E., & Saputra, D. I. S. (2015). Pengembangan Media Pembelajaran Mengenal Organ Pencernaan Manusia Menggunakan Teknologi Augmented Reality. *Jurnal Buana Informatika*, 6(2), 2. Advance online publication. DOI: 10.24002/jbi.v6i2.404

Schneckenberg, D. (2010). Overcoming Barriers for E-learning in Universities— Portfolio Models for E-competence Development of Faculty. *British Journal of Educational Technology*, 41(6), 979–991. DOI: 10.1111/j.1467-8535.2009.01046.x

Shalhoub-Kevorkian, N. (2008). The Gendered Nature of Education under Siege: A Palestinian Feminist Perspective. *International Journal of Lifelong Education*, 27(2), 179–200. DOI: 10.1080/02601370801936341

Sherif, K. (2014). Education in the Middle East: Challenges and Opportunities. .DOI: 10.1057/9781137396969_9

Sinha, C. (2020). Women in the Bahrain Financial Sector: Opportunities, challenges and strategic choices. *Social Change*, 50(1), 44–60. DOI: 10.1177/0049085719901069

Snae, C., & Brückner, M. (2008). Web-based Evaluation System for Online Courses and Learning Management Systems. *2nd IEEE International Conference on Digital Ecosystems and Technologies*, 332-339. DOI: 10.1109/DEST.2008.4635208

Swanwick, T. (2013). Understanding Medical Education (Evidence, Theory and Practice). *Technology-enhanced learning. 149–160*. DOI: 10.1002/9781118472361.ch11

Tamtam, A., Gallagher, F., Olabi, G. A., & Sumsun, N. (2010). Implementing English Medium Instruction (EMI) for Engineering Education in Arab World and Twenty-First Century Challenges. *International Symposium for Engineering Education, University College Cork: Ireland*. Url:https://www.ucc.ie/ucc/depts/foodeng/isee2010/pdfs/Papers/Tamtam%20et%20al.pdf

Thom, J., Millen, D., & DiMicco, J. (2012). Removing Gamification from an Enterprise SNS. *Proceedings of the ACM 2012 Conference on Computer Supported Cooperative Work.* https://doi.org/DOI: 10.1145/2145204.2145362

Tlaiss, H. A. (2014). Women's Entrepreneurship, Barriers and Culture: Insights from the United Arab Emirates. *The Journal of Entrepreneurship*, 23(2), 289–320. DOI: 10.1177/0971355714535307

Tuomi, I., Cachia, R., & Villar Onrubia, D. (2023). On the Futures of Technology in Education: Emerging Trends and Policy Implications. *Publications Office of the European Union, Luxembourg.*, JRC134308. Advance online publication. DOI: 10.2760/079734

Unger, K., Schwartz, D., & Foucher, J. (2013). Increasing Employee Productivity through Gamification and Blended Learning. In T. Bastiaens & G. Marks (Eds.), *Proceedings of E-Learn 2013--World Conference on E-Learning in Corporate, Government, Healthcare, and Higher Education (pp. 2538-2545).* Las Vegas, NV, USA: *Association for the Advancement of Computing in Education (AACE).* Retrieved April 19, 2024 from https://www.learntechlib.org/primary/p/115272/

UNICEF. (2021). Education Annual Report UNICEF. [https://www.unicef.org/sudan/media/8546/file/UNICEF%20Sudan-Education-%20Report%20(2021).pdf]

UNICEF. Analyse Budgétaire: Education, Période 2010-2021. (2022, March). https://www.unicef.org/tunisia/media/6121/file/Education%20Budget%20Brief-2022.pdf

Wiseman, A. W., & Anderson, E. (2012). ICT-integrated Education and National Innovation Systems in the Gulf Cooperation Council (GCC) Countries. *Computers & Education*, 59(2), 607–618. DOI: 10.1016/j.compedu.2012.02.006

Zaatari, R. (2013). A Reading of Syrian Indicators in the Global Report on the Gender Gap, the National Competitiveness Observatory.

Zawacki-Richter, O., Bozkurt, A., Alturki, U., & Aldraiweesh, A. (2018). What Research Says about MOOCS – An Explorative Content Analysis. *International Review of Research in Open and Distance Learning*, 19(1). Advance online publication. DOI: 10.19173/irrodl.v19i1.3356

KEY TERMS AND DEFINITIONS

Equality: When everyone gets the same thing, regardless of needs. Does not account for additional obstacles and barriers for certain individuals and groups.

Equity: When people get what they need, which may differ amongst individuals and groups to ensure the same opportunities.

Feminism: The belief that females should be treated equally to males.

Sexism: When a person or group asserts superiority over another person or group because of sexual identity.

Social Justice: Ensuring everyone has what they need to live a fulfilling life economically, socially, and politically. SOme social justice movements include feminism and anti-racism.

Socioeconomic Status: Includes income, educational level/achievement, financial security, and status/class in society (APA, 2017).

Systemic Barriers: Barriers that place unequal value on certain groups that affect daily life.

Chapter 9
Understanding LMS Usage in Higher Education:
Examining the Interplay of Demographic and Usage Factors in UTAUT

Juby Thomas
https://orcid.org/0000-0003-2167-0620
Kristu Jayanti College, India

Vishnu Achutha Menon
https://orcid.org/0000-0003-4028-3685
Institute for Educational and Developmental Studies, India

T. K. Sateesh Kumar
https://orcid.org/0000-0002-8406-409X
Kristu Jayanti College, India

Lijo P. Thomas
Kristu Jayanti College, India

ABSTRACT

This chapter employs a quantitative survey methodology utilizing the Unified Theory of Acceptance and Use of Technology (UTAUT) questionnaire as the primary research instrument. The questionnaire was administered to 363 students in higher education institutions across Karnataka, India, representing diverse demographic backgrounds. Purposive sampling was employed to ensure the inclusion of students

DOI: 10.4018/979-8-3693-3904-6.ch009

from various geographic settings within Karnataka. Data collection took place over five months, from January 2023 to May 2023, using online surveys administered through Google Forms. It examines the mediating role of psychological, socio-demographic (gender, location, education), and economic/behavioural (pattern of use and purpose of use) variables. Independent variables, including Performance Expectancy (PE), Effort Expectancy (EE), Social Influence (SI), and Facilitating Conditions (FC), were tested for their impact on dependent variables, Behavioural Intention (BI), and Attitude toward using technology (AT).

INTRODUCTION

The role of technology in Indian education is undergoing significant scrutiny within academic discourse. Technological advancements have precipitated a profound transformation in pedagogical practices across all tiers of the Indian educational system. This transformation is characterized by a shift towards more dynamic and interactive learning methodologies, facilitated by the integration of digital tools and resources. One salient aspect of technology's influence on Indian education is its potential to mitigate geographical disparities and enhance access to quality education. The proliferation of digital devices and internet connectivity has democratized educational opportunities, particularly for marginalized and remote communities, by providing them with access to educational resources and expertise previously beyond their reach. Technology is reshaping instructional practices within Indian classrooms. These technological interventions facilitate adaptive learning pathways, accommodating diverse learning preferences and promoting independent inquiry.

Moreover, technology has revolutionized assessment practices in Indian education. Digital assessment tools, online evaluations, and adaptive learning platforms enable real-time feedback, empowering educators to tailor instruction to individual student needs and intervene promptly when necessary. Technology serves as a catalyst for collaboration and knowledge dissemination within the Indian educational landscape. Online forums, collaborative platforms, and virtual classrooms facilitate seamless communication and collaboration among students and educators, transcending geographical boundaries and promoting collective learning experiences. However, the effective integration of technology in Indian education necessitates strategic planning, infrastructural development, and professional capacity-building initiatives. Addressing issues such as the digital divide, ensuring equitable access to technology, and providing comprehensive training and support to educators are imperative for maximizing the transformative potential of technology in Indian education.

The discernible disparity between the knowledge and skillsets imparted within educational institutions and those requisite for contemporary workforce demands and societal contexts represents a significant challenge. This incongruity has been notably accentuated by the rapid proliferation of information technology (IT), fundamentally altering the dynamics of knowledge dissemination. Information and communication technology (ICT), consequently, assumes a pivotal role in addressing these disparities from the perspectives of educators, students, and governmental entities (Jena & Goswami, 2013). Educationally, ICT serves as a potent tool for enriching pedagogical methodologies and enhancing the educational milieu. Educators can utilize ICT to diversify instructional strategies, integrate multimedia resources, and engender interactive learning environments conducive to accommodating diverse learning modalities. Moreover, the integration of ICT enables educators to cultivate digital literacy and critical thinking skills among students, thus preparing them adeptly for the exigencies of the contemporary digital milieu. For students, ICT affords unprecedented access to an expansive reservoir of information and educational resources, transcending the conventional constraints of traditional classroom settings. Online platforms, digital repositories, and interactive learning modules empower students to engage in autonomous learning endeavours, collaborative ventures, and experiential learning pursuits. ICT equips students with requisite digital competencies and adaptability crucial for navigating the complexities of contemporary employment landscapes and contributing meaningfully to societal advancement. By prioritizing the integration of ICT within educational frameworks and infrastructure, governmental bodies can nurture a digitally proficient workforce primed for driving innovation, entrepreneurship, and sustainable development. Governmental initiatives aimed at ameliorating the digital divide and ensuring universal access to ICT underscore a commitment to inclusivity and equitable participation in the digital era.

HIGHER EDUCATION AND COMMUNICATION TECHNOLOGY (ICT)

The higher education in information and communication technology (ICT) within India exhibits a notable inclination towards Western paradigms, characterized by an emphasis on instrumental and technocratic approaches. This observation underscores a prevailing trend wherein educational curricula, methodologies, and priorities are often influenced by Western models and perspectives, reflecting a broader trend of globalization and cross-cultural exchange in educational practices. The Western-centric orientation of higher ICT education in India manifests in several dimensions. Firstly, curricular content and pedagogical approaches tend to prioritize Western theories, frameworks, and case studies, often at the expense of indigenous knowledge systems and contextual relevance. This results in a disconnect between academic discourse and local socio-cultural realities, hindering the holistic development of students and limiting the applicability of their knowledge in real-world contexts. The instrumental nature of higher ICT education in India underscores a predominant focus on technical proficiency and skill acquisition, often overlooking broader societal, ethical, and humanistic dimensions of technology. This instrumental approach reinforces a narrow conception of technology as a means to an end, prioritizing technical competencies over critical inquiry, creativity, and interdisciplinary perspectives essential for addressing complex societal challenges (Ezer, 2006). Higher ICT education in India tends to adopt a technocratic orientation, wherein technological solutions are perceived as panaceas for socio-economic development and governance challenges. This technocratic mindset overlooks the inherent socio-political dimensions of technology and neglects considerations of equity, access, and sustainability in technological interventions. Consequently, the pursuit of technological advancement may exacerbate existing disparities and marginalize marginalized communities, perpetuating inequities rather than inclusive development.

Learning Management System

A Learning Management System (LMS) is a software application or platform that plays a pivotal role in the management and delivery of educational content and resources, particularly in the context of higher education. The utilization of LMS by students in their academic pursuits can be attributed to several significant factors. Primarily, LMS serves as a centralized repository, affording students convenient and organized access to critical course materials, including lecture notes, readings, and multimedia resources, thereby ensuring the availability of essential information for their academic endeavors. Moreover, LMS streamlines the process of assignment and project submissions, enabling students to submit their work electronically. This feature not only simplifies the submission process but also facilitates the efficient tracking and evaluation of students' submissions by both the students themselves and their instructors. LMS platforms incorporate a suite of communication tools, such as discussion boards and messaging systems, promoting collaborative and interactive engagement between students and instructors. These communication tools serve as conduits for students to seek clarification, pose questions, and engage in substantive course-related discussions. LMS offers online assessment and quiz functionalities, allowing students to undertake tests from diverse locations with internet connectivity. This feature augments flexibility and convenience in academic assessment processes. LMS systems encompass gradebook functionalities that empower students to monitor their academic progress, view their grades, and receive constructive feedback on their assignments and assessments, thereby enhancing their self-assessment and overall learning experience. LMS also provides a platform for resource sharing, enabling instructors to share supplementary resources, links, and documents, thereby enriching the depth and breadth of the educational experience. The time and location flexibility inherent in LMS empowers students to access course materials and complete assignments at their discretion, accommodating the diverse schedules and commitments of modern learners.

According to the findings of Alshehri et al. (2020), the usability component of the Learning Management System (LMS), specifically its interactive features, played a pivotal role in shaping students' willingness and eagerness to engage with the system. Their research underscored the significance of user-friendly interfaces and interactive functionalities in teaching positive attitudes and intentions towards LMS adoption among students (Alshehri et al., 2020). In the context of implementing blended learning for distance education, it is imperative to prioritize individuals' attitudes towards technology and their level of experience. This emphasis on technology attitude and experience ensures a more effective integration of Learning Management Systems (LMS) into the educational process. By recognizing and addressing learners' comfort levels, proficiency, and perceptions regarding technology, educators can tailor their approaches to smoother and more successful transition to blended learning modalities in distance education settings (Bervell & Umar, 2018). Thomas et al. (2023) used the SMDS and TIAS, finding moderate to high social media dependency and Instagram addiction among participants, with variations based on gender, region, and locality. Students used Instagram while engaging with the Learning Management System. `

Studies suggest that there exists a positive correlation between an individual's level of education and their likelihood of accepting new learning management systems (LMS). As educational attainment increases, individuals tend to exhibit a greater openness and receptiveness towards adopting innovative educational technologies. This trend can be attributed to various factors, including higher levels of familiarity with technology, increased adaptability to new learning methodologies, and a deeper understanding of the benefits that advanced LMS platforms can offer in facilitating learning and knowledge dissemination. Therefore, educational institutions and organizations seeking to introduce new LMS solutions may find higher acceptance rates and smoother transitions among individuals with higher educational qualifications (Claar, 2014). Virtual Reality is considered the future of education, it offers immersive experiences that can enhance learning in various subjects, from science and history to vocational training and medical education (Kunnumpurath et al., 2024).

Objectives

1. To examine the relationships between the variables of the UTAUT model, including Psychological (dependent variable), demographic, and usage variables (independent variables), in the context of LMS.
2. To analyze the direct and indirect mediation of demographic and usage variables between the UTAUT variables and psychological variables, specifically, Behavioural Intention and Attitude Towards LMS usage, within the context of LMS.
3. To investigate the overall effect of the mediation of demographic and usage variables on the relationship between the UTAUT variables and psychological variables.

Review of Literature

Rahman (2019) emphasized that higher education students possess a strong understanding of Learning Management Systems (LMS) and appreciate the advantages that LMS offers in facilitating their learning experiences. LMS has become an integral part of postgraduate students' learning processes (Rahman et al., 2019). Adzharuddin (2013) underscored the significance of collecting student feedback concerning LMS usage, particularly given its mandatory incorporation into lecture settings. LMS has been adopted globally by numerous universities to bridge the gap between students and lecturers, transcending the constraints of the traditional classroom (Adzharuddin, 2013). LMS primarily functions as a didactic support system for in-person classes (Leone et al., 2020). Both instructors and students hold the teaching and learning tools within the LMS in high regard (Lonn & Teasley, 2009). Learning management systems, falling within the first and second categories, have seen exponential growth, as educational institutions, training centers, and universities increasingly embrace ready-made LMS solutions. Mohd Kasim & Khalid (2016) underscored the pervasive use of Learning Management Systems as an e-learning tool that significantly enhances students' learning experiences and the construction of their understanding of various subjects.

Faculty members perceive LMS as a valuable educational tool that positively impacts their classes, making it a vital and well-suited learning tool in higher education (Al Amoush & Sandhu, 2019). A robust LMS should have the capability to centralize and automate administrative tasks, provide self-service and self-guided services, efficiently assemble and deliver learning content, consolidate training initiatives on a scalable web-based platform, support portability and adhere to standards, personalize content, and enable knowledge reuse (Barbieru et al., 2014). LMS plays a pivotal role in increasing learner motivation, promoting interactive learning, offering valuable feedback, and providing support throughout the learning process. Instructors should allocate sufficient time for students to process their LMS output, especially considering that many of them are working students (F. Agustin, 2022). The perceived usefulness and ease of use of LMS are critical factors influencing the frequency of its use and its recommendation to others (Candra et al., 2023). Researchers advocate for comprehensive training for university faculty and students in the effective utilization of LMS, given its role as a software tool designed to manage user learning interventions (Valsamidis et al., 2012). The effectiveness of the LMS system and students' motivation exhibit a significant correlation with their academic performance success, emphasizing the importance of developing mobile learning management systems to facilitate mobile-supported educational services in higher education (Sampson & Zervas, 2012). LMS stands as the most widely accepted ICT-based tool in the contemporary educational system. The perceived usefulness of LMS has resulted in a strong behavioural intention to use it among learners (Wuttke & Henke, 2008). Recognized as a useful and user-friendly platform for constructing personalized learning environments, the LMS serves as an essential component of the modern education landscape (Ros et al., 2013).

Samaila (2022) focused on postgraduate students and identified performance expectancy, social influence, and effort expectancy as factors influencing their intention to use LMS. Hu (2019) compared the factors affecting LMS use on computers and mobile devices and found that perceived usefulness, perceived ease of use, social influence, and facilitating conditions were significant determinants in both contexts. Collectively, these studies emphasize the critical roles of performance expectancy, effort expectancy, perceived usefulness, and social influence in shaping the behavioural intention and usage of LMS by both instructors and postgraduate students. Instructors' perceived usefulness emerges as the most significant predictor of their behavioral intention to use LMS (Cigdem & Topcu, 2015). In the context of blended learning in distance education, technology attitude and experience are pivotal considerations, with perceived usefulness standing as the strongest predictor of students' continuance intention to use LMS (Ashrafi et al., 2022).

Moreover, the influence of perceived resources is particularly substantial on usage behaviour (Kaewsaiha & Chanchalor, 2021). Enhancements in multimedia features and interactivity within the system have the potential to boost perceived usefulness and ease of use among learners (Cigdem & Ozturk, 2016). Demographic factors play a role in students' adoption of LMS. Attitudes toward use, perceived usefulness, perceived ease of use, technological complexity, perceived self-efficacy, and subjective norms have been identified as the primary determinants of faculty members' behavioural intention to use LMS (Lavidas et al., 2022). The hypothesis that excitement affects behavioural intentions using the LMS was rejected (Rehy &

Tambotoh, 2022). A strong significant relationship is reported between perceived usefulness and attitude toward mobile Learning Management Systems (m-LMS) (Mukminin et al., 2020). Perceived usefulness and expectation-confirmation play a pivotal role in predicting satisfaction (Joo et al., 2016).

In terms of students' actual use of LMS, performance expectancy, effort expectancy, and institutional support exert positive impacts (Buabeng-Andoh & Baah, 2020). Stronger relationships are observed between perceived usefulness and behavioral intention, perceived ease of use and perceived usefulness, and self-efficacy and perceived ease of use (Sánchez-Prieto et al., 2017). Subjective norms and personal innovativeness are identified as having the most significant effects on the behavioural intention to use LMS (Abbas, 2022). The correct cognition of information emerges as a critical factor in user's cognition dimensions related to the Learning Management System (Ho et al., 2019). Differences from the previous system have been noted to affect the perception of the system (Coleman & Mtshazi, 2017). Behavioural intention is found to influence the actual use of mobile marketing services among Generation Y (Ismail et al., 2022). Learning style is also identified as an influencing factor in perceptions of ease of use, usefulness, willingness, and usage behaviour regarding the adoption of a web-based learning system (Lu, 2012).

MEDIATION ANALYSIS

1. Total Effect:

- H10: There is no significant total effect of the IVs (PE, EE, SI, FC) on the AT when mediated through the demographic and usage variables.
- H1a: There is a significant total effect of the IVs (PE, EE, SI, FC) on the AT when mediated through the demographic and usage variables.
- H20: There is no significant total effect of the IVs (PE, EE, SI, FC) on the BI when mediated through the demographic and usage variables.
- H2a: There is significant total effect of the IVs (PE, EE, SI, FC) on the BI when mediated through the demographic and usage variables.

2. Direct Effect:

- H30: There is no significant direct effect of the IVs on the AT after controlling for the demographic and usage variables.

- H3a: There is a significant direct effect of the IVs on the AT after controlling for the demographic and usage variables.
- H40: There is no significant direct effect of the IVs on the BI after controlling for the demographic and usage variables.
- H4a: There is a significant direct effect of the IVs on the BI after controlling for the demographic and usage variables.

3. Indirect Effect:

The above hypothesis testing, paves for understanding the impact of each mediating effect between the IVs and main DV i.e., BI. Below is the hypothesis developed for testing the validation of the mediation effect.

- H50: There is no significant indirect effect of the IVs on the BI through the demographic and usage variables.
- H5a: There is a significant indirect effect of the IVs on the BI through the demographic and usage variables.
- H60: There is no significant indirect effect of the IVs on the BI through the demographic and usage variables.
- H6a: There is a significant indirect effect of the IVs on the BI through the demographic and usage variables.

Theoretical Background

Venkatesh undertook a comprehensive analysis by amalgamating eight distinct theoretical frameworks with the purpose of prognosticating the adoption, acceptance, and utilization of emerging technologies. These frameworks encompass the Diffusion of Innovation Theory, Technology Acceptance Model, Theory of Reasoned Action, Theory of Planned Behaviour, Social Cognitive Theory, the Model of PC Utilization, and the Motivation Model, (Chao,2019). The Unified Theory of Acceptance and Use of Technology (UTAUT), as articulated by Venkatesh, Michael G. Morris, Gordon B. Davis, and Fred D. Davis in their seminal work titled 'User Acceptance of Information Technology: Toward a Unified View,' serves as a pivotal reference. The principal objective of the UTAUT is to provide insights into human behavioural patterns concerning technology acceptance and user intentions for the utilization of information systems (Venkatesh et al., 2003).

Figure 1. UTAUT Model

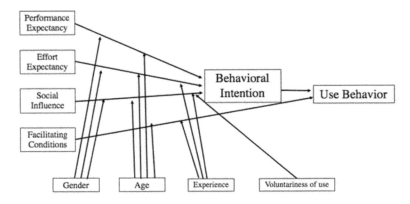

Table 1. Variables in UTAUT

Independent Variable (IV)	Dependent Variable (DV)	Mediating Variable (MV)
Performance expectancy (PE)	Attitude toward using technology (AT)	Gender
Effort expectancy (EE)	Behavioural intention to use the system (BI)	Education
Social influence (SI)		Locality
Facilitating conditions (FC)		Purpose of use
		Pattern of Use

The variable definitions are

1. Performance Expectancy refers to the extent to which an individual holds the belief that employing the system will lead to enhancements in their job performance.
2. Effort Expectancy is characterized by the level of simplicity associated with the utilization of the system.
3. Social Influence is the measure of an individual's perception regarding the extent to which influential figures in their social sphere endorse the adoption of the new system.
4. Facilitating Conditions pertain to an individual's assessment of the presence of a conducive organizational and technical framework that supports the effective use of the system.
5. Behavioural Intentions encompass the actions, efforts, and intentions regarding the adoption and utilization of the technology.

6. Use Behaviour reflects one's disposition or inclination toward employing the technology.

Methodology

The authors employed a survey methodology, utilizing the UTAUT (Unified Theory of Acceptance and Use of Technology) questionnaire as the primary research instrument. The questionnaire was administered to 363 students enrolled in higher education institutes across Karnataka, India. The sample comprised 183 females and 180 males, with diverse demographic backgrounds, including 238 participants from urban areas, 80 from semi-urban areas, and 45 from rural areas. Purposive sampling was used to select participants based on specific criteria, ensuring representation from various geographic settings within Karnataka. Data were collected through online surveys conducted via Google Forms over five months, from January 2023 to May 2023. This approach facilitated efficient data collection from a diverse and geographically dispersed participant pool attending higher education institutions in Karnataka. The study explored the mediating role of psychological, socio-demographic (gender, location, education), economic, and behavioral variables (usage patterns, purposes) in the context of the UTAUT model. Independent variables such as Performance Expectancy (PE), Effort Expectancy (EE), Social Influence (SI), and Facilitating Conditions (FC) were examined for their impact on dependent variables including Behavioral Intention (BI) to use the system and Attitude Toward Using Technology (AT).

Analysis

Total Effect

The total effects of independent variables (IVs)—Performance Expectancy (PE), Effort Expectancy (EE), Social Influence (SI), and Facilitating Conditions (FC)—on users' attitudes and behavioral intentions toward technology adoption. It considers these effects within the framework of demographic characteristics and usage patterns as mediators. Hypotheses H1$0$ and H2$0$ propose that there are no significant total effects of IVs on Attitude Toward Using Technology (AT) and Behavioral Intention (BI) respectively, when mediated through demographic and usage variables. In contrast, hypotheses H1a and H2a hypothesize significant total effects, suggesting a direct impact of IVs on AT and BI even after accounting for demographic and usage influences.

Table 2 . Total effects

			Estimate	Std. Error	z-value	p	95% Confidence Interval	
							Lower	Upper
PE	→	**AT**	**0.330**	**0.045**	**7.263**	**< .001**	**0.152**	**0.506**
SI	→	AT	0.304	0.052	5.818	< .001	0.161	0.455
SI	→	AT	0.393	0.044	8.875	< .001	0.253	0.528
FC	→	AT	0.002	0.047	0.037	0.971	-0.126	0.125
PE	→	BI	0.137	0.075	1.836	0.066	-0.040	0.339
EE	→	BI	0.178	0.086	2.064	0.039	0.005	0.356
SI	→	BI	0.124	0.073	1.706	0.088	-0.040	0.321
FC	→	BI	0.343	0.078	4.415	< .001	0.155	0.545

Note. Delta method standard errors, bias-corrected percentile bootstrap confidence intervals, ML estimator.

Table 2 explains there is statistically significant total effect (p value is <0.05 z value > 1.96) viz., PE on AT (<0.001 & 7.263); EE on AT (<0.001 & 5.818); SI on AT (<0.001 & 8.875), thus supporting H1a. However, the FC is not significant (0.976 & 1.836) on AT. The dependent variables viz., BI is impacted significantly by EE (0.039 & 2.064); FC (0.001 & 4.415), thus theses test supports the H2a. In conclusion, these results support the H2a and infer that there is significant direct impact of DV on IVs. Indeed, there are results, which shows insignificant impact of SI (p value 0.08 and z value 1.706), PE (p value 0.971 and z value 0.037).

Direct Effect

This chapter investigates the direct effects of independent variables (IVs) on users' attitudes and behavioral intentions toward technology adoption, while controlling for demographic characteristics and usage patterns. Specifically, hypotheses H30 and H40 propose that there are no significant direct effects of IVs on Attitude Toward Using Technology (AT) and Behavioral Intention (BI) respectively, after accounting for demographic and usage variables. In contrast, hypotheses H3a and H4a posit that significant direct effects exist between IVs and AT, as well as IVs and BI, even when demographic and usage factors are taken into consideration. These hypotheses aim to deepen our understanding of how various predictors influence users' perceptions and intentions regarding technology adoption within the studied context.

Table 3. Direct effects

			Estimate	Std. Error	z-value	p	95% Confidence Interval	
							Lower	Upper
PE	→	AT	0.174	0.032	5.522	< .001	0.086	0.282
EE	→	AT	0.181	0.036	5.055	< .001	0.096	0.271
SI	→	AT	0.167	0.032	5.246	< .001	0.075	0.264
FC	→	AT	0.008	0.032	0.243	0.808	-0.066	0.085
PE	→	BI	0.114	0.077	1.480	0.139	-0.079	0.322
EE	→	BI	0.165	0.087	1.897	0.058	-0.015	0.329
SI	→	BI	0.097	0.077	1.257	0.209	-0.076	0.283
FC	→	BI	0.341	0.078	4.367	< .001	0.147	0.528

Note. Delta method standard errors, bias-corrected percentile bootstrap confidence intervals, ML estimator.

Table 3 presents the results of direct effects analysis using the Unified Theory of Acceptance and Use of Technology (UTAUT) model. It examines the relationships between key predictors—Performance Expectancy (PE), Effort Expectancy (EE), Social Influence (SI), and Facilitating Conditions (FC)—and two dependent variables: Attitude Toward Using Technology (AT) and Behavioral Intention to Use (BI). The findings reveal that PE, EE, and SI significantly influence AT, with coefficients of 0.174, 0.181, and 0.167 respectively, all showing strong positive relationships ($p <$ .001). In contrast, FC does not significantly affect AT ($p = 0.808$). For BI, PE and EE show marginal positive relationships, with coefficients of 0.114 and 0.165 ($p = 0.139$ and $p = 0.058$ respectively), while SI does not have a significant effect ($p = 0.209$). FC, however, significantly influences BI with a coefficient of 0.341 ($p <$ .001). These results highlight the differential impacts of UTAUT predictors on users' attitudes and behavioral intentions toward technology adoption in the study context.

Indirect Effect

The validation of the mediation effect involves testing hypotheses related to the indirect effects of independent variables (IVs) on Behavioral Intention (BI) through demographic and usage variables. Specifically, H5*0* and H6*0* propose that there is no significant indirect effect of IVs on BI through these variables, while H5*a* and H6*a* predict the presence of a significant indirect effect. These hypotheses aim to elucidate how demographic characteristics and patterns of usage mediate the relationship between IVs, such as Performance Expectancy and Effort Expectancy, and users' intentions to adopt technology.

Table 4. Indirect effects

					Estimate	Std. Error	z-value	p	95% Confidence Interval	
									Lower	Upper
PE	→	**Gender**	→	**AT**	**-8.401×10⁻⁴**	**0.002**	**-0.441**	**0.659**	**-0.008**	**0.002**
PE	→	Education	→	AT	-4.289×10⁻⁴	0.003	-0.149	0.881	-0.008	0.005
PE	→	Locality	→	AT	9.165×10⁻⁵	0.002	0.044	0.965	-0.005	0.007
PE	→	Purpose of use	→	AT	0.121	0.027	4.405	< .001	0.042	0.213
PE	→	Pattern of Use	→	AT	0.036	0.014	2.661	0.008	0.005	0.076
EE	→	Gender	→	AT	-5.441×10⁻⁴	0.001	-0.378	0.705	-0.011	0.001
EE	→	Education	→	AT	-0.004	0.004	-0.924	0.355	-0.018	0.002
EE	→	Locality	→	AT	9.778×10⁻⁴	0.002	0.392	0.695	-0.003	0.014
EE	→	Purpose of use	→	AT	0.094	0.031	3.040	0.002	0.026	0.175
EE	→	Pattern of Use	→	AT	0.033	0.015	2.164	0.030	0.006	0.080
SI	→	Gender	→	AT	0.002	0.003	0.470	0.638	-0.003	0.013
SI	→	Education	→	AT	0.004	0.004	1.108	0.268	6.734×10⁻⁴	0.015
SI	→	Locality	→	AT	-9.813×10⁻⁵	0.002	-0.049	0.961	-0.007	0.005
SI	→	Purpose of use	→	AT	0.163	0.028	5.871	< .001	0.086	0.256
SI	→	Pattern of Use	→	AT	0.057	0.015	3.917	< .001	0.026	0.107
FC	→	Gender	→	AT	-0.002	0.004	-0.473	0.636	-0.015	0.004
FC	→	Education	→	AT	-0.004	0.004	-1.098	0.272	-0.016	4.802×10⁻⁴
FC	→	Locality	→	AT	4.328×10⁻⁴	0.002	0.199	0.842	-0.003	0.011
FC	→	Purpose of use	→	AT	9.644×10⁻⁴	0.027	0.035	0.972	-0.059	0.055
FC	→	Pattern of Use	→	AT	-0.002	0.013	-0.116	0.908	-0.033	0.027
PE	→	Gender	→	BI	0.005	0.006	0.803	0.422	-0.003	0.029
PE	→	Education	→	BI	-8.572×10⁻⁴	0.006	-0.149	0.881	-0.022	0.010
PE	→	Locality	→	BI	2.711×10⁻⁵	6.346×10⁻⁴	0.043	0.966	-0.008	0.009
PE	→	Purpose of use	→	BI	0.012	0.020	0.584	0.559	-0.028	0.061
PE	→	Pattern of Use	→	BI	0.008	0.013	0.630	0.528	-0.018	0.043
EE	→	Gender	→	BI	0.003	0.006	0.542	0.588	-0.004	0.030
EE	→	Education	→	BI	-0.007	0.008	-0.870	0.384	-0.036	0.005
EE	→	Locality	→	BI	2.892×10⁻⁴	0.002	0.146	0.884	-0.008	0.015

continued on following page

Table 4. Continued

									95% Confidence Interval	
					Estimate	Std. Error	z-value	p	Lower	Upper
PE	→	Gender	→	AT	-8.401×10^{-4}	0.002	-0.441	0.659	-0.008	0.002
EE	→	Purpose of use	→	BI	0.009	0.016	0.579	0.563	-0.018	0.056
EE	→	Pattern of Use	→	BI	0.007	0.012	0.622	0.534	-0.013	0.043
SI	→	Gender	→	BI	-0.009	0.009	-1.032	0.302	-0.038	0.003
SI	→	Education	→	BI	0.008	0.008	1.018	0.309	-0.002	0.038
SI	→	Locality	→	BI	-2.902×10^{-5}	6.234×10^{-4}	-0.047	0.963	-0.010	0.008
SI	→	Purpose of use	→	BI	0.016	0.027	0.586	0.558	-0.037	0.082
SI	→	Pattern of Use	→	BI	0.013	0.020	0.640	0.522	-0.028	0.060
FC	→	Gender	→	BI	0.011	0.010	1.061	0.289	-0.005	0.046
FC	→	Education	→	BI	-0.008	0.008	-1.010	0.313	-0.041	0.002
FC	→	Locality	→	BI	1.280×10^{-4}	0.001	0.123	0.902	-0.007	0.012
FC	→	Purpose of use	→	BI	9.295×10^{-5}	0.003	0.035	0.972	-0.010	0.014
FC	→	Pattern of Use	→	BI	-3.327×10^{-4}	0.003	-0.114	0.909	-0.019	0.010

Note. Delta method standard errors, bias-corrected percentile bootstrap confidence intervals, ML estimator.

Table 4 presents the indirect effects of various variables on attitudes (AT) and behavioral intention (BI) through intermediate variables. Perceived Ease of Use (PE) shows significant positive effects on AT through both Purpose of Use (Estimate = 0.121, p < 0.001) and Pattern of Use (Estimate = 0.036, p = 0.008). Effort Expectancy (EE) also positively influences AT through Purpose of Use (Estimate = 0.094, p = 0.002) and Pattern of Use (Estimate = 0.033, p = 0.030). Similarly, Social Influence (SI) significantly affects AT through Purpose of Use (Estimate = 0.163, p < 0.001) and Pattern of Use (Estimate = 0.057, p < 0.001). However, Facilitating Conditions (FC) do not show significant indirect effects on attitudes or behavioral intentions via any intermediaries, suggesting they might have a more direct or different path of influence. For Behavioral Intention (BI), none of the indirect paths through intermediaries are significant, indicating that the effects of PE, EE, SI, and FC on BI might be direct or mediated by factors not included in this analysis. The indirect effects of PE, EE, and SI on AT via Purpose of Use and Pattern of Use are statistically significant, highlighting that how individuals use technology (purpose and pattern) is crucial in shaping their attitudes when mediated by these factors. This analysis underscores the importance of understanding the pathways through which various factors influence attitudes and behavioral intentions towards technology.

The primary objectives of this study are to analyze the impact of several mediators, specifically Gender, Education, Locality (demographic factors), Purpose of Use, and Pattern of Use (usage). It is worth noting that both demographic and usage variables play a significant mediating role between the independent variables (IV) and Behavioral Intention (BI), as indicated in the table above. The results encompass the Confidence Interval, which does not include zero, along with a z-value exceeding 1.96. Consequently, it is appropriate to retain the null hypothesis (H50). Looking at the data presented in Table 4, we observe that the indirect effect (mediation) is highly significant between PE, EE, and SI on AT through the usage variables (with p-values ranging from 0.000 to 0.0 and z-values exceeding 1.96). This lends strong support to H6a. The discussion is justified in the plot below:

Figure 2. Path plot

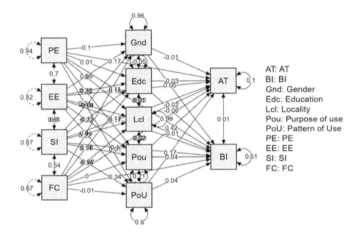

Discussions

In contemporary educational discourse, digital literacy has ascended to the status of a fundamental 21st-century skillset requisite for students' scholastic attainment and future prospects. With technology pervading nearly all facets of contemporary existence, adeptness in maneuvering digital tools, platforms, and information reservoirs has become indispensable for proficient communication, discerning critical thinking, and effective problem-solving. Digital literacy encapsulates a multifaceted array of competencies empowering students to proficiently access, scrutinize, synthesize, and ethically employ digital information. Ranging from rudimentary computer aptitudes such as keyboarding and interface navigation to more intricate proficiencies like information fluency, cybersecurity acumen, and digital citizenship, digital literacy furnishes students with the necessary knowledge and proficiencies to thrive in the contemporary digitally mediated milieu. Digital literacy encourages a culture of continual learning and adaptability, endowing students with the capacity to continually assimilate novel knowledge and proficiencies in response to evolving technological paradigms. In an epoch typified by accelerated technological progression, the capacity for autonomous learning and judicious utilization of digital resources assumes paramount importance for personal and vocational advancement.

Digital literacy transcends the confines of academic purview, permeating diverse dimensions of students' lives encompassing social interactions, civic participation, and vocational preparedness. Proficiency in digital literacy enables students to actively engage in digital communities, critically interrogate digital media, and responsibly navigate the intricacies of the digital realm with ethical discernment. Educators assume a pivotal role in nurturing digital literacy proficiencies among students by integrating technology into pedagogical practices, affording experiential learning opportunities, and inculcating digital citizenship principles through deliberate instruction and modelling. By equipping students with digital literacy proficiencies, educators empower them to navigate the complexities of the digital epoch with confidence, resilience, and a sense of authorship.

The establishment of a collaborative teaching and learning environment stands as a crucial imperative for maintaining a low dropout rate and effectively managing the growing demand for education amidst increasing learner populations and expanding teaching obligations within the framework of India's educational system. This necessity underscores the pivotal role of Information and Communication Technology (ICT) as a facilitative tool in navigating the multifaceted challenges confronting the nation's educational landscape. Central to the endeavour of creating a collaborative teaching and learning milieu is the cultivation of an inclusive and participatory educational ethos, wherein educators, learners, and stakeholders engage synergistically in the co-creation and dissemination of knowledge. The integration of ICT tools and platforms serves to enhance the efficacy of collaborative learning initiatives by transcending geographical barriers, temporal constraints, and logistical impediments.

Virtual learning environments, online collaborative tools, and digital communication platforms facilitate seamless interaction, knowledge sharing, and collaborative problem-solving among educators and learners, thereby enriching the quality and accessibility of education. ICT-enabled solutions offer innovative avenues for addressing the escalating demand for education while alleviating strain on educational resources and infrastructure. Through the adoption of online learning platforms, digital courseware, and remote teaching methodologies, educational institutions can extend their reach, accommodate diverse learner populations, and optimize teaching efficiency without compromising educational quality. However, realizing the full potential of ICT in collaborative teaching and learning environment necessitates concerted efforts in terms of infrastructure development, capacity building, and policy support. Investment in robust ICT infrastructure, professional development initiatives for educators, and regulatory frameworks conducive to ICT integration are imperative for harnessing the transformative power of technology in education.

The comprehensive analysis of the Unified Theory of Acceptance and Use of Technology (UTAUT) model has yielded significant insights into the complex web of relationships between various variables. With a primary focus on Perceived Ease of Use (PE), Effort Expectancy (EE), Social Influence (SI), and Facilitating Conditions (FC), the research objectives encompassed the examination of total effects, direct effects, and indirect effects through the mediation of demographic and usage variables. The key findings of this analysis provide valuable contributions to the understanding of technology acceptance and usage behaviour. Firstly, we confirmed the significant total effects of PE, EE, and SI on Attitude (AT), in line with our initial hypotheses (H1a). These results underscore the influence of these factors on users' attitudes towards technology adoption. However, it's worth noting that Facilitating Conditions (FC) did not exhibit a significant impact on AT, suggesting that the mere presence of supportive conditions may not be enough to sway users' attitudes. Moreover, Behavioural Intention (BI) was found to be significantly influenced by Effort Expectancy (EE) and Facilitating Conditions (FC), supporting our expectations (H2a). Yet, Social Influence (SI) and Perceived Ease of Use (PE) did not demonstrate significant direct effects on BI. This indicates that factors related to social influence and ease of use may indirectly affect behavioural intention through other variables within the UTAUT model.

A crucial aspect of this study is the exploration of mediation effects through demographic and usage variables. Our analysis revealed that these variables play a pivotal mediating role in the relationship between the Independent Variables (IVs) and Behavioural Intention (BI). The mediation effects are supported by Confidence Intervals that do not include zero and z-values exceeding 1.96, confirming the retention of the null hypothesis (H50). Of particular significance is the highly significant mediation observed between Perceived Ease of Use (PE), Effort Expectancy (EE), and Social Influence (SI) on Attitude (AT) through 'Usage variables.' This implies that users' perceptions of ease of use, effort expectancy, and social influence indirectly influence their attitudes towards technology adoption, with 'Usage variables' acting as mediators.

CONCLUSIONS

This chapter provides a comprehensive examination of the Unified Theory of Acceptance and Use of Technology (UTAUT) model, revealing the complex interplay between key factors such as Perceived Ease of Use (PE), Effort Expectancy (EE), Social Influence (SI), and Facilitating Conditions (FC). The findings highlight the significant roles these factors play in shaping Attitudes (AT) and Behavioral Intentions (BI) towards technology use. The study also emphasizes the importance of demographic and usage variables as mediators in these relationships. These insights enhance our understanding of technology acceptance and usage behavior, offering valuable implications for effectively implementing and promoting technology adoption.

RECOMMENDATIONS

Based on the findings of this study, several recommendations can be made to enhance technology acceptance and usage. Focus on improving user experience by simplifying interfaces and providing intuitive designs, making technology more accessible and user-friendly. Comprehensive training and support should be offered to further enhance ease of use. Effort expectancy can be improved by providing clear instructions, detailed guides, tutorials, and responsive customer support to help users understand and use the technology effectively. Social influence can be promoted through social networks by utilizing influencers and early adopters to endorse the technology, as peer recommendations and testimonials significantly impact acceptance. Facilitating usage through supportive conditions is crucial. Ensuring robust infrastructure, such as reliable internet access and technical support, will help facilitate smooth technology use. It is also important to identify and mitigate potential obstacles that might hinder technology adoption, such as financial constraints or accessibility issues. Targeting specific user groups by considering demographic factors allows for tailored marketing and support strategies. Recognizing that factors like gender, education level, and locality can influence technology acceptance is essential. Additionally, analyzing how different user groups interact with the technology and adapting features to meet their specific needs and preferences can be beneficial.

Highlighting the purpose and benefits of the technology by clearly communicating its practical advantages and positive outcomes can motivate potential users. Ensuring that the technology aligns with users' personal and professional goals enhances its perceived usefulness. Encouraging positive attitudes towards the technology through positive messaging and real-life success stories can shape favorable perceptions. Finally, it is important to continuously monitor and adapt by regularly collecting feedback from users to identify areas for improvement and make necessary adjustments. Staying updated with emerging trends and technological advancements ensures the technology remains relevant and competitive. By implementing these recommendations, organizations can enhance the acceptance and effective use of technology, leading to higher satisfaction and better outcomes for users.

Conflict of interest

Nil

Contribution

All authors have contributed equally.

Data Availability

Data is available on request from the corresponding author.

References

Abbas, H. (2022). Behavioral intention to use as a factor in a learning management system in Kuwait. *International Journal of Virtual and Personal Learning Environments*, 12(1), 1–21. DOI: 10.4018/IJVPLE.307018

Adzharuddin, N. (2013). Learning management system (LMS) among university students: Does it work? *International Journal of E-Education e-Business e-. Management Learning.* Advance online publication. DOI: 10.7763/IJEEEE.2013.V3.233

Agustin, F., L., & Santa Rosa City, Laguna Philippines 4026. (. (2022). Modified Learning Management System: Making A difference in E-learning this new normal. *International Multidisciplinary Research Journal*, 4(2), 21–29. DOI: 10.54476/iimrj47

Al Amoush, A. B., & Sandhu, K. (2019). LMS tools and data analysis approaches: Similarities and differences. In *Educational and Social Dimensions of Digital Transformation in Organizations* (pp. 65–76). IGI Global. DOI: 10.4018/978-1-5225-6261-0.ch004

Alshehri, A. J., Rutter, M., & Smith, S. (2020). The effects of UTAUT and usability qualities on students' use of learning management systems in Saudi tertiary education. *Journal of Information Technology Education*, 19, 891–930. DOI: 10.28945/4659

Ashrafi, A., Zareravasan, A., Rabiee Savoji, S., & Amani, M. (2022). Exploring factors influencing students' continuance intention to use the learning management system (LMS): A multi-perspective framework. *Interactive Learning Environments*, 30(8), 1475–1497. DOI: 10.1080/10494820.2020.1734028

Barbieru, D., Roceanu, I., Beligan, D., & Radu, C. (2014). DEVELOPING LEARNING MODULES FOR LMS. *ELearning and Software for Education.*

Bervell, B., & Umar, I. N. (2018). Utilization decision towards LMS for blended learning in distance education: Modeling the effects of personality factors in exclusivity. *Knowledge Management & E-Learning. International Journal (Toronto, Ont.)*, •••, 309–333. DOI: 10.34105/j.kmel.2018.10.018

Buabeng-Andoh, C., & Baah, C. (2020). Determinants of students' actual use of the learning management system (LMS): An empirical analysis of a research model. *Advances in Science Technology and Engineering Systems Journal*, 5(2), 614–620. DOI: 10.25046/aj050277

Candra, S., Limantoro, H. S., & Loang, O. K. (2023). Students' attitudes and behaviors influence learning management system adoption. *Proceedings of the 2023 9th International Conference on Frontiers of Educational Technologies*. DOI: 10.1145/3606150.3606162

Chao, C.-M. (2019). Factors determining the behavioral intention to use mobile learning: An application and extension of the UTAUT model. *Frontiers in Psychology*, 10, 1652. Advance online publication. DOI: 10.3389/fpsyg.2019.01652 PMID: 31379679

Cigdem, H., & Ozturk, M. (2016). Factors affecting students' behavioral intention to use LMS at a Turkish post-secondary vocational school. *International Review of Research in Open and Distance Learning*, 17(3). Advance online publication. DOI: 10.19173/irrodl.v17i3.2253

Cigdem, H., & Topcu, A. (2015). Predictors of instructors' behavioral intention to use learning management system: A Turkish vocational college example. *Computers in Human Behavior*, 52, 22–28. DOI: 10.1016/j.chb.2015.05.049

Claar, C. (2014). Student acceptance of learning management systems: A study on demographics. *Issues in Information Systems*, 15(1), 409–417. DOI: 10.48009/1_iis_2014_409-417

Coleman, E., & Mtshazi, S. (2017). Factors affecting the use and non-use of Learning Management Systems (LMS) by academic staff. *South African Computer Journal = Suid-Afrikaanse Rekenaartydskrif*, 29(3). Advance online publication. DOI: 10.18489/sacj.v29i3.459

Ezer, J. F. (2006). *The interplay of institutional forces behind higher ICT education in India*. London School of Economics.

Ho, H.-C., Wang, M.-T., Shih, S.-C., Kuo, C.-H., & Tsai, C.-P. (2019). A study on the user cognitive model of learning management system. In *Lecture Notes in Electrical Engineering* (pp. 193–202). Springer Singapore.

Hu, X., & Lai, C. (2019). Comparing factors that influence learning management systems use on computers and on mobile. *Information and Learning Science*, 120(7/8), 468–488. DOI: 10.1108/ILS-12-2018-0127

Ismail, M., Razak, R. C., Hakimin Yusoff, M. N., Wan Zulkiffli, W. F., & Wan Mohd Nasir, W. M. N. (2022). The determinants of mobile marketing services acceptance among Gen-Y consumers. *International Journal of Criminology and Sociology*, 9, 2277–2284. DOI: 10.6000/1929-4409.2020.09.271

Jena, R. K., & Goswami, R. (2013). Information and communication technologies in Indian education system. *International Journal of Knowledge Society Research*, 4(1), 43–56. DOI: 10.4018/jksr.2013010104

Joo, Y. J., Kim, N., & Kim, N. H. (2016). Factors predicting online university students' use of a mobile learning management system (m-LMS). *Educational Technology Research and Development. Educational Technology Research and Development*, 64(4), 611–630. DOI: 10.1007/s11423-016-9436-7

Kaewsaiha, P., & Chanchalor, S. (2021). Factors affecting the usage of learning management systems in higher education. *Education and Information Technologies*, 26(3), 2919–2939. DOI: 10.1007/s10639-020-10374-2

Kunnumpurath, B., Menon, V. A., & Paul, A. (2024). ChatGPT and virtual experience. In Advances in computational intelligence and robotics book series (pp. 32–50). DOI: 10.4018/979-8-3693-4268-8.ch003

Lavidas, K., Komis, V., & Achriani, A. (2022). Explaining faculty members' behavioral intention to use learning management systems. *Journal of Computers in Education*, 9(4), 707–725. DOI: 10.1007/s40692-021-00217-5

Leone, R., Mesquita, C., & Lopes, R. (2020). Use of learning management system (LMS): A study in a Brazilian and Portuguese universities. *Proceedings of the 12th International Conference on Computer Supported Education*. DOI: 10.1007/978-3-030-58459-7

Lonn, S., & Teasley, S. D. (2009). Saving time or innovating practice: Investigating perceptions and uses of Learning Management Systems. *Computers & Education*, 53(3), 686–694. DOI: 10.1016/j.compedu.2009.04.008

Lu, H. K. (2012). Learning styles and acceptance of e-learning management systems: An extension of behaviour intention model. *International Journal of Mobile Learning and Organisation*, 6(3/4), 246. DOI: 10.1504/IJMLO.2012.050044

Mohd Kasim, N. N., & Khalid, F. (2016). Choosing the right Learning Management System (LMS) for the higher education institution context: A systematic review. [IJET]. *International Journal of Emerging Technologies in Learning*, 11(06), 55. DOI: 10.3991/ijet.v11i06.5644

Mukminin, A., Habibi, A., Muhaimin, M., & Prasojo, L. D. (2020). Exploring the drivers predicting behavioral intention to use m-learning management system: Partial least square structural equation model. *IEEE Access : Practical Innovations, Open Solutions*, 8, 181356–181365. DOI: 10.1109/ACCESS.2020.3028474

Rahman, M. J. A., Daud, M. Y., & Ensimau, N. K. (2019). Learning management system (LMS) in teaching and learning. *International Journal of Academic Research in Business & Social Sciences*, 9(11). Advance online publication. DOI: 10.6007/IJARBSS/v9-i11/6717

Rehy, V. A. A., & Tambotoh, J. J. C.. (2022). Learning Management System acceptance analysis using Hedonic Motivation System Adoption Model. [Rekayasa Sistem Dan Teknologi Informasi]. *Jurnal RESTI*, 6(6), 930–938. DOI: 10.29207/resti.v6i6.4233

Ros, S., Hernandez, R., Robles-Gomez, A., Caminero, A. C., Tobarra, L., & Ruiz, E. S. (2013). Open service-oriented platforms for personal learning environments. *IEEE Internet Computing*, 17(4), 26–31. DOI: 10.1109/MIC.2013.73

Samaila, K., Khambari, M. N. M., Kumar, J. A., & Masood, M. (2022). Factors influencing postgraduate students' intention to use learning management system. *Tuning Journal for Higher Education*, 9(2), 151–176. DOI: 10.18543/tjhe.2177

Sampson, D. G., & Zervas, P. (2012). Mobile learning Management Systems in Higher Education. In *Higher Education Institutions and Learning Management Systems* (pp. 162–177). IGI Global. DOI: 10.4018/978-1-60960-884-2.ch008

Sánchez-Prieto, J. C., Olmos-Migueláñez, S., & García-Peñalvo, F. J. (2017). MLearning and pre-service teachers: An assessment of the behavioral intention using an expanded TAM model. *Computers in Human Behavior*, 72, 644–654. DOI: 10.1016/j.chb.2016.09.061

Thomas, L. P., Chaudhary, R., Thomas, J., & Menon, V. A. (2023). Assessing Instagram Addiction and Social Media Dependency among Young Adults in Karnataka. *Studies in Media and Communication*, 11(6), 72. DOI: 10.11114/smc.v11i6.6102

Valsamidis, S., Kazanidis, I., Kontogiannis, S., & Karakos, A. (2012). An approach for LMS assessment. *International Journal of Technology Enhanced Learning*, 4(3/4), 265. DOI: 10.1504/IJTEL.2012.051544

Venkatesh, V., Morris, M. G., Davis, G. B., & Davis, F. D. (2003). User acceptance of information technology: Toward a unified view. *Management Information Systems Quarterly*, ●●●, 425–478.

Wuttke, H.-D., & Henke, K. (2008). LMS-coupled simulations and assessments in a digital systems course. *2008 Tenth IEEE International Symposium on Multimedia*. DOI: 10.1109/ISM.2008.99

Chapter 10
Reshaping Higher Education in MENA with Generative AI:
A Systematic Review

Nadia Mohammed Nasser Abubaker
University of Aden, Yemen

SeyedMohammad Kashani
https://orcid.org/0009-0005-9232-0451
Iowa State University, USA

Awad M. Alshalwy
Omar Al-Mukhtar University, Libya

Ali Garib
https://orcid.org/0000-0002-8331-7120
Rice University, USA

ABSTRACT

The appearance of generative artificial intelligence (AI) has led to a paradigm shift in education worldwide, positioning the Middle East and North Africa (MENA) region between traditional pedagogy and technological innovations. To further explore this region's educational practices with generative AI, this chapter conducted a systematic review of research articles published between 2022 and 2024 on the MENA's integration of generative AI in higher education. Using qualitative thematic analysis, four major themes emerged: positive perceptions despite the lack of training, AI-assisted pedagogy, inevitable innovation reshaping educational norms, and challenges identified for successful generative AI integration. Despite the generative

DOI: 10.4018/979-8-3693-3904-6.ch010

AI adoption in the MENA region, these implementations, still in the early stage, face several challenges that reflect the complexities of integrating generative AI in a region fraught with contextual hurdles and accustomed to traditional pedagogical practices, especially in under-resourced contexts. The chapter concludes with pedagogical implications.

INTRODUCTION

The Middle East and North Africa (MENA) region stands at a critical juncture in the recent advancements in higher education, with generative artificial intelligence (AI) leading a new era of academic innovation. To explore how these advancements are shaping higher education in MENA, this chapter conducts a systematic review of research articles published between 2022 and 2024 to provide an in-depth understanding of the integration and impact of generative AI technologies in the practices of the higher education sector across this diverse region.

The focus on MENA is particularly important given its unique socio-economic, cultural status, as well as its technological practices, which present both opportunities and challenges for the adoption of such generative AI tools in education. Generative AI, characterized by its ability to produce content, solve problems, and generate insights through learning from vast datasets (Aydın & Karaarslan, 2022; Brown et al., 2020; Mitrović et al., 2023), offers unprecedented possibilities for enhancing teaching methodologies (Chapelle, 2024; Hubbard, 2023; Krügel, et al., 2023), student engagement (Berber Sardinha, 2024; Garib & Coffelt, 2024; Gao et al., 2022), personalized learning experiences, and operational efficiencies in teachers' practices in higher education institutions (Cardon et al., 2023; Garib, et al., 2024) as well as shaping teacher-educators course design and uses of generative AI tools (Melek & Schmidt-Crawford, 2024; Schmidt-Crawford et al., 2023). In light of these practices, this chapter systematically explored how generative AI technologies are being employed within the MENA region to reshape educational practices with the uses of such tools, ranging from the augmentation of traditional pedagogies to the streamlining of administrative processes.

Through a qualitative thematic analysis of recent research studies published between 2022 and 2024, this investigation revealed four primary themes: positive perceptions despite the lack of training, AI-assisted pedagogy, the role of generative AI as an inevitable innovation driving transformative changes in education, and the numerous challenges that accompany its integration within specific MENA contexts. Despite the optimism towards generative AI's potential in education, caution against overlooking the challenges inherent in the implementation of such technologies is encouraged due to its potential contextual and pedagogical challenges (Angeli,

2024; Kern, 2024), especially within the MENA region (Garib & Schmidt-Crawford, 2024). These challenges include issues of infrastructure readiness, digital literacy gaps among educators and students, cultural nuances affecting technology adoption, concerns surrounding data privacy and security, and country-level bans on educational technologies (Xiao et al., 2023). However, these impacting factors can differ based on the resourcefulness of the specific contexts under study, which we will refer to as well-resourced and under-resourced countries in the region.

Well-Resourced Contexts

In well-resourced contexts within the MENA region, typically found in urban and affluent areas, higher education institutions benefit from ample resources, including state-of-the-art technology, well-equipped facilities, and substantial funding. This environment facilitates more integrations of generative artificial intelligence (AI) technologies into educational practices. Technology integration in education has always been associated with increased ubiquity and interactivity (Garib, 2021), but with the appearance of generative AI, such associated interactivity is exceeding expectations. Recent studies (Sharawy, 2023; UNESCO, 2022; Karam, 2023; Garib & Schmidt-Crawford, 2024; Al-Mughairi & Bhaskar, 2024) shed light on the steps taken for using generative AI for personalized learning experiences, locally adaptive assessment methodologies, and intelligent tutoring practices and systems designed to meet the needs of MENA students.

With robust infrastructure and sufficient funding, higher education institutions can be better positioned to invest in generative AI initiatives that can, in turn, enhance teaching, research, and administrative processes (Chan, 2023). Furthermore, research, such as Dhawan and Batra (2021) and Akinwalere and Ivanov (2022) among others, stress on the transformative impact of generative AI in administrative functions within well-resourced institutions. Therefore, with adequate resources, using AI-powered tools for student learning, support services, and academic development can facilitate the learning and teaching processes, improve administrative efficiency, and enhance the overall student experience (Onesi-Ozigagun, et al., 2024). However, an important question remains: would these generative AI tools have the same impact on students' learning and teachers' practices in under-resourced contexts?

Under-Resourced Contexts

Under-resourced contexts, including rural areas and marginalized communities, face many challenges in adopting generative AI technologies due to the limited access to basic educational resources and weakened infrastructures (Bond et al., 2024; Crompton & Burke, 2023), and the MENA region is no exception. Nurunnabi et al.

(2023) stressed the need for more interdisciplinary research approaches, curricula reform, and ethical considerations to effectively integrate generative AI into teaching and learning while addressing infrastructural challenges and enhancing teachers' technical knowledge in the MENA region. Under-resourced contexts in MENA lack adequate funding, technological infrastructure, and digital literacy (Garib, 2022; Al-Jaro, 2023). Such limitations can exacerbate the digital divide and hinder the effective widespread adoption of generative AI in education in MENA.

Challenges such as inadequate access to electricity, internet connectivity, and computing devices pose major barriers to integrating generative AI into educational practices. Garib (2022) and Parsaiyan and Gholami (2023) highlight the disparities in educational resources and infrastructure across the MENA region and emphasize the urgent need to address these inequities to advanced technological tools, such generative AI, in technology-enhanced education.

Initiatives aimed at generative AI integration in under-resourced contexts can include prioritizing equitable access to technology and establishing capacity-building for educators (Chikotie et al., 2023). Therefore, understanding ways to address these challenges and bridging the digital divide is an area worthy of further exploration. To address this need, this chapter explores the most recent developments of generative AI integration in both MENA well-resourced and under-resourced contexts to highlight the potential benefits and challenges of AI-enhanced education.

Importance of the Current Research Study

This systematic review holds significance for exploring and understanding the MENA region's higher education current practices and norms with generative AI. By synthesizing recent scholarly literature on the integration of generative AI in higher education, this research study provides valuable insights into the opportunities, challenges, and emerging norms shaping educational practices in the MENA region. The findings of this chapter contribute to advancing scholarly understanding of the role of generative AI in transforming teaching, learning, and administrative processes within higher education institutions across the MENA region. By identifying key themes through qualitative thematic analysis, this research offers an overview of how generative AI technological advancements are reshaping educational systems and practices, from traditional pedagogies to administrative operations. Additionally, this research study sheds light on the nuanced challenges facing the successful integration of generative AI in education within specific MENA contexts.

By acknowledging the disparities between well-resourced and under-resourced contexts, this study highlights strategies that account for diverse socio-economic, cultural, and technological practices across the region. These insights can be of informative value to policy decisions, which guide institutional investments and supplement the design interventions aimed at promoting equitable access to AI-assisted education for all learners. Furthermore, this research study serves as a call to action for educators, policymakers, and stakeholders to address the digital divide and ensure that the benefits of generative AI-assisted education can be accessible to teachers and learners from all backgrounds and resources.

This chapter's pedagogical implications provide guidance for teachers in MENA's well-resourced and under-resourced contexts on the integration of generative AI in higher education. Addressing such practices lays the groundwork for future research, policy, and practice aimed at using the potential of generative AI to advance educational outcomes and opportunities. Therefore, this chapter is guided by the research question: How is generative AI reshaping higher education in the Middle East and North Africa?

METHODOLOGY OF ANALYSIS

This systematic review followed a structured approach to identify, analyze, and synthesize the collected research studies on the impact of generative artificial intelligence (AI) in higher education across the Middle East and North Africa (MENA) region. The review was guided by the application of systematic review guidelines in both Chong and Reinders's (2021) and Bahroun et al.'s (2023) analysis for transparency and replicability.

Search Criteria

We systematically searched academic databases, including the Middle East Journal of Research in Education and Social Sciences, the Arab Society of English Language Studies, and Google Scholar for studies published between January 2022 and December 2024. Keywords used in the search included "generative AI," "higher education," and "MENA region," along with specific generative AI technologies like "GPT-3," "GPT-4," "GPT-4-o," "ChatGPT," "AI in education," and variations thereof. Because this process targeted specifically studies that mentioned MENA, the search resulted in collecting 31 research studies only.

Screening and Selection

The initial search yielded 31 articles. After removing studies that were non-empirical and did not examine higher education, the articles were screened for relevance and eligibility, which reduced the pool to 17 articles. Due to text accessibility, the total number of selected articles were 16 articles (see Figure 1). These 16 articles specifically discuss the integration of generative AI in educational settings within the MENA region.

Data Extraction and Relevance Assessment

Data extracted from the articles included author, year of publication, generative AI technology used, macro and micro educational context, study objectives, methodology, findings, and implications for future research. The relevance of each study to the review's main goals was carefully assessed. That is, we made sure that each article is relevant to the topic of our chapter: the use of generative AI within MENA's higher education. Such assessment guided the researchers in conducting a consistent synthesis of the findings.

Synthesis of Data

We employed a qualitative thematic analysis (Braun & Clarke, 2006; Creswell & Creswell, 2017; Creswell & Poth, 2018) to explore and examine the synthesized findings across the collected studies. Themes were identified based on the frequency of occurrence and pertinence to the research questions about generative AI's role in reshaping higher education in MENA.

Figure 1. Data collection and selection procedure

DISCUSSION OF FINDINGS

An Overview

While the Economy Middle East reports an unprecedented surge into the adoption of generative AI in MENA, with investment estimated to reach $23.5 billion by 2030 (Garcia, 2023), research in this area is still in its early stages. More specifically, the United Arab Emirates and Saudia Arabia are the two leading countries in MENA to invest heavily in generative AI infrastructure and development. Both nations view generative AI as a strategic priority to diversify their economies away from oil dependency (Al-Qarni, 2024). In the United Arab Emirates, initiatives like the Dubai National Strategy for AI 2031 aim to position the city as a hub for generative AI technology and innovation globally. Similarly, Saudi Arabia's Vision 2030 includes investments in digital technologies, including generative AI, to stimulate economic growth and public sector efficiency. However, research on these goals remains limited within these two countries, as seen in the systematic review in this study. With that being stated, we anticipate more relevant research to be published in the future.

The findings of this chapter indicate no relevant publications were identified between January 2022 and September 2023. The studies included in the current analysis were published between October 2023 and April 2024. This timeline highlights the rapid progression and ongoing development in the field, reflecting how recent innovations or changes in the study of generative AI in MENA is growing in the region (see Table 1). More importantly, this rapid increase of research studies on generative AI in MENA indicates a gap in early-stage research, which requires more in-depth exploration. Table 1 provides an overview of the 16 studies analyzed in this chapter, distinguished by a theme of the relevant focus for each study.

Table 1. Overview of the Collected Studies

Theme	Author(s)	Overview
The influence of generative AI on higher education	Al-Zahrani (2023)	The study examined how generative AI affects research practices and the ethical implications in higher education in Saudi Arabia. Using a survey of 505 higher education students to examine their views on generative AI tools, positive attitudes and the transformative potential of these technologies in academic research were highlighted. Further training, support, and ethical considerations are needed.
Impact of AI on academic writing	Aljuaid (2024)	Examined the integration of generative AI tools into academic writing instruction in higher education, highlighting their potential to replace traditional methods and discussing the implications for instructional quality and academic integrity.

continued on following page

Table 1. Continued

Theme	Author(s)	Overview
Evaluation of AI translation tools	Aldawsari (2024)	Assessed the advancements in AI-powered machine translation, specifically focusing on the accurate translation of Arabic colloquial expressions. The study compared the performance of Bing AI Chat, Google Translate, and Bing Translator, highlighting the challenges and opportunities for improvement in machine translation systems.
Future of EFL Teaching and learning	Qutub, et al. (2023)	Investigated the future of English as a Foreign Language (EFL) teaching and learning in the context of the Fourth Industrial Revolution in the MENA region, focusing on the impact of educational technologies and digital innovations on teaching practices and learner readiness.
Integration of AI in grammar teaching	Kucuk (2024)	Analyzed the benefits and concerns of using ChatGPT in grammar learning and teaching for EFL students at Tishk International University in Erbil, Iraq. The study compared traditional teacher and book-centered grammar education with ChatGPT-assisted methods.
Perceptions of AI in research writing	Mudawy (2024)	Investigated the attitudes and perceptions of EFL faculty members at Majmaah University regarding the integration of AI tools in the research writing process, using mixed-methods research including questionnaires and interviews.
Perceptions of AI in education	Syarhin & Akmal (2024)	Examined the perceptions of instructors, students, and administrative staff on the role of AI in education in the Sultanate of Oman, providing insights into the extent of AI usage and guidance for future educational plans through focus group discussions.
Impact of AI on vocabulary development	Mugableh (2024)	Compared the impact of ChatGPT-generated exercises versus traditional exercises on Saudi EFL students' vocabulary size and word family strength, providing empirical results on ChatGPT's role in second language vocabulary development at Jouf University.
Impact of AI on academic writing	Al-Zubaidi et al. (2024)	Mapped out the impact of ChatGPT on academic writing at Moroccan universities. The study involved a questionnaire targeting university students and educators to gather insights on the effects of ChatGPT on academic writing quality and practices.
Role of AI in knowledge and power production	Ahmed & Mahmood (2024)	Analyzed how ChatGPT responded to controversial and debatable questions, exploring whether the generative AI model was influenced by any discourses. The study employed Foucault's discourse analysis and Fairclough's Critical Discourse Analysis to examine the impact of language production on power and knowledge production.
Engagement with AI-assisted writing	Moussa & Belhiah (2024)	Explored the dynamics of Moroccan undergraduate EFL learners' engagement with AI-supported writing tools, focusing on how these tools impact writing quality and student interaction with generative AI in writing assignments. The study uses a quasi-experimental design with business law undergraduates at the International University of Rabat.

continued on following page

Table 1. Continued

Theme	Author(s)	Overview
Translation of separable phrasal verbs	Alosaimi & Alawad (2024)	Explored ChatGPT's ability to translate separable phrasal verbs, which posed challenges due to their structure. The study evaluated the effectiveness of ChatGPT in producing clear and accurate translations of these complex verb forms.
Comparison of AI and human writing	Ali (2024)	Offered a multidimensional comparative analysis of the linguistic characteristics in the introduction sections of dissertations produced by ChatGPT and Saudi authors. The study investigated the linguistic variations and relationship between AI-generated and human-written content, using extensive linguistic analysis.
AI Chatbots for EFL essay writing: a paradigm shift in language pedagogy	Pitychoutis (2024)	The study explored the integration of generative AI chatbots into EFL essay writing, underscoring a significant shift in language pedagogy. By focusing on immediate, personalized feedback from AI, the research highlighted how these digital tools can revolutionize traditional teaching methods and accommodate diverse learning styles. The findings suggest that AI chatbots both enhances learners' writing skills and promotes learner autonomy and facilitates linguistic usage/application.
ChatGPT and academic writing self-efficacy: unveiling correlations and technological dependency among postgraduate students	Bouzar et al. (2024)	This article investigated the impact of ChatGPT on academic writing self-efficacy among postgraduate students in Morocco. The study finds that ChatGPT users exhibit higher self-efficacy in writing than non-users, with the technology providing substantial feedback that boosts confidence and writing skills. The research emphasizes the need for a balanced approach to technology use in academic settings, advocating for tools like ChatGPT to complement traditional educational methods rather than replace them.
Integration of generative AI techniques and applications in student behavior and cognitive achievement in Arab higher education	Jaboob et al. (2024)	This study explored the impact of generative AI techniques and applications on student behavior and cognitive achievement in Arab higher education. Conducted in universities across Oman, Jordan, and Yemen with 768 participants, the findings indicated that generative AI technologies enhanced cognitive achievements by personalizing learning and adapting to student behaviors. The research highliighted the transformative role of generative AI in educational settings and suggested further integration to use these benefits fully.

The integration of generative AI across various stages of higher education in the MENA region reveals a transformative potential that both challenges traditional pedagogical methods and offers new avenues for academic enhancement. The studies in the review collectively highlight the role that generative AI technologies are beginning to play in reshaping educational practices in a region that has mostly been accustomed to traditional teaching. Interestingly, the analyzed studies in this chapter were conducted in a few MENA countries, including Saudi Arabia (Al-Zahrani, 2023; Ali, 2024; Aljuaid, 2024; Aldawsari, 2024; Alosaimi & Alawad, 2024; Qutub, et al., 2023; Mugableh, 2024; Mudawy, 2024), Iraq (Ahmed & Mahmood, 2024; Kucuk, 2024), Kuwait (Pitychoutis, 2024), Morocco (Al-Zubaidi et al.,

2024; Bouzar et al., 2024; Moussa & Belhiah, 2024), Oman (Jaboob et al., 2024; Syahrin & Akmal, 2024), and Jordan and Yemen (Jaboob et al., 2024). Notably, Saudi Arabia has the largest number of AI-related studies, which is consistent with its generative AI-investment efforts.

The following sections provide a detailed overview of the emerging themes from the data, followed by their pedagogical implications. These themes included studies highlighting positive perceptions of generative AI despite the lack of training, as well as AI-assisted pedagogical practices in the field of composition instruction followed by evaluative practices of generative AI. Two additional futuristic themes also emerged: inevitable innovation reshaping educational systems and norms and challenges identified for successful AI integration.

POSITIVE PERCEPTIONS, YET TRAINING LAGS

One observation worth highlighting is the generally positive reception towards generative AI technologies among MENA students in all studies (e.g., Al-Zahrani, 2023; Jaboob et al., 2024). For example, in Morocco, Moussa and Belhiah (2024) reported that "students' perceptions of AI writing tools were positive, particularly regarding their ease of access, flexibility, and user-friendliness" (p. 150). In Jordan, Oman, and Yemen, Jaboob et al. (2024) confirmed that "generative AI techniques and applications have a positive and significant impact on student behavior and cognitive achievement" (p. 8). This acceptance is in teachers' favor, as it can facilitate teachers' successful integration of generative AI in their academic settings. Such finding suggests that students are ready for an upgraded version of education to adapt to and benefit from AI-assisted learning. The positive reception of generative AI was not only observed among the students. Teachers also exhibited positive perceptions of these tools. For instance, in Saudi Arabia, Mudawy's (2024) findings revealed that "most EFL teachers perceive integrating AI tools positively, believing they can improve efficiency and quality in the research writing process. However, more familiarity with existing AI applications is needed to ensure their active usage" (p. 181). This finding aligns with the findings of the current literature, which emphasize the need for increased familiarity with generative AI tools to fully realize their potential (Chapelle, 2024; Garib & Coffelt, 2024). Without adequate training to familiarize teachers and students with such technological tools, teachers and students may continue to misunderstand the potential of generative AI technologies, which can result in teachers placing strict banning policies on using generative AI while students would eventually miss an opportunity to learn from and with these technologies. Therefore, providing training on such an unprecedentedly transformative technology should not be an optional task, but a requirement.

Many of the analyzed studies (68.75%) called for and highlighted the need for further teacher and student training and ethical guidelines on using generative AI. This call for training is in the same domain with other research in the literature (Garib & & Schmidt-Crawford, 2024; Melek & Schmidt-Crawford, 2024) that stresses the need for educational transformation, including reviewing and updating the teaching curriculum. For instance, 11 studies called for the establishment of teacher training programs, but interestingly, with these calls, the researchers also highlighted the need for educational reform. Such transformation is to review and update the teaching curriculum. In line with this claim, in Saudi Arabia, Qutub et al., (2023) stated that "the curriculum needs a thorough review, and modular training should be provided to the teaching faculty to be familiar with the inventions in the field of language educational technology, to gain the maximum support of digital resources and applications" (p. 83). Also in Saudi Arabia, Aljuaid (2024) stressed that "training instructors on AI tools and pedagogy could promote best practices and solve emerging" whereas "training students on AI tools could help them comprehend these tools' pros and cons" (p. 38). Aljuaid's statement is a confirmation of the need to train teachers and students alike to ensure best practices in using generative AI.

Aligned with the recent literature (Al-Mughairi & Bhaskar, 2024; Angeli, 2024; Chapelle, 2024; Garib & Coffelt, 2024; Karam, 2023; Onesi-Ozigagun, et al., 2024), teachers in MENA also need training to adapt to and effectively integrate these technologies into their teaching practices. In Oman, Jordan, and Yemen, Jaboob et al. (2024) stated that "there is a need for faculty members to upskill themselves to effectively integrate AI into teaching methodologies. Overall, while the integration of AI in higher education poses challenges, it holds immense potential to transform education and foster a more dynamic learning environment that prepares students for an ever-evolving professional landscape" (p. 9). Such potential is worthy of nation-wide training, which redefines education, leading to a major change in curriculum design and simply educational practices within the MENA region. As for students, they need to be trained to take generative AI content with a 'grain of salt' approach so that they do not believe everything generative AI generates for them. Since "there is no escape from generative AI's growing presence in education" (Garib & Coffelt, p. 9), a critical approach is needed to help students engage with these tools and, most importantly, be critical thinkers of generative AI content to ensure that they use these tools in a supplementary role in their learning rather than as an unquestioned source of knowledge, as Chapelle (2024) warned that "we caution students not to let the AI befriend them, not to believe its lies, and not to take its stolen language" (p. 539).

These findings are consistent with calls in the literature for teacher-educators to supply adequate generative AI-focused training to teachers (Angeli, 2024; Kern, 2024; Garib & Schmidt-Crawford, 2024; Melek & Schmidt-Crawford, 2024). The need for training on generative AI indicates that while the potential of generative AI is recognized, there is a clear need to develop frameworks that ensure these tools are used responsibly and effectively. Otherwise, one could hypothetically imagine a scenario where students would completely rely on generative AI to do all their work for them, and teachers would use generative AI to grade the AI-completed work, resulting in a cycle of academic content being written by AI and graded by AI. Such practices could severely hurt the goal of education in the first place, which can possibly lead to a lack of genuine learning and a critical thinking crisis among students. However, a question remains unanswered, would effective training impact the way teachers and students perceive and use generative AI in their pedagogical practices? This can be an area for future research to explore the impact of AI training on students' and teachers' pedagogical practices.

AI-ASSISTED PEDAGOGY

With the appearance of generative AI, all eyes are on pedagogical practices. The way generative AI tools are used in schools and colleges could inform future practices with these technologies. From the analysis of the data in this study, two subthemes emerged: AI-assisted composition instruction and evaluating generative AI for pedagogical practices.

AI-assisted Composition Instruction

Out of the 16 studies, seven explored the use of generative AI tools in the writing classroom. These seven studies focused on the impact of generative AI in academic writing instruction in the MENA region. Such exploration provides a preliminary examination of how generative AI technologies are reshaping composition instruction practices in MENA. For example, in Morocco, Bouzar et al. (2024) explored the influence of ChatGPT use on academic writing self-efficacy among 148 postgraduate students in Fez and Meknes, Morocco. The findings showed that ChatGPT users reported higher self-efficacy in writing compared to non-users. Furthermore, writing self-efficacy predicted the duration of ChatGPT use, and increased use frequency was associated with greater reliance on ChatGPT. These findings suggest that ChatGPT can enhance writing self-efficacy by providing continuous feedback and fostering a sense of accomplishment, although they also highlight potential risks of over-reliance on the tool. The study recommends longitudinal research to further investigate the evolving impact of ChatGPT and other AI tools on academic writing across different educational levels. Also in Morocco, Moussa and Belhiah (2024) conducted a quasi-experimental study at the International University of Rabat to investigate the impact of AI-assisted writing tools on Moroccan undergraduate EFL learners. The study included 62 Business Law undergraduates, divided into a focus group that received structured generative AI training and a control group without such training. The findings showed that generative AI assistance positively impacted language proficiency, creativity, organizational skills, and vocabulary use in student-written assignments. More specifically, the focus group exhibited notable improvements in proficiency levels. Both groups demonstrated enhanced creativity and organization in their writing. ChatGPT was predominantly preferred by the participating students. The study shows the transformative potential of generative AI in enhancing writing skills while highlighting the need for continuous innovation and adaptation to evolving user preferences. Al-Zubaidi et al. (2024) conducted another study in Moroccan universities to explore the impact of ChatGPT on academic writing. Using a questionnaire distributed to 180 university students and educators, the study found that while ChatGPT was valued for its ability to save time, provide feedback, and assist with grammar and structure, there were alarming concerns regarding academic integrity, creativity, and the potential for misuse without proper guidance. The study highlighted the need for ethical guidelines and training to ensure the responsible use of ChatGPT in academic contexts.

Research also covered AI-assisted pedagogy in more resourced countries, such as Saudi Arabia and Kuwait. Three studies explored generative AI in composition instruction in Saudi Arabia, which reflects the increasing interest in innovating the teaching practices in this context. For instance, Mudawy (2024) conducted a study at Majmaah University to investigate the perceptions of EFL faculty members regarding the integration of generative AI applications into the research writing process. Data from 40 EFL teachers through questionnaires and interviews showed that most participants had positive attitudes toward using generative AI tools, acknowledging their potential to improve efficiency, accuracy, and overall quality in research writing. However, there is a noted need for increased familiarity with existing generative AI technologies and more targeted training and support to ensure effective integration. The study highlights the importance of ethical use, balancing generative AI automation with human expertise, and the major impact of ongoing training and support on successful AI tool integration in research writing. In the same vein, Ali (2024) conducted a comparative study at Prince Sattam bin Abdulaziz University in Saudi Arabia, to analyze linguistic differences in dissertation introductions produced by ChatGPT and those written by Saudi authors. Using the Multidimensional Analysis Tagger (MAT), the study examined over 150 linguistic features. The findings indicated that ChatGPT-generated introductions were more informational, explicit, and less narrative and argumentative compared to human-written introductions. Notably, human-written content was more abstract, whereas ChatGPT-produced text was more concrete. The study highlights interesting linguistic variations, suggesting the constant need for human intervention in any work completed by generative AI tools given its limitations.

Aljuaid (2024) conducted a systematic review at Taif University in Saudi Arabia to investigate the impact of generative AI tools on academic writing instruction in higher education. The study explored whether generative AI tools are replacing traditional academic writing courses and examined their potential benefits and drawbacks. The findings showed that while generative AI tools, such as Grammarly and ChatGPT, could assist with grammar, style, and initial idea generation, they, interestingly, could not replace the skill development offered by traditional academic writing courses. Aljuaid also reported that such courses teach critical thinking, research, citation, argumentation, creativity, and ethics, which generative AI tools currently lack. However, these findings could perhaps reflect an attachment to traditional teaching norms to which both teachers and students are accustomed. Further research is needed to explore this potential bias and to confirm the role of generative AI tools in academic writing instruction.

In Kuwait, Pitychoutis (2024) explored the integration of generative AI chatbots in enhancing English as a foreign language (EFL) essay writing, which shows a major shift in language pedagogy at the American University of the Middle East in Kuwait. The study reviewed the efficacy of generative AI chatbots in providing immediate, personalized feedback to support EFL learners. Utilizing theoretical frameworks such as constructivist learning, communicative language teaching, and the input hypothesis, the study highlighted the pedagogical benefits and challenges of generative AI chatbots, including promoting learner autonomy and providing a safe space for linguistic experimentation. Empirical evidence indicated that AI chatbots could improve writing skills, but the study also acknowledged limitations such as potential over-reliance on technology, data privacy concerns, and the need for transparency in generative AI algorithms. The findings suggest that while such AI chatbots offer promising advancements in language education, ethical and methodological considerations are crucial for their effective and responsible use. Pitychoutis provided implications for future research directions to optimize the integration of generative AI chatbots in EFL curricula.

Interestingly, these findings overall emerged from studies that were mostly conducted in well-resourced countries, which could be indicative of an active research agenda aimed at understanding and effectively using generative AI tools. Such findings confirm the advantages that well-resourced contexts have in adopting advanced technologies (Sharawy, 2023; UNESCO, 2022; Karam, 2023). However, the limited research in under-resourced countries is concerning; these contexts urgently need to assess and address the needs of their teachers and students regarding generative AI. Without this understanding, there is a risk of widespread misuse of such tools, potentially worsening existing challenges and creating further complications in these already fraught environments.

Evaluating Generative AI for Pedagogical Practices

Evaluating generative AI tools for pedagogical practices is one effective method for ensuring the suitability and applicability of such technologies in specific contexts, whether well-resourced or under-resourced. For example, Aljuaid's (2024) study reported that generative AI tools are positioned to redefine instructional methods, which specifically aligns with current research developing new practices to develop innovative writing and communication pedagogy (Cardon et al., 2023; Garib & Coffelt, 2024; Garib et al., 2024). The potential of generative AI to replace traditional teaching methods brings forth discussions on maintaining instructional quality and academic integrity. This transition to generative AI-assisted learning environments requires careful consideration to preserve educational standards and foster an environment where generative AI complements rather than overshadows the traditional or accustomed teaching methodologies. Yes, you have read that statement correctly. Generative AI should not eradicate currently existing teaching and learning norms at least during this initial stage of its integration into existing curricula. Bringing a completely new perspective to educational systems plagued with traditional methods can create additional challenges for teachers' practices and for students to change their own perceptions. However, blending generative AI as a component of teachers' existing teaching methods can organically result in gradual change, leading to more focused AI-based pedagogical practices (Garib et al., 2024). The discussion in the current chapter does not advocate for maintaining traditional teaching methods but rather calls for a gradual change in introducing generative AI into educational practices to avoid misuse, resistance, overreliance, or even misunderstanding the limitations of generative AI tools.

It is no secret that generative AI tools also exhibit limitations. For example, the challenges highlighted in Aldawsari's (2024) research in Saudi Arabia, where accurately translating Arabic colloquial expressions using generative AI tools such as Google Translate and Bing Translator, illustrate the limitations of current generative AI technologies for languages other than English. However, such limitations can be a good learning opportunity for students to critically reflect on and understand the capabilities and limitations of generative AI, which can result in developing critical perspectives on how to use such tools. Besides being a learning opportunity for students, these challenges emphasize the necessity for ongoing improvements in generative AI algorithms to ensure that generative AI tools can effectively support educational activities, particularly in linguistically diverse settings like the MENA region.

Returning back to the integration of generative AI tools, the adoption of these technologies in grammar teaching and vocabulary development (Kucuk, 2024; Mugableh, 2024) shows that generative AI can enhance language learning by providing personalized and immediate feedback. These findings suggest that generative AI tools support traditional learning outcomes and perhaps potentially accelerate and deepen learning through tailored educational experiences, but how would teaching faculty perceive such change? To explore faculty's perception of generative AI in research writing, Mudawy (2024) highlighted a spectrum of attitudes, which highlights the importance of addressing the concerns and expectations of educational stakeholders when integrating new technologies. These findings stress that the adoption of generative AI tools needs to be more inclusive and considerate of the diverse needs within academic communities.

The analysis of generative AI's integration in higher education across the MENA region reveals a complex interplay between the fast-growing technological adoption and the enduring influence of traditional educational practices. The current systematic review brings to light how generative AI is a transformative force, that is expected to reshape educational systems and norms, yet its integration comes with challenges that pinpoint the region's unique educational and cultural systems. To expand on these points, the following discussion highlights the remaining themes that emerged in the findings: inevitable innovation reshaping educational systems and norms and challenges identified for successful AI integration.

Inevitable Innovation Reshaping Educational Systems and Norms

The integration of generative AI, as illustrated by various studies in this systematic review (e.g., Alosaimi & Alawad, 2024; Pitychoutis, 2024; Mudawy, 2024), has great potential in enhancing educational practices by introducing methods that cater to personalized learning experiences. For instance, the use of generative AI in academic writing and grammar instruction points to a broader trend toward customized learning paths that accommodate individual student needs more effectively than traditional methods. Aljuaid (2024) and Kucuk (2024) reflect this educational shift, highlighting generative AI's potential to enhance student engagement and academic outcomes through tailored feedback and interactive learning scenarios with constant human intervention.

The adoption of generative AI tools for language translation and vocabulary development (Alosaimi & Alawad, 2024; Aldawsari, 2024; Mugableh, 2024), discourse analysis (Ahmed & Mahmood 2024), and even research practices (Al-Zahrani,

2023) demonstrate the capacity of generative AI to address specific linguistic and pedagogical practices in various educational settings. Such widespread involvement of generative AI in almost all aspects of higher education invites for a profound change and reconsideration of the goal, delivery, and design of education.

In support of this needed change, Qutub et al. (2023) call for a complete transformation of current pedagogical practices due to the futuristic and revolutionary impacts of this technology. More specifically, to examine the future of EFL teaching in the MENA region, Qutub et al. discuss the Fourth Industrial Revolution (4IR), which is the integration of innovative yet transformative technologies like "generative AI, robotics, the Internet of Things (IoT), genetic engineering, quantum computing, and other emerging technologies" (p. 67). Such exploration includes the integration of educational technologies to address the demands of 4IR. Qutub et al. explain that "[4IR], with the emergence of educational technologies and digital innovations, makes it essential for the Higher Education sector to review the teaching-learning practices to reshape the futuristic plans for 21st-century learners" (p. 67). However, with the current status quo of institutional policies and contextual barriers in MENA, can achieving this transformation be feasible? Perhaps future research could provide an answer to this question.

Although the generative AI advancements mark the end of the one-size-fits-all teaching approaches and enforce a new reality where adaptive and student-centered education is the new normal, such shifts in education can come with a wide array of challenges, especially in under-resourced contexts.

Challenges Identified for Successful AI Integration

Despite the potential benefits, the integration of generative AI in the MENA region's higher education faces several challenges. All the 16 analyzed studies highlighted possible challenges with generative AI, including technological limitations aligning to the Arabic language, as shown in AI's struggles with accurate translation of local Arabic dialects and expressions, the broader issue of infrastructural readiness within educational institutions, and students' possible overreliance on these technologies.

Examples of such challenges include Pitychoutis (2024), whose study reported that the "challenges such as ensuring pedagogical soundness…maintaining learner motivation and addressing ethical implications…related to data privacy and overreliance on technology. These difficulties emphasize the importance of developing sound methodological frameworks and ethical guidelines for integrating AI chatbots into language education" (p. 204). In the same domain, Qutub et al. (2023) explained that one contextual challenge that restricts the integration of generative AI is the existing curricula, stating that "careful curriculum revision because the resources are often reported as outdated" since "the present EFL curriculum and materials in many institutions still do not completely meet the current needs" (p. 67). In Oman, Jordan, and Yemen, Jaboob et al. (2024) explained that "culture plays a significant role in shaping people's values, beliefs, and attitudes towards technology. Therefore, when developing AI systems or designing applications for different regions or countries, it is essential to consider the local culture to ensure acceptability and effectiveness" (p. 2).

The integration of generative AI also brings to the surface ethical and practical considerations that are essential components of the integration of such technology. Addressing the ethical and responsible practices with generative AI can help teachers better understand the potential and limitations of using such tools, which, in turn, can assist teachers in establishing more realistic expectations of students' use of generative AI. What teachers still need to solidify in their students' perceptions of generative AI is that these tools are used to build, assist, enhance, and make a difference in educational practices, rather than damaging the educational systems, cheating, replacing teachers, or diminishing education altogether. Not clarifying such potential misconceptions about generative AI can be damaging to students' intentions to learn or even pursue education. Additionally, teachers' attempts to ban generative AI in education can be regarded as a misguided initiative, as Garib and Coffelt (2024) warned that "restricting students' use of generative AI is not the solution; it is, in fact, a missed opportunity" (p. 9).

Pedagogical Implications and Moving Forward

The findings from the systematic review suggest that for generative AI to be effectively integrated into the educational systems within the MENA region, an approach considering each unique context locally is necessary. Such an approach needs to address and incorporate the local norms of educational values while embracing innovative practices. Why is it important to incorporate local norms with generative AI in MENA specifically? Introducing and integrating generative AI with local educational values adds purpose and meaning to its use in such contexts. Additionally, blending such an interactive technology with the current existing teaching methods, either interactive or even traditional, can facilitate teachers' efforts in introducing and integrating such technologies without resistance from the students or confusing teachers' own teaching practices. For generative AI to bring about substantial changes in education, it will require time and ongoing efforts over multiple generations of teachers and students.

We hope that policymakers in the MENA region avoid repeating past mistakes adopting generative AI practices from Europe or North America without considering local contexts (Farag & Yacoub, 2023). Such an approach might not yield effective learning outcomes in the MENA region due to its unique cultural, linguistic, and infrastructural differences. Tailoring generative AI to local contexts ensures that the technology supports rather than supplants the cultural and educational frameworks already in place.

Furthermore, adapting generative AI tools to meet local educational needs can bridge the gap between global technological advancements and regional educational practices. This approach can enhance the relevance and accessibility of AI-assisted learning, making it more applicable and effective for students in the region. For instance, generative AI applications can be customized to better understand and process local dialects and idioms in language learning, in an effort to improve the quality of language education and make learning experiences more engaging and culturally relevant. However, to successfully achieve this integration, there needs to be substantial investment in training educators to use generative AI tools effectively. The call for training is supported by findings from 11 studies in our review, which highlighted the need for structured generative AI training to enhance student engagement and effective learning outcomes.

Moving forward, the detailed discussion of findings and the themes identified from the current systematic review of generative AI integration in higher education within the MENA region offer several practical pedagogical implications. These implications can help educators, policymakers, and academic institutions to navigate the challenges and use the potential of generative AI effectively. For example, one urgent starting point pointed out in the studies (e.g., Aljuaid, 2024; Kucuk, 2024) is the need to familiarize students with generative AI tools so that they understand the potential benefits and harms of such tools, which, in turn, can develop their critical AI literacy (Tate et al., 2023; Ng et al., 2021). Developing responsible generative AI users/consumers is the key to the ethical use of such technologies.

Incorporating generative AI into educational practices in the MENA region has brought an opportunity for outdated curricula (Qutub et al., 2023) to be upgraded. There has never been a better time for such an overdue initiative. Besides upgrading the curricula, the successful integration of generative AI in education also relies heavily on the underlying technological infrastructure. Investments in reliable internet connectivity, along with the necessary hardware and software, are essential. Equitable access to these technologies *must also be a priority*, which provides all students, regardless of their socio-economic background, with equal opportunities to benefit from AI-assisted education.

CONCLUSION

The integration of generative AI in higher education across the MENA region has both transformative potential and restricting challenges. This systematic review highlights the need for upgrading outdated curricula and creating localized approaches that account for the unique socio-economic, cultural, and technological contexts in the region. Although well-resourced countries demonstrate promising advancements in AI-assisted educational practices, under-resourced contexts are likely to face various difficulties such as infrastructural limitations and digital literacy gaps. To gain the potential benefits of generative AI, training for teachers and students is needed to use such tools responsibly and effectively with whatever means available at their disposal. Despite the challenges, generative AI is reshaping education for a brighter future in the Middle East and North Africa.

REFERENCES

Ahmed, T. N., & Mahmood, K. A. (2024). A Critical Discourse Analysis of ChatGPT's Role in Knowledge and Power Production. *Arab World English Journal (AWEJ)*, 184-196. https://dx.doi.org/DOI: 10.24093/awej/ChatGPT.12

Al-Jaro, M. S. (2023). A qualitative case study of EFL student teachers' teaching practice during practicum. *BRU ELT JOURNAL, 1*(1), 29–42. https://doi.org/DOI: 10.14456/bej.2023.3

Al-Mughairi, H. and Bhaskar, P. (2024). Exploring the factors affecting the adoption AI techniques in higher education: insights from teachers' perspectives on ChatGPT. *Journal of Research in Innovative Teaching & Learning,* 2397-7604. https://doi.org/ DOI: 10.1108/JRIT-09-2023-0129

Al-Qarni, M. A. (2024, July 12). For global AI competitiveness, US and Saudi Arabia have similar strategies. *Arab News.* https://www.arabnews.com/node/2548196/ %7B%7B

Al-Zubaidi, K. O., Jaafari, M., & Touzani, M. (2024). Impact of ChatGPT on Academic Writing at Moroccan Universities. *Arab World English Journal (AWEJ),* 20-30.

Aldawsari, H. A. H. (2024). Evaluating Translation Tools: Google Translate, Bing Translator, and Bing AI on Arabic Colloquialisms. *Arab World English Journal (AWEJ),* 237-251. https://dx.doi.org/DOI: 10.24093/awej/ChatGPT.16

Ali, (2024). Locating the Intersection of Generative Artificial Intelligence and Human English Writing Skills: A Comparative Study. *Arab World English Journal (AWEJ),* 120-130.

Aljuaid, H. (2024). The Impact of Artificial Intelligence Tools on Academic Writing Instruction in Higher Education: A Systematic Review. *Arab World English Journal (AWEJ)*, 26-55.

Alosaimi, B. A. A., & Alawad, N. A. (2024). Evaluation of the Translation of Separable Phrasal Verbs Generated by ChatGPT. *Arab World English Journal (AWEJ),* 282-291.

Angeli, C. (2024, March). Implementing Technological Pedagogical Content Knowledge Amid Uncertain Conditions: Advancements in Comprehending Contextual Factors.

Aydın, Ö., & Karaarslan, E. (2022). OpenAI ChatGPT generated literature review: Digital twin in healthcare. In Ö. Aydın (Ed.), *Emerging Computer Technologies 2*, 22–31. İzmir Akademi Dernegi. http://dx.doi.org/DOI: 10.2139/ssrn.4308687

Bahroun, Z., Anane, C., Ahmed, V., & Zacca, A. (2023). Transforming education: A comprehensive review of generative artificial intelligence in educational settings through bibliometric and content analysis. *Sustainability (Basel)*, 15(17), 12983. DOI: 10.3390/su151712983

Berber Sardinha, T. (2024). AI-generated vs human-authored texts: A multidimensional comparison. *Applied Corpus Linguistics, 4*(1), 100083-. https://doi.org/DOI: 10.1016/j.acorp.2023.100083

Bond, M., Khosravi, H., De Laat, M., Bergdahl, N., Negrea, V., Oxley, E., Pham, P., Chong, S. W., & Siemens, G. (2024). A meta systematic review of artificial intelligence in higher education: A call for increased ethics, collaboration, and rigour. *International Journal of Educational Technology in Higher Education*, 21(1), 4. DOI: 10.1186/s41239-023-00436-z

Bouzar, A., EL Idrissi, K., & Ghourdou, T. (2024). ChatGPT and Academic Writing Self-Efficacy: Unveiling Correlations and Technological Dependency among Postgraduate Students. *Arab World English Journal (AWEJ),* 225-236. https://dx.doi.org/DOI: 10.24093/awej/ChatGPT.15

Braun, V., & Clarke, V. (2006). Using thematic analysis in psychology. *Qualitative Research in Psychology*, 3(2), 77–101. DOI: 10.1191/1478088706qp063oa

Brown, T., Mann, B., Ryder, N., Subbiah, M., Kaplan, J. D., Dhariwal, P., Neelakantan, A., Shyam, P., Sastry, G., Askell, A., Agarwal, S., Herbert-Voss, A., Krueger, G., Henighan, T., Child, R., Ramesh, A., Ziegler, D., Wu, J., Winter, C., & Amodei, D. (2020). Language models are few-shot learners. *Advances in Neural Information Processing Systems*, 33, 1877–1901.

Cardon, P., Fleischmann, C., Aritz, J., Logemann, M., & Heidewald, J. (2023). The challenges and opportunities of AI-assisted writing: Developing AI literacy for the AI age. *Business and Professional Communication Quarterly*, 0(0), 257–295. Advance online publication. DOI: 10.1177/23294906231176517

Chan, C. K. Y. (2023). A comprehensive AI policy education framework for university teaching and learning. *International Journal of Educational Technology in Higher Education*, 20(1), 38. DOI: 10.1186/s41239-023-00408-3

Chapelle, C. A. (2024). Open generative AI changes a lot, but not everything. *Modern Language Journal*, 108(2), 534–540. DOI: 10.1111/modl.12927

Chikotie, T. T., Watson, B. W., & Watson, L. R. (2023, October). Systems Thinking Application to Ethical and Privacy Considerations in AI-Enabled Syndromic Surveillance Systems: Requirements for Under-Resourced Countries in Southern Africa. In Pan African Conference on Artificial Intelligence (pp. 197-218). Cham: Springer Nature Switzerland.

Chong, S. W., & Reinders, H. (2021). A methodological review of qualitative research syntheses in CALL: The state-of-the-art. *System*, 103, 102646. DOI: 10.1016/j.system.2021.102646

Creswell, J. W., & Creswell, J. D. (2017). *Research design: Qualitative, quantitative, and mixed methods approaches* (5th ed.). SAGE Publications.

Creswell, J. W., & Poth, C. N. (2018). *Qualitative inquiry and research design: Choosing among five approaches* (4th ed.). Sage publications.

Crompton, H., & Burke, D. (2023). Artificial intelligence in higher education: The state of the field. *International Journal of Educational Technology in Higher Education*, 20(1), 22. DOI: 10.1186/s41239-023-00392-8

Farag, I. M., & Yacoub, M. (2023). Teachers' appreciation of ELT policies and practices in Egypt. In Ekembe, E. E., Harvey, L., & Dwyer, E. (Eds.), *Interface between English language education policies and practice: Examples from various contexts* (pp. 59–83). SpringerLink. DOI: 10.1007/978-3-031-14310-6_4

Gao, C. A., Howard, F. M., Markov, N. S., Dyer, E. C., Ramesh, S., Luo, Y., & Pearson, A. T. (2022). Comparing scientific abstracts generated by ChatGPT to original abstracts using an artificial intelligence output detector, plagiarism detector, and blinded human reviewers. bioRxiv, 2022-12. https://doi.org/DOI: 10.1101/2022.12.23.521610

Garcia, A. (2023). *Generative AI in MENA to hit $23.5 billion by 2030*. Economy Middle East. Retrieved May 1, 2024, from https://economymiddleeast.com/news/generative-ai-in-mena-to-hit-23-5-billion-by-2030/

Garib, A. (2021). [Software reviewLearn Languages with Music: Lyrics Training App Review]. *Teaching English as a Second Language Electronic Journal (TESL-EJ), 24*(4). https://tesl-ej.org/pdf/ej96/m1.pdf

Garib, A. (2022). "Actually, it's real work": EFL teachers' perceptions of technology-assisted project-based language learning in Lebanon, Libya, and Syria. *TESOL Quarterly*, 57(4), 1434–1462. DOI: 10.1002/tesq.3202

Garib, A., Coffelt, T., Alshalwy, A., & Kashani, S. (2024). ChatGPT: Can students really get away with speechcraft? In Elmoudden, S., & Wrench, J. S. (Eds.), *The Role of Generative AI in the Communication Classroom*. IGI Global. DOI: 10.4018/979-8-3693-0831-8.ch007

Garib, A., & Coffelt, T. A. (2024). DETECTing the anomalies: Exploring implications of qualitative research in identifying AI-generated text for AI-assisted composition instruction. *Computers and Composition*, 73, 102869. DOI: 10.1016/j.compcom.2024.102869

Garib, A., & Schmidt-Crawford, D. (2024, March). TPACK's Contextual Knowledge: Exploring EFL Teachers' Technological Pedagogical Practices in Iran, Libya, Syria, Tunisia, and Yemen. In P. Mishra, M. Phillips, E. Baran, M. Koehler, J. Harris, & M. Williams. (2024, March). *Part 2: The past, present, and most importantly the future of TPACK*. In Society for Information Technology & Teacher Education International Conference (pp. 2443-2448). Association for the Advancement of Computing in Education (AACE). https://punyamishra.com/wp-content/uploads/2024/03/TPACK-symposium-SITE24.pdf

Hubbard, J. (2023). The pedagogical dangers of AI detectors for the teaching of writing. *Composition Studies*, 51(2). https://compstudiesjournal.com/2023/06/30/the-pedagogical-dangers-of-ai-detectors-for-the-teaching-of-writing/

Karam, J. (2023). Reforming Higher Education Through AI. In Azoury, N., & Yahchouchi, G. (Eds.), *Governance in Higher Education*. Palgrave Macmillan., DOI: 10.1007/978-3-031-40586-0_12

Kern, R. (2024). Twenty-first century technologies and language education: Charting a path forward. *Modern Language Journal*, 108(2), 515–533. DOI: 10.1111/modl.12924

Krügel, S., Ostermaier, A., & Uhl, M. (2023). The moral authority of ChatGPT. *arXiv. Preprint.* https://doi.org//arXiv.2301.07098 (Accessed May 4, 2023).DOI: 10.48550

Kucuk, T. (2024). ChatGPT Integrated Grammar Teaching and Learning in EFL Classes: A Study on Tishk International University Students in Erbil, Iraq. *Arab World English Journal (AWEJ),* 100-111. https://dx.doi.org/DOI: 10.24093/awej/ChatGPT.6

Melek, Z., & Schmidt-Crawford, D. (2024, March). GenAI in Teacher Education: Teacher Educators' Views on AI in Pre-service Teacher Education. In Society for Information Technology & Teacher Education International Conference (pp. 817-825). Association for the Advancement of Computing in Education (AACE).

Mishra, P., Phillips, M., Baran, E., Koehler, M., Harris, J., & Williams, M. (2024, March). Part 1: The past, present, and most importantly the future of TPACK. In Society for Information Technology & Teacher Education International Conference (pp. 2443-2448). Association for the Advancement of Computing in Education (AACE).

Moussa, A., & Belhiah, H. (2024). Beyond Syntax: Exploring Moroccan Undergraduate EFL Learners' Engagement with AI-Assisted Writing. *Arab World English Journal (AWEJ)*, 138-155. https://dx.doi.org/DOI: 10.24093/awej/ChatGPT.9

Mudawy, A. M. A. (2024). Investigating EFL Faculty Members' Perceptions of Integrating Artificial Intelligence Applications to Improve the Research Writing Process: A Case Study at Majmaah University. *Arab World English Journal (AWEJ)*, 180-191.

Mugableh, M. I. (2024). The Impact of ChatGPT on the Development of Vocabulary Knowledge of Saudi EFL Students. *Arab World English Journal (AWEJ)*, 280-290.

Ng, D. T. K., Leung, J. K. L., Chu, S. K. W., & Qiao, M. S. (2021). Conceptualizing AI literacy: An exploratory review. *Computers and Education: Artificial Intelligence*, 2, 100041. DOI: 10.1016/j.caeai.2021.100041

Nurunnabi, M., Mitchell, C., Koubaa, A., & Hoke, T. (2023). Sustainable Development Goals and AI integration into Curricula in the MENA Region. Report. Prince Sultan University

Onesi-Ozigagun, O., Ololade, Y. J., Eyo-Udo, N. L., & Ogundipe, D. O. (2024). Revolutionizing education through AI: A comprehensive review of enhancing learning experiences. *International Journal of Applied Research in Social Sciences*, 6(4), 589–607. DOI: 10.51594/ijarss.v6i4.1011

Parsaiyan, S. F., & Gholami, H. (2023). Practicing to sing in chorus: Challenges and opportunities of collaborative inquiry-based learning in an Iranian EFL secondary school context. *Language Teaching Research*: LTR, 136216882311520-. https://doi.org/DOI: 10.1177/13621688231152037

Pitychoutis, K. M. (2024). Harnessing AI Chatbots for EFL Essay Writing: A Paradigm Shift in Language Pedagogy. *Arab World English Journal (AWEJ)*, 197-209. https://dx.doi.org/DOI: 10.24093/awej/ChatGPT.13

Schmidt-Crawford, D. A., Lindstrom, D. L., & Thompson, A. D. (2023). AI in teacher education: What's next? *Journal of Digital Learning in Teacher Education*, 39(4), 180–181. DOI: 10.1080/21532974.2023.2247308

Tate, T., Doroudi, S., Ritchie, D., & Xu, Y. (2023). Educational research and AI-generated writing: Confronting the coming tsunami. *EdArXiv Preprint*. https://doi.org/DOI: 10.35542/osf.io/4mec3

Xiao, P., Chen, Y., & Bao, W. (2023). Waiting, banning, and embracing: An empirical analysis of adapting policies for generative AI in higher education. *arXiv preprint arXiv:*2305.18617.

Chapter 11
An Interactive Study of International Online Collaboration Between Spanish and Moroccan Universities

Aránzazu Gil Casadomet
https://orcid.org/0000-0003-2339-7429
Autonomous University of Madrid, Spain

Imane El Imadi
https://orcid.org/0000-0001-9076-5039
University of Hassan II Casablanca, Morocco

Mohamed Radid
https://orcid.org/0000-0002-8082-2009
University of Hassan II Casablanca, Morocco

ABSTRACT

This chapter describes a cooperative study that looked at the effects of online international collaboration on intercultural and academic development, conducted by universities in Morocco and Spain. It is designed to determine how cross-cultural initiatives affect students' academic development and intercultural competency. It involved 200 students and examined issues including time zones and technological differences while assessing the efficacy of online cooperation through a mixed-methods approach that includes questionnaires, interviews, and content analysis. The theoretical framework emphasizes mutual understanding and the role of tech-

DOI: 10.4018/979-8-3693-3904-6.ch011

nology in removing obstacles. It borrows from theories of collaborative learning and intercultural communication. Initial results demonstrate beneficial effects on communication and cultural understanding, highlighting the need of cross-cultural education in developing globally competent pupils in the face of growing digital interconnection.

INTRODUCTION

Higher education institutions must prepare students to thrive as competent global citizens capable of navigating multiple cultural landscapes in an age of unparalleled global connection. The results of a cooperative study between universities in Spain and Morocco are presented in this article with the intention of examining the effects of online international collaboration on students' academic development and intercultural competences. The main objectives of our research are to assess the results of international academic projects and to discuss the potential and problems that come with them.

This chapter has three main goals: first, to investigate the concrete impacts of virtual international collaboration on students' academic growth; second, to evaluate the subtle intercultural competency development of those involved in cross-cultural academic collaborations;

and third, to recognize the pedagogical and logistical difficulties encountered in putting cross-border educational projects into practice and offer answers. Through the use of a mixed-methods approach that includes questionnaires and interviews, our study offers a thorough assessment of the transformative potential of online cooperation in higher education.

By utilizing well-established ideas of technology-mediated education, intercultural communication, and collaborative learning, this study adds to the conversation on globalized education and the development of globally competent individuals from diverse cultural backgrounds. The significance of cooperative academic endeavors in promoting understanding and information sharing among individuals from different cultural backgrounds is highlighted by theories of collaborative learning. Intercultural communication frameworks highlight the importance of good communication in successful international collaborations, offering insights into the challenges of cross-cultural relationships.

Furthermore, theories of technology-mediated education emphasize how digital technologies can break down barriers of distance and enable meaningful cross-cultural interactions in learning environments.

The goal of this joint project between universities in Spain and Morocco is to provide insightful information about the effects of international online collaboration in higher education. We emphasize the vital significance of fostering cross-cultural understanding and collaboration as necessary components of preparing students for global citizenship in an interconnected world by exploring the experiences of a varied cohort of students. Fostering cultural competency and collaboration is essential for producing flexible and culturally aware global citizens who can thrive in our more interconnected global society as digital connectivity continues to reduce geographic barriers.

By presenting concrete data on the advantages and difficulties of online international collaboration in higher education, this work closes a large vacuum in the literature. Through the evaluation of these projects' effects on intercultural competences and academic growth, we add to the current conversation on successful teaching strategies in a globalized setting. The ramifications of our research's findings extend to educators, politicians, and institutional leaders who aim to improve cross-cultural learning opportunities and foster the growth of graduates who possess cultural competence and are capable of navigating the intricacies of our globalized society.

The transformative potential of online international collaboration in higher education is demonstrated by this collaborative research endeavor between universities in Spain and Morocco. Our study highlights the significance of fostering cross-cultural understanding and collaboration in order to educate students for global citizenship. This is achieved by analyzing the experiences of students involved in cross-cultural academic partnerships. In the digital age, where borders are increasingly hazy, cultivating cultural competency and teamwork is crucial to producing global citizens who are flexible, sensitive to cultural differences, and able to thrive in a variety of interrelated contexts.

1. REVIEW OF LITERATURE

In the context of cross-border academic partnerships, intercultural communication is essential for promoting effective collaboration and understanding among people with different cultural backgrounds (Gudykunst & Kim, 2017). The literature on intercultural communication provides insightful information about the difficulties and solutions related to cross-cultural communication in educational contexts.

Bennett (1993) developed the Developmental Model of Intercultural Sensitivity (DMIS), a well-known framework that outlines the phases of the development of intercultural competence from ethnocentrism to ethnorelativism. For students participating in cross-cultural academic collaborations, this approach emphasizes the value of self-awareness, empathy, and flexibility in negotiating cross-cultural interactions (Chen & Starosta, 2000).

A framework for comprehending cultural variations in communication styles, values, and behaviors is provided by Hofstede (2001) and Hall (1976)'s Cultural Dimensions Theory. These aspects, which affect how people from different cultures view and approach communication, include individuality vs. collectivism, power distance, uncertainty avoidance, and masculinity vs. femininity (Hofstede, 2001).

Ting-Toomey's (2017) recent work highlights the importance of relational dialectics and facework in intercultural communication, providing techniques for resolving disputes and preserving cordial relationships across cultural divides. Effective communication and conflict resolution are critical for fruitful collaboration in cross-cultural academic relationships, which is where this research is most pertinent (Ting-Toomey, 2017).

The literature on intercultural communication competency highlights the necessity of cultural sensitivity, adaptation, and effective communication skills in fostering trust and mutual understanding among cross-border academic initiative participants (Deardorff, 2006). Students can improve their capacity to negotiate intricate cultural dynamics and make valuable contributions to collaborative efforts in higher education environments by cultivating intercultural competence (Deardorff, 2006).

All things considered, the literature on intercultural communication offers insightful theoretical frameworks and useful tactics for promoting intercultural understanding and productive communication in cross-cultural academic collaborations. Teachers can foster meaningful relationships and improve the educational experiences of culturally varied student groups by incorporating these findings into the planning and execution of cross-border educational projects.

1.3. Role of Technology in Facilitating Global Academic Partnerships

Transformative ways to cross-cultural collaboration and eliminating geographic boundaries are made possible by technology-mediated education, which has a significant impact on higher education (Bates, 2019). The body of research on technology in education offers insightful information about how to employ digital tools and platforms to improve the efficacy of international academic partnerships and promote cross-cultural interactions.

Students from other countries can participate in shared academic activities and projects through online learning environments, such as virtual classrooms and collaborative platforms (Means et al., 2014). These settings make use of both synchronous and asynchronous communication capabilities to promote knowledge sharing and in-person encounters across student groups from different cultural backgrounds (Hrastinski, 2008).

According to Cavanaugh et al. (2009), web-based technologies for collaboration, like virtual whiteboards, instant messaging, and video conferencing, facilitate easy communication and teamwork even when people are geographically separated. By encouraging participation, developing intercultural understanding, and facilitating cooperative problem-solving, these technologies improve the efficacy of online international collaboration (Dillenbourg, 2013).

Lai et al. (2020) conducted a study that examines the application of augmented reality (AR) and virtual reality (VR) technologies in international education. The study emphasizes the potential of these technologies to foster immersive learning environments and mitigate cultural differences. According to Li et al. (2020), these cutting-edge technologies present creative approaches to get students involved in cross-cultural exchanges and improve their comprehension of various points of view.

Digital resources and multimedia tools have a crucial role in facilitating language acquisition and the development of intercultural communication skills, as shown by the literature on technology-enhanced language learning (Stockwell, 2010). With the use of these materials, students can hone their language abilities in real-world cross-cultural settings and gain confidence while interacting with classmates from various cultural backgrounds (Stockwell, 2010).

Study on technology-mediated learning emphasizes how revolutionary digital technologies may be for advancing cross-cultural exchanges and international academic collaborations in higher education. Through the use of cutting-edge technologies, instructors may help students from culturally varied backgrounds collaborate effectively online across borders, break down barriers based on geography, and increase intercultural understanding.

1.4. Challenges and Solutions in Implementing Cross-Border Educational Initiatives

Cross-border educational projects provide unique problems that must be carefully considered and strategically planned to ensure their success and long-term sustainability. Previous studies provide significant perspectives on the diverse obstacles faced in international cooperation and provide creative approaches to tackle these intricacies.

Cross-border educational projects frequently face major obstacles due to logistical issues, including time zone differences, language impediments, and limits in technical infrastructure (Altbach & Knight, 2007). Wanner and Palmer's (2015) research emphasizes the significance of efficient project management and communication tactics in reducing logistical obstacles and guaranteeing smooth collaboration between involved establishments.

Pedagogical problems originate from variations in curricular demands, teaching pedagogies, and educational institutions among nations (Leask, 2015). Researchers stress that in order to support successful teaching and learning experiences in cross-border academic partnerships, faculty development programs, curriculum alignment, and culturally sensitive pedagogical techniques are essential (De Vita, 2012).

Cultural barriers can impede cooperation and mutual understanding between participants. These barriers can include variations in beliefs, communication styles, and academic conventions (Deardorff, 2006). To foster cultural competency and enable meaningful interactions in cross-border educational situations, various strategies have been suggested, including intercultural training, peer mentorship programs, and cross-cultural conversation efforts (Beelen & Jones, 2015).

Cross-border educational efforts also confront a significant financial sustainability barrier, which is especially important when it comes to supporting international cooperation and maintaining long-term partnerships (Wende, 2009). Studies underscore the significance of strategic alliances, varied financing streams, and cost-sharing arrangements in bolstering enduring cross-border endeavors in higher education (Altbach & Knight, 2007).

Fostering institutional commitment to internationalization initiatives and negotiating complicated cross-border interactions require collaborative governance frameworks and institutional leadership (Knight, 2004). Research by Marginson (2012) emphasizes how important leadership is in pushing agendas for strategic internationalization and creating a climate of global participation in academic institutions.

Cross-border educational endeavors present a variety of problems that can be overcome, as evidenced by the literature. Through creative thinking and cooperative methods, educators and institutions can improve the efficiency and influence of cross-border cooperation in higher education by tackling logistical, pedagogical, cultural, and financial issues.

2. RESEARCH QUESTIONS

This chapter provides answers two important questions where the challenges of cross-border education and the function of technology in promoting international academic collaborations are among the main topics of the study that are covered by these research questions. They can help you focus the paper and offer a framework for dealing with the challenges of international online collaboration in higher education.

What are the biggest pedagogical, cultural, and logistical obstacles that organizations and students encounter when engaging in cross-border learning projects, and what are the best ways to overcome these obstacles in order to foster successful online international collaboration in higher education?

In particular, how can the use of technology-mediated education help students from different cultural backgrounds develop intercultural understanding and overcome geographical barriers in online international collaboration? How does this affect the effectiveness of cross-cultural interactions and communication?

3. METHODOLOGY

3.1. Design of Research

Mixed-Methods Approach: Use a mixed-methods research design to collect information on the effects of online international collaboration on intercultural and academic growth, including both quantitative and qualitative data.

Questionnaire for Survey: Create and distribute a structured survey to the 200 students from both universities in the cohort. Quantitative information about students' opinions about the impact of online collaboration on intercultural competencies and academic progress will be gathered through the questionnaire.

In-Depth Interviews: Hold semi-structured interviews with a carefully chosen group of people who have a range of experiences and backgrounds. The interviews, which will center on the lived experiences and perceptions of the participants, will offer qualitative insights on the difficulties and advantages of cross-cultural collaboration.

Selecting Participants

Sampling Strategy: To ensure representation from a range of academic disciplines, cultural backgrounds, and levels of online collaborative experience, choose participants from the cohort of 200 students using purposive sampling.

Students who have actively participated in online international collaboration activities should be included in order to obtain a variety of viewpoints regarding the impact of these initiatives.

4. METHODS FOR COLLECTING DATA

Administration of the Survey: Send out the questionnaire to respondents online, stressing the value of truthful and deliberate answers. Maintain privacy and anonymity to promote open communication.

Procedure for Interviews: Conduct in-depth interviews with participants through video conference or in-person to get their detailed perspectives on online cooperation. Ask open-ended questions to examine difficulties, advantages, and ideas for development.

Analyzing Data

Quantitative Analysis: Use descriptive statistics (such as means and frequencies) to analyze survey data and find trends and patterns on how online international collaboration affects academic development and intercultural abilities. Qualitative analytic: Using thematic analytic approaches, transcribe and code interview data to identify reoccurring themes, issues, and solutions related to cross-cultural collaboration that participants have mentioned.

5. THEORETICAL FRAMEWORK

Collaborative Learning Theories: To help with the interpretation of results pertaining to the development of shared knowledge and mutual understanding, frame the study within the framework of collaborative learning theories.

Theories of Intercultural Communication: Use frameworks for intercultural communication to examine the dynamics of cross-cultural encounters and the communication styles seen in virtual teams.

Technology-Mediated Education Theories: Apply these theories to comprehend how digital tools help to develop cross-cultural connections and dissolve geographical barriers.

Ethical Considerations: Prior to data collection, acquire informed consent from each participant, guaranteeing their voluntary involvement and the confidentiality of their answers. Respect ethical standards for research involving human participants, especially when conducting it in cross-cultural settings.

6. FINDINGS

Table 1. Impact of Online International Collaboration on Academic Growth(Survey Results)

Academic Growth Indicator	Percentage of Students Reporting Positive Impact
Increased Knowledge Acquisition	85%
Enhanced Critical Thinking	78%
Improved Problem-Solving Skills	72%

The table displays the percentage of students who indicate favorable impacts on academic growth markers as a result of online international collaboration. Participating in cross-border academic initiatives led to improved problem-solving skills (72%) and greater critical thinking (78%), according to the majority of participants.

Table 2. Development of Intercultural Competencies (Interview Insights)

Intercultural Competency	Rating (Scale: 1-5)
Cultural Awareness	4.2
Communication Skills	4.4
Openness to Diversity	4.0

This table shows ratings (on a scale of 1 to 5) for the development of intercultural competencies among students participating in online international collaboration. It was evident from the participants' considerable improvements in communication skills (ranked 4.4), openness to variety (rated 4.0), and cultural awareness (rated 4.2) that they were better able to negotiate and value cultural differences.

Table 3. Challenges Faced in Cross-Border Academic Initiatives (Survey Results)

Challenge	Frequency of Mention (%)
Time Zone Differences	65%
Language Barriers	58%
Technology Infrastructure Gaps	42%

The frequency of issues identified by participants highlights the practical obstacles that need to be overcome. Language hurdles (58%), time zone disparities (65%), and deficiencies in technology infrastructure (42%) were found to be the most frequent constraints affecting the success of cross-border academic collaboration.

Table 4. Benefits of Online Collaboration for Intercultural Development (Mixed-Methods Insights)

Perceived Benefits	Qualitative Insights
Exposure to Diverse Perspectives	"Interacting with peers from different cultures broadened my worldview."
Enhanced Cross-Cultural Communication	"I feel more confident communicating across cultural boundaries now."

This table presents qualitative insights that highlight the advantages of online international collaboration as viewed by participants. As evidenced by participant response, exposure to a variety of viewpoints enlarged participants' worldviews, and improved cross-cultural communication skills enabled them to converse effectively across cultural barriers.

Table 5. Analysis of Collaborative Projects

Project Outcome	Quality Rating (Scale: 1-10)
Co-created Research Paper	8.5
Virtual Group Presentation	7.9
Collaborative Problem-Solving Task	8.2

This table presents the quality ratings that throw light on the results of virtual collaboration initiatives. Positive evaluations were given to collaborative problem-solving activities (ranked 8.2), virtual group presentations (rated 7.9), and co-created research papers (rated 8.5), highlighting the effectiveness of online platforms in supporting significant group work and knowledge co-creation.

7. DISCUSSION

The data presented in Table 1 illustrates the significant positive impact of online international collaboration on various aspects of students' academic growth. Engaging in cross-border academic initiatives exposes students to varied perspectives and fresh knowledge, hence expanding their learning experiences. This is supported by the high percentage of students (85%) who reported enhanced knowledge acquisition. This result emphasizes the advantages of collaborative contacts in broadening students' academic horizons, which is consistent with theories of collaborative learning.

The significant percentages for improved critical thinking (78%) and problem-solving abilities (72%), in addition, demonstrate the cognitive advantages of cross-cultural cooperation. Collaborative assignments probably encourage students to use higher-order thinking skills by pushing them to examine difficult issues from several perspectives and come up with creative solutions. These results highlight the importance of international online collaboration in education for developing critical thinking abilities that are necessary for both lifetime learning and academic performance.

The beneficial effects on academic development noted in this research point to the revolutionary possibilities of virtual international cooperation in higher education. Participating in cross-cultural academic collaborations fosters critical thinking and problem-solving skills in addition to improving students' knowledge acquisition. Students who work with peers from many cultural origins are exposed to a variety of viewpoints and acquire the skills needed to navigate challenging global issues.

The findings in Table 1 highlight the necessity of incorporating online international collaboration into higher education curricula to improve students' academic experiences and cultivate critical cognitive skills. In order to prepare students for success in a globalized environment, educators and institutions should use cross-cultural collaboration to foster active learning, critical thinking, and problem-solving skills. Subsequent investigations ought to delve deeper into the precise processes by which virtual cooperation impacts academic development and pinpoint efficacious approaches to maximize its pedagogical advantages.

Participants in online international cooperation have made considerable progress in essential intercultural competences, as indicated by the scores shown in Table 2. The average scores for communication skills (4.4), openness to variety (4.0), and cultural awareness (4.2) show significant improvement in students' capacity to recognize and negotiate cultural differences.

These results highlight the value of successful cross-cultural communication and understanding, which is significant in the context of intercultural communication theories. The noted advancements imply that virtual cross-border cooperation aids in the acquisition of critical intercultural competencies required for effective global citizenship and work interaction in multicultural environments.

The transformational impact of online international collaboration on students' cultural awareness and communication abilities is emphasized by the growth of intercultural competencies, as indicated in Table 2. Students who interact with peers from other backgrounds improve their ability to respectfully and efficiently communicate across cultural boundaries, which helps to create a workforce that is more inclusive and capable of working anywhere in the world.

The results presented in Table 2 highlight the significance of virtual international cooperation in fostering intercultural abilities that are essential for thriving in the globalized world of today. Teachers and educational institutions can encourage cultural awareness, efficient communication, and an acceptance of diversity in their pupils by utilizing cross-cultural encounters. Best practices for incorporating intercultural learning into online collaboration projects should be investigated further, and the long-term effects on students' intercultural abilities should be evaluated.

Students taking part in online cross-border academic initiatives face practical hurdles, which are highlighted by the frequency of challenges found in Table 3. Language hurdles (58%), time zone variations (65%), and gaps in technology infrastructure (42%) were found to be the main obstacles affecting how effective collaborative initiatives are.

These difficulties are a reflection of how difficult cross-cultural cooperation may be and how thoughtful interventions are required to maximize results. Time zone disparities can make it difficult to coordinate and communicate in real time, necessitating asynchronous collaboration techniques and flexible scheduling. Effective communication may be hampered by language limitations, which emphasizes the value of cultural awareness and language support in cross-border encounters. Gaps in technology infrastructure also highlight the necessity of strong technical support and fair access to digital resources in order to enable smooth cross-border cooperation.

To improve the success of online international collaboration initiatives, it is critical to solve logistical, linguistic, and technological limitations, as indicated by the problems listed in Table 3. Proactive steps including developing adaptable communication techniques, offering linguistic resources, and making investments in inclusive digital infrastructure are necessary to overcome these obstacles.

The difficulties listed in Table 3 highlight the difficulties associated with international academic projects and the need for focused interventions to foster productive cooperation. To ensure fair participation and meaningful involvement in online international collaboration, educators and institutions need to take creative approaches to addressing time zone differences, language difficulties, and technological disadvantages. Future research should concentrate on creating workable methods to lessen these difficulties and maximize the benefits of cross-cultural cooperation for students' educational experiences.

Table 4 presents qualitative insights that emphasize the perceived advantages of online international collaboration for participants' intercultural development. Students' worldviews were widened by exposure to varied viewpoints, as demonstrated by remarks like "My worldview was widened by interacting with peers from different cultures." This shows that cross-cultural encounters help students improve both personally and professionally by fostering a deeper awareness and appreciation of cultural variety.

There were also reports of improved cross-cultural communication abilities, with comments such as "I feel more confident communicating across cultural boundaries now." This suggests that working together virtually develops the good communication skills required for interacting with people from different cultural backgrounds and creating inclusive connections.

Table 4 shows that online international collaboration has a significant impact on students' intercultural growth. Students who are exposed to a variety of viewpoints are more likely to be sensitive to cultural differences and to develop cross-cultural communication abilities. These advantages support the development of globally competent people who can flourish in multicultural settings.

The results presented in Table 4 highlight the importance of virtual international cooperation in promoting students' cross-cultural growth. Cross-cultural encounters are a valuable tool for educators and institutions to foster cultural knowledge, empathy, and effective communication skills. Subsequent studies ought to investigate methods for optimizing the cross-cultural advantages of virtual cooperation and evaluate their enduring influence on learners' cross-cultural proficiencies and worldwide perspectives.

The quality ratings that are shown in Table 5 shed light on the results of group tasks that are carried out virtually. Co-authored research papers scored an impressive 8.5 out of 10, demonstrating effective scholarly cooperation and co-creation of knowledge. This shows that students from diverse cultural backgrounds can engage in meaningful group work and information exchange using online platforms.

A positive quality rating of 7.9 was also given to virtual group presentations, which showed strong communication and teamwork abilities during joint presentations. Likewise, cooperative problem-solving assignments obtained an 8.2 quality rating, emphasizing the effective utilization of cooperative methods to tackle intricate problems.

Students involved in cross-border academic efforts can effectively support collaborative learning and knowledge co-creation through online platforms, as evidenced by the quality ratings presented in Table 5. Through collaborative projects, students can hone critical abilities in communication, teamwork, and problem-solving while utilizing a range of viewpoints to accomplish common objectives.

The results displayed in Table 5 highlight the educational benefit of cooperative initiatives in virtual international cooperation. Teachers can create cooperative learning exercises that foster critical thinking, multicultural communication, and teamwork. In order to maximize student learning outcomes and boost the efficacy of online international collaboration initiatives, more study should examine creative approaches to planning and evaluating collaborative projects in virtual contexts.

CONCLUSION

Higher education has a critical role to play in helping students become global citizens and promoting cross-cultural understanding in an era of growing global interconnection. This study has examined the complex world of online international collaboration between institutions in Morocco and Spain, investigating how it affects collaborative project outcomes, intercultural competencies, academic advancement, and obstacles. This study's mixed-methods methodology, which includes interviews, questionnaires, and qualitative analysis, has given researchers important new insights into the challenges and possibilities of international academic collaboration in the digital era.

This study had three main objectives: to find out how online international collaboration affects students' academic growth; to evaluate the subtle intercultural competency development; and to pinpoint obstacles and suggest fixes for fruitful cross-border academic endeavors. As a direct result of cross-cultural academic partnerships, a sizable percentage of students reported increased knowledge acquisition, enhanced critical thinking, and improved problem-solving skills. These findings highlight the transformative impact of online collaboration on students' academic growth.

Higher scores for cultural awareness, communication abilities, and openness to diversity further demonstrated the participants' growing intercultural capabilities. Participating in cross-cultural exchanges via virtual platforms has enhanced students' capacity to maneuver through many cultural environments, successfully communicate across boundaries, and appreciate cultural diversity, essential skills for global citizenship and professional success.

However, the survey also revealed problems associated with cross-border academic activities, such as time zone disparities, language barriers, and gaps in technical infrastructure. These real-world challenges highlight the necessity of technological assistance, cultural sensitivity, and strategic preparation in order to maximize the success of virtual international collaboration and guarantee fair participation from students with varying backgrounds.

Notwithstanding the obstacles, the advantages of virtual cooperation for intercultural growth were significant, as suggested by qualitative observations emphasizing participants' increased cross-cultural communication abilities and exposure to a variety of viewpoints. The collaborative projects' quality ratings emphasized even more the educational value of online platforms in promoting meaningful group work, cross-border collaborative problem-solving, and knowledge co-creation.

In conclusion, this collaborative research between Spanish and Moroccan universities has provided a nuanced understanding of online international collaboration in higher education.

This chapter highlights the significance of fostering cross-cultural understanding and collaboration among students and adds insightful information to the conversation on globalized education by analyzing the effects, difficulties, and advantages of cross-border academic efforts. The results of this study highlight the necessity for higher education institutions to prioritize cross-cultural engagement and make use of online platforms in order to prepare students to be proficient and culturally competent global citizens, as the world becomes smaller due to increased digital connectedness. In the future, educators and organizations can build on these discoveries to create creative educational strategies and cooperative projects that support students' academic development, global perspectives, and intercultural learning in an interconnected world.

LIMITATIONS

Sampling Bias: Students from universities in Spain and Morocco made up the study's sample, which could not be entirely typical of the world's higher education sector. The findings' limited generalizability and potential inability to fully represent the varied experiences of students from different cultural backgrounds and geographic locations are due to this sample bias.

Self-Reporting Bias: Information gathered via questionnaires and interviews is dependent on participants' self-reported responses, which can contain biases like recall bias or social desirability bias. The reported effects of online cooperation on academic advancement and intercultural abilities may contain mistakes due to participants' overstatement or understatement of their experiences.

Language and Cultural Differences: Participants in the study came from a variety of linguistic and cultural backgrounds, which could have presented difficulties with language comprehension, survey question interpretation, and cultural nuances in responses. These variations might have had an effect on the consistency and correctness of the data gathered, which would have affected the conclusions' validity and dependability.

Technology Restrictions: The study's digital tools and online collaboration platforms may have had usability problems, compatibility problems, connectivity problems, or other technical difficulties. These technological limitations might have had an impact on participants' experiences and participation in group projects, which could have changed the study's results.

Short-Term Focus: The study's time period might have made it more difficult to document the long-term impacts of virtual international cooperation on students' intercultural competency and academic development. The study mostly ignored prospective long-term changes or developments in favor of concentrating on the effects and perceptions that were felt right away.

Institutional background: The institutional background and organizational elements that could affect the success of online international collaboration projects were not thoroughly examined in this study. Although they weren't thoroughly investigated in this study, elements including administrative rules, teacher participation, and institutional support may have a big impact on how students experience their education and perform.

Researcher Bias: In spite of attempts to remain impartial, bias among researchers may have affected the gathering, evaluating, and interpretation of data. The study process may have been unintentionally influenced by the researchers' own ideas, preconceived notions, or theoretical viewpoints, which could have an effect on the reliability and validity of the findings.

Cross-Cultural Differences in Interpretation: The way that data and findings were interpreted may have been impacted by variations in participants' and research-ers' cultural conventions, values, and communication methods. Cultural variations in the comprehension of study questions, concepts, or techniques may have had an impact on the precision and breadth of the information gathered.

REFERENCES

Altbach, P. G., & Knight, J. (2007). The internationalization of higher education: Motivations and realities. *Journal of Studies in International Education*, 11(3-4), 290–305. DOI: 10.1177/1028315307303542

Barkley, E. F., Cross, K. P., & Major, C. H. (2014). *Collaborative learning techniques: A handbook for college faculty*. John Wiley & Sons.

Beelen, J., & Jones, E. (2015). Redefining internationalization at home. In Beelen, J., & de Wit, H. (Eds.), *Internationalization at Home: A Position Paper* (pp. 7–12). European Association for International Education.

Bennett, M. J. (1993). Towards ethnorelativism: A developmental model of intercultural sensitivity. In Paige, R. M. (Ed.), *Education for the intercultural experience* (pp. 21–71). Intercultural Press.

Cavanaugh, C., Gillan, K. J., Kromrey, J., Hess, M., & Blomeyer, R. (2009). *The effects of distance education on K–12 student outcomes: A meta-analysis*. Learning Point Associates.

Chen, G. M., & Starosta, W. J. (2000). The development and validation of the intercultural sensitivity scale. *Human Communication*, 3(1), 1–15.

De Vita, G. (2012). *Enhancing the student experience in business and management, hospitality, leisure, tourism*. Routledge.

Deardorff, D. K. (2006). Identification and assessment of intercultural competence as a student outcome of internationalization. *Journal of Studies in International Education*, 10(3), 241–266. DOI: 10.1177/1028315306287002

Dillenbourg, P. (2013). Collaboration in computer-supported collaborative learning. In Spector, J. M., Merrill, M. D., Elen, J., & Bishop, M. J. (Eds.), *Handbook of research on educational communications and technology* (pp. 409–438). Springer.

Hall, E. T. (1976). *Beyond culture*. Anchor Press.

Hofstede, G. (2001). *Culture's consequences: Comparing values, behaviors, institutions, and organizations across nations*. Sage Publications.

Hrastinski, S. (2008). Asynchronous and synchronous e-learning. *EDUCAUSE Quarterly*, 31(4), 51–55.

Johnson, D. W., & Johnson, R. T. (2009). An educational psychology success story: Social interdependence theory and cooperative learning. *Educational Researcher*, 38(5), 365–379. DOI: 10.3102/0013189X09339057

Kreijns, K., Kirschner, P. A., & Jochems, W. (2013). Identifying the pitfalls for social interaction in computer-supported collaborative learning environments: A review of the research. *Computers in Human Behavior*, 29(1), 40–55.

Leask, B. (2015). *Internationalizing the curriculum*. Routledge. DOI: 10.4324/9781315716954

Li, L., Yu, F., & Shang, J. (2020). Design and implementation of cross-border AR and VR system in international education. *Future Generation Computer Systems*, 103, 171–181.

Marginson, S. (2012). *International education as self-formation: Morphing a profit-making business into an intercultural experience*. Lecture presented at the Ninth Annual Edward Said Memorial Lecture, Columbia University.

Means, B., Toyama, Y., Murphy, R., Bakia, M., & Jones, K. (2014). *Evaluation of evidence-based practices in online learning: A meta-analysis and review of online learning studies*. US Department of Education.

Piaget, J. (1970). *Science of education and the psychology of the child*. Orion Press.

Slavin, R. E. (1995). *Cooperative learning: Theory, research, and practice*. Prentice Hall.

Stockwell, G. (2010). Using mobile phones for vocabulary activities: Examining the effect of the platform. *Language Learning & Technology*, 14(2), 95–110.

Ting-Toomey, S. (2017). Intercultural conflict competence. In *The International Encyclopedia of Intercultural Communication*. Wiley.

Vygotsky, L. S. (1978). *Mind in society: The development of higher psychological processes*. Harvard University Press.

Wanner, T., & Palmer, E. (2015). Personalizing learning: Exploring student and teacher perceptions about flexible learning and assessment in a flipped university course. *Computers & Education*, 88, 354–369. DOI: 10.1016/j.compedu.2015.07.008

Wende, M. C. (2009). Internationalization of higher education: A historical perspective. In Deardorff, D. K., de Wit, H., Heyl, J. D., & Adams, T. (Eds.), *The Sage handbook of international higher education* (pp. 3–27). Sage Publications.

Chapter 12
Enhancing Undergraduate Skills Through Interdisciplinary Data Projects and Technologies

Wanchunzi Yu

Bridgewater State University, USA

Xiangrong Liu

https://orcid.org/0009-0000-1602-1154

Bridgewater State University, USA

ABSTRACT

In response to the fast-growing demand for data manipulation skills, it is crucial that the undergraduate curriculum evolves to integrate various technologies. This chapter delves into the authors' initiatives to incorporate data visualization, analysis tools, and artificial intelligence (AI) into the interdisciplinary undergraduate curriculum, Statistical Consulting, and Data Visualization undergraduate courses cross-listed by the Department of Mathematics and Department of Management. Two projects serve as examples of this integration: a survey data analysis project from participants of Collaborative University Business Experiences (CUBEs) at Bridgewater State University (BSU), and a Chinese Solar Photovoltaic Rooftop (PV) Adoption project, undertaken by a BSU interdisciplinary faculty-student research team in China. The results, findings, and presentations of students showcased in this paper underscore the significance of incorporating technologies into the teaching process, especially in the interdisciplinary curriculum.

DOI: 10.4018/979-8-3693-3904-6.ch012

1. INTRODUCTION

In preparing students from diverse backgrounds and majors to effectively work with data, a key emphasis lies in highlighting the critical aspects of employing technologies to present findings. This includes the creation of interactive dashboards designed for audiences, whether they are well-versed in statistical terminology and concepts or not. In all our courses, we utilized a diverse array of statistical, mathematical, and management models, complemented by an assortment of statistical software tools. These tools included Tableau, PowerBI, R, Python, as well as AI technologies such as ChatGPT. For instance, we demonstrated to students the seamless conversion of programming code from R to Python using ChatGPT, showcasing the practical applications of these tools in interdisciplinary contexts.

In all our interdisciplinary courses, students are tasked with completing group projects. These projects require students to create both PowerPoint Slideshows and Interactive Dashboards, deliver oral presentations to clients (if applicable), and subsequently upload their work onto their GitHub and Tableau Public pages. This approach allows students to consistently include the links to their GitHub and Tableau Public pages at the forefront of their resumes when pursuing job opportunities. The projects and examples they undertake hold significant meaning and importance, as emphasized by HR professionals invited to our courses. HR discussions shed light on the essential skill sets required for students to secure interview opportunities and job offers. Through this integrated approach, students are not only equipped with practical skills in data analysis and presentation but are also guided on how to effectively market these experiences to potential employers.

In the following sections, this chapter demonstrates how to integrate technology into interdisciplinary teaching. It includes project-based learning with digital tools, collaborative learning platforms, and field trips. The project results in students' success such as skill enhancement, undergraduate research publication, and good placement.

2. SOLAR POWER INDUSTRY PROJECTS- DATA COLLECTION THROUGH UNDERGRADUATE RESEARCH ABROAD TRIPS (FIELD TRIPS)

The China Solar PV Adoption Project was started with two undergraduate Abroad Trips, sponsored by the Office of Undergraduate Research, Adrian Tinsley Program (ATP), and the Center of International Engagement. In the summer of 2014, Dr. Liu led four undergraduate students from the Management Department and Math Department to conduct basic marketing research on the solar panel industry in China. Again, in the Summer of 2016, Dr. Liu co-led the second research trip with Dr. Tran from Economics with another four students from Management and Economics to conduct more in-depth research. For both trips, faculty members submitted the proposal; called for and selected students for participation' planned the 21-day trip; co-designed questionnaires for manufacturers, installers, and residential and college students; filed IRB applications; directed students to input the data; and helped them with analysis of it.

To enrich students' experiences in China, the trips included a professional conference, a trade show, a manufacturing facility tour in the solar industry, and additional cultural exposure. Students learned much throughout the trip- students benefited from the experience, they built connections in the solar industry and developed strong research skills and soft skills. The SNEC conference in Shanghai is the largest industrial conference in this field. Students had a chance to meet with professionals, listen to talks by experts, and build connections. The speakers discussed cutting-edge research, current government policy, international trade influence, and the outlook for this industry. The conference also organized a facility tour to local businesses. The team went to the largest solar panel manufacturers in the world, including Canadian Solar and GCL Solar, to visit production lines and observe the demonstration projects in Shanghai Industrial Park. Attendance at this conference provided students with a great introduction to this field, on which they will continue to build. A trade show was taking place at the same time as the SNEC conference. More than 300 manufacturers in the supply chain of solar power panels were in attendance. Their products ranged from raw materials, such as silicon; to final products, such as the solar panel. With all this first-hand experience, students gained an excellent foundational understanding of the industry. This exhibition also provided an opportunity for students to conduct surveys with manufacturers. The team collected 80 surveys from the manufacturers within three days.

In Beijing and later back in Shanghai, the team collected data collection from local Chinese residents. Using questionnaires, we conducted interviews to understand their opinions regarding the rooftop solar system and their willingness to adopt it in the future on their own rooftops. Since college students are the primary potential customers for the solar industry, we created a separate survey to have a close look at their purchasing intention and interests. This questionnaire also examined the knowledge level of sustainability and clean energy. The findings have the potential to entice Chinese professors to redesign their curricula to incorporate sustainability.

Over 21 days, the team collected primary data through approximately 600 surveys distributed to college students, and manufacturers, and other residents of China. I continued to direct and work very closely with our students. I identified the major relevant literature, co-wrote a literature review with them, taught them fundamental data analysis techniques, and helped them get their papers published in the Undergraduate Review.

This project in Summer 2016 used Hofstede's Culture Theory (2012) and environmental behavior factors to demonstrate the impact consideration of culturally driven practices in China can have in solar PV distributed system adoption. The theory includes six dimensions of national culture – power distance, individualism, masculinity, uncertainty avoidance, pragmatism, and indulgence – widely used to explain the cross-cultural social practices of economic/business phenomena. With limited research focusing on this area previously, this study served to bridge the gap between cultural consideration and technological adoption, a growing need globally, particularly in the solar PV field.

The final success can be seen from the student researchers' publications and the offer for their graduate study. A few student research groups eventually published their work (Sun and Spicer, 2016; Zheng and Prince, 2015; E. Amoako and J. Wilson, 2017) in the BSU Undergraduate Review. Some students extended the research results in their honors thesis (Sun 2015 and Bell 2017). One of the student researchers was also able to pursue her Ph.D. study at Drexel University because of the abroad trip and the engagement in further research.

3. PROJECT EMBEDDED COURSE- STATISTICAL CONSULTING

We further integrated this research project into our undergraduate course teaching so that more students can benefit from this research.

The China Solar PV Adoption Project delves into the intricate interplay of cultural factors, environmental beliefs, norms, and barriers that influence decisions regarding solar PV adoption. This investigation is based on data collected from 351 college students in China. On the other hand, the Collaborative University Business Experiences (CUBEs) project sheds light on the importance of integrating real-world client projects into coursework. This project explored the significance of such involvement through survey data, which includes responses from 227 individuals including students, faculty, employers, and Human Resources (HR) representatives. Both datasets from these projects were rich with real-life data, each posing its unique challenges, including the common occurrence of missing values. These challenges provided invaluable learning opportunities for students as they navigated the complexities of data analysis and interpretation within an interdisciplinary context.

To enhance student comprehension of the project, we initiated a comprehensive literature review catering to individuals with diverse backgrounds. Through reading the classic papers in the area (Hofstede 1984 &2004) and the most recent literature (Labay and Kinnear 1981; Faiers and Neame 2006; Gadenne et al. 2011; Chen 2014;

Alipour et al. 2021) served to acquaint students with the interdisciplinary nature of scientific research, spanning various fields of study. Following the examination of 20 papers and reading materials, students realized how research had been developed over time and synthesized the literature review. This step improved students' skills of information collection, literacy understanding and synthesizing and critical thinking.

Following the literature review, we taught students about cultural factors, Hofstede's culture's consequences, and environmental factors. While this topic might be familiar to management students, it likely presented a new and intriguing concept for the science majors. Liu et al (2015) mentioned several mixed implications of this cultural perspective on the adoption of a distributed solar power system. The recent paper published by Ang, Fredriksson, and Sharma (2020) discussed how individualism influences the adoption of clean energy. The questionnaire consisted of varieties of items designed to detect whether they significantly affect the solar PV panel adoption status.

Our subsequent stage involved educating students on the significance of hypotheses and guiding them on how to formulate and address these hypotheses effectively. Based on prior studies and the selected factors, this study proposed the following hypotheses:

- H1: The cultural factors are associated with the environmental factors (beliefs, barriers & norms).
- H2: The general environmental belief (environmental adaptation) is associated with environmental norms.
- H3: The environmental barrier (professional assistance) is associated with environmental norms.
- H4: The cultural factors significantly affect the current adoption status of solar PV panel.
- H5: The environmental factors (belief, barrier & norms) significantly affect the current solar PV panel adoption status.

We guided students to find appropriate statistical tools in conducting hypothesis test. The Multivariate Analysis of Variance (MANOVA) is also applied to test Hypothesis 2 and Hypothesis 3, the environmental norms are considered as the dependent variables, and the general environmental belief and environmental barrier are the independent variables. To examine which factors may significantly affect the current solar PV panel adaptation status, students realized that a logistic regression analysis is appropriate since the adaptation status is a binary variable.

Our final step involved guiding students to draw conclusions from the data analysis, interpret findings from various aspects using their own background knowledge, and explore potential avenues for future studies that may spark interest. Our data indicated the following major findings to students: some norms such as price norms and action norms are significantly associated with some cultural factors such as individualism, long-time orientation, and masculinity; while environmental adaptation and professional assistance factors are only significantly associated with individualism and masculinity In terms of the culture trait of individualism, our results are consistent with Ang, Fredriksson, and Sharma (2020)'s work. Students also realized some limitations such as convenience samples with only college students, which might influence the accuracy level of the conclusion. Therefore, this points to the future research direction to include household data. Meanwhile, the current analysis is based on the current installation. More research could be done about which factors influenced the intention for PV rooftop installation in the next five and ten years. Some students mentioned their interests in collecting data from different countries in future research. This step also provided students with further development in their critical thinking skills.

4. IMPLEMENTING TECHNOLOGY IN TEACHING

In preparing students from diverse backgrounds and majors to effectively work with data, a key emphasis lies in highlighting the critical aspects of employing technologies to present findings. This includes the creation of interactive dashboards designed for audiences, whether they are well-versed in statistical terminology and concepts or not. In all our courses, we utilized a diverse array of statistical, mathematical, and management models, complemented by an assortment of statistical software tools. These tools included Tableau, PowerBI, R, Python, as well as AI technologies such as ChatGPT. For instance, we demonstrated to students the seamless conversion of programming code from R to Python using ChatGPT, showcasing the practical applications of these tools in interdisciplinary contexts.

As mentioned above, in this interdisciplinary course, students were tasked with completing group projects. These projects required students to create both Power-Point Slideshows and Interactive Dashboards, deliver oral presentations to clients (if applicable), and subsequently upload their work onto their GitHub and Tableau Public pages. This approach allows students to consistently include the links to their GitHub and Tableau Public pages at the forefront of their resumes when pursuing job opportunities. The projects and examples they undertook held significant meaning and importance, as emphasized by HR professionals who were invited to our courses. HR discussions shed light on the essential skill sets required for students to secure interview opportunities and job offers. Through this integrated approach, students were not only equipped with practical skills in data analysis and presentation but were also guided on how to effectively market these experiences to potential employers.

We provided step-by-step instructions for grouping students from different majors to conduct a scientific research project using survey data on China's solar PV panels. Subsequently, we encouraged students to apply their learning and insights by working on another real-life survey dataset, CUBEs data. Remarkably, students were able to generate similar reports by leveraging their own findings and experiences. The results, findings, and presentations highlighted in this paper highlighted the importance of integrating technology into the teaching process, particularly within interdisciplinary curricula.

5. CONCLUSION

This chapter examines our current practices of incorporating a research project into our interdisciplinary course teaching. Students had the opportunity to understand and appreciate the emerging clean energy technology of solar power panel adoption. They conducted a close examination of both the technological and human aspects, including cultural perspectives and international components. Students also applied advanced data analysis tools, using real-world data to enhance their skills in the digital world. Students were intrigued by the interdisciplinary topic including economic, social, and environmental concerns and improved their skills along the rigorous research process.

6. FUTURE STUDY

Despite the evident skill improvements and successful projects, it is essential to conduct a formal assessment of student skills to establish a baseline for future development. Additionally, while the Statistical Consulting course has a limited enrollment, it would be beneficial to incorporate similar projects into larger classes with a wider audience.

REFERENCES

Alipour, M., Salim, H., Stewart, R. A., & Sahin, O. (2021). Residential solar photovoltaic adoption behavior: End-to-end review of theories, methods and approaches. *Renewable Energy*, 170, 471–486. DOI: 10.1016/j.renene.2021.01.128

Amoako, E., & Wilson, J. T. (2017). Environmental behavior factors influencing the outlook of Chinese college students on the domestic adoption of solar photovoltaic technology. *Undergraduate Review*, 13(1), 7–30.

Ang, J. B., Fredriksson, P. G., & Sharma, S. (2020). Individualism and the adoption of clean energy technology. *Resource and Energy Economics*, 61, 101180. DOI: 10.1016/j.reseneeco.2020.101180

Bell, A. Cultural Factors Influencing Chinese Residents and Students' Views on Solar Photovoltaic Rooftop Adoption. In *BSU Honors Program Theses and Projects*. Item 207. 2017. Available at: https://vc.bridgew.edu/honors_proj/207

Chen, K. K. (2014). Assessing the effects of customer innovativeness, environmental value and ecological lifestyles on residential solar power systems install intention. *Energy Policy*, 67, 951–961. DOI: 10.1016/j.enpol.2013.12.005

Faiers, A., & Neame, C. (2006). Consumer attitudes towards domestic solar power systems. *Energy Policy*, 34(14), 1797–1806. DOI: 10.1016/j.enpol.2005.01.001

Gadenne, D., Sharma, B., Kerr, D., & Smith, T. (2011). The influence of consumers' environmental beliefs and attitudes on energy saving behaviors. *Energy Policy*, 39(12), 7684–7694. DOI: 10.1016/j.enpol.2011.09.002

Hofstede, G. (1984). Culture's consequences: International differences in work-related values (Vol. 5). sage.

Hofstede, G., Hofstede, G. J., & Minkov, M. (2005). *Cultures and organizations: Software of the mind* (Vol. 2). Mcgraw-hill New York.

Labay, D. G., & Kinnear, T. C. (1981). Exploring the consumer decision process in the adoption of solar energy systems. *The Journal of Consumer Research*, 8(3), 271–278. DOI: 10.1086/208865

Liu, X., Sun, Y., & Kaloustian, T. S. (2015). Cultural Factors Influencing Domestic Adoption of Solar Photovoltaic Technology: Perspectives from China. China Media Research, 11(4).

Sun, Y. (2015). Exploring residents' attitudes toward solar photovoltaic system adoption in China.

Sun, Y. (2015). Exploring residents' attitudes toward solar photovoltaic system adoption in China.

Zheng, B., & Prince, P. E. (2015). Purchasing efficiency measurement of selected chinese pv panels using data envelopment analysis (DEA). *Undergraduate Review*, 11(1), 148–155.

Afterword

As dreadful as it was, the COVID-19 epidemic motivated us to do something that would benefit teaching and learning in higher education. Hence the idea of writing a series of books to address education, philosophy, technology, student success, assessment, leadership, global engagement, artificial intelligence, and other relevant topics. Hence, the first successful book and SCOPUS Index *"The Role of Educators as Agents and Conveyors for Positive Change in Global Education"*, was born and published in 2023 by the IGI-Global. As authors, we are excited to build on that momentum. Our first book was based on the idea of peer-reviewing the papers submitted for the *13th International Conference on Education: Educators as Agents for Change*, held in Fez, Morocco, in June 2022.

Continuing this endeavor, we have decided to grab the same opportunity of assembling the best-read papers from the *15th International Conference on Education: Innovative Technologies Transforming the Future of Higher Education,* which was Organized jointly by Bridgewater State University (BSU), Bridgewater, MA, USA, Sidi Mohamed Ben Abdalla University (USMBA) Morocco, and the Faculty of Education Sciences, Tafila Technical University (TTU), Jordan. This 15th International Conference took place at BSU on June 24-25, 2024. A proposal was submitted to IGI-Global who consented to the idea that this new volume reflects the latest advancements and use of innovative technologies, particularly focusing on the impact of Artificial Intelligence Tools. Our proposal to IGI-Global was approved, as it aligns with the current trends and transformative changes in the educational landscape. Thus emerged our second volume of the series *"Emerging Technologies Transforming Higher Education: Instructional Design and Student Success"*. The contributors represent a wide range of countries and from various reputable colleges and universities.

Our current volume includes twelve chapters contributed by scholars from diverse parts of the world. These chapters align with the three themes identified in the book, 1) Defining and exploring instructional technologies, 2) Improving Instruction and Learning with Technology, and 3) Instructional Technologies' Global Impact.

1. Defining and Exploring Instructional Technologies

Four chapters were included under this theme of exploring instructional technologies. AI tools continue to evolve, adding new features, and facilitating learning and teaching. It is noted that for the first time in higher education especially, the students are ahead of the faculty in their use of AI Tools for their basic paper writing, computer software program coding, graphic design with slides, self-grammar correction, and research papers with citations, to name a few. It is time that the faculty catch up to the students' innovative genius of using these AI tools in their assignments and paper submissions. Exploring instructional technologies is very critical nowadays. They are continually evolving and changing fast. This theoretical discussion revolves around one main point: It is not whether students and faculty are using AI software, but which software and for what purposes. Drs. Rao and Al-Obaidi aim to provide a comprehensive understanding of various AI applications in learning, writing, research, and pedagogy. Apart from this, they investigate the advantages and challenges of these AI tools, their functionalities, benefits, drawbacks, and the ethical sensitivities surrounding their implementation.

A few discipline-based AI tools are being launched continually across the globe. While these limited selective AI tools share a common goal of enhancing academic pursuits, they differ in their specific functionalities and areas of focus. Browsing sources from across the web, September 2024, here are some of the selected AI tools prevalent in the market. More prevalent and widely used AI tools in higher education include ChatGPT, QuillBot, Copilot (formerly Bing Chat), Gemini, Consensus, Canva, Perplexity, Cognii, Curipod, Resume Worded, Tome, Gradescope, Quizlet, Grammarly, and Easy AI Checker. Another leading finding indicates that higher education institutions (HEIs) are in critical need of upgrading existing regulations and introducing new policies to manage and integrate AI and its open sources in classes, management, scheduling, creating syllabi, and the whole operation of teaching and learning. Continuous research, open dialogue, and responsible implementation strategies are essential to harness the full potential of AI in higher education while mitigating its risks and challenges. In the next chapter, Ms. Sommer examines how university professors manage expectations for essay writing and support students' writing development in their classes using AI platforms such as ChatGPT and Grammarly. The findings are designed to assist university boards, teacher educators, and preservice teachers in making informed decisions regarding AI in postsecondary classrooms. The idea is that university professors should support students' writing development in their classes by thoughtful integration of AI Tools to complement traditional teaching methods. Finally, there is a need for additional longitudinal studies on the long-term effects of AI integration in education and comparative analyses of different AI tools and platforms.

It is essential to grasp the ever-changing nature of AI in academic settings and how it impacts teaching methods, academic honesty, and the overall educational experience. AI chatbots have become increasingly popular among students in higher education because of their user-friendly interface and their ability to provide timely feedback on academic tasks. However, the growing dependence on AI chatbots has resulted in a surge in academic dishonesty and a decrease in students' critical thinking abilities. Educators, developers, and researchers must work together to ensure that chatbots improve learning outcomes and are consistent with educational objectives. Successful integration of these AI tools depends on a balance between innovation and responsibility, empowering both educators and learners in their pursuit of knowledge.

To stay competitive and relevant in the ever-evolving field of education, it is imperative that our faculty continually acquire new skills, upgrade existing ones, and engage in professional development. The chapter utilized a phenomenological transcendental design with ten participants. Qualitative data was collected through a semi-structured questionnaire and focus group discussions (FGD). The study identified several emerging themes related to transformational instruction practices, implementation of flexible learning, and their impact on students' university experience.

2. Improving Instruction and Learning with Technology

Information and communication technologies (ICT) refers to technologies that give access to information through Telecommunication. Virtual learning and teaching environments, adopting digital tools, and communication platforms could facilitate interaction, knowledge sharing, and collaborative problem-solving among educators and learners, enriching the quality and accessibility of education.

Several chapters endeavor to contribute meaningful insights to the discourse on technology integration in education, offering valuable perspectives for educators, policymakers, and researchers. For example, the authors investigated the correlation between the employment of innovative technologies in teaching and the teachers' management of both time and class. Through an opinion poll of teachers of various disciplines at Sidi Mohamed Ben Abdellah University of Fez, Morocco, the chapter presents an insight into the benefits and downsides of technology integration and dependence in Moroccan higher education.

The interconnectivity between technology in classrooms and instructions invokes the idea of combining qualitative and quantitative analysis approaches to address socioeconomic diversity and equity in higher education. The mixed approaches ensure that the findings are well-rounded and grounded in numerical data and rich narrative analysis. Recognizing and embracing diversity in the classroom requires understanding students' socioeconomic, cultural, and linguistic differences and tailoring teaching methods accordingly. This includes using diverse instructional materials, fostering inclusive classroom discussions, and promoting representation in course content. This is to emphasize that educators are expected to employ various strategies to foster an inclusive learning environment. These include differentiated instruction, culturally responsive teaching, and the use of multiple teaching utilities to acclimatize diverse learning styles. Improving instruction and learning with technology does not exclude the implementation of AI even in elementary science education for teachers and students. Shawn O'Neill concluded his chapter that through AI tools, teachers can develop customized, creative, and diverse science lessons that spark interest, encourage thinking, and equip students for the demands of a world driven by technological advancements.

3. Instructional Technologies and Crossing Boundaries

This theme addresses the impact of technology on learning and teaching in higher education across the world. Instructional technologies are no longer confined to the lucky advanced regions but instead spread their wings more broadly. Admittedly, higher education institutions vary in their systems and financial abilities to acquire technologies, yet they have managed to take advantage of the available Instructional Technologies.

Higher education institutions throughout the world succeed in adopting transformative ways to establish cross-cultural collaboration and eliminate geographic boundaries. Indeed, technology-mediated education has a significant impact on higher education. In addition, Miss Ouelfatmi, Dr. Alaoui, and Dr. Boivin, the authors of Chapter 8, pointed out that the rise of demand for digital skills has become a crucial part of 21st-century skills. Technology has reshaped students' engagement with course material, academic networks, and access to resources and led to the implementation of technology-enhanced learning.

Higher education institutions worldwide have successfully embraced transformative methods for cross-cultural collaboration and overcoming geographic barriers through technology-mediated education, significantly impacting higher education in terms of transferring and sharing knowledge, involving students, and creating a platform for collaboration among educators. The employment of digital tools and platforms to improve the efficacy of international academic partnerships and promote cross-cultural interactions has become the norm for education. Cross-border educational efforts are in full display to overcome the financial, linguistic, and cultural barriers between students, teachers, and administrators. T

The chapters under this theme demonstrate that Engaging in cross-border academic initiatives exposes students to varied perspectives and fresh knowledge, expanding their learning experiences. A high percentage of students (85%) reported enhanced knowledge acquisition by joining online international courses like the adaptation of Collaborative Online International Learning (COIL). It is a testimony of the advantages of collaborative contacts in broadening students' academic horizons, which is consistent with theories of collaborative learning and literature review.

CONCLUSION

Collaborating with insightful scholars from Canada, India, Morocco, the Philippines, Spain, the United States, and Yemen was both a powerful experience and a welcoming challenge for us as volume editors. We managed this intellectual task by prioritizing cross-educational, cultural, and linguistic engagement. We put to test our abilities to understand and incorporate the significant contribution of colleagues who came from different cultural, social, and ethnic backgrounds. The result of this academic test was incredible and carefully selected chapters that are designed to lay solid ground for our book "Emerging Technologies Transforming Higher Education: Instructional Design and Student Success"

In the future, educators and organizations can build on these discoveries to create creative educational strategies and cooperative projects that support students' academic development, global perspectives, and intercultural learning in an interconnected world. We hope that in the future, educators, policymakers, and stakeholders can leverage these digital discoveries to develop innovative educational strategies that support students' academic development, global awareness, and cross-cultural learning in an interconnected world.

Compilation of References

Abbas, H. (2022). Behavioral intention to use as a factor in a learning management system in Kuwait. *International Journal of Virtual and Personal Learning Environments*, 12(1), 1–21. DOI: 10.4018/IJVPLE.307018

Abenes, R., & Malibiran, A. L. (2020). Filipino diaspora in the light of Louis Althusser's concept of ideology. *The URSP Research Journal*, 6(1), 21–30.

Aburub, I., & Assaf, D. (2022). *Digital Transformation of Higher Education in Palestine: Employment, Obstacles, and Trends*. Baltic Journal of Law & Politics., DOI: 10.2478/bjlp-2022-002041

Acar, H., Akar, M., & Acar, B. (2016). Value orientations of social workers. *Kastamonu Education Journal.*, 24(1), 97–118.

Adeva, P. K. (2023, April 5). *Will AI chatbots take over education?* Philippine Collegian. https://phkule.org/article/813/will-ai-chatbots-take-over-education

Adisa, K., Byrd, A., Flores, L., Gibson, A., Green, D., Hassel, H., Johnson, S., Kirschenbuam, M., Lockett, A., Mathews, E., & Mills, A. (2023). MLA-CCCC joint task force on writing and AI working paper: Overview of the issues, statement of principles, and recommendations. *Humanities Commons.*https://hcommons.org/app/uploads/sites/1003160/2023/07/MLA-CCCC-Joint-Task-Force-on-Writing-and-AI-Working-Paper-1.pdf

Adler, N. (2004). Shaping history: Global Leadership in The Twenty-First Century. In Scullion, H., & Lineham, M. (Eds.), *International human resource management: A critical text* (pp. 281–297). Palgrave.

Adzharuddin, N. (2013). Learning management system (LMS) among university students: Does it work? *International Journal of E-Education e-Business e-. Management Learning*. Advance online publication. DOI: 10.7763/IJEEEE.2013.V3.233

Afsar, B. S., Asad, S., & Syed, I. A. (2019). The mediating role of transformational leadership in the relationship between cultural intelligence and employee voice behavior: A case of hotel employees. *International Journal of Intercultural Relations*, 69, 66–75. DOI: 10.1016/j.ijintrel.2019.01.001

Agustin, F., L., & Santa Rosa City, Laguna Philippines 4026. (. (2022). Modified Learning Management System: Making A difference in E-learning this new normal. *International Multidisciplinary Research Journal*, 4(2), 21–29. DOI: 10.54476/iimrj47

Ahmad, I., Samsugi, S., & Irawan, Y. (2022). Penerapan Augmented Reality Pada Anatomi Tubuh Manusia Untuk Mendukung Pembelajaran Titik Titik Bekam Pengobatan Alternatif. *Jurnal Teknoinfo*, 16(1), 46. Advance online publication. DOI: 10.33365/jti.v16i1.1521

Ahmad, S. F., Han, H., Alam, M. M., Rehmat, M., Irshad, M., Arrano-Munoz, M., & Ariza-Montez, A. (2023). Impact of artificial intelligence on human loss in decision making, laziness and safety in education. *Humanities & Social Sciences Communications*, 10(1), 1–14. DOI: 10.1057/s41599-023-01787-8 PMID: 37325188

Ahmed, T. N., & Mahmood, K. A. (2024). A Critical Discourse Analysis of ChatGPT's Role in Knowledge and Power Production. *Arab World English Journal (AWEJ)*, 184-196. https://dx.doi.org/DOI: 10.24093/awej/ChatGPT.12

Ainscow, M., Booth, T., & Dyson, A. (2006). *Improving schools, developing inclusion*. Routledge. DOI: 10.4324/9780203967157

Akgun, S., & Greenhow, C. (2022). Artificial intelligence in education: Addressing ethical challenges in K-12 settings. *AI and Ethics*, 2(3), 431–440. DOI: 10.1007/s43681-021-00096-7 PMID: 34790956

Al Amoush, A. B., & Sandhu, K. (2019). LMS tools and data analysis approaches: Similarities and differences. In *Educational and Social Dimensions of Digital Transformation in Organizations* (pp. 65–76). IGI Global. DOI: 10.4018/978-1-5225-6261-0.ch004

Al Mansoori, A., Ali, S., Pasha, S. A., Alghizzawi, M., Elareshi, M., Ziani, A., & Alsridi, H. (2023). Technology Enhanced Learning Through Learning Management System and Virtual Reality Googles: A Critical Review. *Studies in Systems, Decision and Control*, 557–564. DOI: 10.1007/978-3-031-28314-7_48

Al Marzouqi, H. A., & Forster, N. (2011). An Exploratory Study of the Under-representation of Emirate Women in The United Arab Emirates' Information Technology Sector. *Equality, Diversity and Inclusion*, 30(7), 544–562. DOI: 10.1108/02610151111167016

Al-Alawi, A. I. l. (2016, July). Status of Bahraini Women in The Banking and Financial Sector: Challenges and Opportunities. *Journal of International Women's Studies*, 17(4), 210–228.

Alamin, A., Muthanna, A., & Alduais, A. (2022). A Qualitative Evidence Synthesis of The K-12 Education Policy Making in Sudan and the Need for Reforms. *SAGE Open*, 12(1), 215824402110710. DOI: 10.1177/21582440211071081

Al-Ansari, Y., Pervan, S. & Xu, J. (2013). Innovation and Business Performance of SMEs: The Case of Dubai. *Education, Business and Society: Contemporary Middle Eastern Issues*, Vol. 6Nos 3/4, pp. 162-180.

Aldawsari, H. A. H. (2024). Evaluating Translation Tools: Google Translate, Bing Translator, and Bing AI on Arabic Colloquialisms. *Arab World English Journal (AWEJ),* 237-251. https://dx.doi.org/DOI: 10.24093/awej/ChatGPT.16

Aldridge, M. (2015). Modelling mindful practice. Reflective Practice. *International and Multidisciplinary Perspectives.* DOI: 10.1080/14623943.2015.1023278

Alexander, S. (2020). Flexible Learning in Higher Education. *International Encyclopedia of Education. 441–447.* DOI: 10.1016/B978-0-08-044894-7.00868-X

Alghariani, M. (2024). Libyan Women: Examining Their Educational Reality and Contribution to Economic Development.

Ali, (2024). Locating the Intersection of Generative Artificial Intelligence and Human English Writing Skills: A Comparative Study. *Arab World English Journal (AWEJ),* 120-130.

Ali, F., Choy, D., Divaharan, S., Tay, H. Y., & Chen, W. (2023). Supporting self-directed learning and self-assessment using TeacherGAIA, a generative AI chatbot application: Learning approaches and prompt engineering. *Learning: Research and Practice*, 1–13. https://doi.org/DOI: 10.1080/23735082.2023.2258886

Alipour, M., Salim, H., Stewart, R. A., & Sahin, O. (2021). Residential solar photovoltaic adoption behavior: End-to-end review of theories, methods and approaches. *Renewable Energy*, 170, 471–486. DOI: 10.1016/j.renene.2021.01.128

Al-Jaro, M. S. (2023). A qualitative case study of EFL student teachers' teaching practice during practicum. *BRU ELT JOURNAL, 1*(1), 29–42. https://doi.org/DOI: 10.14456/bej.2023.3

Aljuaid, H. (2024). The Impact of Artificial Intelligence Tools on Academic Writing Instruction in Higher Education: A Systematic Review. *Arab World English Journal (AWEJ)*, 26-55.

Almasri, N., Tahat, L., Skaf, S., & Masri, A. A. (2019). *A Digital Platform for Supervised Self-Directed Learning in Emergencies: The Case of The Syrian Crisis. Technology, Pedagogy and Education*, 28(1), 91–113. DOI: 10.1080/1475939X.2019.1568293

Almelhem, S., Almshhor, E., Alabdullah, S., Kadan, B., Alzoabi, M., & Jhar, A. (2022). Factors Affecting Gender Balance In Higher Education In Northwest Syria: Challenges And Potential Actions. *International Journal of Educational Research Open*, 3, 100164. DOI: 10.1016/j.ijedro.2022.100164

Al-Mughairi, H. and Bhaskar, P. (2024). Exploring the factors affecting the adoption AI techniques in higher education: insights from teachers' perspectives on ChatGPT. *Journal of Research in Innovative Teaching & Learning,* 2397-7604. https://doi.org/ DOI: 10.1108/JRIT-09-2023-0129

Alosaimi, B. A. A., & Alawad, N. A. (2024). Evaluation of the Translation of Separable Phrasal Verbs Generated by ChatGPT. *Arab World English Journal (AWEJ)*, 282-291.

Al-Qarni, M. A. (2024, July 12). For global AI competitiveness, US and Saudi Arabia have similar strategies. *Arab News*. https://www.arabnews.com/node/2548196/ %7B%7B

Al-Rahmi, W., Aldraiweesh, A., Yahaya, N., Bin Kamin, Y., & Zeki, A. M. (2019). Massive Open Online Courses (MOOCs): Data on Higher Education. *Data in Brief*, 22, 118–125. DOI: 10.1016/j.dib.2018.11.139 PMID: 30581914

Alsakkaf, R. (Sept 29, 2023) https://medium.com/lampshade-of-illumination/resume -worded-ccd8331158f3

Alsalem, A. S. (2018). Curriculum orientations and educational philosophies of high school Arabic teachers. *International Education Studies*, 11(4), 92–95. DOI: 10.5539/ies.v11n4p92

Alshaikh, M. (2020). Developing cybersecurity culture to influence employee behavior: A practice perspective. [CrossRef]. *Computers & Security*, 98, 102003. DOI: 10.1016/j.cose.2020.102003

Alshehri, A. J., Rutter, M., & Smith, S. (2020). The effects of UTAUT and usability qualities on students' use of learning management systems in Saudi tertiary education. *Journal of Information Technology Education*, 19, 891–930. DOI: 10.28945/4659

Alston, E. (Feb 28, 2024) https://zapier.com/blog/how-to-use-google-bard/

Altbach, P. G., & Knight, J. (2007). The internationalization of higher education: Motivations and realities. *Journal of Studies in International Education*, 11(3-4), 290–305. DOI: 10.1177/1028315307303542

Alzaabi, I., Ramírez-García, A., & Moyano, M. (2021). Gendered STEM: A Systematic Review and Applied Analysis of Female Participation in STEM in The United Arab Emirates. *Education Sciences*, 11(10), 573. DOI: 10.3390/educsci11100573

Alzahrani, L. (2023). Analyzing Students' Attitude and Behavior Toward Artificial Intelligence Technologies in Higher Education. [IJRTE]. *International Journal of Recent Technology and Engineering*, 11(6), 65–73. DOI: 10.35940/ijrte.F7475.0311623

Al-Zubaidi, K. O., Jaafari, M., & Touzani, M. (2024). Impact of ChatGPT on Academic Writing at Moroccan Universities. *Arab World English Journal (AWEJ)*, 20-30.

Amoako, E., & Wilson, J. T. (2017). Environmental behavior factors influencing the outlook of Chinese college students on the domestic adoption of solar photovoltaic technology. *Undergraduate Review*, 13(1), 7–30.

Angeli, C. (2024, March). Implementing Technological Pedagogical Content Knowledge Amid Uncertain Conditions: Advancements in Comprehending Contextual Factors.

Ang, J. B., Fredriksson, P. G., & Sharma, S. (2020). Individualism and the adoption of clean energy technology. *Resource and Energy Economics*, 61, 101180. DOI: 10.1016/j.reseneeco.2020.101180

Annuš, N. (2024). Education in the Age of Artificial Intelligence. *TEM Journal*, 13(1), 404–413.

Annuš, N., Csóka, M., & Paksi, D. (2023). Learning Management Systems and Their Possibilities in Education - Case of Slovakia. 17th International Technology, *Education and Development Conference*, 6981-6986. Doi: DOI: 10.21125/inted.2023.1896

Appleton, L. A. (1993). *Educational Development in Western Libya, 1942-1952: A Critical Assessment of the Aims*. Methods and Policies of the British Military Administration.

Artificial Intelligence Blog https://www.artificial-intelligence.blog/ai-news/from-bard-to-gemini-a-look-at-the-evolution-of-googles-ai-assistant. Accessed on July 16, 2024.

Artificial intelligence in education. (2023). *UNESCO*. https://www.unesco.org/en/digital-education/artificial-intelligence

Ashour, S. (2020). Quality Higher Education is the Foundation of a Knowledge Society: Where Does the UAE Stand? *Quality in Higher Education*, 26(2), 209–223. Advance online publication. DOI: 10.1080/13538322.2020.1769263

Ashrafi, A., Zareravasan, A., Rabiee Savoji, S., & Amani, M. (2022). Exploring factors influencing students' continuance intention to use the learning management system (LMS): A multi-perspective framework. *Interactive Learning Environments*, 30(8), 1475–1497. DOI: 10.1080/10494820.2020.1734028

Asma U.l., Hosna, L., & Mahmud Hamid, T. (2021). A Review of the relationship of Idealized Influence, Inspirational Motivation, Intellectual Stimulation, and Individual Consideration with Sustainable Employees Performance. *International Journal of Progressive Sciences and Technologies*

Awa-abuon, J. (2023). How to Reduce AI Hallucination With These 6 Prompting Techniques. https://www.makeuseof.com/how-to-reduce-ai-hallucination/

Aydın, Ö., & Karaarslan, E. (2022). OpenAI ChatGPT generated literature review: Digital twin in healthcare. In Ö. Aydın (Ed.), *Emerging Computer Technologies 2*, 22–31. İzmir Akademi Dernegi. http://dx.doi.org/DOI: 10.2139/ssrn.4308687

Ayodele, T. (2010). Machine Learning Overview. .DOI: 10.5772/9374

Bahroun, Z., Anane, C., Ahmed, V., & Zacca, A. (2023). Transforming education: A comprehensive review of generative artificial intelligence in educational settings through bibliometric and content analysis. *Sustainability (Basel)*, 15(17), 12983. DOI: 10.3390/su151712983

Bala, K., & Colvin, A. (2023). *Generative Artificial Intelligence for Education and Pedagogy*.

Banilower, E. R., Smith, P. S., Malzahn, K. A., Plumley, C. L., Gordon, E. M., & Hayes, M. L. (2018). *Report of the 2018 NSSME*. Horizon Research, Inc.

Banks, J. A. (2015). *Cultural diversity and education: Foundations, curriculum, and teaching* (6th ed.). Routledge. DOI: 10.4324/9781315622255

Banzuelo, N. (2023). What Filipino students are saying about ChatGPT. *Business-World Online.* https://www.bworldonline.com/technology/2023/04/19/517952/what-filipino-students-are-saying-about-chatgpt/

Barbieru, D., Roceanu, I., Beligan, D., & Radu, C. (2014). DEVELOPING LEARNING MODULES FOR LMS. *ELearning and Software for Education.*

Barkley, E. F., Cross, K. P., & Major, C. H. (2014). *Collaborative learning techniques: A handbook for college faculty.* John Wiley & Sons.

Barret, L., & Long, V. (2012). *The Moore Method and the Constructivist Theory of Learning: Was R. L. Moore a Constructivist?* Taylor and Francis., DOI: 10.1080/10511970.2010.493548

Barton, G. M., & Ryan, M. (2014). Multimodal approaches to reflective teaching and assessment in higher education: A cross disciplinary approach in creative industries. Higher Education Research & Development, 33, 409–424. *International Studies on Educational Management..*DOI: 10.1080/07294360.2013.841650

Baskerville, R., & Siponen, M. (2002). An information security meta-policy for emergent organisations. [Google Scholar] [CrossRef] [Green Version]. *Logistics Information Management*, 15(5/6), 337–346. DOI: 10.1108/09576050210447019

Bates, T. (2017). *The 2017 national survey of online learning in Canadian post-secondary education: methodology and results.* International Journal of Education and Technology., DOI: 10.1186/s41239-018-0112-3

Beatman, A. (Dec 14, 2023) https://azure.microsoft.com/en-us/blog/azure-openai-service-powers-the-microsoft-copilot-ecosystem/#:~:text=Copilot—powered%20by%20Microsoft%20Azure,infrastructure%20from%20cloud%20to%20edge

Beelen, J., & Jones, E. (2015). Redefining internationalization at home. In Beelen, J., & de Wit, H. (Eds.), *Internationalization at Home: A Position Paper* (pp. 7–12). European Association for International Education.

Bell, A. Cultural Factors Influencing Chinese Residents and Students' Views on Solar Photovoltaic Rooftop Adoption. In *BSU Honors Program Theses and Projects.* Item 207. 2017. Available at: https://vc.bridgew.edu/honors_proj/207

Ben Salah, M., Chambru, C., & Fourati, M. (2022). The colonial Legacy of Education: Evidence from Tunisia. SSRN *Electronic Journal.* https://doi.org/DOI: 10.2139/ssrn.4101795

Benjamin, L. T. (1988). A History of Teaching Machines. *The American Psychologist*, 43(9), 703–712. DOI: 10.1037/0003-066X.43.9.703

Ben-Khalifa, T. (2024). A Critical Perspective to Higher Education in the 21st Century Tunisia: The Problems of the Present and the Challenges of the Future. Trends in Education and Educational Studies, 1(1), 1-13 ceiling or sticky floor? *Journal of North African Studies*, 28(4), 976–1005. DOI: 10.1080/13629387.2022.2113992

Bennett, M. J. (1993). Towards ethnorelativism: A developmental model of intercultural sensitivity. In Paige, R. M. (Ed.), *Education for the intercultural experience* (pp. 21–71). Intercultural Press.

Berber Sardinha, T. (2024). AI-generated vs human-authored texts: A multidimensional comparison. *Applied Corpus Linguistics, 4*(1), 100083-. https://doi.org/DOI: 10.1016/j.acorp.2023.100083

Berkeshchuk, I. S., Shcherbak, I. V., Shkvorchenko, N. M., Masytska T. E. & Chornyi, I. V. (2020). Modern Technologies and Applications of ICT in the Training Process of Teachers-Philologists. *International Journal of Higher Education*. Vol. 9, No. 7; 2020 URL: https://doi.org/.DOI: 10.5430/ijhe.v9n7p84

Bervell, B., & Umar, I. N. (2018). Utilization decision towards LMS for blended learning in distance education: Modeling the effects of personality factors in exclusivity. *Knowledge Management & E-Learning. International Journal (Toronto, Ont.)*, ●●●, 309–333. DOI: 10.34105/j.kmel.2018.10.018

Bhattacharya, S. (2022). Artificial intelligence, human intelligence, and the future of public health. *AIMS Public Health*, 9(4), 644–650. DOI: 10.3934/publichealth.2022045 PMID: 36636147

Blanck, R., & Balch, D. E. (2024). Mitigating Hallucinations in LLMs for Community College Classrooms: Strategies to Ensure Reliable and Trustworthy Ai-Powered Learning Tools. Faculty Focus Daily, May 15, 2024._https://www.facultyfocus .com/articles/teaching-with-technology-articles/mitigating-hallucinations-in-llms -for-community-college-classrooms-strategies-to-ensure-reliable-and-trustworthy -ai-powered-learning-tools/?st=FFdaily;sc=FF240515;utm_term=FF240515& mailingID=6501&utm_source=ActiveCampaign&utm_medium=email&utm _content=Mitigating%20Hallucinations%20in%20LLMs%20for%20Community %20College%20Classrooms%3A%20Strategies%20to%20Ensure%20Reliable%20 and%20Trustworthy%20AI-Powered%20Learning%20Tools&utm_campaign= FF240515 Accessed: May 15, 2024.

Blank, R. K. (2013). *What is the impact of decline in science instructional time in elementary school?* Council of Chief State School Officers.

Boamah, S., Spence, K., Wong, C., & Clarke, S. (2018). Effect of transformational leadership on job satisfaction and patient safety outcomes. *Nursing Outlook*, 66(2), 180–189. Advance online publication. DOI: 10.1016/j.outlook.2017.10.004 PMID: 29174629

Bohr, D., & Kearns, R. (2016). The role of faculty development in promoting inclusive teaching. *Journal of Higher Education Policy and Management*, 38(1), 57–70.

Bond, M., Khosravi, H., De Laat, M., Bergdahl, N., Negrea, V., Oxley, E., Pham, P., Chong, S. W., & Siemens, G. (2024). A meta systematic review of artificial intelligence in higher education: A call for increased ethics, collaboration, and rigour. *International Journal of Educational Technology in Higher Education*, 21(1), 4. DOI: 10.1186/s41239-023-00436-z

Booth, T., & Ainscow, M. (2011). *The index for inclusion: A guide to school development led by inclusive values*. Centre for Studies on Inclusive Education.

Borasi, R. Miller, E. David; Vaughan-Brogan, Patricia; DeAngelis, Karen; Han, Yu. Jung & Sharon, Mason. (2024). *An AI Wishlist from School Leaders*. Phi Delta Kappa, May 1, 2024, 47-58. https://web-p-ebscohost-com.libserv-prd.bridgew.edu/ehost/pdfviewer/pdfviewer?vid=3&sid=e4171dce-a14d-40f5-97f4-303c18f16832%40redis

Bouchara, A. (2022). Les femmes à l'université marocaine: des trajectoires fractures. Observatoire Francophone pour le developpement inclusif par le genre. Cahiers de recherche OFDIG, no 02-2022. ISBN: 978-2-9821216-1-4.

Bouzar, A., EL Idrissi, K., & Ghourdou, T. (2024). ChatGPT and Academic Writing Self-Efficacy: Unveiling Correlations and Technological Dependency among Postgraduate Students. *Arab World English Journal (AWEJ)*, 225-236. https://dx.doi.org/DOI: 10.24093/awej/ChatGPT.15

Braidotti, R. (2019). A Theoretical Framework for the Critical Post-humanities. *Theory, Culture & Society*, 36(6), 31–61. DOI: 10.1177/0263276418771486

Braun, V., & Clarke, V. (2006). Using thematic analysis in psychology. *Qualitative Research in Psychology*, 3(2), 77–101. DOI: 10.1191/1478088706qp063oa

Brom, C., Cihon, T. M., & Buchtová, M. (2020). Ethical Considerations for Teachers Using AI Technologies in Education. *Journal of Information Technology Education*, 19, 209–241.

Brooks, C., & Grajek, S. (2020). Faculty Readiness to Begin Fully Remote Teaching. er.educause.edu/blogs/2020 /3/faculty-readiness-to-begin-fully-remote-teaching

Brown, J. M. (2017). Novice elementary science teachers' experiences of self-efficacy, anxiety, and frustration. *Journal of Science Teacher Education*, 28(1), 65–86.

Brown, T., Mann, B., Ryder, N., Subbiah, M., Kaplan, J. D., Dhariwal, P., Neelakantan, A., Shyam, P., Sastry, G., Askell, A., Agarwal, S., Herbert-Voss, A., Krueger, G., Henighan, T., Child, R., Ramesh, A., Ziegler, D., Wu, J., Winter, C., & Amodei, D. (2020). Language models are few-shot learners. *Advances in Neural Information Processing Systems*, 33, 1877–1901.

Brue, M. (July 20, 2023). https://www.forbes.com/sites/moorinsights/2023/07/20/microsoft-puts-ai-chat-to-work-with-bing-chat-enterprise/?sh=1a8eb6a219b1

Bruns, W. (Oct 26, 2023). https://easyaichecker.com/blog/2023/10/the-ethics-of-ai-detection-and-humanizing-a-comprehensive-analysis/

Bryd, D., & Alexander, M. (2020). Investigating special education teachers' knowledge and skills: Preparing general teacher preparation for professional development. *Journal of Pedagogical Research*. *https://doi.org/.*DOI: 10.33902/JPR.2020059790

Buabeng-Andoh, C., & Baah, C. (2020). Determinants of students' actual use of the learning management system (LMS): An empirical analysis of a research model. *Advances in Science Technology and Engineering Systems Journal*, 5(2), 614–620. DOI: 10.25046/aj050277

Bullock-Rest, N. E. (2020). Artificial Intelligence in Education: A Literature Review. *Journal of Research on Technology in Education*, 52(1), 88–112.

Cairns, D., Sears, J., & Rehmat, A. P. (2011). The effect of inquiry-based science instruction on student achievement. *Journal of Science Education and Technology*, 20(5), 602–608.

Callo, E., & Yazon, A. (2020). Exploring the Factors Influencing Faculty and Students' Readiness on Online Teaching and Learning as an Alternative Delivery Model for the New Normal. https://www.hrpub.org/journals/article_info.php?aid=9556

Callo, E., Yazon, A., & Briones, M. (2020). *LSPU Primer on Facilitation Flexible Learning: Migrating to the New Normal*. LSPU Board Resolution No. 061 Series of 2020.

Candra, S., Limantoro, H. S., & Loang, O. K. (2023). Students' attitudes and behaviors influence learning management system adoption. *Proceedings of the 2023 9th International Conference on Frontiers of Educational Technologies*. DOI: 10.1145/3606150.3606162

Cardon, P., Fleischmann, C., Aritz, J., Logemann, M., & Heidewald, J. (2023). The challenges and opportunities of AI-assisted writing: Developing AI literacy for the AI age. *Business and Professional Communication Quarterly*, 0(0), 257–295. Advance online publication. DOI: 10.1177/23294906231176517

CAST. (2018). *Universal design for learning guidelines version 2.2.* CAST.

Cavanaugh, C., Gillan, K. J., Kromrey, J., Hess, M., & Blomeyer, R. (2009). *The effects of distance education on K–12 student outcomes: A meta-analysis.* Learning Point Associates.

Celik, I. (2023). Emotional intelligence. *Computers in Human Behavior*, 138. Advance online publication. DOI: 10.1016/j.chb.2022.107468

Chamdimba, P., Ahed-Ahmad, B., Ouedraogo, A., Mizunoya, S., Angieri, R., Amaro, D., Mishra, S., & Kelly, P. (2022). Palestine Education Fact Sheets https://data.unicef.org/wp-content/uploads/2022/12/2022Palestine-Education-Fact-Sheet-2022FINAL.pdf

Chan, C. K. Y. (2023). A comprehensive AI policy education framework for university teaching and learning. *International Journal of Educational Technology in Higher Education*, 20(1), 38. DOI: 10.1186/s41239-023-00408-3

Chan, C. K. Y., & Hu, W. (2023). Students' Voices on Generative AI: Perceptions, Benefits, and Challenges in Higher Education. *International Journal of Educational Technology in Higher Education*, 20(1), 43. Advance online publication. DOI: 10.1186/s41239-023-00411-8

Chao, C.-M. (2019). Factors determining the behavioral intention to use mobile learning: An application and extension of the UTAUT model. *Frontiers in Psychology*, 10, 1652. Advance online publication. DOI: 10.3389/fpsyg.2019.01652 PMID: 31379679

Chapelle, C. A. (2024). Open generative AI changes a lot, but not everything. *Modern Language Journal*, 108(2), 534–540. DOI: 10.1111/modl.12927

Chaudhry, I. S., Sarwary, S. M., Refae, G. E., & Chabchoub, H. (2023). Time to Revisit Existing Student's Performance Evaluation Approach in Higher Education Sector in a New Era of ChatGPT — A Case Study. *Cogent Education*, 10(1), 2210461. Advance online publication. DOI: 10.1080/2331186X.2023.2210461

Chen, B., Wu, Z., & Zhao, R. (2023). From Fiction to Fact: The Growing Role of Generative AI in Business and Finance. SSRN *Electronic Journal.* DOI: 10.2139/ssrn.4528225

Chen, C. (2023). *AI Will Transform Teaching and Learning. Let's Get it Right.* (March 9, 2023), Stanford University, Human-Centered Artificial Intelligence https://hai .stanford.edu/news/ai-will-transform-teaching-and-learning-lets-get-it-right

Chen, G. M., & Starosta, W. J. (2000). The development and validation of the intercultural sensitivity scale. *Human Communication*, 3(1), 1–15.

Cheng, E., & Wang, T. (2022). C.K.; Wang, Tianchong. (2022). Institutional Strategies for Cybersecurity in Higher Education Institutions. *Information (Basel)*, 13(4), 192. DOI: 10.3390/info13040192

Chen, K. K. (2014). Assessing the effects of customer innovativeness, environmental value and ecological lifestyles on residential solar power systems install intention. *Energy Policy*, 67, 951–961. DOI: 10.1016/j.enpol.2013.12.005

Chen, N. S., Clarebout, G., & Kim Chwee, D. N. (2020). AI meets AI: Exploring the applications of artificial intelligence for authentic assessment. *Computers & Education*, 157, 103982. DOI: 10.1016/j.compedu.2020.103982

Chen, Y., & Yu, S. (2021). Artificial Intelligence Applications in K-12 Education: A Systematic Review. *Journal of Educational Computing Research*, 59(1), 126–148.

Chi, C. (2023, July 19). Should ChatGPT be banned in schools? UP crafts 'responsible' AI use guidelines. *Philstar.com*. https://www.philstar.com/headlines/2023/07/19/2282226/should-chatgpt-be-banned-schools-crafts-responsible-ai-use-guidelines

Chikotie, T. T., Watson, B. W., & Watson, L. R. (2023, October). Systems Thinking Application to Ethical and Privacy Considerations in AI-Enabled Syndromic Surveillance Systems: Requirements for Under-Resourced Countries in Southern Africa. In Pan African Conference on Artificial Intelligence (pp. 197-218). Cham: Springer Nature Switzerland.

Chong, J. L., Tan, P., & Felix, B. (2012). IT governance in collaborative networks: A socio-technical perspective. Pac. Asia J. Assoc. Inf. Syst. 4, 31–48. [Google Scholar] [CrossRef] [Green Version CNET. (2024, April 11). ChatGPT Glossary: 42 AI Terms That Everyone Should Know. https://www.cnet.com/tech/computing/chatgpt-glossary-42-ai-terms-that-everyone-should-know/

Chong, S. W., & Reinders, H. (2021). A methodological review of qualitative research syntheses in CALL: The state-of-the-art. *System*, 103, 102646. DOI: 10.1016/j.system.2021.102646

Cigdem, H., & Ozturk, M. (2016). Factors affecting students' behavioral intention to use LMS at a Turkish post-secondary vocational school. *International Review of Research in Open and Distance Learning*, 17(3). Advance online publication. DOI: 10.19173/irrodl.v17i3.2253

Cigdem, H., & Topcu, A. (2015). Predictors of instructors' behavioral intention to use learning management system: A Turkish vocational college example. *Computers in Human Behavior*, 52, 22–28. DOI: 10.1016/j.chb.2015.05.049

Claar, C. (2014). Student acceptance of learning management systems: A study on demographics. *Issues in Information Systems*, 15(1), 409–417. DOI: 10.48009/1_iis_2014_409-417

Cohen, A. M., & Brawer, F. B. (2008). *The American community college* (5th ed.). Jossey-Bass.

Colebook, C. (2017). *What Is This Thing Called Education?* Sage Journal., DOI: 10.1177/1077800417725357

Coleman, E., & Mtshazi, S. (2017). Factors affecting the use and non-use of Learning Management Systems (LMS) by academic staff. *South African Computer Journal = Suid-Afrikaanse Rekenaartydskrif*, 29(3). Advance online publication. DOI: 10.18489/sacj.v29i3.459

Coleman, R., & Ringrose, J. (2013). *Deleuze and Research Methodologies*. Taylor and Francis. DOI: 10.1515/9780748644124

Conole, G. (2015). Designing Effective MOOCs. Educational Media International, 52(4), 239–252. https://doi.org/. *Current Issues in Comparative Education*, 20(1), 45–67.DOI: 10.1080/09523987.2015.1125989

Conway, A. (May 07, 2024). https://www.xda-developers.com/microsoft-copilot/#:~:text=Copilot%20was%20developed%20by%20Microsoft,you%20can%20use%20it%20freely

Cordeschi, R. (2017). AI turns fifty: Revisiting its origins. *Applied Artificial Intelligence*, 21(4-5), 259–279. DOI: 10.1080/08839510701252304

Cortellazzo, L., Bruni, E., & Zampieri, R. (2019). The Role of Leadership in a Digitalized World. *A Review.Frontiers in Psychology*, 10, 1938. Advance online publication. DOI: 10.3389/fpsyg.2019.01938 PMID: 31507494

Creswell, J. W. (2015). *Qualitative inquiry & research design: Choosing among five approaches*. Sage Journal.

Creswell, J. W., & Creswell, J. D. (2017). *Research design: Qualitative, quantitative, and mixed methods approaches* (5th ed.). SAGE Publications.

Creswell, J. W., & Poth, C. N. (2018). *Qualitative inquiry and research design: Choosing among five approaches* (4th ed.). Sage publications.

Crompton, H., & Burke, D. (2023). Artificial intelligence in higher education: The state of the field. *International Journal of Educational Technology in Higher Education*, 20(1), 22. DOI: 10.1186/s41239-023-00392-8

Dalati, S. (2021). Factors Affecting Syrian Female Researchers' Experience During Crisis: Inductive Approach. *Business. Management and Economics Engineering*, 19(01), 91–110. DOI: 10.3846/bmee.2021.13232

Davis, C. (2024). Artificial Intelligence is the Most. AVTechnology Guide, 2024. https://issuu.com/futurepublishing/docs/avtechnology_june_guide_2024_0035?fr=sYWZmOTc0ODQ2NDY

de l'Éducation, C. S. de la Formation et de la Recherche Scientifique (CSEFRS). (2021). Enseignement au temps de covid au maroc. Rapport thématique. ISBN : 978-9920-785-37-2.

De Vita, G. (2012). *Enhancing the student experience in business and management, hospitality, leisure, tourism*. Routledge.

DeAngelo, L., & Franklin, J. (2020). Financial aid and student success: A comprehensive analysis. *Higher Education Research & Development*, 39(4), 673–689.

Deardorff, D. K. (2006). Identification and assessment of intercultural competence as a student outcome of internationalization. *Journal of Studies in International Education*, 10(3), 241–266. DOI: 10.1177/1028315306287002

Deterding, S., Sicart, M., Nacke, L., O'Hara, K., & Dixon, D. (2011). Gamification: Using Game-Design Elements in Non-Gaming Contexts. In Proceedings of the 2011 Annual Conference Extended Abstracts on Human Factors In Computing Systems - CHI EA '11 (p. 2425). *New York, USA: ACM Press*. DOI: 10.1145/1979742.1979575

Di Stasio, M., & Miotti, B. (2021). Perspectives for School: Maker Approach, Educational Technologies and Laboratory Approach, New Learning Spaces. *Makers at School, Educational Robotics and Innovative Learning Environments*, 3–9. DOI: 10.1007/978-3-030-77040-2_1

Dillenbourg, P. (2013). Collaboration in computer-supported collaborative learning. In Spector, J. M., Merrill, M. D., Elen, J., & Bishop, M. J. (Eds.), *Handbook of research on educational communications and technology* (pp. 409–438). Springer.

Dimitriadis, G. (2020). Evolution in Education: Chatbots. *Homo Virtualis*, 3(1), 47–54. DOI: 10.12681/homvir.23456

Diprose, L. (May 09, 2019) https://medium.com/consensus-ai/consensus-update-5 -the-consensus-app-dff638b21eac

Dixon-Román, E. (2021). *Social epistemology and the pragmatics of assessment.* Sage Journal.

Doraiswamy, P. M., Blease, C., & Bodner, K. (2020). Artificial intelligence and the future of psychiatry: Insights from a global physician survey. *Artificial Intelligence in Medicine*, 102, 101753. DOI: 10.1016/j.artmed.2019.101753 PMID: 31980092

Dron, J. (2022). Educational technology: What it is and how it works. *AI & Society*, 37(1), 155–166. Advance online publication. DOI: 10.1007/s00146-021-01195-z

Dryden-Peterson, S. (2015). *The Educational Experiences of Refugee Children in Countries of First Asylum.* Migration Policy Institute., Retrieved from https://www .migrationpolicy.org/sites/default/files/publications/FCD_ Dryen-PetersonFINAL-WEB.pdf

Dziuban, C. (2018). Blended learning: the new normal and emerging technologies. Front. *Education. Educational technology journal. /.*DOI: 10.1186/s41239-017-0087-5

Elabbar, D.A. (2017). Libyan Political Conflict: Effects on Higher Education Development.

Elazhari, E. S. (2021). Cultural Impact on Social Position and Women's Education in Libya. [IJSRP]. *International Journal of Scientific and Research Publications*, 11(4), 425–427. DOI: 10.29322/IJSRP.11.04.2021.p11257

El-Bushra, J., El-Karib, A., & Hadjipateras, A. (2002). *Gender-Sensitive Programme Design and Planning in Conflict-Affected Situations.* ACORD.

Elias, T. (2021). Artificial Intelligence in Education: Theoretical and Practical Considerations. *Educational Technology Research and Development*, 69(1), 105–128.

Elkhatat, A. M., Elsaid, K., & Almeer, S. (2023). Evaluating the efficacy of AI content detection tools in differentiating between human and AI-generated text. *International Journal for Educational Integrity*, 19(17), 17. Advance online publication. DOI: 10.1007/s40979-023-00140-5

Elmoazen, Ramy & López-Pernas, Sonsoles & Misiejuk, Kamila & Khalil, Mohammad & Wasson, Barbara & Saqr, Mohammed. (2023). Reflections on Technology-enhanced Learning in Laboratories: Barriers and Opportunities.

Emmanuel, W. (2020). Online learning in the time of COVID-19: A Computer Science Educator's Point of View. https://arete.ateneo.edu/connect/online-learning-in-the-time-*of-covid19-a-computer-science-educators-point-ofview?-4kGhBbzL-5wp8vCiczqCnqX4*

Engelmann, S., & Carnine, D. (1991). *Theory of instruction: Principles and applications*. ADI Press.

Escofet, A., & Marimon, M. (2010). Web 2.0 and Collaborative Learning in Higher Education. *Web-Based Education*, 699–714. DOI: 10.4018/978-1-61520-963-7.ch047

Eutsler, L., & Long, C. S. (2021). Preservice Teachers' Acceptance of Virtual Reality to Plan Science Instruction. *Journal of Educational Technology & Society*, 24(2), 28–43. https://www.jstor.org/stable/27004929

Exploring the Trend and Potential Distribution of Chatbot in Education: A Systematic Review - Volume 13 Number 3 (Mar. 2023) - ijiet. (n.d.). https://www.ijiet.org/show-186-2428-1.html

Ezer, J. F. (2006). *The interplay of institutional forces behind higher ICT education in India*. London School of Economics.

Faiers, A., & Neame, C. (2006). Consumer attitudes towards domestic solar power systems. *Energy Policy*, 34(14), 1797–1806. DOI: 10.1016/j.enpol.2005.01.001

Farag, I. M., & Yacoub, M. (2023). Teachers' appreciation of ELT policies and practices in Egypt. In Ekembe, E. E., Harvey, L., & Dwyer, E. (Eds.), *Interface between English language education policies and practice: Examples from various contexts* (pp. 59–83). SpringerLink. DOI: 10.1007/978-3-031-14310-6_4

Ferguson, L. (2022). The lack of science education in elementary schools: An interdisciplinary concern.

Ferguson, C., Green, P., Vaswani, R., & Wu, G. (2013). Determinants of effective information technology governance. [Google Scholar] [CrossRef]. *International Journal of Auditing*, 17(1), 75–99. DOI: 10.1111/j.1099-1123.2012.00458.x

Filsecker, M., & Hickey, D. T. (2014). A Multilevel Analysis of The Effects of External Rewards on Elementary Students' Motivation, Engagement and Learning in an Educational Game. *Computers &amp. Computers & Education*, 75, 136–148. DOI: 10.1016/j.compedu.2014.02.008

Firat, M. (2023). What ChatGPT means for universities: Perceptions of scholars and students. *Journal of Applied Learning and Teaching*, 6(1).

Fives, H., Lacatena, N., & Gerard, L. (2015). *Teachers' beliefs about teaching (and learning)*. Routledge.

Flayols, A., Jongerius, D., & Bel-Air, F. (2019) Tunisia: Education, Labour Market, Migration. *The Dutch Ministry of Foreign Affairs*, 9 Apr. 2019.

Florian, L., & Black-Hawkins, K. (2011). Exploring inclusive pedagogy. *British Educational Research Journal*, 37(5), 813–828. DOI: 10.1080/01411926.2010.501096

Flower, A., McKenna, J. W., & Haring, C. D. (2017). Behavior and classroom management: Are teacher preparation programs preparing our teachers? *Preventing School Failure*, 61(2), 163–169. DOI: 10.1080/1045988X.2016.1231109

Flower, L., & Hayes, J. R. (1981). A cognitive process theory of writing. [REMOVED HYPERLINK50 FIELD]. *College Composition and Communication*, 32(4), 365–387. DOI: 10.58680/ccc198115885

Fortune (April 11, 2024). Hallucinations are the bane of AI-driven insights. Here's what search can teach us about trustworthy responses, according to Snowflake's.

Fortune, M.F., Spielman, M., & Pangelinan, D.T. (2021). Students' Perceptions of Online or Face-to-Face Learning and Social Media in Hospitality, Recreation and Tourism. *Journal of Tourism and Management*.

Francisco, C., & Barcelona, M. (2020). Effectiveness of an Online Classroom for Flexible Learning. *International Journal of Academic Multidisciplinary Research*.

Fűrész, E., Szabóné Tóth, É., Tóth, K., & Amariei, D. (2023). Adult Education's Role in Rural Development and Women's Empowerment in Tunisia and Hungary: Exploring Cross-Regional Collaboration, Growth Opportunities, and Gender-Inclusive Strategies. *Studia Mundi – Economica, 10*(1), 14–25. https://doi.org/DOI: 10.18531/sme.vol.10.no.1.pp.14-25

Gadenne, D., Sharma, B., Kerr, D., & Smith, T. (2011). The influence of consumers' environmental beliefs and attitudes on energy saving behaviors. *Energy Policy*, 39(12), 7684–7694. DOI: 10.1016/j.enpol.2011.09.002

Gallagher, K. (2019). Challenges and Opportunities in Sourcing, Preparing and Developing a Teaching Force for the UAE. *Education in the United Arab Emirates*, 127–145. DOI: 10.1007/978-981-13-7736-5_8

Gao, C. A., Howard, F. M., Markov, N. S., Dyer, E. C., Ramesh, S., Luo, Y., & Pearson, A. T. (2022). Comparing scientific abstracts generated by ChatGPT to original abstracts using an artificial intelligence output detector, plagiarism detector, and blinded human reviewers. bioRxiv, 2022-12. https://doi.org/DOI: 10.1101/2022.12.23.521610

Garcia, A. (2023). *Generative AI in MENA to hit $23.5 billion by 2030*. Economy Middle East. Retrieved May 1, 2024, from https://economymiddleeast.com/news/generative-ai-in-mena-to-hit-23-5-billion-by-2030/

Garcia, R. A., & Rodriguez, M. S. (2021). Challenges in elementary science education: The absence of formal curriculum. *Elementary Education Journal*, 38(3), 301–315.

Gardner, H. (2006). "Multiple Intelligences: New Horizons in Theory and Practice." *Basic Books,* https://a.co/d/hkd8AP2

Garib, A. (2021). [Software reviewLearn Languages with Music: Lyrics Training App Review]. *Teaching English as a Second Language Electronic Journal (TESL-EJ), 24(*4). https://tesl-ej.org/pdf/ej96/m1.pdf

Garib, A., & Schmidt-Crawford, D. (2024, March). TPACK's Contextual Knowledge: Exploring EFL Teachers' Technological Pedagogical Practices in Iran, Libya, Syria, Tunisia, and Yemen. In P. Mishra, M. Phillips, E. Baran, M. Koehler, J. Harris, & M. Williams. (2024, March). *Part 2: The past, present, and most importantly the future of TPACK*. In Society for Information Technology & Teacher Education International Conference (pp. 2443-2448). Association for the Advancement of Computing in Education (AACE). https://punyamishra.com/wp-content/uploads/2024/03/TPACK-symposium-SITE24.pdf

Garib, A. (2022). "Actually, it's real work": EFL teachers' perceptions of technology-assisted project-based language learning in Lebanon, Libya, and Syria. *TESOL Quarterly*, 57(4), 1434–1462. DOI: 10.1002/tesq.3202

Garib, A., & Coffelt, T. A. (2024). DETECTing the anomalies: Exploring implications of qualitative research in identifying AI-generated text for AI-assisted composition instruction. *Computers and Composition*, 73, 102869. DOI: 10.1016/j.compcom.2024.102869

Garib, A., Coffelt, T., Alshalwy, A., & Kashani, S. (2024). ChatGPT: Can students really get away with speechcraft? In Elmoudden, S., & Wrench, J. S. (Eds.), *The Role of Generative AI in the Communication Classroom*. IGI Global. DOI: 10.4018/979-8-3693-0831-8.ch007

Gay, G. (2018). *Culturally responsive teaching: Theory, research, and practice* (3rd ed.). Teachers College Press.

Gedera, D., Williams, J., & Wright, N. (2015). Identifying factors influencing students' motivation and engagement in online courses. In Koh, C. (Ed.), *Motivation, leadership and curriculum design*. Springer., DOI: 10.1007/978-981-287-230-2_2

Gillwald, A., & Partridge, A. (2022). Gendered Nature of Digital Inequality - UN Women. https://www.unwomen.org/sites/default/files/2022-12/BP.1_Alison%20 Gillwald.pdf

Goby, V., & Erogul, M. (2011). Female Entrepreneurship in The United Arab Emirates: Legislative Encouragements and Cultural Constraints. *Women's Studies International Forum*, 34(4), 329–334. DOI: 10.1016/j.wsif.2011.04.006

Gravel, J., Gravel, M. D., & Osmanlliu, E. (2023). Learning to fake it: Limited responses and fabricated references provided by ChatGPT. *Mayo Clinic Proceedings. Digital Health*, 1(3), 226–234. Advance online publication. DOI: 10.1016/j. mcpdig.2023.05.004

Greene, R. T. (2023, April 24). *The pros and cons of using AI in learning: Is ChatGPT helping or hindering learning outcomes?* eLearning Industry. https:// elearningindustry.com/pros-and-cons-of-using-ai-in-learning-chatgpt-helping-or -hindering-learning-outcomes

Greene, M. (1968). Technology and the Human Person. *Teachers College Record*, 69(4), 385–393. DOI: 10.1177/016146816806900404

Guhanarayan, V. (2023). 4 Ways to Prevent AI Hallucinations. https://www.makeuseof .com/prevent-ai-hallucination/

Gupta, S., & Chen, Y. (2022) "Supporting Inclusive Learning Using Chatbots? A Chatbot-Led Interview Study," *Journal of Information Systems Education*: Vol. 33: Iss. 1, 98-108.*arXiv (Cornell University)*. https://doi.org//arxiv.2306.03823DOI: 10.48550

Gurin, P., Dey, E. L., Hurtado, S., & Gurin, G. (2002). Diversity and higher education: Theory and impact on educational outcomes. *Harvard Educational Review*, 72(3), 330–367. DOI: 10.17763/haer.72.3.01151786u134n051

Hall, E. T. (1976). *Beyond culture*. Anchor Press.

Hammad, W., & Hallinger, P. (2017). *A systematic review of conceptual models and methods used in research on educational leadership and management in Arab societies*. Taylor and Francis., DOI: 10.1080/13632434.2017.1366441

Hancock, R. S. B., Azhar, S., Mezei, S., Aas, M. B., & Gijsbertsen, B. (2023). Reconsidering Education Policy in the Era of Generative AI. Global Solutions. Retrieved from https://www.global-solutions-initiative.org/policy_brief/reconsidering-education-policy-in-the-era-of-generative-ai/

Han, J. (2020). Changes in attitudes and efficacy of AI learners according to the level of programming skill and project interest in AI project. *Journal of The Korean Association of Information Education.*, 24(4), 391–400. DOI: 10.14352/jkaie.2020.24.4.391

Haraki, O. A., & Drwish, D. H. (2023). The Impact of the Syrian Conflict on the Educational and Behavioral Development of Students: Insights from Intermediate School Teachers in Homs City. *PáGinas De EducacióN/Páginas De Educación, 16*(2), 85–110. DOI: 10.22235/pe.v16i2.3172

Hattie, J. (2009). *Visible learning: A synthesis of over 800 meta-analyses relating to achievement.* Routledge.

Hew, K. F., & Cheung, W. S. (2014). Students' and Instructors' Use of Massive Open Online Courses (MOOCs): Motivations and Challenges. *Educational Research Review*, 12, 45–58. DOI: 10.1016/j.edurev.2014.05.001

Hijazi, S. (2020). *International Outreach for university post-crisis.* QS Intelligence Unit.

Hofstede, G. (1984). Culture's consequences: International differences in work-related values (Vol. 5). sage.

Hofstede, G. (2001). *Culture's consequences: Comparing values, behaviors, institutions, and organizations across nations.* Sage Publications.

Hofstede, G., Hofstede, G. J., & Minkov, M. (2005). *Cultures and organizations: Software of the mind* (Vol. 2). Mcgraw-hill New York.

Ho, H.-C., Wang, M.-T., Shih, S.-C., Kuo, C.-H., & Tsai, C.-P. (2019). A study on the user cognitive model of learning management system. In *Lecture Notes in Electrical Engineering* (pp. 193–202). Springer Singapore.

Holmes, W., Bialik, M., & Fadel, C. (2019). Artificial Intelligence. In *Education Promises and Implications for Teaching and Learning*. The Center for Curriculum Redesign.

Hong, B., & Ghanavati, A. (2022). The Virtual Laboratory: A Natural Vehicle for Simulation in Engineering Education. *ASEE-NE 2022 Proceedings*. DOI: 10.18260/1-2--42213

Hrastinski, S. (2008). Asynchronous and synchronous e-learning. *EDUCAUSE Quarterly*, 31(4), 51–55.

Huang, J. (2021). An Internet of Things evaluation Algorithm for Quality Assessment of Computer-Based Teaching. *Mobile Information Systems*, 2021, 9919399. DOI: 10.1155/2021/9919399

Huang, R., Zmud, R. W., & Price, R. L. (2010). Influencing the effectiveness of IT governance practices through steering committees and communication policies. [Google Scholar] [CrossRef]. *European Journal of Information Systems*, 19(3), 288–302. DOI: 10.1057/ejis.2010.16

Hubbard, J. (2023). The pedagogical dangers of AI detectors for the teaching of writing. *Composition Studies*, 51(2). https://compstudiesjournal.com/2023/06/30/the-pedagogical-dangers-of-ai-detectors-for-the-teaching-of-writing/

Hung, M., Chou, C., Chen, C., & Own, Z. (2020). Learner readiness for online learning: Scale development and student perceptions. *Elsevier. 3 (55).*https://www.sciencedirect.com/science/article/abs/pii/S0360131510001260?via% *3Dihub*

Hu, X., & Lai, C. (2019). Comparing factors that influence learning management systems use on computers and on mobile. *Information and Learning Science*, 120(7/8), 468–488. DOI: 10.1108/ILS-12-2018-0127

Ibrahimov, V. (Sept 14, 2023) https://medium.com/@aiVugar/consensus-ask-ai-questions-and-obtain-conclusions-from-research-papers-48f80a8c717

Ilieva, G., Yankova, T., Dimitrov, A., Bratkov, M., & Angelov, D. (2023). Effects of Generative Chatbots in Higher Education. *Information (Basel)*, 14(9), 492. DOI: 10.3390/info14090492

Illanes, P., Law, J., Sarakatsannis, J., Sanghvi, S., and Mendy, *A. (2020). Coronavirus and the Campus: How Can US Higher Education Organize to Respond?* McKinsey and Company.

Iqbal, N., Ahmed, H., & Azhar, K. (2023). Exploring Teachers' Attitudes towards Using Chat GPT. *Global Journal for Management and Administrative Sciences.*, 3(4), 97–111. Advance online publication. DOI: 10.46568/gjmas.v3i4.163

Iqbal, U., & Ralf, B. (2013). *Textbook of Educational Philosophy.* Kanishka Publishers.

Irwin, C., Ball, L., Desbrow, B., & Leveritt, M. (2017). Students' perceptions of using Facebook as an interactive learning resource at university. *Australasian Journal of Educational Technology*, 28(7), 1221–1232.

Ismail, M., Razak, R. C., Hakimin Yusoff, M. N., Wan Zulkiffli, W. F., & Wan Mohd Nasir, W. M. N. (2022). The determinants of mobile marketing services acceptance among Gen-Y consumers. *International Journal of Criminology and Sociology*, 9, 2277–2284. DOI: 10.6000/1929-4409.2020.09.271

Jabeen, F., & Faisal, M. N. (2018). Imperatives for Improving Entrepreneurial Behavior Among Females in the UAE. *Gender in Management*, 33(3), 234–252. DOI: 10.1108/GM-03-2016-0042

Jackson, C. J. (2020). Transformational leadership and gravitas: 2000 years of no development? *Personality and Individual Differences*, 156, 109760. DOI: 10.1016/j.paid.2019.109760

Jaitly, A. (2024). *Engaging Minds, Empowering Futures: How AI is Revolutionizing Education and Keeping Students Hooked*. LinkedIn. March 22, 2024. https://www.linkedin.com/pulse/engaging-minds-empowering-futures-how-ai-education-keeping-jaitly-2oplc/

Jena, R. K., & Goswami, R. (2013). Information and communication technologies in Indian education system. *International Journal of Knowledge Society Research*, 4(1), 43–56. DOI: 10.4018/jksr.2013010104

Jenkins, K. (2020). *Towards impactful energy justice research: Transforming the power of academic engagement*. PLOS Journal., DOI: 10.1016/j.erss.2020.101510

Jenkins, M., Browne, T., Walker, R., & Hewitt, R. (2011). The development of Technology Enhanced Learning: Findings from a 2008 Survey of UK Higher Education Institutions. *Interactive Learning Environments*, 19(5), 447–465. DOI: 10.1080/10494820903484429

Johnson, A. (2018). The impact of deficient science content knowledge on lesson planning and delivery. *Journal of Teacher Education*, 69(3), 245–258.

Johnson, D. W., & Johnson, R. T. (2009). An educational psychology success story: Social interdependence theory and cooperative learning. *Educational Researcher*, 38(5), 365–379. DOI: 10.3102/0013189X09339057

Johnston, A. C., & Hale, R. (2009). Improved security through information security governance. [Google Scholar] [CrossRef]. *Communications of the ACM*, 52(1), 126–129. DOI: 10.1145/1435417.1435446

Jones, S. (July 02, 2024) https://edrawmind.wondershare.com/ai-features/tome-ai-review.html

Joo, Y. J., Kim, N., & Kim, N. H. (2016). Factors predicting online university students' use of a mobile learning management system (m-LMS). *Educational Technology Research and Development. Educational Technology Research and Development*, 64(4), 611–630. DOI: 10.1007/s11423-016-9436-7

Kabilan, M. K., Ahmad, N., & Abidin, M. J. Z. (2020). Facebook: An online environment for learning of English in institutions of higher education? *The Internet and Higher Education*, 13(4), 179–187. DOI: 10.1016/j.iheduc.2010.07.003

Kaewsaiha, P., & Chanchalor, S. (2021). Factors affecting the usage of learning management systems in higher education. *Education and Information Technologies*, 26(3), 2919–2939. DOI: 10.1007/s10639-020-10374-2

Kamelia, L. (2015). Perkembangan Teknologi Augmented Reality Sebagai Media Pembelajaran Interaktif Pada Mata Kuliah Kimia Dasar. *JURNAL ISTEK*, 9(1). https://journal.uinsgd.ac.id/index.php/istek/artic le/view/184

Karam, J. (2023). Reforming Higher Education Through AI. In Azoury, N., & Yahchouchi, G. (Eds.), *Governance in Higher Education*. Palgrave Macmillan., DOI: 10.1007/978-3-031-40586-0_12

Karina, B., & Kastuhandani, F. (2024). Preservice English teachers' lived experience in using AI in teaching preparation. *Journal Ilmiah Pendidikan*, 5(1), 550–568. Advance online publication. DOI: 10.51276/edu.v5i1.767

Karnad, A. (2014). *Trends in educational technologies*. The London School of Economics and Political Science.

Kashina, A. (2021). "Gender Equality in Tunisia: Current Trends" JOSSTT 1(01):04. DOI: https://doi.org/DOI: 10.52459/josstt1140721

Kaur, D. P., Kumar, A., Dutta, R., & Malhotra, S. (2022). The Role of Interactive and Immersive Technologies in Higher Education: A Survey. *Journal of Engineering Education Transformations*, 36(2), 79–86. DOI: 10.16920/jeet/2022/v36i2/22156

Kennedy, M., & Dunn, T. J. (2018). Improving the Use of Technology Enhanced Learning Environments in Higher Education in the UK: A Qualitative Visualization of Students' Views. *Contemporary Educational Technology*, 9(1). Advance online publication. DOI: 10.30935/cedtech/6212

Kern, R. (2024). Twenty-first century technologies and language education: Charting a path forward. *Modern Language Journal*, 108(2), 515–533. DOI: 10.1111/modl.12924

Kezar, A., & Maxey, D. (2014). *Understanding the role of organizational culture in change management*. Jossey-Bass.

Khan, S., & Khan, S. (2023, April 17). AI Chatbots for Education: How They are Supporting Students and Teachers? - EdTechReview. *EdTechReview*. https://www.edtechreview.in/trends-insights/trends/ai-chatbots-for-education-how-they-are-supporting-students-and-teachers/

Kim, S., & Lee, Y. (2021). Basic study for the development of artificial intelligence literacy instrument. *Proceedings of the Korean Association for Computer Education Conference, 25*(2(A)), 59–60.

King, M. R. (2023). A conversation on artificial intelligence, chatbots, and plagiarism in higher education. *Cellular and Molecular Bioengineering*, 16(1), 1–2. DOI: 10.1007/s12195-022-00754-8 PMID: 36660590

Kirkwood, A., & Price, L. (2013). Technology-enhanced Learning and Teaching in Higher Education: What is 'Enhanced' and How Do We Know? A Critical Literature Review. *Learning, Media and Technology*, 39(1), 6–36. Advance online publication. DOI: 10.1080/17439884.2013.770404

Klímová, B., & Seraj, P. M. I. (2023). The use of chatbots in university EFL settings: Research trends and pedagogical implications. *Frontiers in Psychology*, 14, 1131506. Advance online publication. DOI: 10.3389/fpsyg.2023.1131506 PMID: 37034959

Knight, J. F., Carley, S., Tregunna, B., Jarvis, S., Smithies, R., de Freitas, S., Dunwell, I., & Mackway-Jones, K. (2010). Serious Gaming Technology in Major Incident Triage Training: A Pragmatic Controlled Trial. *Resuscitation*, 81(9), 1175–1179. DOI: 10.1016/j.resuscitation.2010.03.042 PMID: 20732609

Kooli, C. (2023). Chatbots in Education and Research: A Critical Examination of ethical implications and solutions. *Sustainability (Basel)*, 15(7), 5614. DOI: 10.3390/su15075614

Kotrlik, J. W., & Redmann, D. H. (2009). A trend study: Technology Adoption in The Teaching-Learning Process by Secondary Agriscience Teachers-2002 And 2007. *Journal of Agricultural Education*, 50(2), 62–74. DOI: 10.5032/jae.2009.02062

Kreijns, K., Kirschner, P. A., & Jochems, W. (2013). Identifying the pitfalls for social interaction in computer-supported collaborative learning environments: A review of the research. *Computers in Human Behavior*, 29(1), 40–55.

Kucuk, T. (2024). ChatGPT Integrated Grammar Teaching and Learning in EFL Classes: A Study on Tishk International University Students in Erbil, Iraq. *Arab World English Journal (AWEJ),* 100-111. https://dx.doi.org/DOI: 10.24093/awej/ChatGPT.6

Kumar, L., Singh, P., & Tiwari, D. (2024). Use and Utility of Modern Technology in Learning and Teaching. *Atharv Publication, Bhopal* (M.P.) ISBN: 978-93-94945-60-9

Kumar, J. A. (2021). Educational chatbots for project-based learning: Investigating learning outcomes for a team-based design course. *International Journal of Educational Technology in Higher Education*, 18(1), 65. Advance online publication. DOI: 10.1186/s41239-021-00302-w PMID: 34926790

Kunnumpurath, B., Menon, V. A., & Paul, A. (2024). ChatGPT and virtual experience. In Advances in computational intelligence and robotics book series (pp. 32–50). DOI: 10.4018/979-8-3693-4268-8.ch003

Kysela, J., & Štorková, P. (2015). Using Augmented Reality as a Medium for Teaching History and Tourism. *Procedia: Social and Behavioral Sciences*, 174, 926–931. DOI: 10.1016/j.sbspro.2015.01.713

Labadze, L., Grigolia, M., & Machaidze, L. (2023). Role of AI chatbots in education: Systematic literature review. *International Journal of Educational Technology in Higher Education*, 20(1), 56. Advance online publication. DOI: 10.1186/s41239-023-00426-1

Labay, D. G., & Kinnear, T. C. (1981). Exploring the consumer decision process in the adoption of solar energy systems. *The Journal of Consumer Research*, 8(3), 271–278. DOI: 10.1086/208865

Labus, A., Simić, K., Vulić, M., Despotović-Zrakić, M., & Bogdanović, Z. (2012). An Application of Social Media in E-learning 2.0. *25th Bled Econference - Edependability: Reliable And Trustworthy Estructures, Eprocesses, Eoperations And Eservices For The Future, Proceedings, 557-572.*

Lacy, L. (2023). Hallucinations: Why AI Makes Stuff Up and What's Being Done About It.

Ladson-Billings, G. (1995). Toward a theory of culturally relevant pedagogy. *American Educational Research Journal*, 32(3), 465–491. DOI: 10.3102/00028312032003465

Lambert, J., & Stevens, M. (2023). Chat GPT and generative AI technologies: A mixed bag of concerns and new opportunities. *Computers in the Schools*, 1—25. https://doi.org/DOI: 10.1080/07380569.2023.2256710

Lavidas, K., Komis, V., & Achriani, A. (2022). Explaining faculty members' behavioral intention to use learning management systems. *Journal of Computers in Education*, 9(4), 707–725. DOI: 10.1007/s40692-021-00217-5

Lawrence Hall of Science. (2011). Elementary school teachers' perceptions and practices in science education (Press release). Retrieved from https://www.lawrencehallofscience.org/press_releases/elementary_school_teachers_perceptions_and_practices_in_science_education

Leask, B. (2015). *Internationalizing the curriculum*. Routledge. DOI: 10.4324/9781315716954

Leone, R., Mesquita, C., & Lopes, R. (2020). Use of learning management system (LMS): A study in a Brazilian and Portuguese universities. *Proceedings of the 12th International Conference on Computer Supported Education*. DOI: 10.1007/978-3-030-58459-7

Lewandowski, J. (2023). The applications and challenges of chatbots in education. *TS2 SPACE*. https://ts2.space/en/the-applications-and-challenges-of-chatbots-in-education

Lidén, A., & Nilros, K. (2020). *Percieved benefits and limitations of chatbots in higher education*. DIVA. https://www.diva-portal.org/smash/record.jsf?pid=diva2%3A1442044&dswid=1887

Li, L., Yu, F., & Shang, J. (2020). Design and implementation of cross-border AR and VR system in international education. *Future Generation Computer Systems*, 103, 171–181.

Lin, C., Yu, C., Shih, K., & Wu, Y. (2021). STEM based Artificial Intelligence Learning in General Education for Non-Engineering Undergraduate Students. *Journal of Educational Technology & Society*, 24(3), 224–237.

Lingard, L. (2023). Writing with ChatGPT: An illustration of its capacity, limitations & implications for academic writers. *Perspectives on Medical Education*, 12(1), 261–270. Advance online publication. DOI: 10.5334/pme.1072 PMID: 37397181

Li, S., Wang, C., & Wang, Y. (2024). Fuzzy evaluation model for physical education teaching methods in colleges and universities using artificial intelligence. *Scientific Reports*, 14(1), 4788. DOI: 10.1038/s41598-024-53177-y PMID: 38413670

Literacy rate, Adult Total for Bahrain. *FRED*. (2024, June 4). https://fred.stlouisfed.org/series/SEADTLITRZSBHR

Liu, X., Sun, Y., & Kaloustian, T. S. (2015). Cultural Factors Influencing Domestic Adoption of Solar Photovoltaic Technology: Perspectives from China. China Media Research, 11(4).

Liubchak, V. O., Zuban, Y. O., & Artyukhov, A. E. (2022). Immersive Learning Technology for Ensuring Quality Education: Ukrainian University Case. *CTE Workshop Proceedings, 9*, 336–354. https://doi.org/DOI: 10.55056/cte.124

Liu, D., Valdiviezo-Díaz, P., Riofrio, G., Sun, Y.-M., & Barba, R. (2015). Integration of Virtual Labs into Science E-learning. *Procedia Computer Science*, 75, 95–102. DOI: 10.1016/j.procs.2015.12.224

Livingstone, S. (2012). Critical Reflections on the Benefits of ICT in Education. *Oxford Review of Education*, 38(1), 9–24. DOI: 10.1080/03054985.2011.577938

Lo, C. K. (2023). What Is the Impact of ChatGPT on Education? A Rapid Review of the Literature. *Education Sciences*, 13(4), 410. DOI: 10.3390/educsci13040410

Lone, A. A (2015). Reconstruction of Islamic Education: with special reference to AllamaIqbal's Educational philosophy. FUNOON. *International Journal of Multidisplinary Research- Vol. I, Issue 2.*

Lone, S. (2015). *Impact of childlessness on life and attitudes towards continuation of medically assisted reproduction and/or adoption.* Taylor and Francis., DOI: 10.3109/14647273.2015.1006691

Lonn, S., & Teasley, S. D. (2009). Saving time or innovating practice: Investigating perceptions and uses of Learning Management Systems. *Computers & Education*, 53(3), 686–694. DOI: 10.1016/j.compedu.2009.04.008

Lopez, T., & Qamber, M. (2022). The benefits and drawbacks of implementing chatbots in higher education : A case study for international students at Jönköping University (Dissertation).https://urn.kb.se/resolve?urn=urn:nbn:se:hj:diva-57482

Luckin, R., Holmes, W., Griffiths, M., & Forcier, L. B. (2016). *Intelligence unleashed. An argument for AI in education.* Pearson.

Lüftenegger, M. (2020). Multiple Social and Academic Achievement Goals: Students' Goal Profiles and Their Linkages. *Journal of Experimental Education.* Advance online publication. DOI: 10.1080/00220973.2022.2081959

Lu, H. K. (2012). Learning styles and acceptance of e-learning management systems: An extension of behaviour intention model. *International Journal of Mobile Learning and Organisation*, 6(3/4), 246. DOI: 10.1504/IJMLO.2012.050044

Lv, Z. (2023). Generative Artificial Intelligence in the Metaverse Era. *Cognitive Robotics*, 3, 208–217. DOI: 10.1016/j.cogr.2023.06.001

Mahdi, M. (2015). *IbnKhaldun's Philosophy of History: A Study in the Philosophic Foundation of the Science of Culture*. Routledge.

Maier, S. (2013). *From the Classroom to the Boardroom: Enhancing Women's Participation in The GCC Workforce. Policy Note 4.* Mohammed Bin Rashid School of Government.

Maina, A. (Oct 26, 2023) https://alphanmaina.medium.com/tome-ai-use-ai-to-transform-your-ideas-into-appealing-visuals-131c7dade7f4

Maldonado, A. (April 29, 2024). https://studentbridgew.sharepoint.com/SitePages/Artificial-Intelligence-Summit.aspx

Malik, A. R., Pratiwi, Y., Andajani, K., Numertayasa, I. W., Suharti, S., Darwis, A., & Marzuki, . (2023). Exploring Artificial Intelligence in Academic Essay: Higher Education Student's Perspective. *International Journal of Educational Research Open*, 5, 100296. DOI: 10.1016/j.ijedro.2023.100296

Maper, S. (2024). Analysing Barriers to Girls' Education Outcomes in South Sudan. *Texila International Journal of Management*, 10(1), 1–7. DOI: 10.21522/TIJMG.2015.10.01.Art001

Marginson, S. (2012). *International education as self-formation: Morphing a profit-making business into an intercultural experience*. Lecture presented at the Ninth Annual Edward Said Memorial Lecture, Columbia University.

Margolis, R. J. (1963). *Do Teaching Machines Really Teach?* Redbook.

Mark, B. (2018) Benefits and challenges of doing research: Experiences from Philippine public school teachers. *Issues in Educational Research*https://www.iier.org.au/iier28/ullaabs.html

Marr, B. (March 19, 2023). https://www.forbes.com/sites/bernardmarr/2023/05/19/a-short-history-of-chatgpt-how-we-got-to-where-we-are-today/?sh=633d8a14674f#open-web-0

Martin, F., Budhrani, K., & Wang, C. (2019). *Examining Faculty Perception of Their Readiness to Teach Online*. Online Learning Journal. DOI: 10.24059/olj.v23i3.1555

Marzano, R., & Marzano, J. (2003a). *Classroom management that works: Research based strategies for every teacher*. Association for Supervision and Curriculum Development.

Marzuki, W., Widiati, U., Rusdin, D., Darwin, , & Indrawati, I. (2023). The impact of AI writing tools on the content and organization of students' writing: EFL teachers' perspective. *Cogent Education*, 10(2), 2236469. Advance online publication. DOI: 10.1080/2331186X.2023.2236469

Maslej, N; Fattorini, L; Brynjolfsson, F; Etchemendy, J; Ligett, K; Lyons, T; Manyika, J; Ngo, H; Niebles, J.C; Paril, V; Shoham, Y; Wald, R; Clark, J. and Perrault, R. (2023). The AI Index 2023 Annual Report. Stanford University: AI Index Steering Committee, Institute for Human-Centered-AI.

McClure, R. (2021). Community engagement in higher education: Bridging the gap. *Journal of Community Engagement and Higher Education at Indiana State University*, 13(2), 22–35.

Means, B., Toyama, Y., Murphy, R., Bakia, M., & Jones, K. (2014). *Evaluation of evidence-based practices in online learning: A meta-analysis and review of online learning studies*. US Department of Education.

Melek, Z., & Schmidt-Crawford, D. (2024, March). GenAI in Teacher Education: Teacher Educators' Views on AI in Pre-service Teacher Education. In Society for Information Technology & Teacher Education International Conference (pp. 817-825). Association for the Advancement of Computing in Education (AACE).

Mercado, J., & Picardal, J. P. (2023). Virtual Laboratory Simulations in Biotechnology: A Systematic Review. *Science Education International*, 34(1), 52–57. DOI: 10.33828/sei.v34.i1.6

Metcalfe, B. D. (2006). Exploring cultural dimensions of gender and management in the Middle East. *Thunderbird International Business Review*, 48(1), 93–107. DOI: 10.1002/tie.20087

Metz, C. (March 21, 2023). https://www.nytimes.com/2023/03/21/technology/google-bard-guide-test.html

Miles, R., Al-Ali, S., Charles, T., Hill, C., & Bligh, B. (2021). Technology Enhanced Learning in the MENA Region: Introduction to the Special Issue. *Studies in Technology Enhanced Learning*, 1(2). Advance online publication. DOI: 10.21428/8c225f6e.df527b9d

Miller, G. D. (2002). *Peace, value, and wisdom*. Brill Rodopi., DOI: 10.1163/9789004496071

Mishra, P., Phillips, M., Baran, E., Koehler, M., Harris, J., & Williams, M. (2024, March). Part 1: The past, present, and most importantly the future of TPACK. In Society for Information Technology & Teacher Education International Conference (pp. 2443-2448). Association for the Advancement of Computing in Education (AACE).

Mishra, P., & Koehler, M. J. (2006). Technological Pedagogical Content Knowledge: A Framework for Teacher Knowledge. *Teachers College Record*, 108(6), 1017–1054. DOI: 10.1111/j.1467-9620.2006.00684.x

Mohd Kasim, N. N., & Khalid, F. (2016). Choosing the right Learning Management System (LMS) for the higher education institution context: A systematic review. [IJET]. *International Journal of Emerging Technologies in Learning*, 11(06), 55. DOI: 10.3991/ijet.v11i06.5644

Mollick, E. (2023). My Class Required AI. Here's What I've Learned so Far. https://www.oneusefulthing.org/p/my-class-required-ai-heres-what-ive

Mosly, A. (2022). *Education in the GCC: Developments and Trends*. Gulf Research Center.

Moussa, A., & Belhiah, H. (2024). Beyond Syntax: Exploring Moroccan Undergraduate EFL Learners' Engagement with AI-Assisted Writing. *Arab World English Journal (AWEJ)*, 138-155. https://dx.doi.org/DOI: 10.24093/awej/ChatGPT.9

Mücahit, G. (2022). *The Advantages and Disadvantages of Using Artificial Intelligence in Mental Health Services*. Journal of Human & Society / İnsannsan ve Toplum. September 1, 2022

Mudawy, A. M. A. (2024). Investigating EFL Faculty Members' Perceptions of Integrating Artificial Intelligence Applications to Improve the Research Writing Process: A Case Study at Majmaah University. *Arab World English Journal (AWEJ)*, 180-191.

Mugableh, M. I. (2024). The Impact of ChatGPT on the Development of Vocabulary Knowledge of Saudi EFL Students. *Arab World English Journal (AWEJ)*, 280-290.

Mukminin, A., Habibi, A., Muhaimin, M., & Prasojo, L. D. (2020). Exploring the drivers predicting behavioral intention to use m-learning management system: Partial least square structural equation model. *IEEE Access : Practical Innovations, Open Solutions*, 8, 181356–181365. DOI: 10.1109/ACCESS.2020.3028474

Mullis, I. V. S., Martin, M. O., & Loveless, T. (2016). 20 Years of TIMSS International Trends in Mathematics and Science Achievement, Curriculum, and Instruction. Retrieved from http://timssandpirls.bc.edu/timss2015/international-results/timss2015/wpcontent/uploads/2016/T15-20-years-of-TIMSS.pd

Najim, D. M. (2023). Challenges Facing Palestinian Women in Assuming Leadership Positions in Higher Education Institutions: Glass Ceiling. *International Conference on Gender Research, 6*(1), 192–200. DOI: 10.34190/icgr.6.1.1136

Naldoza, N. (2020, April). Online Teaching and Learning Preparedness. *Survey.* https://docs.google.com/forms/d/e/1FAIpQLSfU_i57h19jgASOby9PeWZtrpNeYw FIc8ApdBkhFAcOxj5uA/viewform

Nalliah, S., & Idris, N. (2014). Applying the learning theories to medical education: A commentary. International E-Journal of Science. *Medical Education*, 8(1), 50–57.

Nasrullah, S., & Saqib Khan, M. (2015). The Impact of Time Management on the Students' Academic Achievements. *Journal of Literature, Languages and Linguistics.* ISSN 2422-8435 An International Peer-reviewed Journal Vol.11, 2015.

National Academies of Sciences, Engineering, and Medicine. (2021). Science and Engineering in Preschool Through Elementary Grades: The Brilliance of Children and the Strengths of Educators. Washington, DC: The National Academies Press.

National Center for Education Statistics. (2016). *The Nation's Report Card: 2015 Science*. U.S. Department of Education.

National Research Council. (2012). *A framework for K-12 science education: Practices, crosscutting concepts, and core ideas*. The National Academies Press.

National Science Teaching Association. (2018). Position statement: The Next Generation Science Standards (NGSS). Retrieved from https://www.nsta.org/position -statement-next-generation-science-standards-ngss

Ng, D. T. K., Leung, J. K. L., Chu, S. K. W., & Qiao, M. S. (2021). Conceptualizing AI literacy: An exploratory review. *Computers and Education: Artificial Intelligence*, 2, 100041. DOI: 10.1016/j.caeai.2021.100041

Nguyen, M. H., & Nguyen, T. H. (2014). The Influence of Leadership Behaviors on Employee Performance in the Context of Software Companies in Vietnam. *Advances in Management & Applied Economics*, 4(3), 157–171.

Nhavkar, V. (2023). Impact of Generative AI on IT Professionals. *International Journal for Research in Applied Science and Engineering Technology*, 11(7), 15–18. Advance online publication. DOI: 10.22214/ijraset.2023.54515

Nieto, S., & Bode, P. (2018). *Affirming diversity: The sociopolitical context of multicultural education* (7th ed.). Pearson.

Ning, Y., Zhang, C., Xu, B., Zhou, Y., & Wijaya, T. (2024). AI-TPACK: Exploring the relationship between knowledge elements. *Sustainability (Basel)*, 16(3), 978. Advance online publication. DOI: 10.3390/su16030978

Njuguna, S. (July 24, 2023). https://www.linkedin.com/pulse/how-i-use-resume -worded-make-my-winning-one-samuel-njuguna/

Nkisi-Orji, I., Naeem, U., Mbah, G. C. E., & Munshi, A. A. (2019). Intelligent evaluation of learners' interaction records in simulation-based computer science education. *International Journal of Information and Communication Technology Education*, 15(3), 1–13. DOI: 10.4018/IJICTE.2019070101

Nolan, R.; McFarlan, F.W. (2005). Information technology and the board of directors. Harv. Bus. Rev. 2 83, 96. [Google Scholar]

Nurunnabi, M., Mitchell, C., Koubaa, A., & Hoke, T. (2023). Sustainable Development Goals and AI integration into Curricula in the MENA Region. Report. Prince Sultan University

Nyakan, B. A., Getange, K. N., & Onchera, P. O. (2018). Influence of principals' management competencies on supervision of instruction in public secondary schools in Homabay County, Kenya. *International Journal of Novel Research in Education and Learning*, 5(3), 1–6. www.noveltyjournals.com

O'Sullivan, A., Rey, M. E., and Mendez, J. G. (2011). Opportunities and Challenges in the MENA Region. *The Arab World Competitiveness Report, 2011-2012*.

Okonkwo, C. W., & Ade-Ibijola, A. (2020). Chatbots applications in education: A systematic review. *Computers and Education: Artificial Intelligence*, 2, 100033. DOI: 10.1016/j.caeai.2021.100033

Onesi-Ozigagun, O., Ololade, Y. J., Eyo-Udo, N. L., & Ogundipe, D. O. (2024). Revolutionizing education through AI: A comprehensive review of enhancing learning experiences. *International Journal of Applied Research in Social Sciences*, 6(4), 589–607. DOI: 10.51594/ijarss.v6i4.1011

Onia, S. I. (2021b). Girls' Education Policy in Sudan: Challenges and Prospects. *MANAGERE : Indonesian Journal of Educational Management*, 3(3), 196–210. DOI: 10.52627/ijeam.v3i3.175

Osborne, J., & Dillon, J. (2008). *Science education in Europe: Critical reflections*. The Nuffield Foundation.

Owoc, L., Rodriguez, A., & Kim, S. (2021). The role of AI in amplifying and extending human teaching. *Journal of Educational Technology & Society*, 24(3), 112–129.

Panigrahi, A., & Joshi, V. (2020). Use of Artificial Intelligence in Education. *The Management Accountant Journal.*, 55(5), 64–67. DOI: 10.33516/maj.v55i5.64-67p

Park, W., & Kwon, H. (2024). Implementing artificial intelligence education for middle school technology education in Republic of Korea.(2023). *International Journal of Technology and Design Education*, 34(1), 109–135. DOI: 10.1007/s10798-023-09812-2 PMID: 36844448

Parsaiyan, S. F., & Gholami, H. (2023). Practicing to sing in chorus: Challenges and opportunities of collaborative inquiry-based learning in an Iranian EFL secondary school context. *Language Teaching Research*: LTR, 136216882311520-. https://doi.org/DOI: 10.1177/13621688231152037

Pelaez, J., Smith, K., & Chen, L. (2022). The debate on using AI to augment or replace teacher instruction. *Artificial Intelligence in Education Journal*, 15(2), 87–104.

Perkins, R. (2020). *Higher education and social mobility: What does research tell us?* Routledge.

Petrina, S. (2004). Sidney Pressey and the Automation of Education, 1924-1934. *Technology and Culture*, 45(2), 305–330. DOI: 10.1353/tech.2004.0085

Pham, S. T. H., & Sampson, P. M. (2022). The development of artificial intelligence in education: A review in context. *Journal of Computer Assisted Learning*, 38(5), 1408–1421. DOI: 10.1111/jcal.12687

Piaget, J. (1970). *Science of education and the psychology of the child*. Orion Press.

Pitychoutis, K. M. (2024). Harnessing AI Chatbots for EFL Essay Writing: A Paradigm Shift in Language Pedagogy. *Arab World English Journal (AWEJ)*, 197-209. https://dx.doi.org/DOI: 10.24093/awej/ChatGPT.13

Pompea, M., & Russo, M. (2023). Challenges in elementary science education: Limited time, resources, and teacher confidence. *Elementary Science Journal*, 20(1), 45–62.

Porter, J. (2005). *Media Literacy* (3rd ed.). Sage Publications, Inc.

Presswire, E. (June 9, 2023) https://www.wate.com/business/press-releases/ein-presswire/638444700/easy-ai-checker-launches-free-app-to-quickly-flag-plagiarism-and-ai-generated-content/

Prokofyev, K. G., Zmyzgova, T. R., Polyakova, E. N., & Chelovechkova, A. V. (2019). Transformation of the education system in a digital economics. *Proceedings of the 1st International Scientific Modern Management Trends and the Digital Economy: From Regional Development to Global Economic Growth*, Yekaterinburg, 614-619. Doi: DOI: 10.2991/mtde-19.2019.123

Rahman, M. J. A., Daud, M. Y., & Ensimau, N. K. (2019). Learning management system (LMS) in teaching and learning. *International Journal of Academic Research in Business & Social Sciences*, 9(11). Advance online publication. DOI: 10.6007/IJARBSS/v9-i11/6717

Ramadan, M., Hwijeh, F., Hallaj, O. A., Salahieh, S., & Diab, M. (2021). The Status of Gender Equality and Women's Rights in Syria.

Rashed, R. (2017). *Structure*. Gender, Tribalism, And Workplace Power In Libya.

Rashid, M., & Mamunar, R. (2018). Social Media Advertising Response and its Effectiveness: Case of South Asian Teenage Customers. Social Media Advertising Response and its Effectiveness: Case of South Asian Teenage Customers. *Global Journal of Management and Business Research*, 18(4), 9–16. https://journalofbusiness.org/index.php/GJMBR/article/view/249

Rauf, M., Ahmad, M., & Iqbal, Z. (2013). Al-Farabi's Philosophy of Education. http://muslimheritage.com/article/al-farabis-doctrine-education-betweenphilosophy-and-sociological-theory?page=1clxxvii

Razzak, N. A. (2017). E-Learning and National Innovation in Bahrain: Opportunities, Challenges, and Future Developments. (April 2-3, 2017).

Redding, S., & Corbett, J. (2018). *Shifting school culture to spark rapid improvement: A quick start guide for principals and their teams*. WestEd.

Rehy, V. A. A., & Tambotoh, J. J. C.. (2022). Learning Management System acceptance analysis using Hedonic Motivation System Adoption Model. [Rekayasa Sistem Dan Teknologi Informasi]. *Jurnal RESTI*, 6(6), 930–938. DOI: 10.29207/resti.v6i6.4233

Rideout, V. (2016). Measuring time spent with media: The Common Sense census of media use by US 8- to 18-year-olds. *Journal of Children and Media*, 10(1), 138–144. Advance online publication. DOI: 10.1080/17482798.2016.1129808

Ridge, N., Kippels, S., & ElAsad, S. (2017). Fact Sheet: Education in the United Arab Emirates and Ras Al Khaimah. Sheikh Saud bin Saqr Al Qasimi Foundation for Policy Research.

Riegle-Crumb, C., King, B., & Irizarry, Y. (2023). Decline in interest and engagement in science among middle and high school students. *Journal of Research in Science Teaching*, 50(3), 374–392.

Roblyer, M. D., & Doering, A. H. (2014). Integrating Educational Technology into Teaching. Pearson. Allyn and Bacon. ISBN. 0135130638, 9780135130636. M Rose, G. (January, 2015). Innovation and Information Technology. DOI:. In book: Wiley Encyclopedia of ManagementDOI: 10.1002/9781118785317.weom070007

Roose, K. (Feb 16, 2023) https://www.nytimes.com/2023/02/16/technology/bing-chatbot-microsoft-chatgpt.html

Rosário, A. & Dias, J. (2022). Learning Management Systems in Education: Research and Challenges. .DOI: 10.4018/978-1-6684-4706-2.ch003

Rosenshine, B. (2012). Principles of instruction: Research-based strategies that all teachers should know. *American Educator*, 36(1), 12–19.

Ros, S., Hernandez, R., Robles-Gomez, A., Caminero, A. C., Tobarra, L., & Ruiz, E. S. (2013). Open service-oriented platforms for personal learning environments. *IEEE Internet Computing*, 17(4), 26–31. DOI: 10.1109/MIC.2013.73

Rothrock, R. A., Kaplan, J., & Van Der Oord, F. (2018). The board's role in managing cybersecurity risks. [Google Scholar]. *MIT Sloan Management Review*, 59, 12–15.

Rudolph, J., Tan, S., & Tan, S. (2023). ChatGPT: Bullshit spewer or the end of traditional assessments in higher education? *Journal of Applied Learning and Teaching*, 6(1). Advance online publication. DOI: 10.37074/jalt.2023.6.1.9

Ryan, G. (2018). Introduction to positivism, interpretivism, and critical theory. *Nurse Researcher*, 25(4), 14–20. Advance online publication. DOI: 10.7748/nr.2018. e1466 PMID: 29546962

Saeverot, H., Reindal, S., & Wivestad, S. (2013). *Introduction: Reconnecting with Existentialism in an Age of Human Capital*. Philpapers.

Sahin, M. (2015). Essentialism in philosophy, psychology, education, social and scientific scopes. *Journal of Innovation in Psychology, Education and Didactics*.

Salem, O. (2023). Education And Challenges in Palestine. (Gendered Impact within Women, Peace And Security). *MIFTAH*. http://www.miftah.org/Display.cfm?DocId=26830&CategoryId=13

Salovey, P., & Mayer, J. D. (1990). Emotional intelligence. Emotion, Cognition, and Personality, 9(3), *Science Direct,* 185—211. DOI: 10.1016/0160-2896(93)90010-3

Samaila, K., Khambari, M. N. M., Kumar, J. A., & Masood, M. (2022). Factors influencing postgraduate students' intention to use learning management system. *Tuning Journal for Higher Education*, 9(2), 151–176. DOI: 10.18543/tjhe.2177

Sampson, D. G., & Zervas, P. (2012). Mobile learning Management Systems in Higher Education. In *Higher Education Institutions and Learning Management Systems* (pp. 162–177). IGI Global. DOI: 10.4018/978-1-60960-884-2.ch008

Sánchez-Prieto, J. C., Olmos-Migueláñez, S., & García-Peñalvo, F. J. (2017). MLearning and pre-service teachers: An assessment of the behavioral intention using an expanded TAM model. *Computers in Human Behavior*, 72, 644–654. DOI: 10.1016/j.chb.2016.09.061

Sandu, R. (2020). Adoption of AI-Chatbots to enhance student learning experience in higher education in India. *ResearchGate*. https://www.researchgate.net/publication/338868551_Adoption_of_AI-Chatbots_to_Enhance_Student_Learning_Experience_in_Higher_Education_in_India

Sangwan, S. (July 14, 2021). https://yourstory.com/2021/07/chicago-jaipur-ai-startup-quillbot-one-stop-writing-platform

Saputro, R. E., & Saputra, D. I. S. (2015). Pengembangan Media Pembelajaran Mengenal Organ Pencernaan Manusia Menggunakan Teknologi Augmented Reality. *Jurnal Buana Informatika*, 6(2), 2. Advance online publication. DOI: 10.24002/jbi.v6i2.404

Schmidt-Crawford, D. A., Lindstrom, D. L., & Thompson, A. D. (2023). AI in teacher education: What's next? *Journal of Digital Learning in Teacher Education*, 39(4), 180–181. DOI: 10.1080/21532974.2023.2247308

Schmidt, D. A., Baran, E., Thompson, A. D., Mishra, P., Koehler, M. J., & Shin, T. S. (2009). Technological Pedagogical Content Knowledge (TPACK): The Development and Validation of an Assessment Instrument for Preservice Teachers. *International Society for Technology in Education (ISTE)*, 800.336.5191. *JRTE*, 42(2), 123–149.

Schneckenberg, D. (2010). Overcoming Barriers for E-learning in Universities—Portfolio Models for E-competence Development of Faculty. *British Journal of Educational Technology*, 41(6), 979–991. DOI: 10.1111/j.1467-8535.2009.01046.x

Selwyn, N. (2019). What's the Problem with Learning Analytics? *Journal of Learning Analytics*, 6(3), 11–19. DOI: 10.18608/jla.2019.63.3

Serkan, Ü., Reyhan, A., & Korkmaz, F. (2017). Exploring Teaching Profession from a Sociological Perspective: Evidence from Turkey. Universal. *The Journal of Educational Research*, 5(5), 874–880. DOI: 10.13189/ujer.2017.050519

Shalhoub-Kevorkian, N. (2008). The Gendered Nature of Education under Siege: A Palestinian Feminist Perspective. *International Journal of Lifelong Education*, 27(2), 179–200. DOI: 10.1080/02601370801936341

Shelley, M. (2017). *Frankenstein; the Modern Prometheus. Amazon Classics.* Kindle Edition.

Sherif, K. (2014). Education in the Middle East: Challenges and Opportunities. .DOI: 10.1057/9781137396969_9

Silviera, T., & Lopes, H. (2023). Intelligence across humans and machines: A joint perspective. *Frontiers in Psychology*, 14, 1209761. Advance online publication. DOI: 10.3389/fpsyg.2023.1209761 PMID: 37663348

Sim, J., & Mengshoel, A. M. (2022). Metasynthesis: Issues of empirical and theoretical context. *Quality & Quantity*, 57(4), 3339–3361. DOI: 10.1007/s11135-022-01502-w

Singh, R. (2021). Information Communication Technology. https://www.researchgate.net/publication/350087090_INFORMATION_COMMUNICATION_TECHNOLOGY

Singh, J. (July 12, 2023). https://cointelegraph.com/news/what-is-quillbot

Sinha, C. (2020). Women in the Bahrain Financial Sector: Opportunities, challenges and strategic choices. *Social Change*, 50(1), 44–60. DOI: 10.1177/0049085719901069

Sj. (2023, August 30). ChatGPT in the Philippines: A revolution in AI and education - TechSergy. *TechSergy*. https://techsergy.com/chatgpt-in-the-philippines/

Slavin, R. E. (1995). *Cooperative learning: Theory, research, and practice*. Prentice Hall.

Slepankova, M. (2021). *Possibilities of Artificial Intelligence in Education : An Assessment of the role of AI chatbots as a communication medium in higher education*. DIVA. https://www.diva-portal.org/smash/record.jsf?pid=diva2%3A1617720&dswid=6364

Smith, J. K., & Brown, L. M. (2020). The role of artificial intelligence in curriculum development in elementary science education. *Journal of Educational Technology*, 45(2), 201–215.

Snae, C., & Brückner, M. (2008). Web-based Evaluation System for Online Courses and Learning Management Systems. *2nd IEEE International Conference on Digital Ecosystems and Technologies*, 332-339. DOI: 10.1109/DEST.2008.4635208

Soccorsi, L. (2013). Instilling a personal teaching philosophy in preservice teachers: Vitally important but not always easy to achieve. *Journal of Student Engagement: Education Matters*, 3(1), 21–28.

Spremić, M., & Šimunic, A. (2018). Cyber security challenges in digital economy. In *Proceedings of the World Congress on Engineering*, London, UK, 4–6 July 2018; International Association of Engineers: Hong Kong, China, pp. 341–346. [Google Scholar]

Stepanechko, O., & Kozub, L. (2023). English Teachers' Concerns About the Ethical Use of Chatgpt by University Students. *Grail of Science*, 25(25), 297–302. DOI: 10.36074/grail-of-science.17.03.2023.051

Stephens, K. (2019). *Teacher Dispositions and Their Impact on Implementation Practices for the Gifted*. Sage Journal. DOI: 10.1177/1076217519862330

Sternberg, R. (2022). Intelligence. *Dialogues in Clinical Neuroscience*, 14(1), 19–27. DOI: 10.31887/DCNS.2012.14.1/rsternberg PMID: 22577301

Stockwell, G. (2010). Using mobile phones for vocabulary activities: Examining the effect of the platform. *Language Learning & Technology*, 14(2), 95–110.

Sullivan, M., Kelly, A., & McLaughlan, P. (2023). ChatGPT in Higher Education: Consideration for Academic Integrity and Student Learning. *Journal of Applied Learning & Teaching*, 6(1), 31–40.

Sullivan, S. (April 03, 2023). https://sulliwrites.medium.com/grammarly-can-slightly -change-your-articles-a-i-content-score-aff21b30271e

Sun, Y. (2015). Exploring residents' attitudes toward solar photovoltaic system adoption in China.

Swanwick, T. (2013). Understanding Medical Education (Evidence, Theory and Practice). *Technology-enhanced learning. 149–160*. DOI: 10.1002/9781118472361.ch11

Sweller, J., Ayres, P., & Kalyuga, S. (2011). *Cognitive load theory*. Springer. DOI: 10.1007/978-1-4419-8126-4

Tai, R. H., Liu, C. Q., Maltese, A. V., & Fan, X. (2006). Planning early for careers in science. *Science*, 312(5777), 1143–1144. DOI: 10.1126/science.1128690 PMID: 16728620

Tamtam, A., Gallagher, F., Olabi, G. A., & Sumsun, N. (2010). Implementing English Medium Instruction (EMI) for Engineering Education in Arab World and Twenty-First Century Challenges. *International Symposium for Engineering Education, University College Cork: Ireland.* Url:https://www.ucc.ie/ucc/depts/foodeng/isee2010/pdfs/Papers/Tamtam%20et%20al.pdf

Tate, T., Doroudi, S., Ritchie, D., & Xu, Y. (2023). Educational research and AI-generated writing: Confronting the coming tsunami. *EdArXivPreprint.* https://doi.org/DOI: 10.35542/osf.io/4mec3

TechEd Maven Consulting. (2024). Embracing AI in Education: Understanding Its Impact. https://www.linkedin.com/posts/teched-maven-consulting_ai-future-of-teaching-and-learning-reportpdf-activity-7097776305177317376-Q6SG/

Tengi, M. L., Mansor, M., & Hashim, S. (2017). A Review Theory of Transformational Leadership for School. *International Journal of Academic Research in Business & Social Sciences*, 7(3). Advance online publication. DOI: 10.6007/IJARBSS/v7-i3/2847

Texas &M University, & the Center for Teaching Excellence. (2024). *Generative AI syllabus statement considerations.* https://cte.tamu.edu/getmedia/1d5e4ef6-97f1-4065-987f-3c9dfecbb7bd/TAMU-CTE_GenAI-SyllabusStatementConsiderations.pdf

Thomas, L. P., Chaudhary, R., Thomas, J., & Menon, V. A. (2023). Assessing Instagram Addiction and Social Media Dependency among Young Adults in Karnataka. *Studies in Media and Communication*, 11(6), 72. DOI: 10.11114/smc.v11i6.6102

Thom, J., Millen, D., & DiMicco, J. (2012). Removing Gamification from an Enterprise SNS. *Proceedings of the ACM 2012 Conference on Computer Supported Cooperative Work.* https://doi.org/DOI: 10.1145/2145204.2145362

Ting-Toomey, S. (2017). Intercultural conflict competence. In *The International Encyclopedia of Intercultural Communication.* Wiley.

Tinto, V. (1993). *Leaving college: Rethinking the causes and cures of student attrition.* University of Chicago Press.

Tlaiss, H. A. (2014). Women's Entrepreneurship, Barriers and Culture: Insights from the United Arab Emirates. *The Journal of Entrepreneurship*, 23(2), 289–320. DOI: 10.1177/0971355714535307

Tomlinson, C. A. (2014). *The differentiated classroom: Responding to the needs of all learners* (2nd ed.). ASCD.

Tomlinson, C. A. (2017). *How to differentiate instruction in academically diverse classrooms* (3rd ed.). ASCD.

Trinity College. (2023). *Sample syllabus statement.* https://www.trincoll.edu/ctl/wp -content/uploads/sites/110/2023/09/Sample-Syllabus-Statements-on-AI.pdf

Tuomi, I., Cachia, R., & Villar Onrubia, D. (2023). On the Futures of Technology in Education: Emerging Trends and Policy Implications. *Publications Office of the European Union, Luxembourg.*, JRC134308. Advance online publication. DOI: 10.2760/079734

UNESCO. (2023). ChatGPT and Artificial Intelligence in Higher Education, Quick Start Guide. Document Code: ED/HE/IESALC/IP/2023/12. 1-14.

Unger, K., Schwartz, D., & Foucher, J. (2013). Increasing Employee Productivity through Gamification and Blended Learning. In T. Bastiaens & G. Marks (Eds.), *Proceedings of E-Learn 2013--World Conference on E-Learning in Corporate, Government, Healthcare, and Higher Education (pp. 2538-2545).* Las Vegas, NV, USA: *Association for the Advancement of Computing in Education (AACE).* Retrieved April 19, 2024 from https://www.learntechlib.org/primary/p/115272/

UNICEF. (2021). Education Annual Report UNICEF. [https://www.unicef.org/ sudan/media/8546/file/UNICEF%20Sudan-Education-%20Report%20(2021).pdf]

UNICEF. Analyse Budgétaire: Education, Période 2010-2021. (2022, March). https:// www.unicef.org/tunisia/media/6121/file/Education%20Budget%20Brief-2022.pdf

Valsamidis, S., Kazanidis, I., Kontogiannis, S., & Karakos, A. (2012). An approach for LMS assessment. *International Journal of Technology Enhanced Learning*, 4(3/4), 265. DOI: 10.1504/IJTEL.2012.051544

Van Wyk, M. M., Adarkwah, M. A., & Amponsah, S. (2023). Why All the Hype about ChatGPT? Academics' Views of a Chat-based Conversational Learning Strategy at an Open Distance e-Learning Institution. *Open Praxis*, 15(3), 214–225. DOI: 10.55982/openpraxis.15.3.563

Venkatesh, V., Morris, M. G., Davis, G. B., & Davis, F. D. (2003). User acceptance of information technology: Toward a unified view. *Management Information Systems Quarterly*, ●●●, 425–478.

Viano, A. (2023, April 28). How Universities Can Use AI Chatbots to Connect with Students and Drive Success. *Technology Solutions That Drive Education.* https:// edtechmagazine.com/higher/article/2023/02/how-universities-can-use-ai-chatbots -connect-students-and-drive-success

Vygotsky, L. S. (1978). *Mind in society: The development of higher psychological processes*. Harvard University Press.

Vyse, G. (2024). *How Generative AI is Changing the Classroom*. This report is underwritten by Amazon Web Services (AWS). The Chronicle of Higher Education Inc._https://www.chronicle.com/featured/digital-higher-ed/how-generative-ai-is-changing-the-classroom?utm_campaign=che-ci-cnt-ci-aws-generativeai&utm_medium=em&utm_source=mkto&utm_content=24-06-30-v2&mkt_tok=OTMxLUVLQS0yMTgAAAGUZL5SQT7fpYZvjlqt6F-0qquU3syDw4TKw1Elm-GTQBmZNvmNgONH5y2AEQqJR8DBSngqD1_mpIa6nn5qWX4PY8B9wevYUO1ZZIlL4YNiE1Rn5Uo

Walton Family Foundation. (March 1, 2023). Teachers and Students Embrace ChatGPT for Education, New Survey from Walton Family Foundation Finds._https://www.waltonfamilyfoundation.org/chatgpt-used-by-teachers-more-than-students-new-survey-from-walton-family-foundation-finds

Wang, F., Hannafin, M. J., & Lin, H. (2020). Effects of Artificial Intelligence Integration in Elementary Science Instruction. *Journal of Educational Technology & Society*, 23(3), 174–187.

Wanner, T., & Palmer, E. (2015). Personalizing learning: Exploring student and teacher perceptions about flexible learning and assessment in a flipped university course. *Computers & Education*, 88, 354–369. DOI: 10.1016/j.compedu.2015.07.008

Wardat, Y., Tashtoush, M. A., AlAli, R., & Jarrah, A. M. (2023). ChatGPT: A revolutionary tool for teaching and learning mathematics. *Eurasia Journal of Mathematics, Science and Technology Education*, 19(7), em2286. Advance online publication. DOI: 10.29333/ejmste/13272

Wende, M. C. (2009). Internationalization of higher education: A historical perspective. In Deardorff, D. K., de Wit, H., Heyl, J. D., & Adams, T. (Eds.), *The Sage handbook of international higher education* (pp. 3–27). Sage Publications.

Wilkin, C. L., & Chenhall, R. H. (2010). A review of IT governance: A taxonomy to inform accounting information systems. [Google Scholar] [CrossRef]. *Journal of Information Systems*, 24(2), 107–146. DOI: 10.2308/jis.2010.24.2.107

Williamson, B. (2019). The Hidden Architecture of Higher Education: Building a Big Data Infrastructure for the 'Smarter University'. *International Journal of Educational Technology in Higher Education*, 16(1), 39–57.

Wiseman, A. W., & Anderson, E. (2012). ICT-integrated Education and National Innovation Systems in the Gulf Cooperation Council (GCC) Countries. *Computers & Education*, 59(2), 607–618. DOI: 10.1016/j.compedu.2012.02.006

Woithe, J., & Filipec, O. (2023). *Understanding the Adoption, Perception, and Learning Impact of ChatGPT in Higher Education : A qualitative exploratory case study analyzing students' perspectives and experiences with the AI-based large language model.* DIVA. https://www.diva-portal.org/smash/record.jsf?pid=diva2%3A1762617&dswid=-6729

Wollny, S., Schneider, J., Di Mitri, D., Weidlich, J., Rittberger, M., & Drachsler, H. (2021). Are We There Yet? - A Systematic Literature Review on Chatbots in Education. *Frontiers in Artificial Intelligence*, 4, 654924. DOI: 10.3389/frai.2021.654924 PMID: 34337392

Wuttke, H.-D., & Henke, K. (2008). LMS-coupled simulations and assessments in a digital systems course. *2008 Tenth IEEE International Symposium on Multimedia.* DOI: 10.1109/ISM.2008.99

Xiao, P., Chen, Y., & Bao, W. (2023). Waiting, banning, and embracing: An empirical analysis of adapting policies for generative AI in higher education. *arXiv preprint arXiv:2305.18617.*

Yasin, F., Firdaus, R., & Jani, M. (2013). *Islamic Education.* The Philosophy, Aim, and Main Features.

Yılmaz, K., Altınkurt, Y., & Çokluk, Ö. (2014). Developing the educational belief scale: The validity and reliability study. *Educational Sciences: Theory & Practice*, 11(1), 343–350.

Yue, C., Men, A., Rita, L., & Ferguson, M. (2019). Bridging transformational leadership, transparent communication, and employee openness to change: The mediating role of trust. *Public Relations Review*, 45(3), 101779. DOI: 10.1016/j.pubrev.2019.04.012

Zaatari, R. (2013). A Reading of Syrian Indicators in the Global Report on the Gender Gap, the National Competitiveness Observatory.

Zabala, A. (2014). Q method: A Package to Explore the Human Perspective Using Q Methodology. *The R Journal*, 6(2), 163–173. DOI: 10.32614/RJ-2014-032

Zawacki-Richter, O., Bozkurt, A., Alturki, U., & Aldraiweesh, A. (2018). What Research Says about MOOCS – An Explorative Content Analysis. *International Review of Research in Open and Distance Learning*, 19(1). Advance online publication. DOI: 10.19173/irrodl.v19i1.3356

Zevalsiz, S. (2014). Value Perception of University Students. *International Periodical for Languages. Literature and History of Turkish or Turkic*, 9(2), 1739–1762.

Zhang, J., Oh, Y. J., Lange, P., Yu, Z., & Fukuoka, Y. (2020). Artificial intelligence Chatbot Behavior change model for designing artificial intelligence chatbots to promote physical activity and a healthy diet: Viewpoint. *Journal of Medical Internet Research*, 22(9), e22845. DOI: 10.2196/22845 PMID: 32996892

Zheng, B., & Prince, P. E. (2015). Purchasing efficiency measurement of selected chinese pv panels using data envelopment analysis (DEA). *Undergraduate Review*, 11(1), 148–155.

About the Contributors

Jacquelynne Anne Boivin is an Assistant Professor of Elementary and Early Childhood Education at Bridgewater State University in Bridgewater, MA, USA, where she supervises student teachers, mentors honors thesis projects, and teaches math methods to elementary teacher candidates and seminars on deconstructing racism by integrating schools and decolonizing social studies curricula. She is co-chair of her department's Anti-Racism Matters committee and supports and facilitates student and faculty professional development focused on diversity, equity, and inclusion. She is also co-chair of the College of Education and Health Sciences' Diversity and Equity Steering Committee. She is a former elementary school teacher who uses her experience in the field to contextualize her instruction in teacher-preparation. She is the author of the book, Exploring the Role of the School Principal in Predominantly White Middle Schools: School Leadership to Promote Multicultural Understanding and co-editor of Education as the Driving Force of Equity for the Marginalized, The Role of Educators as Agents and Conveyors for Positive Change in Global Education, and STEM Education Approaches and Challenges in the MENA Region. Her largest passion is authentically connecting academic disciplines with social justice skills and understandings. In her spare time, she enjoys outdoor adventures with her husband, Craig, a warm cup of tea with a good book and her cat, and cooking and baking with locally sourced ingredients.

Jabbar A. Al-Obaidi received his Ph.D. in Communication from the University of Michigan, Ann Arbor, and obtained his master from Hartford University, Connecticut, and a bachelor from Baghdad University. Currently, he is a Professor in the Department of Communication Studies at Bridgewater State University (BSU) and serves as the Academic Director of Global Programs of the Minnock Institute of Global Engagement. Presently at BSU, he serves as the Chair of All University Committee (AUC) at BSU, he is also engaged as the Project Co-Director for the US Department of Education, Undergraduate International Studies and Foreign Languages Program, Grant # P016A200027. He served as the Co-Chair of BSU Steering Committee for Reaccreditation, and Co-Chair of Subcommittee 3: Education, Training, and Continued Learning Opportunities for Faculty, Staff, and Students. Previously, Al-Obaidi served as the director of the Center for Middle East Studies and the chairperson for the Department of Communication Studies. In addition to his extensive teaching and administrative experiences in the US, he taught in Iraq, Jordan, Yemen, United Arab Emirates and China. He is the author or editor of three books: Media Censorship in the Middle East, Broadcast, Internet, and TV Media in the Arab World and Small Nations and Mass Communication. He has published in several peer-reviewed scholarly journals and presented research papers at major national and international conferences around the world. Professor Al-Obeidi's administrative contribution, scholarly work, and teaching cover curriculum and programs, management and leadership, assessment, COIL and virtual teaching, intercultural communication, and media in the Middle East. He also produces and hosts INFOCUS a cable television program and makes documentary films. He organized and participated in numerous workshops and training sessions in intercultural communication, professional development, curriculum assessment, online learning and teaching, and institutional strategic development. Al-Obaidi initiated and facilitated the organization of several international conference on education between BSU and universities in Jordan and Morocco. He worked closely with BSU administration to implement academic international partnerships with many universities in the Middle East and Asia. He led study abroad programs, undergraduate research, and internship and traveled to various countries.

Madhusudana N. Rao obtained his Ph.D. in Geography from Kent State University and is currently a Professor in the Department of Geography at Bridgewater State University (BSU). He is also the Director of the Middle East & North Africa Studies Program, Minnock Institute of Global Engagement. Presently at BSU, he is involved as the Principal Investigator for the US Department of Education, Undergraduate International Studies and Foreign Languages Program, Grant # P016A200027. His practical experience adds value to the teaching and learning environment within the classroom both in the technical and cultural elements of Geographic education. His research interests lay at the intersection of geographic themes such as cultural and environmental sustainability as they relate to climate change, regional development, renewable energy, technology, and emerging economies, especially in the context of the developing world in the mix of globalization. He has published in several peer-reviewed scholarly journals and presented research papers at major national and international conferences around the world. He received research grants from federal and state agencies in the USA. He offers consulting services in geotechnology education to several reputed public and private organizations, which keeps him on the pulse of current topical concerns in the field of educational learning.

***

Vishnu Achutha Menon is an independent journalist, writer, researcher, and an Indian percussionist. He is a recipient of the Junior Scholarship the Ministry of Culture awarded. His research interests are film studies, verbal & nonverbal communication, south Asian performances, Natyasastra, media studies, media analysis techniques, Laban Movement Analysis, and Ethnomusicology.

Sadik Madani Alaoui is a full professor and lecturer in the Department of English Studies at Sidi Mohamed Ben Abdellah University, Fez. He received a B.A. in Psycholinguistics, an M.A. in Language, Culture & Communication, and a Ph.D. in Media and Cultural Studies. He has been teaching English for more than 30 years. Currently, he is the head of English Studies Filiere in Fez. He is teaching General Linguistics, Pragmatics, Media Studies & Cultural Studies, Public Speaking, and Intercultural Communication. He worked as an adjunct professor in a various HEIs such as the ENSAM School of Engineering and ESTM Vocational School, and Al-Akhawayne University in Ifrane. He also a member of the European Scientific Journal Editorial Board. He took part in many M.A. programs in various universities in Morocco. MA in Applied Linguistics at My Ismail University, MA in Language, Communication and Society at FLDM, and MA in DDT Program at the faculty of FSJES of Meknes. His major fields of interests are Applied linguistics; Media and Cultural Studies; Public Speaking and Debating; Cultural Identity issues, and Mass communication Studies. Some of his recent publications are: Madani, A. S., Belfakir, L., & Moubtassime, M. (2020). Globalization, Cultural Identity and Education in the Digital Age. Les presses supercopie de Fez. ISBN: 978-9920-32-405-2; Madani, A, I., & Madani, A. S. (2021). Le Discours de la Rumeur. Actes du colloque International, 1ère Edition. Imprimerie Iqtissad de la FLSH Agadir. ISBN: 978-9920-615-21-1; Madani., A. S., & Chahbane, S. (2023). Deconstructing Gender Stereotypes through Moroccan Facebook Groups: A Netnographic Analysis. Open Journal of Social Sciences, 11, 314-328 https://www.scirp.org/journal/jss ISSN Online: 2327-5960; Madani., A. S., & Aknouche, L. (2022). "Diaspora and the Quest of Moroccanness. In "The Problematics of Identity and Otherness in Contemporary Moroccan Discourse" sous la direction de Mohammed ElKouche. Publications of ROA PRINT, RABAT. ISBN: 978-9920-9231-4-9. Dépôt légal: 2022MO0867 ; Madani., A. S., ER-Radi, H. & Es-soufi, K. (2023). Being a Teacher in a Plurilingual Environment: An Attitudinal Analysis. International Journal of Linguistics, Literature and Translation ISSN: 2617-0299 (Online); ISSN: 2708-0099 (Print). DOI: 10.32996/ijllt; Madani, A. S. (2019). The Value of Reflective Teaching: Benefits and Challenges. Proceedings of 14th International Scientific Forum, ISF, 03-04, October Marrakech, Morocco. European Scientific Institute Publications, Macedonia. ISBN 978-608-4642-71-8

Awad M. Alshalwy is an M.A. student in Applied Linguistics at the Libyan Academy of Postgraduate Studies. He has a bachelor's degree in Geology and another bachelor's degree in English linguistics and literature from Omar Al-Mukhtar University (OMU), Libya. He is an EFL instructor at the Language Center of OMU. His research interests primarily lie in the areas of instructional technology, communication assessment, cultural diversity in language curricula, and content-based and project-based learning.

Edilberto Z. Andal is an Associate Professor V at Laguna State Polytechnic University (LSPU), San Pablo City Campus, San Pablo City, Laguna, Philippines. He is the current Dean of the College of Teacher Education & Graduate Studies and Applied Research (CTE-GSAR). At LSPU, he got a Doctor of Education with a major in Educational Management (2010). Batangas State University (BatSU) awarded him a Master of Education in Industrial Education Management. In 1986, he received an undergraduate degree, a Bachelor of Science in Industrial Education (cum laude), focusing on Electrical Technology. He is an active member of CHED-RQAT in the Region and an accredited member of AACCUP and ISO internal accreditor. In 2022, he was named Best Senior Researcher, acknowledging his active participation in scientific projects. His involvement in various research activities and professional organizations, such as serving as the program head and project manager of the Ideation Design and Development Laboratory (IDD Lab), a collaboration project between LSPU and DOST Region IV-A, and active involvement in research and extension development, mentoring research presentations and publications, qualifies him for the recognition. He is also a pioneering mentor of the ROBOTECH Project for Department of Education (DepED) faculty and students in the Division of San Pablo City, being part of IDD Lab Projects to integrate Robotics technology into the Basic Education Curriculum. His research interests include educational management, industrial education and technology, administration and supervision, and educational leadership and innovation.

Ali Garib is a doctoral candidate in the Applied Linguistics and Technology program at Iowa State University and an ESL lecturer at Rice University. Ali holds an M.A. in Applied Linguistics from Arizona State University and an M.A. in TESOL and Educational Technology from the University of Manchester. Ali's primary research interests span the areas of innovative teaching, technology-assisted project-based language learning, AI-powered teaching, CALL, educational technology, communication skills, and language teacher TPACK practices and professional development. Email: ali.garib@rice.edu I ORCID: 0000-0002-8331-7120

Aránzazu Gil Casadomet holds a PhD in French and Francophone Studies from the Universidad Autónoma de Madrid (UAM), with an extraordinary doctoral prize for her thesis "Aportaciones a una semántica argumentativa y enunciativa" (2016). She holds a degree in French Philology from the UAM and in Sciences du Langage from the Université de Nice-Sophia Antipolis (France), and a Master's degree from both universities. She also holds an Expert Degree in University Teaching Methodology (2021, UAM). She is currently Assistant Professor in the Department of French Philology at the UAM. She teaches undergraduate and master's degree courses, with special emphasis on French language and linguistics, computational and corpus linguistics, and localisation of computer products. She has two five-year teaching periods. In research, she is part of the Language and Communication Sciences Laboratory (TiLc&Com, UAM), and develops projects in French linguistics, argumentative semantics, applied linguistics, lexicography, computational linguistics, and FLE and FOS teaching. Her research covers various areas of French philology and language teaching, and is notable for its multidisciplinary and applied approach. Her most recent work focuses on the semantic-pragmatic analysis of the French language lexicon, exploring the evolution in the description of linguistic subjectivity. In addition, she has addressed the issue of lexical polarity in political and tourist discourses; and the creation of new lexies and the transcription of complex ideas in French and Spanish with the aim of creating a dictionary of neologisms inherent to the media. Her contribution also extends to the teaching of FLE and FOS, participating in research on the development of academic and scientific competence. She has also explored pedagogical strategies, such as the use of micro-video for multimodal discourse and attention to the integration of synophone learners in multicultural classrooms.

Jherwin P. Hermosa is an Associate Professor 3 at the Laguna State Polytechnic University in San Pablo City Campus. He previously served as the Chairperson for the Innovation and Technology Support Office (ITSO). Dr. Hermosa earned his Doctor of Education in Educational Management in 2023 from the same university. He also holds degrees in Philosophy and Theology from Rome, Italy. Dr. Hermosa currently teaches Social Sciences and Philosophical Subjects at both the undergraduate and Graduate Program levels. Additionally, he serves as an editorial board member for the International Review of Social Sciences Research. Dr. Hermosa has authored books such as Foundations of Education (2022) Philosophy of Education (2023) and Advanced Social Philosophy (2024), along with numerous scientific articles and literary works that have been published internationally. He offers specialized thesis assistance to students at both the undergraduate and graduate levels as an advisor, subject matter expert, and technical editor. Currently, he is pursuing a Juris Doctor degree at San Pablo Colleges, College of Law. Dr. Hermosa's research interests primarily focus on the social sciences, philosophy, educational management, and law.

Fate Jacaban-Bolambao, a distinguished educator, began her academic journey as a student assistant for four years at St. Theresa's College-Cebu, culminating in a Bachelor of Secondary Education degree specializing in Mathematics. Her expertise expanded during a six-year tenure as a Grade School Teacher at the same institution, focusing on Math and Computer subjects. Acknowledged for her coaching prowess, Fate received accolades in interschool, regional, and national competitions, including MTG, MTAP, and E-learning contests by leading book companies in the Philippines. Recognizing her proficiency in educational technology, she earned the prestigious Genyo E-learning Award, designating her as the top content creator on the school's Learning Management System (LMS). Fate also secured a position among the top content creators in the National Top 100 Aralinks-CLE and received the Alaga 6 by Phoenix Aralinks Educator Award in 2021, emphasizing her commitment to blended learning. Complementing her achievements, she obtained a Master of Arts in Education major in Mathematics from Cebu Normal University and is currently pursuing a Doctor of Philosophy in Education, majoring in Research and Evaluation. Presently, as an educator in the Department of Education-Mandaue City Division, Fate imparts knowledge in Senior High Research and Mathematics, while actively coaching inter-school research competitions.

SeyedMohammad Kashani is a Ph.D. candidate in Computer Engineering at Iowa State University. He received his B.S. in Electrical Engineering from AmirKabir University of Technology. SeyedMohammad's primary research utilizes machine learning tools in the healthcare industry. His secondary areas of research include cyber security, machine learning, and using quantum computing to improve machine learning techniques. kashani@iastate.edu

Youssef Laaraj is a language teacher, researcher, and opinion writer. He is currently a Professor of English Communication at The Faculty of Sciences and Techniques, Sidi Mohamed Ben Abdellah University. He has been teaching English in various schools and regions across Morocco for more than 15 years. He earned a PhD in Education and Language Policy at Mohammed V University in Rabat in 2021 and published several articles on his major research areas, which include English language Education, Language Policy, and Instruction Technologies.

Xiangrong Liu is a Professor of Management in the Ricciardi College of Business. She specializes in the fields of Operations Management and Supply Chain Management. Professor Liu's research focus is mathematical modeling with applications in supply chain management. Her current research emphasizes such global sustainability issues as remanufacturing, biofuel, pollution emission controls, renewable energy, and sustainable supply chains. Recently, she published in the Journal of the Operational Research Society, Information Systems Education Journal, International Journal of Information and Operations Management Education, Bridgewater Review, and a special issue of China Media Research: Sustainability, Resilience, and Global Communication. Professor Liu serves as Internship Coordinator for Management and Team Leader for Collaborative Undergraduate Business Experiences (CUBEs).

Ouelfatmi Meryem is a third-year doctoral candidate pertaining to CREDIF lab at Sidi Mohamed Ben Abdellah University. Her research interests explore the role of attitudes in the acceptance and use of technology by higher-education students. Her dissertation investigates the subset constructs that influence attitude and therefore, the intention to use technology for educational purposes.

Michel Plaisent is a full professor in the University of Québec at Montréal (Canada). After a bachelor in Information technology, a M.Sc. in project management and a Ph.D. in Information Technology Management, he joined the Business school in 1980 where he held different position while developing his research career, namely IT program director for 6 years. His doctoral research was pioneer as he studied the use of computer mediated communication systems by CEO. Since then, Dr. Plaisent's researches continue to focus human factors of IT, namely cognitive ergonomics, learning problems and personal productivity tools for managers. Among his new researches namely: Education 4.0 concepts and tools, and more broadly the impact of internet on life and society. He has published more than 25 books and more than one hundred of articles in international conferences and academic indexed journals. He is engaged in China EMBA program and he manages for UQAM research collaboration protocols with three South-Asia universities.

Angeline M. Pogoy is a professor VI and the former Vice-president for Research, Extension and Publication, the former Officer in Charge (OIC) of the Center for Research and Development and the former director for the Institute of Research in Instructional Delivery (IRIID) of Cebu Normal University. She has been teaching Professional Education courses, Educational Management courses, Research courses and Mathematics Education courses. She is a senior on-line Flexible Learning Tutor of the SEAMEO INNOTECH. She had been a pre-service teaching mentor and a supervisor of Integrated Laboratory School of the university. She has conducted several researches presented in Singapore, Seoul, Korea, Hong Kong, Taiwan, China, Japan and the Philippines and published in Scopus indexed, ACI and in international referred journals. She has engaged with international universities in Japan, China, Thailand, Vietnam, Taiwan, Singapore and Canada. She is a productive researcher, reviewer and an author.

Tatum Sommer is an undergraduate student at Texas A&M, pursuing a major in English with a passion for education. With a heart dedicated to education and English, Tatum Sommer seeks to positively impact the world of English education by creating awareness of educational gaps and increasing the accessibility of proper English education to all. She first fell in love with research at her job as an undergraduate research assistant with Texas A&M's Education Department. In the future, she aims to pursue a Ph.D. program to gain further knowledge in these fields.

Wanchunzi Yu is an associate professor at Bridgewater State University. She earned her PhD in Statistics from Arizona State University, and then spent two years there as a postdoctoral fellow. Her broad research interests include statistical consulting, design and analysis of experiments, and data science.

Index